Madrid and the Spanish Economy,
(1560–1850)

Madrid and the Spanish Economy, 1560–1850

DAVID R. RINGROSE

University of California Press

Berkeley · Los Angeles · London

University of California Press
Berkeley and Los Angeles, California

University of California Press, Ltd.
London, England

© 1983 by
The Regents of the University of California

Printed in the United States of America

1 2 3 4 5 6 7 8 9

Library of Congress Cataloging in Publication Data

Ringrose, David R.
    Madrid and the Spanish economy, 1560–1850.

    Bibliography: p.
    Includes index.
    1. Madrid (Spain)—Economic conditions.
2. Spain—Economic conditions. I. Title.
HC388.M3R56   330.946′41   82–1971
ISBN 0–520–04311–1   AACR2

This book is dedicated to the memory of my father,
ROBERT GORDON RINGROSE

Contents

List of Tables, Figures, and Maps

Tables

Tables

Tables

Tables

Maps

Maps

Figures

Figures

Acknowledgments

A book as long in the making as this one has been inevitably accumulates many benefactors, both personal and institutional. Let me begin by acknowledging the unfailing dedication of the numerous archivists all over Spain who, in the face of serious limitations imposed by the Franco regime, preserved, organized, and made available as best they could one of the richest archival heritages in the world. The size of this heritage is impressive when one works in the commonly used *Archivo General de Simancas,* the *Archivo General de Indias* (Sevilla), or the *Archivo Histórico Nacional* (Madrid), but it is even more striking when one penetrates to the municipal and provincial collections that are scattered across the country. In particular I wish to indicate my gratitude for the patience and helpfulness of the staff of the *Archivo de la Villa de Madrid*, one of the richest municipal archives in Europe.

Several institutional acknowledgments are in order, since without research support the years in Spain and the attendant travel costs would have been insupportable. Both the Research Council of Rutgers, the State University of New Jersey, and the Research Committee of the Faculty Senate of the University of California, San Diego provided travel funds, computer support, and time for writing and reflection. The *Comisión de Intercambio Cultural Entre España y los Estados Unidos* (Spanish Fulbright Program) made possible two years in Spain as a graduate student and a year as a Faculty Research Fellow. The National Endowment for the Humanities provided an additional year of leave which allowed the final archival work and provided time to begin serious writing.

No acknowledgments can be complete without mention of the professional friends and colleagues who provided useful criticism, advice, and moral support. Among these are my Spanish friends Gabriel Tortella Casares, Gonzalo Anes Álvarez, and Antonio Domínguez Ortiz, who provided valuable orientation to the academic world of Spain. Others crucial to the development of the project were Domenico Sella, Rondo Cameron, Herbert Rowen, and Richard

Herr. Several people provided constructive comments on the manuscript as it evolved, including Robert Ritchie, Woodrow Borah, and Edward Malefakis. As the book reached consideration for publication, I benefited immensely from uncompromising and searching critiques by Elias Tuma and Pablo Fernández Albaladejo and by Michael Weisser, who has provided me with an ongoing debate over the relationship between the two great cities of the Spanish meseta, Madrid and Toledo. My most important professional debt of all is to Kathryn M. Ringrose, who, as professional colleague, research assistant, confidant, and wife provided ongoing criticism and encouragement and subordinated a large part of her own career to this project.

1. Introduction: Madrid and Spain, 1560–1850

Madrid has never possessed a creative culture . . . it has learned from abroad a minimum of badly assimilated things. This acquired culture, . . . this reservoir of culture, comes specifically to Madrid for its needs as a major city, to sustain the sober dignity of a capital. To think that it has ever been able to disseminate its spirit is idiocy. Six kilometers from Madrid the cultural influence of Madrid ends and, without transition or enlightened hinterland, total backwardness begins abruptly.

JOSÉ ORTEGA Y GASSET (1927)[1]

Madrid developed in geographic isolation from the dynamism of the Atlantic world and stood culturally apart from the region that surrounded it. Even in the 1920's, the urban reformer saw it as an incomplete outpost of cultural modernity. To the traditional elites of the interior, it was, because of those incomplete elements of modernity, a potential threat to authority in the countryside. Reformers and conservatives alike considered it an economic and social parasite, filled with politicians, bureaucrats, and servants exploiting the political institutions of the country for their own benefit. All of these perceptions contained an element of truth. But while the city was an isolated cultural outpost, it was also the center of an important and complex set of economic relationships derived from the structure of Spain's empire, from the structures of rural society in the interior, and from the size and economic structure of Madrid itself. The legacy of that relationship has considerable importance for the historical pattern of modern Spain and for the study of urban development everywhere.

Even the most hurried review of urban history reveals considerable differences in the functions that cities have performed. In the pre-industrial world, cities often attained prominence primarily as cultural and political centers—as focal points for the web of connections that provided rural and agricultural civilization with its central authority.[2] Europe, however, was

---

1. José Ortega y Gasset, *La redención de las provincias* (1967), p. 83. In a similar vein, see the description of travel between cities in 1800 given by Antonio Flores in *Ayer, hoy y mañana*, vol. 1, *Ayer o la sociedad de la fe en 1800* (1892), p. 175. Flores describes desolation, wilderness, and a need for armed escorts.
2. Gideon Sjoberg, *The Pre-Industrial City* (1960), pp. 67–77; Max Weber, *The City* (1958), pp. 65–75; Richard M. Morse, "A Prolegomenon to Latin American Urban History" (1972). See also Peter Clark, ed., *The Early Modern Town: A Reader* (1976), ch. 1.

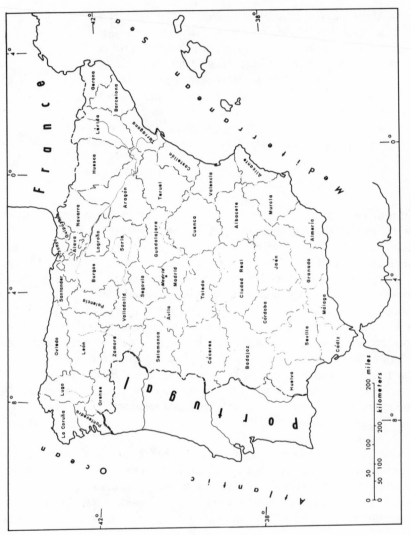

Map 1.1 *Spain: Modern Provinces*

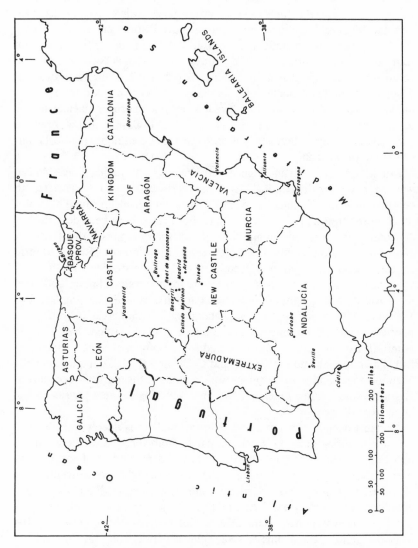

Map 1.2 *Spain: Traditional Regions*

unique in the degree to which it contained commercial cities that organized economic life around market structures rather than political ones. Obviously, the dichotomy between political and commercial cities blurs when applied to specific examples. But the two ideal types—large-scale economic organization and large-scale political organization—are distinct enough so that we can only understand the uniqueness of European commercial cities if we also study the economic impact of the political ones. This is because extensive commercial networks generally required a political framework in order to develop, and that dependence on political power forced commerce to accommodate itself to elite values that gave low priority to economic efficiency as defined by the market. In the case of Madrid and Castile, market-oriented commerce developed, but only as a consequence of continuous political intervention in the economy.

Much as Amsterdam and Venice were archetypical trading cities, Madrid was the model for the political city. From its rise at the end of the sixteenth century until the Napoleonic Wars, Madrid remained an imperial center much in the tradition of imperial Rome. Both cities have been described as economic parasites, consuming the wealth of their empires without directly contributing to the creation of that wealth. Like imperial Rome, Madrid organized and ran a worldwide political and administrative structure and used that political structure as a framework for controlling, taxing, and shaping a widespread system of commercial activity. Madrid was unique, however, since its location kept it from becoming the commercial as well as the political center of its empire. The Spanish political system had a single administrative structure, but it suffered from a pronounced economic dualism. The imperial trade at Seville and Cádiz and the coastal fringes of the Mediterranean and Basque regions were exposed to the maritime economy of Europe, while interior León and Old and New Castile were physically isolated from the sea.

Not surprisingly, economic and cultural dualism is deeply imbedded in Spanish historiography. It is derived partly from the contrast between the maritime provinces and the remote plains and mountains of the interior, partly from the Christian-Moslem struggle of the eighth to the seventeenth centuries, and from the more recent conflict between traditional and post-enlightenment world views.[3] At times the coastal areas were relatively dynamic, while in other periods the Castilian interior asserted authority over the coastal regions.[4] Responding to geographic separation and the differing en-

---

3. Pierre Vilar, *Spain, A Brief History* (1967), pp. 1–3; Jaime Vicens Vives, *Approaches to the History of Spain* (1967), p. xxx; Juan Vilá Valenti, *La peninsula ibérica* (1968), esp. ch. 12, "Los contrastes regionales."

4. Vilar, *Spain*, pp. 16–18.

dowments of coast and interior, two parallel economies were present in Spain until well after the introduction of the railroads in the nineteenth century.

The isolation of the interior is best demonstrated by regional variations in market activity. In the sixteenth century, when the interior was relatively dynamic, year-to-year variations in the prices of basic commodities were more extreme in Old and New Castile than in Valencia on the coast.[5] This is indicative of a lack of integration between interior and coastal markets. The situation had not altered by the end of the eighteenth century; and in the unprecedented crisis of 1804, while wheat prices rose 100% (1799–1804) in the eastern and northern coastal towns, they climbed over 350% in Old Castile and Extremadura.[6] The isolation of interior markets continued far into the nineteenth century, and the sharp regional differences in price levels did not diminish until the 1880's.[7] Clearly it was extremely difficult to move goods around in the interior or to get them into and out of the region.[8]

Consequently, the government in Madrid was perennially faced with accommodating two distinct patterns of economic life within a single political structure. The coastal districts could rely on the maritime trade network for food when domestic supplies failed. Thus they could accept the risk of specialization in export crops and manufacturing, with correspondingly more efficient use of resources. During the difficult seventeenth century these areas escaped demographic crisis, and many coastal zones experienced growing output, population, and commercial activity. On the other hand, the interior was hampered by a precarious climate, poor soil, and isolation from distant supplies when local crops failed. The only product that could bear the cost of transport to the sea and still be profitable was wool. Thus the interior could not risk economic specialization and had to commit its resources to basic food crops as insurance against bad harvests. Constantly threatened by food shortages, the interior was severely limited in its ability to find more efficient ways of organizing production.[9]

5. Earl J. Hamilton, *American Treasure and the Price Revolution in Spain, 1501–1650* (1934), p. 198.

6. Gonzalo Anes, *Las crisis agrarias en la España moderna* (1970), p. 495. The same process is noted in the less severe crisis of 1868 when over a period of 36 months wheat prices rose 50% to 87% in port cities and 150% to 205% in interior districts. See Nicolás Sánchez-Albornoz, *España hace un siglo: Una economia dual* (1968).

7. Nicolás Sánchez-Albornoz, *Los precios agrícolas durante la segunda mitad del siglo XIX*, vol. 1, *Trigo y cebada* (1975), pp.45–46.

8. David R. Ringrose, *Transportation and Economic Stagnation in Spain, 1750–1850* (1970), esp. ch. 6.

9. Everything depended on the fall rains in Old Castile. If they came late, the planting was late and the grain did not ripen until summer heat had begun, producing stunted grain. See Angel García Sanz, *Desarrollo y crisis del Antiguo Régimen en Castilla la Vieja: Economia y sociedad en tierras de Segovia de 1500 a 1814* (1977), p. 24. On the possible types of agrarian change, see Robert Brenner, "The Origins of Capitalist Development: A Critique of Neo-Smithian Marxism" (1977), pp. 38–45.

Economic dualism took its modern form in the seventeenth century as Madrid became a major metropolis. During the sixteenth century the interior dominated the peninsula because of its own demographic vitality and the slow recovery of the Mediterranean after the crises of the late middle ages and Turkish expansion.[10] By the eighteenth century the pattern had reversed and the peripheral regions were far more dynamic.[11] The durability of the central bureaucracy in the seventeenth century, and the apparent successes of the Bourbon monarchy in rebuilding and unifying Spain in the eighteenth, only masked the tensions inherent in the situation. Coastal regions, while not integrated with each other, maintained their common access to the sea. In the sixteenth century the Atlantic fringes participated in the prosperity of the trans-Atlantic empire, but the Mediterranean littoral remained relatively depressed until the last quarter of the century. By the 1650's, however, the economic life of the entire periphery was adjusting to the market system developed by the Dutch and English during the century and a half preceding the Industrial Revolution.

The interior, with its low economic potential, was insulated from this trend. Early sixteenth-century population growth gave way in the later decades to a precarious equilibrium which was soon upset by a series of crises. By 1650 the regional population had fallen substantially, and most cities contained only a fraction of their earlier numbers. The commerce and crafts of the regional economy were reduced to the export of wool, subsistence agriculture, and inter-regional exchanges of basic commodities largely independent of urban services and markets.[12]

The preceding paragraphs do not imply that interior/periphery and subsistence/market economies were parallel dichotomies. Many peripheral areas were lightly touched by maritime trade, while almost every interior hamlet had some tenuous contact with the larger world.[13] The peninsula is best seen as a large mosaic of self-sufficient local economies buttressed by short-range exchanges of basic commodities. This mosaic was crisscrossed by a web of economic connections. Its strands represented the meager inflow of manufac-

10. Antonio Domínguez Ortiz, *The Golden Age of Spain* (1971), pp. 4–9.

11. The *Morisco* rebellion of 1568–69 was the principal event between the *Comuneros* and *Germanías* of the 1520's and the Aragonese revolt of the 1590's. The overt expressions of the tension appear to begin with the revolt of Aragón in 1591–92 over political issues. By the 1630's the question of raising the contributions of the periphery to the Spanish war effort was clearly tied to attempts to reduce peripheral autonomy, an issue only partly settled by the Bourbon conquest of Catalonia in the War of Spanish Succession.

12. Ringrose, *Transportation,* pp. 20–24.

13. See James Casey's comments on the extreme subsistence orientation that persisted in parts of Valencia in the seventeenth century, and Jaime García-Lombardero's comments on the stagnation of eighteenth-century Galicia: James Casey, *The Kingdom of Valencia in the Seventeenth Century* (1979); Jaime García-Lombardero, *La agricultura y el estancamiento económico de Galicia en la España del Antiguo Régimen* (1973), ch. 5.

tures and amenities, the export of the few goods that could bear the cost of transport, and the movement of commodities controlled by the landed elites. Occasionally a few strands joined where a market, bishop, governor, or court dispensed services. Near the coasts, the web was denser as port towns provided the mercantile functions made possible by the sea. The striking feature of this overlay of long-distance economic contact as it reached inland was its orientation to Madrid.[14] The observation that Madrid dominated the economy of the interior is hardly novel, but the implications of the city's function as imperial capital while located in the interior have never been worked out. It is a factor that will go far to explain economics and politics in Spain and the increasing tension between the "two Spains."

The very existence of Madrid as a capital city was the consequence of a political decision. No other city in early modern Europe was as dependent upon administered economic life, and no major city was so poorly located to stimulate market-oriented exchanges.[15] Consequently, Madrid's growth involved a large-scale elaboration of Hecksher's primitive urban mercantilism.[16] While London, Paris, Amsterdam, and Lisbon could all depend on maritime and river shipping, Madrid was the largest city of pre-railroad Europe wholly dependent on primitive overland transportation. This is an important consideration, given the impact of eighteenth- and nineteenth-century canals on freight rates.[17] Spain's lack of transport and dispersed resources explain the rural orientation to subsistence agriculture and make it inconceivable that Madrid could have reached its eighteenth-century size without the conscious allocation of resources from interior, periphery, and empire. The first priority of any state is its own immediate needs, and in this

14. García-Lombardero, *La agricultura de Galicia,* maps 3–13 following p. 80.

15. It is important to avoid the assumption that economic change is best approached through the study of market activity—as do Douglass C. North and Robert Paul Thomas in "An Economic Theory of the Growth of the Western World" (1970)—or that Castile lacked markets. See Josep Fontana Lázaro, *La quiebra de la monarquia absoluta, 1814–1820* (1971), pp. 49–51. Fontana maintains that agriculture was blocked by the lack of market articulation, when the blockage was really due to the nature of the market which Madrid induced. Most of the interior economy was subsistence oriented, and commodity movements were only partly organized by market-defined supply and demand. Thus we must distinguish between market activity and "revenue economy." The latter involved seigneurial rents, tithes, and taxation and administrative allocation of surpluses outside of a market environment, as well as mercantilist political doctrines. See Sir John Hicks, *A Theory of Economic History* (1969), pp. 15–24, 81–100; Max Weber, *Law in Economy and Society* (1954), pp. 33–40; Karl Polanyi, "The Economy as Instituted Process," in *Primitive, Archaic, and Modern Economies* (1968), pp. 139–174; E. W. Fox, *History in Geographic Perspective* (1971), pp. 23–71.

16. Eli Hecksher, *Mercantilism* (1935).

17. In England, on a paved road, a horse could haul about two tons of cargo. The same horse could pull a fifty ton cargo on a canal barge. And in Ohio, for example, the price received by the farmer for his wheat rose 300% in six years along the The Ohio Canal. See Phyllis Deane, *The First Industrial Revolution* (1965), p. 79; Harry N. Scheiber, *The Ohio Canal Era: A Case Study of Government and the Economy, 1820–1861* (1969), p. 192.

case a major city was involved. As political center, Madrid rapidly became the social and financial center for the country's wealthy elites. The result was the addition of a large flow of private income to the resources provided by the state. A superstructure of market-based activity developed to meet urban demands, but the income supporting that market relied on the coercive powers of state and landed classes. By the end of the eighteenth century most nonessentials were supplied by market activity, but municipal and royal agencies continually regulated and bolstered grain, fuel, meat, and wine supplies.

As coordinator of political and social life, market for interior agriculture, and national center of conspicuous consumption, Madrid was a point of contact between the "two Spains." The economic life of the periphery was affected by policy made in Madrid, and a large part of its commerce consisted of relaying imports on to the capital. Once in the interior, however, commerce entered the domain of a privileged elite in a region where the contrast between rich and poor was extreme. There the landed elites acquiesced to commercial reform on the periphery, but only so long as their control of society in the interior was not endangered. Thus the capital created political and commercial contacts between interior and maritime Spain, but in the process created a framework within which disagreement could become confrontation. The political structure of the country was unifying as the economic worlds of Spain moved apart.

If the concept of dualism helps define Madrid's position in Spain, models for the two economies suggest why they were separating. One of these is a conception of economic change conditioned by the fact that before 1800 technology was rudimentary and improved slowly.[18] Pre-industrial economies operated within a limited context, with the principal constraint being the threat of Malthusian over-population. Within those limits, however, agrarian Europe was by no means static, experiencing long cycles of expansion and

18. B. H. Slicher van Bath, *The Agrarian History of Western Europe, A.D. 500–1850* (1963); Emmanuel Le Roy Ladurie, *Les paysans de Languedoc* (1966), vol. 1, pp. 139–328 (in the abridged English edition, *The Peasants of Languedoc* (1976), pp. 111–131); Fernand Braudel, *La Méditerranée et le monde méditerranéen à l'époque de Philippe II* (1966), vol. 1, pp. 326–580 (in the English edition, *The Mediterranean and the Mediterranean World in the Age of Philip II* (1972), vol. 1, pp. 355–605). Slicher van Bath attempts to generalize the cycle for all of Europe; Le Roy Ladurie details it beautifully for fourteenth- to seventeenth-century Languedoc; Braudel uses it to organize the masses of information he has collected on the sixteenth-century Mediterranean.

The nature of the technological ceiling has been questioned, but it remains convincing with regard to Spain. The assumption of technological limits has been attacked by Ester Boserup, and more tentatively by E. A. Wrigley. Douglass North and Robert Thomas also insist on increasing productivity in the seventeenth and eighteenth century, but implicitly refer to northwestern Europe and England. See Ester Boserup, *Conditions of Agricultural Growth* (1965), p. 118; E. A. Wrigley, "Demographic Models and Geography," in *Socio-Economic Models in Geography* (1971), p. 197; North and Thomas, "An Economic Theory."

contraction as well as periods of stability at both high and low population densities. The upper limits were set by the supply of land and a static technology. As population grew, the productivity of additional labor declined until the society was reduced to relative poverty and the death rate matched the birth rate. Technology was a limiting factor in two ways: the best agricultural techniques were extremely rudimentary, with little ability to increase the productivity of labor applied to land; and, although technology changed, it changed much more slowly than the ratio of population to resources.

Under such conditions, a low population-to-land ratio encouraged population growth. This happened over much of Europe in the twelfth century and again in the fifteenth. As population increased, the demand for food grew, prices rose, and the rural economy was encouraged to exploit more and more land for basic foods. Since the newer farmlands tended to be less fertile, diminishing returns set in, and output per laborer declined. As population pressure continued to increase, demand produced an acceleration in the rise of food prices. The general level of nutrition declined, and buying power shifted away from manufactures to foodstuffs. The initial prosperity of an expanding economy became increasingly uneven as demand for nonessential products stagnated. The population, both rural and urban, experienced increasing underemployment and became progressively more susceptible to famine and disease.

As economic conditions deteriorated, political and economic structures underwent increasing stress and became vulnerable to shocks from crop failure, disease, and warfare. Any of these factors could disrupt supply and tax systems and trigger a downward demographic and economic trend. As population growth gave way to decline because of deteriorating conditions, a small drop in the total demand for basic foods produced a relatively rapid decline in food prices. At the same time, the population decline made labor relatively scarce, pushing up wages and rural production costs. These factors forced less fertile land out of food production and encouraged conversion of resources to livestock, labor-saving crops, or raw materials. Primarily used for manufactures, these products were better investments as population declined, since falling food prices allowed the surviving population to use an increasing share of its income for nonessential items. Eventually a new balance was achieved, characterized by lower population density and total production, but with higher productivity and per-capita income.[19]

19. Obviously population change is the principal motor for the model, but as E. A. Wrigley points out in *Population and History* (1969), pp. 77–78, family structure and attitudes toward children can influence demographic patterns so as to generate prolonged periods of stability which create apparent lags in the model. Wrigley cites fifteenth-century England as a case of population stability at low population density. Something similar (albeit for different reasons) may have occurred in the interior of Spain between 1650 and 1750.

Within Spain, crucial elements of this self-limiting cycle continued to operate well into the nineteenth century. Following the plagues of the fourteenth century, Castile's population began to grow, and the first half of the sixteenth century is depicted as a period of general prosperity. The cities of the plateau flourished, industry and commerce were stimulated by rising population and Atlantic expansion, and agriculture spread into marginal zones. After 1560 population growth slowed, rural poverty increased, and the two Castiles experienced a generation of precarious stability. Beginning in the 1590's, a series of subsistence crises and epidemics upset the balance, and by 1650 Castilian population had declined 25%.[20] The demographic situation stabilized in the second half of the seventeenth century, and thereafter the population increased gradually until the 1790's. Castile thus experienced more than a century of relatively slow population growth, reflecting perhaps a more self-contained rural economy than that of the sixteenth century.[21] From about 1790 the interior experienced stagnation that probably continued until around 1840.

A second model, that of "the crisis of the seventeenth century," more clearly delineates the developments on the periphery. This "crisis" model has undergone frequent revision, becoming little more than a loose reference to all of the bad weather, wars, revolutions, and fiscal crises from 1560 to 1715—the antithesis of Braudel's "long sixteenth century." From the attendant discussion, however, there has emerged a clearer perception of the process whereby the maritime and waterborne trade of Europe was integrated into a continent-wide market system of unprecedented geographic scope, carrying capacity, and cheapness of transportation. By 1700 this commercial network was revolutionary in three ways:[22] (1) It unified the trade of the Baltic, Atlantic, and Mediterranean regions to an unprecedented degree. (2) It increasingly dealt with bulky, everyday goods such as wheat, fish, and rough textiles, in addition to the more valuable goods that dominated earlier long-distance trade. (3) As it grew, the market system focused a growing share of Europe's trans-Atlantic and Asian commerce on England and the Netherlands. This trade in hides, cacao, sugar, coffee, tobacco, dye products,

---

20. José Gentil da Silva, *En Espagne: Développement économique, subsistance, déclin* (1965), pp. 104–120; Bartolomé Bennassar, *Recherches sur les grandes épidémies dans le nord de l'Espagne à la fin du XVIᵉ siècle* (1969), pp. 60–82.

21. Anes, *Las crisis agrarias,* pp. 141–142. García Sanz, in *Desarrollo y crisis en Segovia,* pp. 75 and 84, dates the later cycle in Segovia as 1600–1650, decline; 1650–1700, stagnation; 1700–1760, expansion; 1760–1814, stagnation.

22. North and Thomas attribute the growth of the Netherlands and England primarily to market activity, but as in the case of Madrid, the market masks administrative decisions allocating resources to the wars in the north from 1567–1659. Their impact on Northern industry, commerce, and money supply helps explain the Dutch capture of European trade. See

and cotton involved new or once-rare goods with potential mass markets.[23] The unification of the European market system allowed England and Holland to benefit from regional specialization in the rest of Europe on a scale never before possible. The neo-Malthusian cycle of agricultural society no longer applied to Europe as a whole, because the Netherlands and England had become centers for widespread productivity increases through regional specialization and investment in new technology and business techniques. Thus they could counter the negative pressures of population density inherited from the sixteenth century and even increase per-capita wealth by the eighteenth century. Ultimately the new commercial pattern laid the basis for the Industrial Revolution.

These changes altered Spain's position relative to the rest of the continent and increased the possibilities for market orientation in the maritime areas and in the empire. As a result, Vizcaya, Catalonia, Valencia, and the Seville/Cádiz complex began to experience a modest renewal of commercial life in the second half of the seventeenth century. The wool and iron trades of Bilbao expanded, and Pierre Vilar provides evidence that Barcelona and its hinterland experienced a renewal of economic initiative unmatched since the middle ages.[24] As we shall see, by 1700 several other coastal regions were responding to external stimuli at a time when the stagnation of the Spanish interior was notorious.

These developments marked the sharpening of certain features that run through Spanish history. With the exception of Moorish Córdoba and medieval and eighteenth-century Catalonia, Spain has always been an underdeveloped part of Europe. Despite American silver and the development of Castilian industry in the sixteenth century, Spain's European commerce consisted largely of imported luxuries and the manufactures and export of raw materials, foodstuffs, and semi-finished goods. This commerce depended heavily upon Italian, Flemish, or German capital and upon foreign carrying capacity. Spain compensated for this dependence on the advanced parts of Europe by enforcing a similar dependence upon its American colonies and mines. As northern Europe increased its economic efficiency during the crises of the seventeenth century, Spain lost her capacity to function as an active

---

David R. Ringrose, "European Economic Growth: Comments on the North–Thomas Theory" (1972).

23. To comprehend the degree to which the markets of Europe had become integrated, one need only refer to the maps showing evolution of grain prices in Fernand Braudel and Frank Spooner, "Prices in Europe from 1450 to 1750," in *Cambridge Economic History,* vol. 6 (1967), pp. 472–473.

24. Pierre Vilar, *Catalunya dins l'Espanya moderna* (1968), vol. 2, pp. 187–188, 267–289, 373–412; John Lynch, *Spain Under the Hapsburgs* (1969), vol. 2, p. 154.

participant in Atlantic commerce, and her dependence on European and American capital, ships, and goods became more pronounced.[25]

As this dependence developed, it in turn increased the separation between the two peninsular economies. While the economic context of the interior remained unchanged, that of the periphery was being revolutionized. The separation was not sharply geographic. Elements of the maritime economy reached into the interior, as seaports, landed elites, and the capital city exchanged certain goods and services. Despite this link, however, the economies of coast and interior were responding to different situations and were being drawn apart.

Such a statement will not surprise historians familiar with Spain; but if we are to understand the unique role that Madrid played as the urban center where the two Spains came into contact, we have to define the obvious with some care. In the sixteenth century, when maritime trade had not entirely surpassed land transport in efficiency, Castile showed economic development in response to domestic and imperial demand. By the seventeenth century this growth had reached the limits of interior resources, and the balance was shifting to the periphery. Yet one should not underestimate the weight of the interior provinces in the Spanish system. They included a third of Spain's eighteenth-century population, produced almost a third of royal revenue, and produced 60% of the gross agricultural product of the Crown of Castile in 1750. Although the wealth and population of the region were dispersed and heavily committed to subsistence agriculture, they were not negligible.[26]

Madrid was an integral part of both economic worlds, but created little interaction between them. This was not because Madrid lacked commercial significance—in the 1750's the capital's commercial and industrial income exceeded that of Seville and Cádiz combined.[27] The urban economy depended upon the government, which in turn depended upon revenue from the maritime system. Government resources were supplemented by the land rents collected by landowners resident in the city. At the same time, the city drew its basic supplies from the subsistence-oriented economy of the interior, and its luxuries from much farther away. Given the economic structure of the

25. These structures of dependence are discussed relative to Spain in the eighteenth century by Barbara and Stanley Stein, *The Colonial Heritage of Latin America* (1970), pp. 15–26, 86–106.

26. It is difficult to provide totals or comparisons which include the provinces of the Crown of Aragón, since they had a separate tax structure which yielded few economic surveys easily compared with those of Castile. See José Canga Argüelles, *Diccionario de hacienda con aplicación a España* (1834), articles on "Población de España"; Antonio Matilla Tascón, *La única contribución y el catastro de Ensenada* (1947); Pierre Vilar, "Estructures de la societat espanyola cap al 1750" (1970), pp. 15 and 28.

27. Vilar, "Estructures," p. 28.

capital, this had important implications for Spain. It produced the paradox of a growing metropolis which discouraged economic development in its surrounding region, a pattern that requires closer examination.

All cities are supported by the areas around them in return for services they provide, but there is great variety in the functions performed and the resources required.[28] Thus a city can serve as a central place for several functions with several fields of influence that will vary in size with the nature of the function or commodity involved. A city may operate as a transport focus, a break-of-bulk point, or as source of a specialized service. The first two also imply the possibility of an entrepôt function.[29] Some urban functions can extend over longer distances than others, with the result that the landscape will have a hierarchy of central places, the smaller ones providing shorter-range functions for smaller hinterlands while depending upon a larger central place for other purposes. Improved transportation has the effect of strengthening and enlarging the urban fields of larger towns. This reduces the relative importance of subordinate centers, particularly those closest to the larger central place.[30]

The size of a field of influence depends on the cost of distributing the good or service in question, the preference of the consumer for substitutes, and the degree to which the consumer will forego the commodity as the price rises. In general, individual demand for basic foodstuffs is very inelastic as prices rise or fall, while the consumer's demand for luxuries will vary greatly as their prices change relative to real income and the cost of more essential goods.[31] At the same time, the capital cost of producing a good or service affects centrality. A facility requiring a large capital investment is not easily replicated, and therefore will provide that function over a wide geographic range.[32]

In a poor society with rudimentary transport, there is great disparity in the geographic scope of these functional fields of influence. Political and social services based on communication, and commerce involving valuable commodities, can reach a large area from a single center. Exchange of bulky, low-value goods has a smaller range and is carried out by smaller towns distributed across the region. Only improved transportation or subsidization of

28. For a recent theoretical discussion, see Brian J. L. Berry, Edgar C. Conkling, and D. Michael Ray, *The Geography of Economic Systems* (1976), ch. 12, "Local Trade and Urban Hierarchies," pp. 226–242.

29. Chauncy D. Harris and Edward L. Ullman, "The Nature of Cities" (1945), pp. 7–9 (reprinted in Paul K. Hatt and Albert J. Reiss, eds., *Cities and Society* (1957), pp. 237–247).

30. Edward L. Ullman, "A Theory of Location for Cities" (1941), esp. pp. 855–856 (reprinted in Hatt and Reiss, *Cities and Society*, pp. 227–236).

31. Walter Christaller, *Central Places in Southern Germany* (1966), pp. 51–53, 96.

32. Ibid., p. 96.

the central market can widen the field of influence based on such a function.[33] Thus a wealthy society using many services and commodities exhibits a developed urban hierarchy based on differing combinations of distribution and production costs.[34] If, however, the society is poor and transport costly, the urban hierarchy will have only a few central places with fields of influence extending beyond local and regional exchanges, and the volume of activity in those fields will be slight.[35]

The significance of this model is apparent if we look at the economic processes that developed around London. The interactions between London and its English hinterland included urban-rural migration; urban demand for agricultural commodities and manufactures; the requirements of London's re-export markets; the fact that one-sixth of the surrounding area's countrymen had experienced the amenities of London life, and were drawn to produce for the market to obtain them; and the role of a landlord class acclimated to the market and disposed to reorganize their estates to meet urban demand. These factors were reinforced by river transport, coastal trade, and European and trans-Atlantic commerce. Prior to about 1640, the city grew by capturing wealth and urban functions from the rest of England. Thereafter its consumption, exchange, production, and administrative functions provided positive returns to the rest of the country, and by the end of the seventeenth century had been instrumental in ending rural economic isolation.[36]

As imperial capital and largest city in Spain, however, Madrid's most important functions were political rather than industrial or commercial, and the interactions between the capital and its hinterland were quite different from those between London and the rest of England.[37] In the sixteenth century Madrid undermined the economic position and central-place functions of the manufacturing towns of the Spanish interior. In the seventeenth, Madrid encouraged the development of a rural society based on local power, low-order central places, and markets and land usage that left few incentives for the peasant to increase productivity. This reflected the rise of Madrid as center of imperial policy-making, aristocratic socialization, and conspicuous

33. The crucial work on the topic is Walter Christaller's *Central Places*. The conceptual model is laid out in Part I, pp. 14–135. First published in Germany in 1933, the durability of this conceptual framework is documented by its basic role in textbooks of very recent date, e.g., Berry et al., *Geography of Economic Systems*, ch. 12.

34. Christaller, *Central Places*, pp. 101, 119–120, 121.

35. Ibid., p. 121.

36. E. A. Wrigley, "A Simple Model of London's Importance in Changing English Society and Economy, 1650–1750" (1967). A more perceptive geo-economic discussion of the problem is found in Peter Clark and Paul Slack, *English Towns in Transition, 1500–1700* (1976), esp. chs. 1 and 5.

37. On London, see Wrigley, "A Simple Model."

consumption by elites. The capital city extracted resources from all over the interior, both by subsidizing its urban market and by administratively re-directing regional commodity flows. This undermined older commercial and industrial towns in ways that minimized incentives for rural specialization.[38]

When Madrid was expanding in the eighteenth century, urban supply provided the basis for a community of interests among the landed elements, who accumulated rents and primary products; the stewards who actually managed estates; wealthy peasants; and the middlemen of the capital, who collected taxes on government contract, extended credit to the Crown, pro-vided landlords with mortgage money, and contracted for delivery of supplies for capital, court, and military. Common to all these activities was the under-lying reality that Madrid existed because it provided central political and social services. The transition to the nineteenth century modified the balance between these various elements. A Castilian agro-commercial oligarchy crystalized out of the ruins of Spanish society left by foreign and civil wars between 1808 and 1839, and imposed its will on all of Spain for the rest of the nineteenth century. At the same time, the structure of rural power was little changed except for the addition of new urban elements to the landlord class with the sale of Church properties. These "bourgeois" elements imposed a liberal, parliamentary, and centrist regime in Spain on the Anglo-French model.

This study takes the position that the emerging political class of the nine-teenth century was in place by the end of the eighteenth century, over-shadowed by the social and political structure based on the interlocking interests of Madrid, aristocracy, and Cádiz. Oriented to Madrid, the domes-tic agro-commercial group was the inadvertent heir of the ruins of the empire. To preserve their domestic base, these agro-commercial elements coalesced around what became the *Moderado* state. They adopted parliamentary liber-alism as a new rationale for their control of the rural economy. They also accepted the absolutist heritage of centrism that they had once resisted, since it had become essential to the survival of the eighteenth-century commercial and market structures that they depended upon. In the process, interior elites developed a community of interests antagonistic to the modernization of Spain's political and economic life.

In brief, the rise of Madrid between 1560 and 1630 contributed to the decline of the Castilian economy of the sixteenth century. As the capital grew in the context of a stagnant regional economy, population and production fell. After 1610, commercialization of agricultural products in the interior de-pended on the Madrid market. The Thirty Years' War ruined Spain's Euro-

---

38. Ibid., pp. 56–57; Wrigley stresses the importance of improving productivity as opposed to simply expanding output with traditional methods.

pean empire, while her American empire experienced a prolonged depression. During this double crisis in the middle third of the seventeenth century, the capital lost 40% of its population, further depressing the agricultural markets of the region. Sale of jurisdictions and taxes by a desperate Crown expanded the nobility's control of local power. Agriculture compensated for population decline by shifting to less intensive activities, and for market decline by orienting output to local needs. In the eighteenth century the Empire revived and Madrid began to expand, renewing its demand for supplies and expanding administrative and market institutions which drew on the surpluses that landowners extracted from the countryside. Historians have noted the improved prospects of the dominant classes for patronage and wealth in a reviving empire, but have ignored a parallel development in which the same groups were becoming dependent on the sale of agricultural products to the growing capital. This second process produced the characteristic traits of Spain's nineteenth-century agro-commercial oligarchy: close association among agriculture, rural power, dependence on commerce in agricultural products, and the need to shape a national policy in support of that commerce.

Explanations of nineteenth-century Spanish history often give central place to the appearance of a "new oligarchy" out of the chaos of 1808–1839.[39] In fact, the socio-economic ties and habits underlying that "new oligarchy" were a legacy of empire generated by the development of Spain's capital city. Part One of the following study examines the development and structure of the urban economy at the center of this process; Part Two details the economic relationship between Madrid and Castilian agriculture; and Part Three traces the impact on the Castilian urban network and the connections with the peninsular periphery.

39. For versions of this theme, see Juan Beneyto Pérez, *Historia social de España y de Hispanoamérica* (1961), pp. 351–356, 368–393; Raymond Carr, *Spain: 1808–1939* (1966), pp. 196–209, 281–286; José Luis Comellas García-Llera, *Los moderados en el poder, 1844–1854* (1970), pp. 60–80; Richard Herr, *An Historical Essay on Modern Spain* (1971), pp. 87–98; Antoni Jutglar, *Ideologías y clases en la España contemporánea,* vol. 1 (1968), pp. 15–20, 76–87, 101–124; Jaime Vicens Vives, *Manual de historia económica de España* (1967), pp. 553–557, 560–583.

Part One
Madrid

2. Population and Market Trends: A Long-Term Profile

In the three centuries after 1600, the expansion and contraction of economic life in Madrid followed the evolution of the maritime provinces and imperial trade. The result was a constantly changing relationship between the capital and the interior, one measure of which was the constantly fluctuating size of the city. Thus the first step toward an understanding of the relationship of city to region and country is an examination of the basic pattern of the city's growth. This can then be compared with the evolution of the two distinctive economic patterns apparent in Spain.[1] To this end, the rise of Madrid is illustrated through revenues from taxes on market activity in the city and the results are compared with a re-evaluation of available figures for the actual population of the city. This profile of urban growth provides the setting for the city's demographic structure, occupational structure, the distribution of wealth and income,[2] and changes in income and consumption in the city.

Madrid's role in both regional and national economic life is important to our understanding of the eighteenth century, a period when maritime expansion preceded the capital's recovery. This suggests that Madrid's economy relayed the effect of maritime economic change to the interior. This logic also applies to the late sixteenth and early seventeenth centuries, when Madrid's

1. I have explored the problem of Madrid's growth and patterns of food consumption in an earlier article—David R. Ringrose, "Madrid y Castilla, 1560–1850: Una capital nacional en una economía regional," (1969)—deducing population from consumption figures. Here a more extensive use of primary sources allows the population totals to stand by themselves in relation to other aspects of Madrid's development.
2. I have made some preliminary comments on income distribution and the structure of the workforce in David R. Ringrose, "Madrid et l'Espagne du XVIIIᵉ siècle: L'économie d'une capitale politique" (1975), pp. 593–605; see also David R. Ringrose, "Madrid as an Agent of Economic Stagnation in Spain" (1981).

19

growth first paralleled Castilian expansion but then continued against a background of economic stagnation in 1590–1610 and was sustained by peripheral resources, despite serious regional decline, between 1610 and 1640. The possibility that Madrid's growth damaged the regional economy cannot be denied and will be dealt with later.[3] The basic linkages are also apparent in the middle of the seventeenth century when the collapse of Spain's American and European influence coincided with a pronounced contraction of both population and economic activity in the capital.

Among the revenues of the city of Madrid, the *peso mayor y correduría* (weighing and brokerage duties) collected in the main plaza, and the toll at the ferry near Arganda (the *barca de Arganda*) represent two aspects of the city's commercial activity. The *peso* was collected on a wide range of foodstuffs and merchandise sold in the principal markets, but excluded staples such as bread, wine, olive oil, or meat.[4] Such a tax on consumption is inherently sensitive to subsistence crises and changes in real income, because it represents commodities used by the poor when possible, but easily foregone when income fell.

The decennial average of the yield from the *peso* doubled between the 1560's and the decade 1611–20 (see Table 2.1), while the regional price level rose only 45%. Discounting the subsistence crisis of 1626–31 for the moment, the revenue from the *peso* remained high through the early 1620's, and in the 1630's was briefly higher still. Meanwhile the general price level rose about 20%. Depending on the proportion of the revenue that was collected *ad valorem, peso* revenues suggest a long-term increase in regional market activity of 55% to 100% between 1560 and 1620, followed by a slight decline. Since, as will be shown later, per-capita real income was declining after 1620, the decline does not conflict with sustained population growth. *Peso* revenues began to drop in the 1640's as prices continued to rise, and reached very low levels in the 1650's and 1670's. In the first instance prices were also falling, but in 1676–80 they were 30% higher than in 1651–55, indicating an even sharper drop in the real value of any revenue collected *ad valorem.* The nominal low in the 1680's coincided with a subsistence crisis and monetary deflation, so the linkages at that point are obscured. Revenues then stabilized

3. David R. Ringrose, "The Impact of a New Capital City: Madrid, Toledo, and New Castile, 1560–1660" (1973), pp. 761–791. See ch. 11 below.

4. The quality of this type of data is a question that affects many parts of this study. Several filters were present between the reported revenue and actual trade. The revenues were farmed (contracted out to private businesses for collection) and provided a profit to the contractor. Contracts were based on projected rather than actual revenue. Some goods were taxed *ad valorem* while others paid a flat fee, and we have no way of being certain of the balance between the two types. And evasion was chronic. Our assumption is that these variables were in a fairly stable relationship with actual trade; and with allowance for inherent biases where necessary, and for possible margin of error, that the more pronounced trends are trustworthy.

Table 2.1. *Decennial Averages of Tax Revenues*
Reflecting Commercial Activity in Madrid*

Period	Peso Mayor y Correduria		Barca de Arganda	
1561-70	12,646	(4)		
1583-84	19,548	(1)	3,824	(2)
1591-1600	20,815	(9)	7,357	(6)
1601-10	22,529	(2)(a)	11,000	(4)(c)
	11,900	(6)(b)	7,700	(8)(d)
1611-20	24,158	(5)	12,871	(7)
1621-30	18,519	(6)(e)	17,483	(6)
1631-40	22,588	(8)(f)	19,150	(8)
1641-50	19,292	(9)	17,000	(8)
1651-60	11,559	(9)	13,900	(10)
1661-70	14,026	(10)	16,907	(10)
1671-80	10,332	(10)	20,350	(10)
1681-90	11,898	(10)	20,000	(10)
1691-1700	15,012	(10)	16,562	(10)
1701-10	14,980	(10)	19,320	(10)
1711-20	15,509	(10)	20,123	(10)
1721-30	19,698	(10)	20,635	(10)
1731-40	19,302	(10)	21,114	(10)
1741-50	23,182	(6)	22,684	(10)
1751-60	22,000	(5)	26,952	(3)
1761-70	47,723	(5)(g)	26,143	(10)
1771-80	34,006	(10)	24,676	(10)
1781-90	36,041	(4)	29,629	(10)
1791-1800	37,973	(5)	34,999	(10)
1801-10	15,973	(5)	39,100	(10)
1811-20	–	–	25,220	(10)

Sources: See Table A.2.

* All averages given in *reales*. Numbers in parentheses indicate the actual number of years for which figures exist. The *peso* was collected partially in fixed fees, partly *ad valorem*. The *barca* was collected entirely in fixed fees. The same fee schedule recurs in the sources throughout the period discussed.

a. With Court present.

b. Six years, including five when Court absent.

c. Four years, with Court present.

d. Eight years, including four when Court absent.

e. Three of the six years from the prolonged subsistence crisis of 1626-31.

f. Includes 1631, worst year of subsistence crisis of 1626-31.

g. The revenues from the *peso* for 1766-71 are suspiciously high, suggesting an abortive reform in collections. Even if they are set aside, the trend is clear.

until the 1720's, followed by a strong increase that continued through the eighteenth century. The real value of the commerce thus reflected was not eroded by inflation until after 1750.

The *barca de Arganda* was a boat toll collected on a main road from Valencia, Alicante, and Cartagena to Madrid (Map 1.2). It reflected both regional trade and the movement of merchandise and travelers along an important route from the sea to the Spanish capital. In contrast to the *peso mayor,* which reflected regional market activity, the Arganda toll is indicative of the long-distance traffic between Madrid and periphery. It also has the advantage of being based on a toll schedule defined in money terms rather than *ad valorem*, and thus the relationship between revenue and traffic was not affected by price changes.

The growth of toll revenues is startling: from the 1580's to 1611–20 the volume of traffic tripled, and by the 1630's it was five times that of the late sixteenth century. Revenues declined in the middle decades of the century, but recovered by 1670. Between 1670 and 1730, the revenues and presumably traffic were stable except for a recession in the 1690's. Around 1730, when revenue compared with the peak of a century earlier, traffic began to expand, and by the end of the eighteenth century it had nearly doubled.

The trends shown by these two indicators contrast markedly with those recorded for the other towns of the interior.[5] The market activity reflected in the *peso* and the long-distance traffic reflected in the *barca* expanded until the 1620's, but after 1620 *peso* revenues stagnated while toll revenues continued to rise.[6] In either case, the trend contrasts with the collapse of commerce at other urban centers of the interior and parallels the continued high levels of port activity on the periphery. Between 1640 and about 1725, the *peso,* an indicator of the city's ability to consume nonessential products from the interior, dropped to half its high in the 1630's and remained depressed until the 1720's, reflecting urban poverty and reduced population. The boat toll, however, continued to follow the pattern of the maritime regions. The declines are briefer and less severe, and by 1670 traffic had recovered the volume of earlier in the century. This aspect of Madrid's economy was functioning as part of the commercial structure of the Spanish maritime centers, while at the same time Madrid was interacting with the economic structures of the Castilian interior.

This profile of Madrid's evolution is reinforced by the fluctuations of the city's population. Total population is a crude indicator of economic importance, since many of our sources are not very satisfactory, but they do establish some general boundaries for the problem. Associated with market and traffic trends, this picture permits an initial perception of market development from the seventeenth century into the nineteenth century.

The accepted version of Madrid's growth indicates that by mid-sixteenth century Madrid had 20,000 inhabitants. Philip II resided there while heir-

5. See Chapters 10–12 below.
6. In this, Madrid follows the sustained levels of economic activity of the Mediterranean area until mid-seventeenth century; see Fernand Braudel, *The Mediterranean and the Mediterranean World in the Age of Philip II*, vol. 2, pp. 893–894.

apparent, and Madrid became the formal capital in 1560. By 1570 it contained 35,000 people, and the new capital grew steadily under Philip II and Philip III, reaching 65,000 by 1600 and 130,000 in 1620. In this version the city stabilized for the rest of the seventeenth century, until a new phase of expansion brought it to 170,000 inhabitants by 1797. Growth was cut short by the Napoleonic wars, but by 1850 the population had reached 235,000 and in the 1860's it hovered around 290,000.[7] The evolution of both the Castilian economy and the Spanish monarchy, when compared with this version of Madrid's growth, implies that prosperity, decadence, stagnation, overpopulation, depopulation, political success, and political failure all expanded or sustained the city's size.

This implication is difficult to accept unless the city itself contained a source of wealth independent of the country's economy or government. Yet Madrid has always been considered a parasite and an economically unproductive dependency. The capital was invariably described as a city filled with bureaucrats shuffling papers, nobles seeking sinecures and supporting armies of retainers and servants, and the poor and dispossessed fleeing the natural and man-made calamities of rural Castile. While that description is too sharply drawn, it rules out the possibility that the urban economy was somehow independent of the rest of the Spanish world. Moreover, the halving of market revenue and 30% decline in income from the Arganda toll between 1635 and 1660 suggest an urban decline concomitant with the crises of Castile and empire. Similarly, the stability of the same revenues between 1690 and 1720 contradicts the possibility of new urban expansion before 1725. Thus there are inconsistencies in accepted perceptions that require a reevaluation of population figures and of the interaction between the city and the hinterland.

Reexamined in conjunction with trends in the market activity of the city, the same sources indicate that the city's growth was neither constant nor gradual. Its population in the early seventeenth century has been underestimated, while those of the late seventeenth and early nineteenth have been overestimated. In fact, the sources can be interpreted to show that the city grew gradually from 1560 to 1599, and then became a boom town that grew from 65,000 to 175,000 inhabitants in a generation. Subsequently the population fell to about 125,000 by 1685, and stayed there until after the War of the Spanish Succession. Thereafter it grew slowly until the 1750's, before expanding rapidly to 195,000 in 1799. Around 1800 population began to drift

7. An often-quoted version casually tossed off by Jaime Vicens Vives differs, in that he states breezily that the city continued expanding "fabulously" until 1660, "obeying the law of the creation of gigantic urban nuclei in countries with low population density and poor agriculture." See Antonio Domínguez Ortiz, *La sociedad española del siglo XVIII* (1955), pp. 73–74, and *La sociedad española del siglo XVII*, vol. 1 (1963), pp. 129–134; Jaime Vicens Vives, *Manual de historia económica de España*, pp. 400, 402, 564–565.

downward, a trend hastened by the Napoleonic occupation, and as of 1821 the total was no more than 160,000. While it recovered in the 1820's and '30's, the population did not definitively exceed 200,000 until the 1840's. Such striking fluctuations in population, combined with the behavior of market indicators, suggest strong interaction between city and country and require careful examination of the population evidence.

The first step is a review of the heterogeneous population figures that are available and of the calculations based upon them. Not one of the numerous primary sources can be considered exact, and all create problems of interpretation and large margins of error. Thus it is hardly surprising that there is substantial disagreement regarding the population of Madrid at any given time. As Table A.2 demonstrates, estimates for the sixteenth century range from 4,775 inhabitants in 1530 to 30,000 in 1546, and from 14,000 to 40,000 for 1570 alone. Later figures range from 70,000 in 1622–26 to 392,000 in 1646. The discrepancies in later estimates are smaller, since they reflect better censuses, but even the figures for a given year in the nineteenth century can differ by 20%.

These disagreements derive from the nature of the primary sources. Many refer to *vecinos* or registered heads of families, others only to *vecinos pecheros,* or registered taxpayers, since many legal residents were exempt from taxes. Other documents list persons taking confession and communion, with first communion apparently common around the age of 12.[8] Censuses of all inhabitants are available only after 1750. In addition, there are estimates of unknown origin by contemporary observers, censuses of inhabited houses, and figures for the number of "families" in the city.

Converting these heterogeneous figures into population totals has led historians to the use of a number of debatable conventions. The thorniest problem is the relationship between the number of recognized households and actual inhabitants.[9] The literature includes coefficients varying from three to six persons per *vecino,* but the arguments are seldom convincing and the results are of dubious validity for a long period of alternating prosperity and eco-

8. See article "Comunión" in the *Encyclopedia Universal Ilustrada* (n.d.), vol. 14, p. 884.
9. The traditional practice was to multiply *vecinos* by five to obtain total population. This coefficient was used by contemporaries such as Gerónymo de Uztariz and was adopted by Tomás González and Pascual Madoz in the nineteenth century. Modern researchers have proposed coefficients of 4.75, 4.5, and even 4.0. Recent studies based on the figures of Sebastian Miñano, published in 1826, suggest coefficients of 3.88 for Salamanca, 4.29 for Madrid province, and 2.74 for La Mancha. Other provincial coefficients: Burgos, 4.31; Soria, 4.38; Segovia, 4.07; Ávila, 3.92. See Gerónymo de Uztariz, *Theórica y práctica de comercio y de Marina,* (facsimile reprint of 1742 edition, 1968), pp. 34–39; and volumes in the series *La España del Antiguo Régimen,* ed. Miguel Artola: María Dolores Mateos, *Salamanca* (1966), p. 15; María Pilar Calonge Matellanes, Eugenio García Zarza, and María Elena Rodríguez Sánchez, *Castilla la Vieja* (1967), p. 17; María Dolores Marcos González, *Castilla la Nueva y Extremadura* (1971), p. 15.

nomic crisis.[10] The floating, transient element presents a similar problem that everyone acknowledges, but it cannot be quantified. Estimates of transients are often around 20,000 persons, although 30,000 and even 50,000 (in 1597) have appeared plausible at times.[11] There are no real guidelines for this concept, but two corollaries apply: As censuses became more thorough, more of the floating population got counted; also, periods of unrest and urban expansion expand the floating population. Thus a figure of 25,000 transients might be acceptable for the 1620's, but a smaller one fits the 1790's or the early nineteenth century.

A third problem is that of the relationship between *"personas de confesión y comunión"* and total population, whether domiciled or nonresident. It is customary to add 25% to the number of communicants to account for dependents below the age of first communion, and later censuses support this coefficient.[12] Finally, even the conventional adjustments for transients and noncommunicants have not been applied systematically. The situation was further confused by Tomás González's conversion of *casas* and *familias* into *vecinos* to clarify the censuses of the 1590's. Finally, we have the estimates of Ricardo Martorell, who attempted to extrapolate total population from baptism figures without allowing for immigration.[13]

Thus we have a two-part problem: documenting change in urban size requires reliable totals; but to get those totals, we have to work with a variety of questionable sources and estimates. The confusion makes it worthwhile to

10. Sebastian Miñano's figures for Madrid in 1825 suggest 3.64 inhabitants per *vecino* without transients and 4.02 with them. Those ratios appear constant in the mid-nineteenth century, but the Madrid census of 1804 yields 4.0:1 and 4.5:1, suggesting that the average household was larger then. See Marcos González, *Castilla la Nueva,* pp. 18, 19, 83; also see Appendix A.

11. In 1597, authorities estimated over 50,000 persons outside the precept of *"confesión y comunion,"* as can be seen from comments written on the outer cover of Archivo General de Simancas (AGS), *Expedientes de Hacienda,* leg. 121. Later observers and modern historians assume a floating population of 20,000 to 30,000. While some sources lump garrison, poorhouse residents, and religious into a "nonresident" category along with true transients, the censuses of 1804, 1825, and 1845 list 18,000 to 20,000 people in those official nonresident categories, but leave open the question of the truly transient.

12. Although never discussed by contemporaries, this figure appears accurate. The detailed censuses of 1787, 1850, and 1857 allow precise estimates of dependent noncommunicants which offer support for the 25% guess. Assuming that the age of first communion was 12 years (see note 8 above), and given the age distribution of those three censuses, 20% of the resident population would have been excluded by a communicant census, the equivalent of 25% of those over age 12. This indicates a small base for the urban age pyramid compared with region or country (see Chapter 3 below), but it is a characteristic of every Madrid census indicating age distribution.

13. Domínguez Ortiz converts 108,000 communicants in 1617 to only 130,000 inhabitants; while for 1723, with 95,000 communicants, he finds 150,000 inhabitants. Ricardo Martorell Téllez Girón's figure—in *Aportaciones al estudio de la población de Madrid en el siglo XVII (1930)*—of 69,000 inhabitants for the 1620's is far too low, because he made no allowance for immigration. (For citations, see Table A.2.)

set aside the previous estimates and restrict ourselves to figures based upon stable contemporary definitions such as *vecino,* communicant, and inhabitant (see Table 2.2). There is little chance of our finding a single ratio between *vecinos* and total population, but estimates of the number of transients and inhabitants are subject to certain logical premises. An expanding city that is the seat of government will have proportionately more unregistered inhabitants than the same city as capital of a defeated and disorganized state. There also will be more inhabitants per *vecino* when a city is expanding than when it is declining, since prosperity implies more household dependents and domestics. Conversely, the capital of a declining monarchy will have smaller households, many *vecinos* who have departed in its registers, and fewer transients.

The most reliable supplement to Table 2.2 is an extrapolation from communicants to domiciled inhabitants. The censuses of 1787, 1850, and 1857 indicate that for 70 years 20% of the registered population was 12 or younger, the same ratio assumed by contemporaries. Applied to earlier figures for communicants, this allows the estimates of total domiciled population given in Table 2.3.

Even where the sources refer to all inhabitants, adjustments are needed. "Inhabitant" was a juridical concept that excluded several types of resident, including garrison troops, secular clergy, religious communities and their servants, and hospital and poorhouse residents, as well as the transients or *forasteros.* Later censuses, however, often included some of these groups,[14] but if we make the appropriate adjustments to the inhabitant figures in Tables 2.2 and 2.3, we arrive at a set of homogenous estimates that exclude only the unregistered floating element. For 1617 and 1621 the estimate reaches 150,000–155,000; for 1685 and 1723, about 125,000; and for 1769, 140,000. Adding garrison estimates to 1787, 1793, and 1797 brings them to 166,000, 168,000, and 177,000 respectively, bringing them into line with the more complete censuses of 1798, 1799, and 1804. The same procedure reduces the total for 1821 to 150,000. To all of these totals we can add conservative estimates of the truly transient population, reducing the adjustments for the later years to compensate for the improving quality of the sources.[15] Based on all these adjustments of the primary sources, the total population developed as presented in Table 2.4.

14. The figures for 1787, 1797, and 1831 include all of these except the garrison and transients. Those for 1799 and 1804 include the garrison as well, as do the larger figures for some years after 1836. Garrison figures are consistently around 8,000 to 10,000 men. Other undomiciled categories are less consistent, but they run from 4,000 to 10,000 persons until the sale of Church properties in the nineteenth century led to a sharp reduction in the clerical population. All groups tended to fluctuate with the prosperity of the city.

15. Thus, while 20,000 might be a plausible figure for 1621, 10–15,000 is more believable by 1685 or 1723, and by 1800 a more conservative 10,000 estimate is safer.

Table 2.2. *Madrid Population as Reported in Primary Sources*

Year	*Vecinos*	Communicants	Inhabitants
1513	3,000		
1546	6,000		
1594	9,541		
1597	11,857 "familias"	45,422	101,550
1617		108,332	
1621		112,000	
1646	74,435 "vecinos"		
1646	58,669 "contri- buyentes"		
1659			129,653
1685		96,000 over age seven	
1723	24,344	95,473	
1743			111,268
1757	30,626	101,057	109,753
1766	32,745		
1769			121,038
1787			156,672
1793			158,086
1797			167,607
1798			180,300
1799			184,404
1804	39,523		176,374
1817			138,000
1821			135,629
1825	50,336		201,344
1831	49,400		211,127
1836	50,440		224,312
1842			157,397
1842	44,000		194,312
1843	44,980		166,283
1843	55,267		212,225
1845	48,108		206,714
1846			205,848
1847	58,750		215,000
1850			216,571
1851			234,178
1852			236,108
1853			231,866
1857			281,170
1860			292,426
1862			288,373
1864			285,174
1865			283,197
1866			282,976
1868			282,635
1869			292,483

Sources: See Table A.1.

Table 2.3. *Estimated Population of Madrid,
if Communicants Equal 80% of Total
Population**

Year	Communicants	Inhabitants (est.)
1597	45,422	56,778
1617	108,332	135,415
1621	112,000	140,000
1685	96,000	120,000
1723	95,473	119,342
1757	101,057	126,326

Sources: See Table 2.2 and text.
*As population totals, these estimates are roughly
comparable to those of 1743, 1769, 1757, and 1821, and
the domiciled population of 147,000 in the census of
1787. There is little to suggest, however, that the earlier
figures were compiled as carefully, and they probably
understate reality more than the later figures.

Table 2.4. *Selected Estimates of Total
Population, Madrid, 1597-1860*

Year	Population (est.)
1597	65,000
1630	175,000
1685	125,000
1723	130,000
1757	142,500
1769	150,000
1787	175,000
1799	195,000
1821	160,000
1842	200,000
1850	220,000
1860	300,000

Sources: See text and Tables 2.2 and 2.3. For
the problematic late seventeenth century, there
are estimates ranging from 120,000 to 150,000;
see Claude Larquié, "Quartiers et paroisses
urbaines: L'example de Madrid au XVIIe
siècle," p. 168.

These figures (illustrated by Figure 2.1) indicate rapid growth in the reign
of Philip III, a pronounced decline in mid-seventeenth century, accelerating
expansion in the eighteenth century, and sharp contraction in the quarter-
century after 1800. The numbers depart from accepted figures for the early
seventeenth century, where the city's size has been seriously underesti-

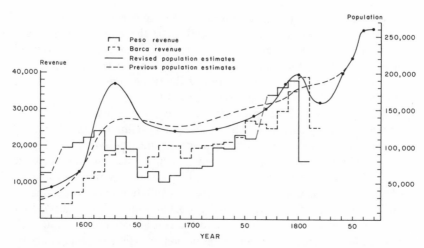

Figure 2.1 *Evolution of Madrid: Population,* Peso *Revenue, and* Barca *Revenue Trends**

*On the *Barca*, see Chapters 10 and 11 below. Revenues are given as decennial averages.

mated.[16] The new estimate for 1800 also exceeds the commonly cited totals based on the censuses of 1787 and 1797, but conforms with municipal data for 1798, 1799, and 1804, which leaves only the floating population open to question. The decline after 1800 becomes correspondingly more pronounced, and in 1817 and 1821 the total was still 20% below that for 1799.[17] Miñano's data for 1825 actually give only 182,000 residents, adding the conventional 20,000 *forasteros* to reach a total of 202,000. The evidence for sustained growth above that level is inconclusive until the 1840's.[18]

The cycle of growth and contraction from 1740 to 1820 is supported by demographic trends in the city.[19] After a strong increase around 1750, the volume of marriages grew slowly but steadily until 1795. Except for a brief

16. Contemporaries certainly had the impression of a crowded city of great size, and Domínguez Ortiz cites a document from the period—Archivo Histórico Nacional (AHN), *Consejos*, leg. 51438, exp. 7—that discusses food supply and assumes a population of 300,000. At least two English observers around 1630 describe a city of 200,000 to 300,000 inhabitants.

17. Gabriel Lovett, *Napoleon and the Birth of Modern Spain* (1965), vol. 2, p. 537; Manuel Espadas Burgos, "El hambre de 1812 en Madrid" (1968). Manuel Cristóbal y Mañas, in *La hacienda municipal de la villa de Madrid* (1901), p. 39, discusses a reduction in tax quotas in 1821 reflecting a 13.5% decline in the legally domiciled civil population since 1797, quoting 156,339 and 135,629 as the population figures.

18. For impressions by close observers, see Alexander Mackenzie, *Two Years in Spain, by a Young American* (1828), pp. 405–409; and Richard Ford, *Handbook for Spain, 1845* (1965), vol. 3, p. 1075.

19. María Carbajo Isla, "Primeros resultados cuantitativos de un estudio sobre la población de Madrid, 1742–1836" (1968).

recovery in 1803–07, it fell sharply until 1815 and had a sharp but brief recovery in 1815–21. Between 1821 and 1840 the number of marriages dropped to a level well below that before 1795. The other demographic indicators reinforce the appearance of decline in the capital after 1800. Distress and poor nutrition are apparent in the rising number of deaths after 1795 and the high mortality figures of 1830–40.

When the city's probable population development is juxtaposed with the tax data in the early part of this chapter, we get a preliminary insight into the evolution of urban demand. The *peso mayor* and the *barca de Arganda* represent different aspects of the urban economy. The first reflects market activity in the main plaza, the second the long-distance communications and trade of Madrid. Despite the possibility that inflation may exaggerate the growth of revenue, *peso* activity had a declining growth rate after 1600, reflecting the absence of the Court and the subsistence crisis of 1607. The next decade, however, shows both rapid urban growth and a temporary improvement in real wages, accompanied by declining food prices and a construction boom.[20]

Population growth remained strong into the 1630's, but *peso* revenues stagnated and their real value declined. Prices rose, real wages fell, and the new immigrants were poor. Urban per-capita income was declining even though the city continued to grow, diverting demand from the less essential commodities taxed at the *peso*. Meanwhile, traffic at Arganda continued to increase into the 1630's, well after *peso* revenues stagnated. The contrast implies that urban per-capita income declined while elite demand remained strong, and thus that income distribution was becoming less equal. The urban markets of rich and poor were separating and the poor were shifting what buying power they had to the most basic commodities. The regionally produced goods of intermediate value were losing their markets even before the city began to contract. Purchasing power for manufactures was gravitating to the small elite that could afford qualitative distinctions and favored imported products.[21]

The reduced population of the late seventeenth and early eighteenth centuries parallels low levels of activity at the *peso* until 1690. For most of 1650–90, *peso* revenues were half those in 1611–20 and did not regain that level until mid-eighteenth century.[22] Population declined nearly 30% between

20. In the decades after 1606, as many as 140 major buildings were under way every year; see Chapter 6 below. On construction, see Claude Larquié, "Quartiers et paroisses urbaines: L'example de Madrid au XVIIᵉ siècle" (1974); and Michel Devèze, *L'Espagne de Philippe IV, 1621–1665: "Siècle d'or et de misère"* (1971), pp. 373–378.

21. For additional evidence of these differing elasticities of demand, see the discussion of food consumption patterns in Ringrose, "Madrid y Castilla," pp. 65–122, and Chapter 6 below.

22. The complexity of price history and the partial dependence of the *peso* on *ad valorem* tariffs make it impossible to infer much in this period, particularly in view of the deflation of

1630 and 1685 and did not rise significantly before the 1720's; yet there is little indication that population decline led to an improvement in urban life.[23] Rather, the deteriorating urban market simultaneously shifted away from nonessential goods and declined in scale.

By contrast, the Arganda toll had returned to its earlier peak by the 1660's and stabilized at the higher level until after 1730. Once the immediate crises of the Thirty Years' War had passed, elite demand and central-place functions were unaffected by population decline. The dualism that Madrid's society and market had developed not only persisted but became more pronounced. The contraction of what had become the only significant urban market in the interior was thus most evident in the demand for regional manufactures and nonessential agricultural products. This has to have been a factor in the persistent trend to local self-sufficiency of seventeenth-century Castile.[24]

Renewed expansion of the capital in the eighteenth century provides other useful inferences regarding Madrid's evolution as a market. The population began to recover after 1720, but growth remained slow until the last third of the century, when there was a marked acceleration. This offers a close parallel with the trend in revenues at the Arganda toll. Since the toll links the capital with Spain's maritime world, the concordance of population and toll revenue suggests that the growth of the capital was derived from prosperity in that larger world.

The impact on Madrid's relationship with the interior is reflected in the *peso* figures. Until the subsistence crisis of 1766–67, the *peso* yield grew more rapidly than either the population or the Arganda toll. During the middle decades of the century, stable food prices and mild prosperity improved real incomes and allowed an increase in urban demand for regional products. By 1770 the trend of *peso* revenue was falling behind that of population. Rising food prices, static money wages, and declining real income for the bulk of the population produced another decline in per-capita ability to purchase nonessential goods. This is reflected in the rising number of urban deaths and the

---

1680. By 1690 the volume of activity may have been expanding faster than revenues suggest. Also, the *peso* decline may be more apparent than real, as rental contracts became longer and less responsive to conditions.

23. Logically the reduced pressure of population on resources ought to have reduced food prices and improved the demand for less essential goods. Whether prices in Madrid followed this line or not, there is no evidence that demand for nonessentials improved. For the theoretical formulation, see Slicher van Bath, *The Agrarian History of Europe,* pp. 132–144, 195–239. For impressions of the life of the seventeenth-century poor, see Charles L. Carlson, "The Vulgar Sort: Common People in Siglo de Oro Madrid" (Ph.D. diss., University of California, Berkeley, 1977).

24. The decline itself was a function of depopulation and declining rents in the interior and of the depressed fortunes of the Spanish monarchy. These reduced the pressures for urban immigration while forcing the elite of the city to cut down on construction and personal service.

declining volume of births and marriages. The growth of the city was aggravating subsistence crises and forcing up regional food prices while restraining Madrid's development as a market for other Castilian goods. Madrid began to lose population as early as 1800, and the drop in market activity as measured by the *peso* was even sharper. Thus the crisis of early nineteenth-century Madrid was under way before the Napoleonic occupation, and follows the spectacular decline in commerce at Cádiz around 1798–99 (see Chapter 10). By 1810 the *peso* yield was half that of 1780–1800, and by 1820 the Arganda toll had dropped 35% in 15 years.

After the turn of the century, we have to project market trends on the basis of population and trends in vital statistics. Total population declined 20% between 1800 and 1821, although the nadir was probably reached in 1812–13 and a recovery under way by the later date.[25] There was a sharp upturn in vital statistics in 1815–21, as families were rebuilt, a large number of marriages took place, and there was an increase in the number of baptisms. At the same time the number of deaths was the lowest in a century.[26] By 1825, when the population may have reached 180,000, baptisms and especially marriages had fallen off dramatically, while the number of deaths was climbing rapidly. The pattern between 1825 and 1835 resembles that of 1790–1803 and allows similar inferences about Madrid's limited capacity to consume other than basic foodstuffs from its hinterland. The big difference now is in the relative penury of the elite and the government after the collapse of the Empire,[27] a situation that did not give way to sustained increases in population and consumption until the 1840's (see Chapter 6).

Tolls, market duties, and population figures give us a preliminary profile of the evolution of Madrid as an urban market. For three centuries the isolated interior supported a capital that ranked among the principal cities of pre-industrial Europe. It constituted the only urban market for Castile's agricultural products and had no alternative sources of supply. Because physical isolation precluded agricultural specialization, the surpluses available for the market were small and widely dispersed. This imposed reliance on an overland transport system of huge geographic scope. Moreover, the size and structure of this market changed over three centuries in response to external factors, and in the process caused important developments in relations between the city and the countryside.

The revised history of Madrid's population development thus acquires

25. See note 9 above.

26. This implies application (possibly risky) to a large city of the mechanisms of post-crisis demographic recovery outlined by E. A. Wrigley in *Population and History*, pp. 68–70.

27. See Josep Fontana Lázaro, "Colapso y transformación del comercio exterior español entre 1792 y 1827: Un aspecto de la crisis de la economía del Antiguo Régimen en España" (1970).

great importance. Madrid experienced two long cycles of expansion and contraction: 1500–1685 and 1685–1825. Thereafter it began a third expansion, sustained after 1850 by the falling transport costs of railroad and steamship. Interpretations of the evolution of the Spanish interior must take into account the manner in which the changes in the capital are linked with the development of the interior. Madrid, therefore, should be studied not only as an extension of the Castilian economy, but also as a determinant of its evolution.[28]

28. The contrast, and some of the inspiration for this work, is found in E. A. Wrigley's "A Simple Model of London's Importance in Changing English Society and Economy, 1650–1750" (1967), and in Peter Clark and Paul Slack, *English Towns in Transition, 1500–1700* (1976), ch.1.

3. Structure and Evolution of the Urban Population

The preceding profile of Madrid's long-term development offers a suggestive but impressionistic framework for analyzing the city's significance. To go beyond that requires examination of the structure of the population, its evolution over time, and the interaction between urban and rural demography. Building upon eighteenth- and nineteenth-century sources, there is evidence to establish the origins of urban population structure in the early seventeenth century.[1]

I. Residents, Immigrants, and Age-Sex Distribution

The striking feature of Madrid's pre-modern demography is the coexistence of two distinct populations within the same city—a stable "core" and a fluctuating "envelope" of immigrants and transients. The dual nature of Madrid's population is illustrated by the urban census of 1850–51, one version of which distinguishes between Madrid-born residents and immigrants by age, sex, and marital status; the resultant population pyramid is shown in Figure 3.1.[2] Only 40% of the population declared itself native to the city or province of Madrid. The age-sex pyramid of the city as a whole shows a huge

1. The censuses used are dated 1757, 1787, 1793, 1804, 1831, 1845, 1850–51, 1857, 1865, and 1869, and are cited in Appendix A. The early baptism figures, dated 1594–98 and 1622–26, are in Ricardo Martorell Téllez Girón, *Aportaciones al estudio de la población de Madrid en el siglo XVII* (1930). Later baptisms, burials, marriages, and foundlings are in María Carbajo Isla, "Primeros resultados cuantitativos de un estudio sobre la población de Madrid, 1742–1836" (1968).
2. There are two tabulations for 1850–51, one distinguishing age, sex, marital status, and whether or not Madrid-born, the other indicating sex and province of origin; both are in AVM, *Secretaría*, sig. 6–61–49. See also Antonio Fernández García, *El abastecimiento de Madrid en el reinado de Isabel II* (1971), p. 148.

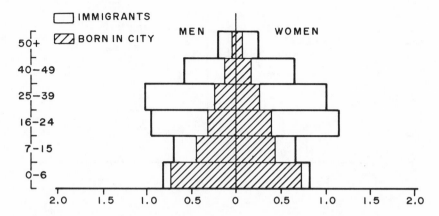

Figure 3.1 *Distribution of the Population of Madrid by Age and Sex, 1850–51*

bulge in the 16–24 and 25–39 age groups, a bulge that is not reflected in the age distribution of Madrid-born residents. Taken as a separate entity, the city-born population has an age-sex distribution similar to that of the population of Old Castile in 1787 (see Figure 3.2). The lowest cohort is wider for the "inner city" than for Castile, but the configuration is the same, and the distortion reflects the city-born children of recent immigrants.[3] While we have no way of measuring the distortion, even a 25% reduction in the 0–6-year cohort would leave a pyramid resembling that of Castile and would be a passable representation of the population of the inner city. It represents that part of the urban society which was stable and self-sustaining despite changing economic conditions.

Less direct evidence of this core/envelope structure is present in the census of 1787.[4] By comparing the age-sex distribution, marriage ratios, and occupational structure of the eight districts of the city, certain demographic traits can be associated with broad occupational categories (see Table 3.1). Since

3. This kind of dual structure is implicit in E. A. Wrigley's discussion of pre-industrial London in "A Simple Model," pp. 45–63. During its rapid growth in the late eighteenth century, Bordeaux experienced a similar influx; see J. P. Poussou, "Les structures démographiques et sociales," in *Histoire de Bordeaux*, vol. 5, *Bordeaux au XVIIIe siècle* (1968), pp. 332–333. A discussion of immigration to various European towns is in Roger Mols, *Introduction à la démographie historique des villes d'Europe du XIV au XVIIIe siècle*, vol. 3, pp. 374–393.

4. This *Censo de Floridablanca*, in RAH in numerous *legajos*, is preserved in the form of summary tallies for every village and town in Spain. The materials for Madrid do not distinguish between city-born and immigrant residents, but they do give age, sex, and marital status by 6 cohorts and list several occupational categories for each of 64 *barrios* grouped in 8 *cuarteles*. For Madrid, there are two separate tabulations from the first half of 1787 (leg. 9/6235).

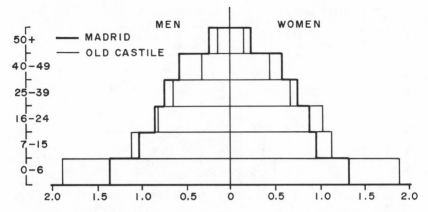

Figure 3.2 *Age/Sex Distribution of the Population of Old Castile (1787) and the City-Born Population of Madrid (1850–51)*
Source: On Old Castile, see María Pilar Calonge Matellanes, Eugenio García Zarza, and María Elena Rodriguez Sánchez, *La España del Antiguo Régimen*, fasc. III, *Castilla la Vieja* (Salamanca: Universidad de Salamanca, 1967), pp. 24–25.

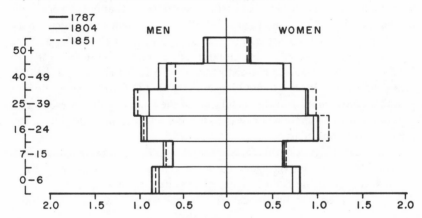

Figure 3.3 *Age/Sex Distribution of the Population of Madrid in 1787, 1804, and 1850–51*

the citywide age-sex pyramid is strikingly like that of 1850–51 (see Figure 3.3), and the relative size of occupational categories is consistent over the long run (see Chapter 5), implications drawn from either census are probably valid for both.

Our initial assumptions are that: (1) nobility, commerce, the professions, government, and artisan industry implied status and activities in the "core" of the city; (2) domestic service *(criados)*, casual labor, and unskilled labor were linked with the transient "envelope;" and (3) these categories exhibited

Table 3.1. Selected Demographic and Occupational Data, by District, Madrid, 1787

District	City Pop.	0-7 yrs.	7-16 yrs.	Percentage of District Population Married and in 25-40 yrs. Cohort: Men	Women	No. Men per 100 Women	Economically Active
San Francisco	15.0%	12.7%	12.2%	67.3%	76.2%	106.2	23.8%
Maravillas	15.5	12.6	10.2	57.0	70.3	102.1	26.7
Barquillo	10.9	12.5	11.1	58.2	71.5	107.4	22.9
Lavapiés	18.5	12.4	11.7	64.2	74.0	101.3	34.5
Afligiados	6.8	11.6	11.6	53.4	72.8	108.1	35.5
San Gerónimo	12.3	10.6	10.4	54.3	61.1	103.1	30.0
Plaza Mayor	15.8	10.5	12.7	52.2	62.9	114.2	32.5
Real Palacio	5.2	9.6	10.5	44.6	59.2	103.9	31.2
All Madrid	100.0%	11.7%	11.3%	57.9%	69.2%	105.6	29.5%

(continued on next page)

Table 3.1. (cont.)

District	Servants	Day Labor	Percentage of Economically Active Population Artisans	Mercantile and Professional	Government	Listed as Hidalgo
San Francisco	32.7%	33.4%	10.8%	4.3%	14.6%	13.0%
Maravillas	39.4	11.4	24.8	4.8	14.5	3.3
Barquillo	42.6	18.9	18.9	4.7	9.4	4.9
Lavapies	23.6	34.5	24.3	5.1	8.9	3.7
Afligiados	59.1	18.8	3.9	1.4	12.5	6.0
San Gerónimo	54.5	7.5	18.9	5.4	13.3	2.6
Plaza Mayor	46.2	17.2	8.4	10.7	12.0	6.0
Real Palacio	33.0	6.3	14.0	6.7	27.6	8.5
All Madrid	39.7%	20.5%	16.1%	5.7%	12.8%	5.8%

Source: Calculations based on census data for 64 barrios in RAH, leg. 9/6235.
Note: Cross-totals will not equal 100% because of an unknown degree of duplication between hidalgo and some other categories. Hidalgos are included as a separate group because they offer a crude proxy for rentier landowners.

distinctive demographic traits.[5] There are striking neighborhood variations in marriage ratios in the 25–40-year cohort, when most marriages took place, and in the relative size of the childhood cohorts (ages 0–6 and 7–16). These differences correspond with the size of the artisan and *criado* portions of the workforce. In three of the four districts where the artisan sector was proportionately large, the younger-childhood cohorts were among the largest in the city. The same three districts (Maravillas, Barquillo, and Lavapies—Map 3.1) also had a very high percentage of married women in the 25–40-year cohort.[6] The fourth artisan *barrio,* San Gerónimo, does not show these traits, but it also contained many domestics. In contrast, the three districts with the largest proportion of domestics in the workforce (Afligiados, San Gerónimo, and Plaza Mayor) had three of the four smallest childhood cohorts and significantly lower male marriage ratios. In two of those three districts, the female marriage ratio was also well below the city average. The artisan sector clearly constituted part of the stable demographic core of the city, while the huge servant class (40% of the workforce in 1787) was part of the demographically weak outer envelope.

The position of smaller urban elements is less clearcut, and requires a closer examination of the districts of San Francisco, Afligiados, Plaza Mayor, and Real Palacio. Each was dominated by one or more groups that were less prominent elsewhere in the city. The district of San Francisco shows the largest childhood cohorts and the highest marriage ratios in the city, despite a low proportion of artisans. The unique factor in this case was the large noble population; 13% of San Francisco's population was classed as *hidalgo,* twice that of any other district. Near the royal palace, the district was centered on the Basilica of San Francisco el Grande and was an important residential area for the nobility. The presence of so many relatively affluent families, with better infant survival rates and strong motives for marrying, helps explain the demographic structure of the district and links the nobility with the city's demographic core.[7]

The small peripheral district of Afligiados apparently functioned as an entry point for immigrants. As with San Francisco, the proportion of artisans was low, but the childhood cohorts were nevertheless relatively large. The

5. A discussion of the elites within the "inner city" as part of this core/envelope model is in A. B. Hibbert, "Medieval Town Patricians" (1953). The definitions and assumptions used in this section are general and serve to relate occupational groups to the dual urban demographic structure.

6. Poussou, in *Bordeaux,* "Les structures," p. 360, provides evidence for this in the high proportion of marriages attributed to the artisan class in the same period.

7. This contrasts sharply with Stone's findings on the English peerage, but this is not surprising. The Spanish *hidalguía* was much larger, including the equivalent of the gentry. In practice we are discussing a fair-sized urban element that was neither aristocratic nor bourgeois (in the economic sense) but primarily a land-owning and rentier group. See Lawrence Stone, *The Crisis of the Aristocracy, 1558–1641* (1965), pp. 161–174.

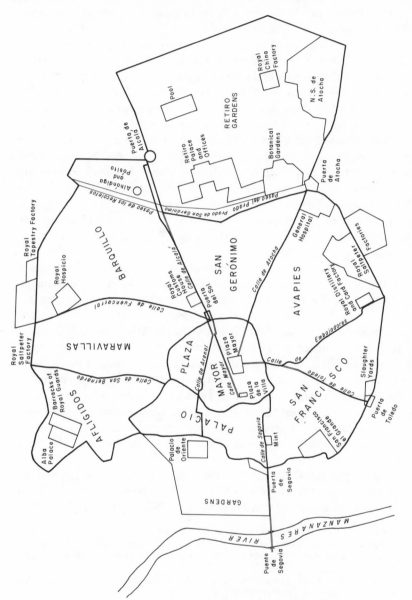

Map 3.1 *Madrid in 1787: Barrios and Points of Interest*

ratio of males to females was the second-highest in the city (108/100), and the percentage of married males aged 25–40 was quite low. On the other hand, the percentage of the population that was noble was fairly large and the percentage of married females was quite high. This implies a fair number of stable and/or semi-rural households with sizable families, in conjunction with a large transient male population, and conveys the impression of an entry point for immigrants into the city. The high proportions of domestics in the workforce and of unmarried men among the adults—far more than the district itself could employ—indicates that many immigrant males resided in the district while working in other *barrios*.

If the district of San Francisco was primarily residential and noble, the Plaza Mayor was dominated by commerce and the professions. Constituting 5.7% of the active population citywide, this sector averaged 5% in six districts and accounted for only 1.5% in peripheral Afligiados, but constituted 10.7% of the active population of Plaza Mayor. The district was also marked by traits that imply small childhood cohorts: a high ratio of males to females (114/100), low marriage ratios, a large proportion of domestics in the workforce (46%), and a very small artisan sector (8.4%). In fact, the 0–6-year cohort is second-smallest in the city, but the 7–16 cohort is the largest. Either family formation declined suddenly around 1780, or important elements had begun to restrict family size (an interesting possibility in eighteenth-century Spain), or else many of the domestics in the district were under the age of 17. Given the concentration of wholesale and retail activity, the last explanation is probably the best. If so, the commercial and professional element, though proportionately large in the district, contributed little to the demographic strength of the "core" of the city. It is worth noting that in Real Palacio, the other district where mercantile and professional elements were important, childhood cohorts were also small.

The district of Real Palacio highlights another element in the urban structure—the bureaucracy. The district was marked by very low marriage ratios, the smallest younger-childhood cohorts of the city, and a male-to-female ratio lower than that of the city as a whole (103.9/100 versus 105.6/100). The percentage of nobles in the population was high and the unskilled and domestic elements quite small. Dominating everything is the fact that over 27% of the economically active population was employed by the Crown. Given the proportion of households that must have been relatively affluent, the proportion of resident *criados* in the workforce is small. Apparently many households had servants who resided in other districts—the reverse of what we saw in Afligiados.

While bureaucrats, merchants, and professionals constituted over a third of Real Palacio's economically active population—far more than in any other district—the younger childhood cohorts and the marriage ratios were the smallest in the city. The origin of the small, modern, middle-class family in Spain has scarcely been discussed, but this suggests some interesting possibilities. One scholar talks of the spread of "bourgeois values," the individualization of women, the eroticization of costume, and the emergence of women as social and cultural arbiters.[8] This echoes the eighteenth-century playwright Ramón de la Cruz, who complained that women increasingly used pages for errands, maids and cooks for domestic work, governesses for child-care, and wet-nurses for their babies.[9] Whether these observations imply a trend strong enough to influence the demographic indicators is debatable, but the relationship is plausible.

The occupational group that has not yet appeared in this analysis is the unskilled day laborer or *jornalero,* 20.5% of the active population. Two very different districts, San Francisco and Lavapies, had the highest proportion of *jornaleros* in the district workforce. Both also had large childhood cohorts, which in San Francisco coincided with noble residence and in Lavapies with a large artisan element. Since the term *jornalero* in an urban context includes anything from a skilled journeyman in a guild to unskilled construction labor, the category is too heterogeneous to relate to our simple core/envelope model, although it does not appear associated with small childhood populations. While no doubt including many recent immigrants, the category was relatively stable and probably represented a socio-economic bridge between the stable core and the transient envelope.

Thus the dual structure evident in 1850–51 was a long-term feature that is suggested by the age distribution and the demographic and occcupational correlations in the census of 1787. The occupational groups of the urban core, while creating a normal population pyramid in 1850–51, did not contribute equally to the demographic basis of that core. The most prolific elements were the artisan class and the nobility—the most clearly "old regime" elements in the city. The merchant, professional, and bureaucratic segments had few children and low marriage rates. The element most readily identified with the outer envelope of the population pyramid of 1850–51, the domestic servant, was typically single and unattached. This was the group most marginal to the urban society and economy; it was also by far the largest component of the workforce.[10]

8. Numerous perceptive comments on the life-style of the upper classes in eighteenth-century Madrid are offered by Pedro Romero de Solis, *La población española en los siglos XVIII y XIX* (1973), pp. 83–103. He considers these as indicators of the development of the modern small middle-class family.

9. Arthur Hamilton, "A Study of Spanish Manners, 1750–1800, from the Plays of Ramón de la Cruz" (1926), pp. 17–25.

10. The clergy has been excluded from this discussion in part because they were not included in contemporary age and sex calculations and their subsequent insertion would have distorted the analysis in this passage. They were supported in large part by endowments, were

The census of 1787 thus elaborates upon and lends chronological perspective to the two-part population structure of 1850–51. The "inner city" consisted of the personnel of long-distance trade, the landed and bureaucratic elites, and the artisan and retail groups that provided their needs. Dependent upon maritime Spain and the state, it operated far-reaching political and commercial fields of influence focused on the capital and shaped the city's demand for nonessential commodities. The "outer city" was economically marginal to that core, sensitive to the latter's fortunes because its services were expendable. It was linked with Madrid's fields of influence in the interior, source of many of its immigrants and of basic necessities.

II. Chronological Perspective on Demographic Structure

A. Seventeenth-Century Origins

The patterns of age distribution, immigration, and occupations point the way to solution of an interpretive problem raised in Chapter 2 regarding the population of Madrid in the seventeenth century, and in the process, provide validity to some long-neglected research and establish the early seventeenth century as the period when Madrid's "core/envelope" pattern of the eighteenth and nineteenth centuries first appeared. In 1931 Ricardo Martorell set forth some unacceptably low estimates for the total population of the capital in the 1620's.[11] He started, however, with carefully compiled figures for baptisms in Madrid in the 1590's and 1620's, using them as a base for a normal population pyramid (see Table B.1) from which he derived his estimated total. It is clear that his mistake was not in his method but in his neglect of immigration as a component of urban population. If we build a population pyramid on the baptism totals for 1622–26 shaped like that of the city-born population of 1850–51 (Figure 3.1), we arrive at an estimated population in 1625 close to that of the city-born element in 1850–51 and to Martorell's estimate for the total population. At the same time, the earlier Madrid had a reputation as the dirtiest and most noisome capital in Europe and had a massive housing problem—conditions that discourage family formation and raise infant mortality.[12] If we then recall that Madrid expanded at

part of the urban "core" professionally, and declined from about 4,000 at the end of the eighteenth century to about 2,000 in the 1850's because of the seizure of religious property and the corresponding loss of an economic base.

Some of the qualitative aspects of migration to the city for domestic service are discussed by Teresa McBride in "Traditional Socialization and the Process of Modernization for Women: Domestic Service in Nineteenth-Century France" (1974 and 1976).

11. Martorell, *Aportaciones*.

12. Ruth Lee Kennedy, "The New Plaza Mayor of 1620 and Its Reflection in the Literature of the Time" (1944), pp. 49, 56; José Deleito y Piñuelo, *Solo Madrid es Corte: La capital de dos mundos bajo Felipe IV* (1953), pp. 127–128.

an unprecedented pace after 1600—even faster than in the 1840's—an "inner city" of 60,000 is a plausible 35% of the estimate of 175,000 inhabitants in 1630 presented in Chapter 2. In this context, Martorell's long-neglected figures for Madrid baptisms fit and help identify and date the origins of Madrid's "core/envelope" pattern to the early seventeenth century.

B. Eighteenth and Nineteenth Centuries

Although Madrid's total population changed considerably, the age-sex structures are remarkably similar for 1787, 1804, and 1850–51 (see Figure 3.3). The high proportion of immigrants in the 1850–51 census appears as a remarkable bulge in the 16–24- and 25–49-year cohorts, giving the age-sex pyramid a pronounced wasp-waisted appearance. This structure is apparent in any pre-modern census of Madrid that contains age or sex data. One is struck by the degree to which Madrid in 1850–51 was structured like Madrid of the eighteenth century, which in turn apparently had not altered in this respect since the early seventeenth century.

A comparison of population pyramids allows additional insights, however. In 1787 and in 1850–51 Madrid had just experienced a period of rapid growth, whereas in 1804 a decline was under way. The 1850–51 census had a larger 7–16 cohort and a significantly higher percentage of females. The share of the population over 50 was smaller, indicating a more rapid rate of immigration in the 1840's than before 1787. The high proportion of women is paralleled by a large decline in the percentage of women who were married and an increase in the number of female domestics. This in turn reflects a change in the nature of household service from mid-eighteenth to mid-nineteenth century (see Table 3.6 for sex and marriage ratios).[13]

By contrast, the census of 1804 illustrates a city in decline. The loss of 5,000 people in five years was not enough to eliminate the bulge in the middle cohorts, but it did alter the age-sex distribution. The relative sizes of the 16–24 and 25–49 age groups declined, while the aged and young became relatively more numerous, despite bad economic conditions. The population structure thus indicates a decline of immigration and an exodus of recent immigrants as economic opportunity faded in the capital. In view of the offhand way in which economic historians of Spain have talked about economic crisis stimulating immigration to the city, the reverse process in the late 1790's suggests the need for reexamination of another old chestnut of Spanish economic history.[14] The city contracted by reducing the marginal "envelope" while the core society continued relatively unaffected, probably

13. Romero de Solis, *La población,* pp. 83–103, definitely finds this sort of change in household life.

14. Jaime Vicens Vives, *Manual de historia económica,* pp. 400–401, is a choice example of this kind of loose analysis.

repeating the pattern of the mid-seventeenth century. Thus the ratio between immigrant and core populations was partly a function of the rate of growth in the years preceding each census. If the "inner city" constituted about 40% in 1850–51, it probably represented slightly more as of 1787, and a yet higher percentage in 1804. On the other hand, given the extremely rapid growth of the capital after 1600, the core population was proportionately smaller in 1630 than in the later examples. This helps explain how Madrid could fluctuate as it did in the seventeenth century without losing its importance to the elites of the country.

C. Urban Comparisons

Important insights into urban immigration emerge from comparison of Madrid's demographic structure with other communities. The massive role of immigration in Madrid's demography is suggested by comparison with the isolated provincial capital of Soria in 1787,[15] and with Barcelona in 1787 and 1863 (see Figures 3.4 and 3.5).[16] One-fifth the size of Madrid, Soria shows a conventional pyramid-shaped age-sex distribution that includes sizable childhood cohorts. There are some anomalies, notably a disproportionately large number of women in the middle age groups. This indicates either female immigration or male outmigration; the first is more likely, and suggests that even a fairly small city had complex demographic relationships with its hinterland.

Barcelona, a commercial and manufacturing port, provides a much more interesting contrast with Madrid. The age-sex distribution indicates the same duality that we have noted for Madrid—in particular, an age pyramid in which the childhood cohorts are small for the rest of the population. The situation is less pronounced than in Madrid, however. The city depended on immigrants for growth, but the larger number of children suggests more opportunities for economic stability and family formation in Barcelona than in Madrid. This reflects the wider range of functions performed by Barcelona as a port, entrepôt, and manufacturing center, in particular the much larger artisan and manufacturing population (see Chapter 4).

D. City and Country

Other aspects of urban immigration are apparent in the population structures of nearby rural communities: the impoverished mountain district of Buitrago, two hill towns in the Real de Manzanares specializing in long-distance carting, and several farming communities in the province of Toledo.

15. RAH, leg. 9/6244, Province of Soria.
16. For 1787, Josep Iglesias, ed., *El cens de Comte de Floridablanca, 1787: Parte de Catalunya* (1968), p. 58; for 1863, Armando Saez Buesa, *La población de Barcelona en 1863 y 1960* (1968), pp. 16–17.

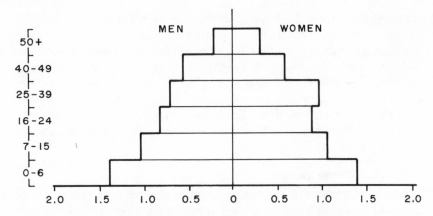

Figure 3.4 *Age/Sex Distribution of the Population of Soria in 1787*

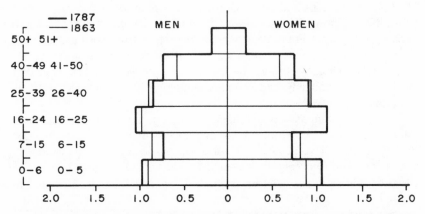

Figure 3.5 *Age/Sex Distributon of the Population of Barcelona in 1787 and 1863*

The poverty-stricken *señorio* of Buitrago (Map 1.2) shows an age-sex distribution that is the reverse image of Madrid (see Figure 3.6).[17] The childhood cohorts are very large, as is the 40–49-year cohort. The 16–24 cohort is relatively small, and that of 25–39 extremely small, documenting a classic case of outmigration from a marginal economy to Madrid. The shrinkage of the more mobile cohorts in Buitrago, as the city grew between 1751 and 1787, further confirms that hypothesis.

The two carting towns of Becerril and Collado Mediano (Map 1.2) had normal childhood cohorts and normal age distribution in the male population

17. *El Antiguo Régimen: El señorío de Buitrago* (1974), pp. 57–58.

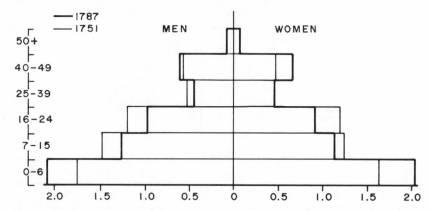

Figure 3.6 *Age/Sex Distribution of the Population of the* Señorio *of Buitrago, 1751 and 1787*

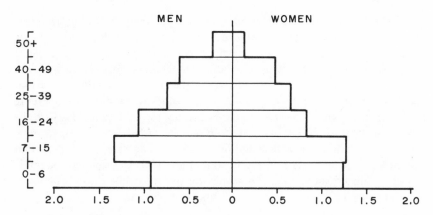

Figure 3.7 *Age/Sex Distribution of the Population of the Carting Towns of Becerril and Collado Mediano in 1787*

(see Figure 3.7).[18] Their active long-haul transport industry and related cattle-raising provided economic niches and kept the young men in the community. Age distribution among the women, however, shows a large deficit in the middle cohorts, implying female outmigration to Madrid.

18. RAH, leg. 9/6226, Province of Guadalajara, for Becerril and Collado Mediano. This sample and the next one cited (Figures 3.7 and 3.8) had abnormally small numbers of male children aged 0–6 in 1787. Appparently New Castile suffered from a serious epidemic of "*fiebres tercianas*" from September 1783 until 1787, with lingering effects until 1791. This might account for the small infant cohorts, and apparently it didn't reach the mountains where Buitrago (Figure 3.6) is located, but this doesn't readily explain the differential impact on the sexes. See Mariano and José Luis Peset, *Muerte en España: Politica y sociedad entre la peste y*

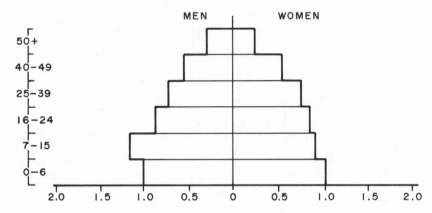

Figure 3.8 *Age/Sex Distribution of the Population of Six Farm Communities in the Madrid-Toledo Region in 1787*

The Toledan farming communities exhibit yet another rural pattern (see Figure 3.8).[19] The old-age cohorts are larger, while the 25–49 cohorts indicate male outmigration. At first glance it appears that the population lived longer, but it is more likely that many men left town temporarily and returned later in life. This is reflected in comments on the manuscript tally sheets that sometimes mention temporary emigration to Madrid, but more often refer to single men working as *criados* in other farming towns. It coincides with the small number of immigrants over 40 in the city in 1850–51. These farming towns show normal age distribution on the female side, suggesting that women tended to remain in the communities. Thus the isolated mountain towns produced young men and women for the city, while the carting towns sent out surplus women and the farm towns surplus men.

III. Geography of Migration

The rural population structures are linked to that of Madrid by the census of 1850–51, which lists all residents of Madrid by sex and province of origin.[20] The importance of cityward migration to the sending provinces is indicated in Table 3.2, which shows the number of Madrid residents from each province as a percentage of the population of that province as of 1857. Five of the six biggest contributors, relative to the population of the sending districts, were near Madrid: Toledo, Guadalajara, Segovia, Ciudad Real, and

el cólera (1972), pp. 76–77. About then (1785–87) there was a pronounced peak in hospital admissions and burials in Madrid; see Carbajo Isla, "Primeros resultados," pp. 81–82.

19. RAH, leg. 9/6226, Province of Guadalajara, and 9/6248–49, Province of Toledo.

20. AVM, *Secretaría*, sig. 6–61–49.

Table 3.2. *Immigrants in Madrid as Percentage of Population of Province of Origin(a)*

Rank	Province	Percentage in Madrid
1	Toledo	3.34%
2	Oviedo	3.28
3	Guadalajara	3.28
4	Segovia	2.35
5	Ciudad Real	2.19
6	Cuenca	1.82
7	Vizcaya	1.80
8	Santander	1.58
9	Lugo	1.41
10	Alava	1.29
11	Logroño	1.25
12	Alicante	1.23
13	Valladolid	1.21
14	Guipúzcoa	1.12
15	Soria	1.11
16	Burgos	1.06

Source: See Table B.2.

a. Based on Madrid censuses of 1850-51 and Spanish census of 1857; modern provincial boundaries. Only provinces registering more than 1.0% are listed.

Cuenca (see Map 3.2). The only peripheral province to make a similar contribution was Oviedo. But if the provinces are ranked by the absolute size of their contingents in the capital, the picture changes (see Table 3.3 and Map 3.3): Oviedo heads the list, and Lugo, Alicante, and Valencia emerge as major contributors. In these cases, however, the contingents were small relative to the sending populations, and the interior provinces still rank as the major contributors to the capital's immigrant population.

The tabulation for 1850–51 also shows that the male/female ratio among immigrants varied considerably depending on age and origin (see Table 3.4). The proportion of males among immigrants (97.2 males/100 females) was higher than for the city as a whole (94.6/100). The two cohorts with the most immigration—ages 16–24 and 25–39—differed most from the average. The 16–24 group had a deficit of males in both immigrant and city-born populations, probably reflecting conscription and its evasion.[21] At the same time, this immigrant cohort included a large number of single women entering domestic service. By contrast the 25–39 cohort was preponderantly male. While the ratio of men to women in the city-born portion of the cohort

21. This can be inferred from the fact that census records for this period were found with tallies of draft-eligible men.

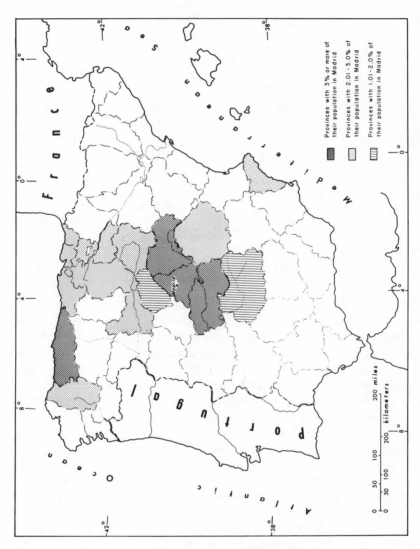

Map 3.2 *Percent of Provincial Populations in Madrid, 1850–51*

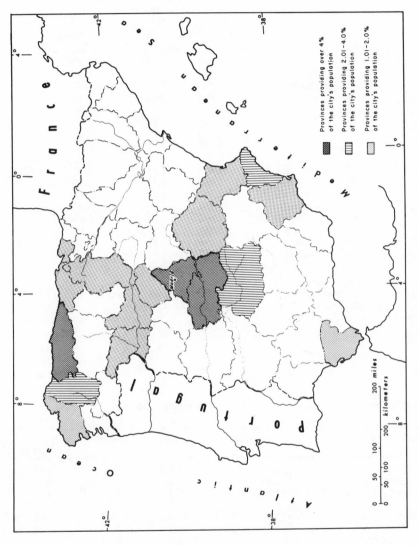

Map 3.3 *Percent of Madrid Population from Provinces, 1850–51*

Provinces providing over 4%
of the city's population

Provinces providing 2.01–4.0%
of the city's population

Provinces providing 1.01–2.0%
of the city's population

Table 3.3. *Origin of Population of Madrid by Province, 1850* (a)

Rank	Province	No. in Madrid	% of Madrid's Pop.	% of Madrid's Immigrant Pop.
1	Oviedo	17,195	7.76%	14.21%
2	Toledo	10,980	4.95	9.07
3	Guadalajara	6,521	2.94	5.39
4	Lugo	5,960	2.69	4.93
5	Ciudad Real	5,349	2.41	4.42
6	Alicante	4,670	2.11	3.86
7	Cuenca	4,178	1.88	3.45
8	Valencia	3,579	1.61	2.96
9	Burgos	3,537	1.60	2.92
10	Segovia	3,458	1.56	2.86
11	Murcia	3,439	1.55	2.84
12	Santander	3,388	1.53	2.80
13	Zaragoza	3,354	1.51	2.77
14	Valladolid	2,943	1.33	2.43
15	Vizcaya	2,881	1.30	2.38
16	Cádiz	2,598	1.17	2.15
17	Coruña	2,377	1.07	1.96

Source: See Table B.2.
a. Based on Madrid censuses of 1850-51. Only provinces contributing more than 1.0% of the city's population are listed.

Table 3.4. *Selected Age and Sex Distribution Figures, Madrid, 1850-51*

Group	Population		Male	Female	No. Males per 100 Females
Total city	216,571	100.0%	48.6%	51.4%	94.6
Madrid-born	80,596	37.2	47.3	52.7	92.0
Born elsewhere	135,975	62.8	49.3	50.7	97.2
Cohort aged 16-24	41,637	100.0%	45.4%	54.6%	83.2
Madrid-born	13,976	33.6	44.1	55.9	79.9
Born elsewhere	27,661	66.4	46.1	53.9	85.5
Cohort aged 25-39	66,710	100.0%	50.3%	49.7%	101.2
Madrid-born	16,528	24.8	48.1	51.9	92.7
Born elsewhere	50,182	75.2	51.0	49.0	104.1

Source: See Tables B.3, B.4, and B.5.

approximated that for all city-born residents (92/100), in the immigrant part of the cohort it was 104.1/100, well above the ratio for the city as a whole.

The immigrant age-sex structure also varied with province of origin, and provides the link with the demographic structures of neighboring communities. Female immigrants were not only younger, but generally came from adjacent provinces, while males tended to be older and were more likely to have come from distant provinces with port cities (see Table 3.5). The migration from 11 provinces was over 55% female, with the percentage as high as 68.7% for Guadalajara; 6 of these 11 provinces were near Madrid and accounted for 14% of the city's entire female population, compared with 4.5% from the 5 distant provinces that sent more women than men (Map 3.4). The importance of nearby provinces as sources of women immigrants to Madrid confirms signs of female outmigration in the hill and mountain areas north and west of Madrid.[22] In contrast, immigrant groups from 9 provinces were over 55% male. The percentage was as high as 74.6% from Oviedo, and the peripheral provinces in this group contributed 12.6% of the total city population of Madrid, while Córdoba, the one interior province with predominantly male migration, contributed only 0.6%.

In summary, with the exception of Oviedo, the provinces contributing the most immigrants relative to their own populations were near Madrid. Female immigrants were most likely to be in the 16–24 cohort and from the interior provinces. The peripheral provinces, on the other hand, sent far more men, and they were likely to be older.

One of the fascinating developments between 1757 and 1850–51 is the evolution of the male/female ratio and the marriage ratio of the 25–39-year cohort (see Table 3.6). In 1757 there were 111.2 men to 100 women, but by 1850–51 this ratio had fallen to 95/100. The change in the sex ratio was paralleled by a more pronounced change in the proportion of women who were married and not yet widowed, which can be traced from 1787. Consistently, few marriages took place below the age of 25. In 1787, only 13.8% of men and 27.7% of women in Madrid between 16 and 24 were married, and by 1850–51 this had dropped to 8.6% for men and 17.4% for women. Thus the important cohort for reproduction is that of ages 25–39. In the 1787 census, 57.9% of men in that age group were married, compared with 69.2% of women. Even these relatively high figures mark a contrast with Soria, where 87% of women and 89% of men in that age cohort were married. By 1850–51

22. This pattern of migration—with skilled and professional persons from relatively long distances and large towns; and unskilled labor, especially women from nearby rural districts, often for domestic service—is evident in many cities. Examples are nineteenth-century Paris, eighteenth-century Bordeaux, and seventeenth-century Amiens; see McBride, "Traditional Socialization"; Poussou, "Les structures," pp. 334–350; and Pierre Deyon, *Amiens, capitale provinciale* (1967), pp. 7–10.

Table 3.5. *Sex Distribution of Migrants to Madrid, 1850-51, by Province*

More than 55% female immigrants		
Province	Number	Female
Guadalajara	6,521	68.7%
Guipúzcoa	1,745	66.7
Vizcaya	2,881	65.0
Avila	1,044	62.6
Navarra	2,041	62.0
Segovia	3,458	61.9
Toledo	10,980	59.7
Cádiz	2,598	59.5
Cuenca	4,178	58.4
Albacete	1,062	55.9
Valladolid	2,943	55.2

More than 55% male immigrants		
Province	Number	Male
Oviedo	17,195	74.6%
Orense	834	72.1
Lugo	5,960	72.1
Pontevedra	790	67.9
Almería	352	65.9
León	1,436	65.2
Coruña	2,377	57.5
Gerona	333	56.5
Córdoba	1,036	55.5

Source: See Table B.2.

the marriage rate for men 25–39 in Madrid had dropped to 53.4%, while that for women had plummeted 16%, to 53.1%. Significantly, the marriage ratio for city-born women remained considerably higher than for the much larger number of immigrant women in the cohort (59.4% versus 52.6%).

IV. Why Migration?

Statistical evidence of migration offers few explanations or motives. Obviously there had to be a pattern of perceived opportunities, local stress, and communications to bring these provincial contingents to the capital. While a detailed study of the question is beyond the scope of this book, a few observations are necessary. Since the late sixteenth century Madrid has been the focal point of a continuous stream of rural emigration. We have little information on the reverse flow, although it is likely that for many immigrants the stay in the capital was temporary. Migration follows established commercial and

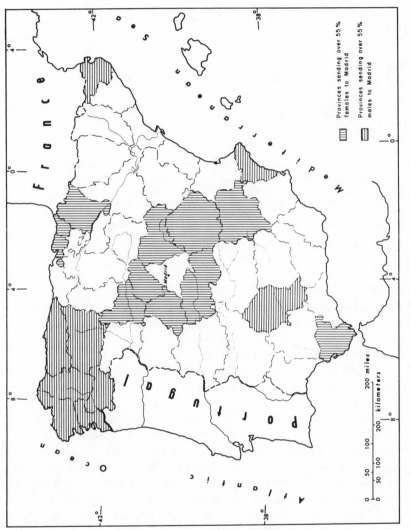

Map 3.4 *Male and Female Migration to Madrid, 1850–51*

Table 3.6. *Sex Distribution and Marriage Ratios in Madrid, 1757-1869*

Year	No. Males per 100 Females	Married Men			Married Women		
		Total	16-24	25-39	Total	16-24	25-39
1757	111.2						
1787	105.6	39.9%	13.8%	57.9%	39.5%	27.7%	69.2%
1793	103.0						
1804	101.2	37.7	12.8(a)	54.8	36.5	20.8(a)	60.1
1831		35.9			29.5		
1845	97.6						
1850	94.6						
1851	96.0	35.1	8.6	53.4	30.4	17.4	53.1
1857	102.4	32.3			30.3		
1865	91.9						
1869	91.9	35.8			31.1		

Sources: For 1787, 1804, and 1850-51, see Tables B.4, B.6, and B.7; for 1757, AGS, *Dirección General de Rentas, Contribución Unica,* leg. 1980; for 1793, Moreau de Jonnes, *Statistique de l'Espagne,* p. 51; for 1831, Mesonero Romanos, *Manual de Madrid,* pp. 44-45; for 1845, AVM, *Secretaría,* sig. 6-61-47; for 1851, Fernández García, *Abastecimiento,* p. 148; for 1857, AVM, *Secretaría,* sigs. 6-62-1 and 6-63-29; for 1865 and 1869, Fernández García, p. 148.

a. This cohort was defined as one year younger in the 1804 census, hence these percentages are a bit low relative to those for 1787 and 1850-51.

communications links, exploiting information and personal contacts in the search for urban niches. In the case of eighteenth- and nineteenth-century Madrid, we can postulate two such networks: one followed the connecting routes to the coastal provinces that provided Madrid's imports, colonial products, and nationally produced luxuries; the other was based on the network of urban-supply commerce that tied the interior provinces to the capital city.[23]

The kinds of niches that immigration offered are fairly obvious. The majority of immigrants remained on the fringes of the city's society and economy, but the male-dominated immigration from the periphery also involved recruitment of personnel for the inner sector. The predominance of Basque names in mercantile activities, in the fish supply, and in the iron trade is but one example. The arrival of Catalan merchants, retailers, and craftsmen is well attested for the later eighteenth century. The eighteenth-century playwright Ramón de la Cruz noted large numbers of immigrants from Asturias, Galicia, Valencia, Catalonia, and Andalusia, observing that most of them were men and were occupied as manservants, produce buyers, and various types of petty middlemen and facilitators. Rather than vagrants, they have the air of purposeful, long-term migrant labor.[24] To this commercially derived network, the nineteenth century added a political one. The parliamentary

23. For the commercial bases of these networks, see Chapters 6 and 7.

24. Arthur Hamilton, "A Study of Spanish Manners," pp. 56–57, 70. Ramón de Mesonero Romanos—in *Obras* (1967), vol. 2, p. 190—describes Castilian food vendors and wandering

system of deputies and elections provided new connections which brought provincials to the capital to feed the *empleomanía* that was one of the city's perennial problems.[25]

A similar pattern is apparent between immigrants from the Castilian hinterland and domestic service and food distribution. As recorded for both 1787 and 1845, domestics accounted for a sizable proportion of all immigrants, while their male/female ratio corresponded with that of migration from the interior provinces. In 1787 domestics constituted 12% of the entire population and 40% of the economically active population. In 1845, despite a 35% growth of the city, the 24,000 domestics constituted 11.5% of the population and 67.6% were female, as was the migration from the provinces near Madrid. This predominantly female migration was most likely to encounter household and casual or temporary unskilled employment.[26] It is hardly surprising, therefore, that the inmates of the poorhouses of the day came primarily from the provinces of Toledo, Guadalajara, Cuenca, Segovia, and Ávila.[27]

The analogous networks of the early seventeenth century are not clearly documented, but the sources of immigration were probably similar. There was a large migration from Toledo after 1610 that made important additions to the commercial and artisan core, despite attempts to send them back to Toledo.[28] There are descriptions of immigrant notables from all over the country, and of nobility seeking to expand access to royal largesse.[29] The *peticiones de vecindad* which will be analyzed in Chapter 5 reflect this type of immigrant. Seventeenth-century guild lists show the patterns of regional names and implied linkages seen later. Not until after 1750 did domestic service shift from male retainers to female domestics, and women may not have been as important in seventeenth-century immigration from nearby regions as they became later. At the same time, seventeenth-century parish

peddlers from Valencia and Aragón. George Rudé identifies this pattern for Paris in "The Growth of Cities and Popular Revolt, 1750–1850, with Particular Reference to Paris" (1973), p. 174.

25. Vicens Vives, *Manual de historia económica,* pp. 443, 504–505; Deyon, *Amiens,* pp. 7–10; Poussou, "Les structures," pp. 334–350; Antonio Flores, *La sociedad de 1850* (1968), p. 85. *Empleomania* was a contemporary term denigrating the perpetual scramble of would-be office-seekers for bureaucratic sinecures in Madrid.

26. This pattern is identical with that observed in Seville; see Juan Ignacio Carmona García, *Una aportación a la demografía de Sevilla en los siglos XVIII y XIX: Las series parroquiales de San Martin (1750–1860)* (1976), pp. 138–139.

27. William Callahan, "Corporate Charity in Spain: The Hermandad del Refugio of Madrid, 1518–1814" (1976), p. 163.

28. Domínguez Ortiz, *La sociedad española del siglo XVII,* vol. 1, pp. 131–132.

29. Michel Devèze, *L'Espagne de Philippe IV (1621–1665),* pp. 263–264; Thomas K. Niehaus, "Population Problems and Land Use in the Writings of the Spanish Arbitristas: Social and Economic Thinkers, 1600–1650" (Ph.D. diss., University of Texas, Austin, 1976), pp. 202–212.

registers feature arrivals from Old Castile, Asturias, and Galicia, demonstrating that the pattern of 1850–51 was very old.[30]

These movements of people in the context of a static society become understandable when seen as a particular type of migration. Cultural anthropologists refer to *transformational migration*, caused by changes in the structure of the sending village, and *institutional migration*, which is a solution to the problems of impartible inheritance or overpopulation. Institutional migration involves regular, often temporary departures to distant but well-known places needing unskilled and semi-skilled labor.[31] The large number of urban immigrants from Asturias, and the heavily female migration from the central provinces, clearly suggest such institutionalized patterns. Thus Madrid's steady absorption of young adults from rural society may help explain the stability of social and economic life in many Castilian villages. Only in the mid-nineteenth century is the appearance of transformational migration to the capital suggested. The accelerated immigration of the 1840's was accompanied by an increase in the relative size of Madrid's economically marginal population and by the growing demand for women as domestics. Given the consistent importance of domestic service in the workforce, the increasing surplus of females, and the decline of marriage ratios, there is evidence of a strong association between the marginal occupations of the city and immigration from nearby provinces. The countryside was producing more surplus population, and some interesting changes in the capital's economy and life-style were taking place.[32]

V. Demographic and Economic Trends After 1740

The chronology of changing conditions and population structure can be further clarified by reference to the volume of births, deaths, and marriages for 1743–1836.[33] The lack of good population totals precludes construction of birth and death rates,[34] and we must be satisfied with analyzing the actual numbers of baptisms, burials, and marriages relative to other trends.[35] These

30. Claude Larquié, "Quartiers et paroisses urbaines," p. 191.

31. Stanley H. Brandes, *Migration, Kinship and Community: Tradition and Transition in a Spanish Village* (1975), pp. 14–15. The case of Galician migration is famous; see Antonio Mejide Pardo, *La emigración gallega intrapeninsular del siglo XVIII* (1960).

32. Some fascinating impressions of this are in Flores, *La sociedad de 1850*.

33. Carbajo Isla, "Primeros resultados."

34. Alexandre Moreau de Jonnes—in *Statistique de l'Espagne* (1834), p. 51—calculated a birth rate of 31.4/1000 and a death rate of 25.0/1000 for Madrid in 1788, the latter being suspiciously low. For 1797 the birth rate varied from 31.3 to 29.4 and the death rate from 29.4 to 26.6, depending on which of the available base figures one chooses. For comparable serial data on Parisian vital indicators, see E. Charlot and J. Dûpaquier, "Mouvement annuel de la population de la ville de Paris de 1670 à 1821" (1967).

35. Rudé, "The Growth of Cities," pp. 182–183, insists on the usefulness of these indicators for documenting deteriorating conditions in Paris at the end of the eighteenth century.

figures reveal several phases in the evolution of Madrid. The prosperity of the 1750's was followed by a crisis in the mid-'60's, a period of changing conditions and growth from 1770 to 1793, a sharp crisis around 1800, and decline until 1812. Demographic recovery marked the first restoration, followed by worsening economic conditions in the capital from 1824 to 1835.

From an average of 4,750 in the 1750's, baptisms fell 10% by 1770, and then stabilized until 1783 with only a slight downward drift. The number of marriages, after a post-crisis jump in 1767, fell sharply by 1770 but subsequently rose steadily and by 1783 was 15% higher than in 1770. The number of burials, around 3,000 in the late 1750's, peaked sharply in the mid-1760's, then oscillated around 4,000 until 1784. Stable mortality levels, rising marriages, declining births, and growing population do not fit together unless we consider the cityward migration of young adults, the majority of whom were women, judging from the declining proportion of men in the city. This explains how marriages and total population could grow without a corresponding increase in the number of burials, but does not explain the decline in baptisms. The latter is confirmed, however, by the number of infants entering the royal foundling home, which also declined through the 1770's. One possible explanation is that factors were working to restrict family size, even though family formation increased. As we have seen, the 1787 census suggests that only the relatively traditional artisan and *hidalgo* classes were associated with large childhood cohorts in their districts, while other groups were associated with smaller numbers of children. Obviously, this is an answer that is a question in its own right; but in general, the period 1770–83 seems to be one of growth and relatively good economic conditions in the city.

This expansive phase continued until 1793, but with growing signs of economic distress in urban society. The number of marriages continued to rise with the influx of adult immigrants, and by 1794 was 22% larger than in 1770. The number of baptisms rose sharply after 1783, reversing the trend of the previous decade: from 4,400 per year between 1774 and 1783, it reached nearly 6,000 in 1793. Admissions to the foundling home experienced an even faster rise, from 650 a year to almost 1,000. The mortality figures are more erratic, rising in the late 1780's and then falling back below the 4,000 level in 1791–92. During 1784–93 Madrid continued to expand, but living conditions were deteriorating and the food supply was becoming precarious as demand grew,[36] causing high food prices and mortality levels. The growth in marriages and baptisms in the early '90's thus reflects family re-formation after the mortality of the late '80's rather than renewed prosperity. Apparently the impact of increasing supply instability was confined to the outer envelope of

36. See Ringrose, *Transportation and Economic Stagnation in Spain, 1750–1850,* pp. 124–127.

the population structure. The inner core of society, while not immune to the crises of 1785–89, recovered rapidly from the effects of the episode. Nevertheless, the 1780's brought a growing public uneasiness about the numbers of vagrants, hangers-on, and unemployed, a sharpening of establishment attitudes toward the poor, and attempts to expel impecunious *pretendientes* from the city.[37]

The year 1793 marks a turning point in the development of the city. Population continued to grow until about 1798, but other indicators show a marked worsening of urban conditions, and even before the subsistence crisis of 1804 the population began to decline. Between 1793 and 1802 marriages dropped sharply and, despite a recovery after 1804, remained low until the Napoleonic occupation. Baptisms declined from the high of 6,000 in 1793 to about 4,700 in 1806—a level comparable to that of the 1750's. Burials, meanwhile, rose rapidly after 1792—and even excluding the crisis of 1804, which killed 11,000 people, were consistently above the previous norm. This is the Madrid depicted by Antonio Flores in his withering description of the perpetual hunger and the *"sopa boba"* that the Old Regime dispensed at the convent doors.[38] Foundling hospital admissions present an even more telling testimony to urban conditions. Despite declining baptisms, the number of foundlings rose from 650 per year in the 1770's to an average of 1,300 in the decade before the French occupation.

Clearly Madrid entered an economic crisis after 1793. The instability of the food supply, apparent in 1785–89, worsened in the 1790's and culminated in the subsistence crisis of 1804. Disruption of trade and diversion of government resources to the war effort undermined the economy of the urban core, and by 1804 population had begun to decline. The immigrant-swollen young adult cohorts contracted and the 0–7 childhood cohort became significantly smaller than in 1787 or 1793. The biggest impact was on the male population in the 25–39 cohort; the crisis apparently displaced men more readily than women, as falling employment combined with the effects or threat of conscription to encourage departure. Thus the fifteen years before the French occupation were marked by rising death and child-abandonment figures and declining birth and marriage totals. The economic base of the city was contracting and marginal groups were being pushed below the subsistence level, discouraging immigration.

The trends of the early nineteenth century are harder to discern, because of gaps in the vital statistics and the quality of the census data. The French occupation was disastrous and brought a subsistence crisis in 1812 far worse than that of 1804.[39] As late as 1821 the population was well below that of the 1790's, even though postwar birth and marriage figures reflect demographic recovery and immigration. In 1814–22 marriages exceeded the previous high of 1784–93, and baptisms regained the 6,000 level by 1821. Death figures were relatively low, reflecting loss of the weaker inhabitants in the preceding crisis. The marginality of the new population is apparent in admissions to the foundling home, which matched those of the late 1790's despite the reduced population. If the city was younger and more fertile in this first restoration, it was also poorer. The balance between the "inner city" and its marginal "envelope" was shifting and the latter was becoming proportionately larger, anticipating the structure of 1850–51.

This is borne out by vital statistics during the second restoration and its aftermath (1824–36) which suggest that urban conditions in the late 1820's were bad and that the 1830's were little better.[40] The average number of marriages in 1822–29 was lower than in any crisis year in the eighteenth century. Marriages did not reach eighteenth-century levels until 1835–36, in the aftermath of an epidemic. Baptisms, however, stayed fairly high, while admissions to the foundling home continued to rise. Burials rose rapidly after the low of the first restoration, reached eighteenth-century levels by the late 1820's, and continued to climb to the epidemic of 1834.

Thus, while Madrid recovered its eighteenth-century maximum by 1825–30, its economic base was weaker, and more of the population was economically marginal and sensitive to economic stress. This dismal situation provided the background for the rapid expansion of the 1840's which will be discussed in Chapter 5.

VI. Implications of Demographic Structure and Change

The dualism of Madrid's population structure and society was a persistent phenomenon from the early seventeenth to the nineteenth centuries. This is not a surprising discovery, since no pre-industrial city could grow rapidly without recruiting immigrants.[41] In the case of Madrid, the urban core constituted barely 40% of the population and provided an even smaller share of the economically active inhabitants. This sector imported, processed, and consumed most of the goods brought to Madrid from outside the Castilian

39. Manuel Espadas Burgos, "El hambre de 1812 en Madrid" (1968).

40. Spain was hit by cholera in 1834–35; but even before that, the figures given by Mesonero Romanos for 1831 include such signs of distress as unusually large numbers of widows and widowers and an unusual shortage of males. Unfortunately the figures lack detail to permit more careful analysis. See Peset and Peset, *Muerte en España*, pp. 216–217, and Ramón de Mesonero Romanos, *Manual de Madrid* (1833), pp. 44–45, "Población de Madrid en 1831."

41. Wrigley, "A Simple Model," pp. 45–63; Mols, *Introduction à la démographie historique*, vol. 3, pp. 374–393.

interior. It staffed the bureaucracy and collected, lived from, and re-distributed most of the taxes, rents, and profits that subsidized the capital. As we will see, the concentrations of wealth were far more extreme than the preceding discussion suggests. Population structure and income distribution thus constitute key aspects of Madrid's impact on the economic history of Castile and Spain.

This duality of urban society reinforces the inferences drawn in Chapter 2. Population trends, prices, and revenue from duties based on regional ex-change suggest that per-capita income declined after 1620. This forced most of the population to shift buying power toward essential commodities not reflected in the *peso* revenues, even as long-distance traffic serving the urban elites continued to expand. The structure of the urban population reinforces this perception and helps explain contradictory trends.

The "inner city" continued to develop after 1620 as long as imperial policy was vigorous (see Chapter 5), but most population growth was due to immi-grants joining the outer "envelope" of casual labor. As urban growth and money supply pushed up food prices, this marginal sector bought less and less that was not essential to survival. The process can be seen in greater detail in the varying elasticities of demand for different foodstuffs, which will be presented in Chapter 6. The same sensitivity to shortage, food prices, and political failure plagued the city in the eighteenth and nineteenth centuries. In 1850–51, 60% of the population consisted of people who had entered the city as young adults (see Figure 3.9), and this 60% included only those immigrants stable enough to be counted by inefficient census-taking. When the market Madrid presented to the interior changed, it was primarily be-

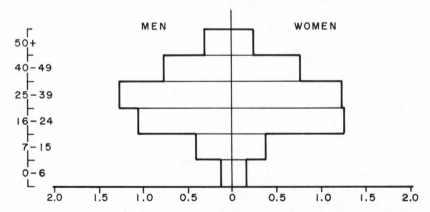

Figure 3.9 *Age/Sex Distribution of the Immigrant Population of Madrid in 1850–51*

cause of conditions affecting the size and well-being of this part of urban society. The significance of those changes is measured by the importance of that market for the rural economy, as will be shown in Chapters 6–9.

The identification of immigrants with the urban poor can easily be overstated, and it is important to note that the immigrant population was more complex than that identification suggests. Two well-defined flows of immigrants came to Madrid: one from the nearby provinces, the other from maritime provinces and port cities. Interior immigration was dominated by relatively young women, while maritime immigrants were older and predominantly male. In the first case, the contacts that brought people to the capital usually channeled them to household service, casual labor, and vending of foodstuffs; the second migration paralleled the links between the "inner city" of Madrid and the maritime world. While there is no doubt that most of the 20,000 Asturians and Gallegos entered marginal niches, immigrants from the periphery were more likely to be found in petty retailing and activities associated with the basic functions of Madrid.

The relative weight of the city-born and immigrant populations varied, depending on the conditions of the maritime economy and the empire. Thus the rapid expansion of Madrid after 1590 established the pattern of an inner city with a normal age-sex structure and a fluctuating envelope of adult immigrants. Initially, the latter sector was proportionately quite large. This imbalance was reduced during the stagnation after 1650, but increased with urban growth after 1750, producing the population pyramid of 1787 (see Figure 3.2). During the subsequent crisis, immigration was throttled back, enhancing the relative importance of the "inner city." In the post-Napoleonic restorations, reconstruction of a poorer urban population took place around an inner core debilitated economically by the collapse of the state and loss of empire. This is reflected in the faster growth of the female population, the relative importance of domestic service, declining marriage ratios, and an increased number of foundlings.

This sheds some light on the question of the degree to which a pre-modern city maintained itself demographically and shows that urban misery and bad living conditions are not the whole answer. Madrid's city-born population was demographically self-supporting with a normal age-sex-distribution pyramid. Its marriage ratios were higher than among immigrants and, in the census of 1787, certain districts where stable occupations predominated had large childhood cohorts. The artisan class and the nobility emerge as the demographically strongest sectors, while the mercantile, professional, and bureaucratic elements had low marriage ratios and small childhood cohorts (see Table 3.1). Thus the more traditional core elements were demographically strongest, not necessarily the most affluent. The "modern" elements had the smaller family associated with modern urban society. As we will see, the distribution of income was extremely uneven in Madrid, but it was not until the nineteenth century that it was accompanied by the signs of misery seen in eighteenth-century Paris and London.

Important city-country relationships emerge from the population structure. We will see that—tied to both the interior and maritime economies of Spain, and to its function as political capital—Madrid attracted its luxuries and manufactures from far beyond the two Castiles. Its food, fuel, building materials, and the rough manufactures used by the poor, however, were drawn from a series of supply zones and areas of urban influence embracing Old and New Castile. The structure of Madrid's population, partly as a result of this dual economic life, embodied various city-country interactions. Thanks to unstable weather, weak market organization, and poor transport, frequent supply crises hit the capital, reducing demand for nonessential goods. When the city expanded, this problem intensified, forcing the urban poor to shift their buying power to basic food with greater frequency, and weakening demand for the rough manufactures. Changes in the economic base of the "inner city" reflected changes in Spain's imperial and maritime resources. Crisis in the traditional structure of power, as in 1793–1808, reduced support for marginal functions and new immigrants. Disruption of that structure, as in mid-seventeenth century and again in 1808–25, damaged the economic base of the capital so that the urban core contracted, reducing the number of artisans and functionaries as well.

People migrate because they see opportunity such as the city offered in the early seventeenth, late eighteenth, and mid-nineteenth centuries. They also migrate because of limited local opportunities. This was a contributing factor in the early seventeenth century and mid-nineteenth century, when a deteriorating rural situation complemented an urban construction boom and relatively stable food supplies. Any circumstances that strengthened the urban core then led to rising population and consumption. This required ever more vigorous intrusions into the rural economy, displacing ever more people to the city, even as urban opportunity was eroded by the erratic prices and declining real wages produced by their arrival. This happened after 1620 and also in the late eighteenth century, and possibly in the nineteenth century.

By 1650 Madrid had become the preeminent city of the entire Spanish interior. Immigration took place in a more stable framework as regional and urban population reached a new equilibrium. There was general prosperity from 1720 to 1750, and urban prosperity as late as 1780. Thereafter urban conditions deteriorated, and by 1800 the balance of forces had reversed and immigration declined. The post-Napoleonic period saw a burst of urban replacement from a disrupted countryside. By the 1840's, a growing rural population and renewed urban prosperity again created a flood of people ready to believe that there were places for them in the great city.

In the long run, Madrid's demand for migrants was unstable, as was the demand for the goods the population consumed. As we will see, the wealthier and more stable part of the urban market depended on distant resources for much of what it consumed, while the huge marginal segments of the population constituted most of the market that Madrid presented to Castile. That market was repeatedly disturbed both by long-term urban growth and by recurrent subsistence crises. This economic dualism—suggested by our long-term profile in Chapter 2, by the structure of urban population, and by the nature of migration to the city—can now be examined more directly.

4. The Urban Economy in the Eighteenth Century: Occupations, Income, and Consumption

The conventional perception of Madrid's economy is summarized succinctly by Ramón de Mesonero Romanos' quip that the capital's most important industry was "the manufacture of reputations (*hacer las reputaciones*) for all parts of the realm," with tailoring and *tertulias* the important support activities.[1] This was a fairly accurate assessment, and government and tailoring were by far the largest industries in the eighteenth-century capital. Mesonero Romanos was not the first to make the observation, and Madrid's economic structure clearly reflects a perennial relationship between its urban functions and the larger world. Its most prominent features were a large, poorly paid service sector and a landed and bureaucratic elite that controlled a huge share of urban income and constituted the focal point for the city's economic life. Madrid's function as a producer of political and social services is starkly outlined in its occupational structure.[2]

I. Occupations

Detailed analysis of wealth and occupation has barely begun for Spain, and there is little work based on tax records, wills, estate inventories, and marriage contracts of the kind well known in England and France.[3] The sources

---

1. Ramón de Mesonero Romanos, *Obras*, vol. 2, p. 217.
2. The result is an even more extreme case of the "residential city" than the Berlin cited by Werner Sombart in *Luxury and Capitalism* (1967), p. 25. On urban functions and occupational structures, see Christaller, *Central Places in Southern Germany.*
3. For a compendium of examples of such work in France, see Adeline Daumard, ed., *Les fortunes françaises au XIXe siècle* (1973), with summaries of work by Daumard on Paris, Félix-Paul Codaccioni on Lille, Georges Dufeux and Jacqueline Herpin on Bordeaux, and Jacques Godechot and Jean Sentou on Toulouse.

used for Madrid in this study are governmental and fiscal in nature, and consequently biased toward underreporting. Nevertheless, the data have compensating advantages, since they come from the Castilian *Catastro* of the 1750's, a source compiled all at one time using standard guidelines, a fact which gives the data a unique coherence. The fact that the *Castastro* measures incomes rather than accumulated wealth also offers wider prospects for understanding the urban economy. The end result is as precise a survey of an urban economic structure as we have for any large pre-modern community.

The occupational structure of mid-eighteenth-century Madrid is summarized in Table 4.1. It is based on an analysis of almost 42,000 income recipients listed in the *Catastro,* and ignores the traditional distinction between lay and clerical populations.[4] The conventional classification into primary, secondary, and tertiary sectors does not tell us much about pre-modern economies, and occupations have been grouped here into more relevant categories.[5] The nearly 42,000 income recipients equal almost 30% of the estimated population of 142,500 for 1757. This is a fairly high proportion, but corresponds with the large adult population documented in Chapter 3 and is reiterated in the census of 1804.

The occupational structure that emerges offers a concrete example in support of our general assumptions about the economic orientation of bureaucratic and patrimonial cities.[6] The landed elite and government employees account for over 10% of income recipients—a figure that includes clerks and doormen as well as royal ministers, widows with rooms to let as well as grandees. If one includes the clergy in the controlling elite, as does Gideon Sjoberg, it accounted for 21.6% of income recipients.[7] The dependence of the city on this elite is apparent in the structure of the rest of the workforce. The legal, medical, and teaching personnel outside of the government, including

4. The same assumption is made by Bartolomé Bennassar, "Medina del Campo: Un example des structures urbaines de l'Espagne au XVIe siècle" (1961), p. 492. See also the discussion of this problem in Adeline Daumard and François Furet, *Structures et relations sociales à Paris au milieu de XVIIIe siècle* (1961), esp. pp. 16–22 and 26–38; and also Michael Katz, "Occupational Classifications in History" (1973).

5. The city had virtually no primary sector. The tertiary sector, if defined to include government, personal service, professions, and mercantile distribution, is too large to contribute to analysis. In an unspecialized pre-modern economy it is impossible to separate processing and manufacturing (secondary activities) from mercantile and personal service (tertiary activities). This is especially true for guilds and food processing. For additional comment on the derivation of occupational and income figures, see Appendix C.

6. For a classic statement on such cities, see Sombart, *Luxury and Capitalism,* pp. 21–35, 107–112. See also the more direct observation of Antonio Flores on *empleomanía* in *La sociedad de 1850,* p. 85.

7. On the directing elites of pre-industrial cities, see Gideon Sjoberg, *The Pre-Industrial City,* p. 110. Sjoberg has been criticized for creating a sociologism and loosely stating the obvious, but his conceptualization, however derivative, is still useful. As will be seen, the inclusion of 21.6% of economically active people within the elite is a considerable overstatement.

Table 4.1. *Distribution of Economically Active Population by Occupational Sector, Madrid, 1757*

Occupational Sector	Number(a)	% of active population
Royal and city government	3,000 (est.)	7.06%
Church-related	4,829 (est.)	11.36
Propertied persons	1,351	3.18
Professions(b)	1,758	4.14
Business and financial	1,952	4.49
Food industries	2,674	6.29
Construction	6,732	15.84
Manufacturing	7,325	17.23
Personal service	12,990	30.86

Sources: See Part I of Appendix C and Table C.1.
a. Because of the way the sources are constructed, the total excludes small groups of clerics, hospital staffs, and possibly untitled persons with income apparently wholly from extra-urban sources.
b. Professions include law, medicine, and teaching.

their assistants and minor employees, constituted just 4% of the workforce. The entire mercantile sector as identified by contemporaries—merchants and agents, clerks and porters—included only 4.5% of the total. This figure includes only part of retail commerce because of the blending of retailing with manufacturing in the guild sector. Some "artisans" were in fact wealthy capitalists with large commercial enterprises; the silversmiths, iron merchants, and other metal suppliers stand out in this regard. Other craftsmen, such as tailors and shoemakers, fit the conception of guildsmen engaged in small-scale production of custom-made products for final consumption. As defined by contemporaries, the artisan sector included 17% of Madrid's economically active population, considerably more than the 12.5% estimated for Castile, and thus reflected the capital's concentration of special markets.[8]

Since the diverse artisan sector included everything from silversmith-jewelers with over 50,000 *reales* in yearly income to apprentices with only 300, a more detailed breakdown is very instructive (see Table 4.2). Well over half of the manufacturing population worked in luxury trades—precious metals, quality clothing, leather goods, and similar products. Classically an industry of transformation to consumer demand, tailoring was the largest craft, with 1,369 individuals. It was followed by shoemaking, a similar craft with 880 masters and employees. The inherent structure of these trades and the small

8. The definition of economically active that produced the 12.5% figure is narrower than the one we have used, and a precise comparison would enhance the importance of the Castilian artisan sector. See *La economía del Antiguo Régimen: La Renta Nacional de la corona de Castilla,* by "Grupo 75" (1977), p. 137.

Table 4.2. *Distribution of Manufacturing Population by Type of Product, Madrid, 1757*

Type of Product	No. of Persons Active	% of Industrial Sector
Quality textiles, leather, final products	3,273	44.7%
Precious metals, jewelry	820	10.7
Mechanical and metallurgical	1,449	19.8
Rough textiles, leather, semi-finished goods	1,296	17.7
Miscellaneous crafts	487	6.6

Sources: See Part I of Appendix C and Table C.1. Section C of Table C.2 illustrates the diversity and number of skilled occupations involved.

size of most other craft guilds shows that the industrial structure was shaped almost entirely by the internal market of Madrid itself—a market that, as we shall see, was extremely narrow. The other large guilds—locksmiths, bakers, carpenters, cabinet-makers, and master builders—were associated with either construction or food supply, activities that by their nature were confined to geographically immediate markets.

Not surprisingly, construction was the largest single industrial activity, with 16% of the workforce. A fourth of construction workers were skilled—master builders, carpenters, window and door makers, stone-cutters, etc.—while the balance consisted of unskilled or semi-skilled day laborers and transporters. The dependence of this industry on government and the monied class is obvious. While we have no study of building activity in eighteenth-century Madrid, it was an age of urban expansion and reconstruction. Only large institutions and the wealthier segments of the elite had sufficient capital for the investments implied. While the participation of the nobility in urban real estate has yet to be explored, it is suggestive that the city's titled residents drew income from urban real estate in excess of 10 million *reales* a year. Assuming that this represented a 5% return, it implies property assets of 200 million *reales*. Thus the construction industry was not just inherently oriented to the urban market, but depended directly on the investment abilities of its wealthy elite.

Food processing, with 6% of the workforce, was also dependent on the urban economy for markets, but in a broader way. Two-thirds of the participants in this sector dealt in basic commodities—the bread, wine, oil, and meat that absorbed most of the buying power of the poor. Here, too, certain industries dominate the scene—notably baking, with 970 persons, and wine distribution, with 487 *taverneros* and *bodegoneros*. Among them, 120 master bakers and the wholesale wine brokers had substantial incomes. The remaining third of the food industry handled luxury foods such as fresh vegetables, milk, eggs, fruit, sugar, and chocolate. In general, the food industry reflected derived demand based on the overall distribution of urban income, rather than the direct demand of the wealthy elites. It is also the economic sector most directly linked with Castilian agriculture and thus has considerable importance in explaining the failure of the Madrid market to stimulate much development in the interior.

By far the largest segment of the workforce (30%) was devoted to service in the literal sense—hairdressers, entertainers, and above all, household servants and unaffiliated men-for-hire *(gente de librea)*. Virtually all descriptions of society in Madrid dwell on the overstaffed noble houses, the use of servants in very modest households, and the hundreds of unattached able-bodied men in the city.[9] The *Catastro* confirms these accounts with an emphasis that makes the most exaggerated accounts credible. It also accords with our previous chapter's evidence of the city's attraction for young and unmarried adults who fit the customary requirements of personal service.

The numerical preeminence of the servant and bureaucratic classes in Madrid's workforce (about 40%) is clear enough, but its importance becomes apparent when Madrid is contrasted with commercial and industrial Barcelona. Although its categories are different from those of the *Catastro,* the census of 1787 reflects the same structural traits in Madrid as the earlier source, and at the same time permits direct comparison of the two cities (see Table 4.3). Thus, while minor differences between the two cities would stand little scrutiny, larger ones provide useful contrasts. The *hidalgo, criado,* and bureaucratic groups as defined in this census constitute 62.7% of the economically active population in Madrid, compared with only 28.7% in Barcelona. Conversely, artisans, manufacturers, and laborers composed only 27.5% of Madrid's workforce, compared with 47.8% in Barcelona. Since the Barcelona census includes the entire *corregimiento,* elimination of the agricultural *labradores* around the city would heighten the contrast.

Madrid's occupational structure clearly shows that the economy was not only shaped by its primary functions, but that the orientation of the economy to those functions was extremely strong. Political and social center of the empire, Madrid had an occupational structure ill-equipped to supply goods and services for the regions of Castile that provided its basic supplies. The structure of the workforce indicates that the city produced little that was not

9. See Charles Kany, *Life and Manners in Madrid, 1750–1800* (1970), pp. 252–261, for a long and descriptive account of the numbers, variety, and life-style of servants in Madrid.

Table 4.3. *Occupational Structures of Madrid(a) and Barcelona(b) in the Census of 1787*

Occupational Category	Madrid		Barcelona	
	No. Active	% of Active Pop.	No. Active	% of Active Pop.
Crown, military	5,566	11.1%	375	1.1%
Hidalgos	8,545	17.1	259	0.8
Rentiers	—	—	5,122	15.0
Inquisition, etc.	69	0.1	764	2.3
Students	734	1.4	2,113	6.3
Professions	854	1.7	441	1.3
Merchants	898	1.8	344	1.0
Artisans, manufactures	7,030	14.0	6,102	18.3
Day laborers	8,928	11.7	9,492	28.5
Criados	17,313	34.5	3,804	11.4
Labradores	102	0.2	3,981	11.7
Registered population	149,546(c)		124,323	
Active population(d)	50,113		33,351	
% of population economically active		33.5%		26.8%

Sources: For Madrid: RAH, *Censo de Floridablanca*, leg. 9/6235. For Barcelona: Josep Iglesias, ed., *El cens de Comte de Floridablanca, 1787: Parte de Catalunya*, pp. 49-51.

a. Madrid figures for 1787 are not directly comparable with those of 1757, because of the differences in the two censuses.

b. Figures for Barcelona are for the *corregimiento*, including nearby rural areas. The population of the city proper was around 95,000.

c. The total registered population of Madrid differs from source to source, depending on whether the first or second tally is used and whether one uses the official totals or those on the *barrio* returns. Totals vary from 147,500 to 149,500.

d. Active population does not here include members of religious communities, secular clergy, nor the transients given in the Barcelona sources. *Hidalgos* are included, although this may involve some double counting, especially in the government-employee category. *Rentistas* do not appear in the Madrid count, and it is assumed that they are subsumed within other categories.

destined for internal consumption, and thus the city contributed few exports to offset the cost of its imports.[10]

II. Income

The domination of the urban economy by political and land-owning elites comes into sharper focus when we examine the distribution of income among

10. An interesting comparison can be made with Mexico City, which was a residential and political center, but also a center for long-distance and interregional trade. See John Kisza, "Mexico City and the Provinces in the Late Colonial Period: The Dynamics of Domination" (paper given at the meeting of the Pacific Coast Branch, American Historical Association, 1978).

Table 4.4. *Distribution of Income by Occupational Sector, Madrid, 1757*

Sector	% of Workforce	% of Urban Income	% of Adj. Income(a)	% of Adj. Income(b)
Government	7.06%	32.08%	22.25%	21.74%
Church	11.36	6.80	4.72	9.22
Hospitals	-?-	1.23	.86	.84
Propertied	3.18	8.73	36.69	35.84
Professions	4.14	3.52	2.44	2.39
Business and finance	4.59	9.05	6.28	6.14
Food industries	6.29	6.54	4.45	4.44
Construction	15.85	5.54	3.84	3.75
Manufacturing	17.23	13.34	9.25	9.04
Service	30.56	11.24	7.80	7.62

Sources: See note 12 and Part II of Appendix C. Table C.2, C.3, and C.4 illustrate the data from which income estimates were compiled.

a. Adjusted for known rental income of titled residents as of 1809, deflated by Hamilton's price indices.

b. Adding to the first adjustment the arbitrary assumption that extra-urban clerical income equaled clerical income from within the city.

occupations, as shown in Table 4.4.[11] The *Catastro* includes only income from sources within the jurisdiction of Madrid and is based on a combination of direct survey and standardized assumptions: Incomes are overstated at the lower levels because of the assumption of regular employment in an economy readily affected by seasonal conditions. Extra-urban income was recorded where it was produced; consequently the income of the rentier class is distorted by the way in which the *Catastro* was compiled. And the income of most nonsalaried persons is also likely to be understated, because officials had to rely on what they were told by people who assumed that the survey was connected with taxes.

The first adjustment in Table 4.4 incorporates estimates of extra-urban income of the city's titled nobility. It is based on municipal sources of 1800–10, deflated by the New Castilian price index. The second adjustment illus-

11. Pre-modern income figures are hard to find, and those of the *Catastro* are subject to many qualifications. These figures are the result of cross-referencing versions of the 1757 *Catastro* of Madrid with adjustments extrapolated from other sources. The results are not comparable to distribution-of-wealth figures because the latter emphasize the propertied classes. Our figures are more comprehensive: they include all social elements within a single frame of reference. For possibilities and limitations of this technique, see Daumard and Furet, *Structures et relations,* and Daumard, *Les fortunes françaises,* esp. the synthesis in ch. 5. It is not clear how well some groups were counted, or how accurate the assumptions about wages were. Given the probability of underreporting in high income groups, and of unstable employment among the poor, the distribution of income was probably more extreme than these figures indicate.

trates the effect of the further assumption that the extra-urban income of religious institutions equaled their urban income, a condition undoubtedly closer to reality than the unadjusted figures. The taxes that supported the Court and the bureaucracy were extra-urban in origin, but are recorded as salaries paid to employees within the city. Among the laboring classes, the conventional daily wages of the *Catastro* match those documented by Earl Hamilton, but the conventions regarding days of employment during the year are questionable.[12] The hierarchy of relative income size thus appears reliable, while the sectoral distribution of income both verifies and explains the occupational structure.

The 10% of the economically active population supported directly by the state and by land-owning received 41% of the income generated in the city and 60% of income after adjustment for extra-urban sources. If the clergy are included in the elite, 21.6% of income recipients controlled 48% of the income generated in Madrid and 64–67% of all disposable income.[13] Given the downward biases in the sources, this has to be a low estimate. The mercantile and professional sectors, with 8.7% of recipients, were credited with 12.5% of the income produced in Madrid. Because no adjustments could be made for their extra-urban income, their share of the adjusted total falls to 8.5%. But this is the class historians look to for rural investment; and to the extent that they had investments outside the city, their relative importance is understated. It is worth noting, however, that their income from urban real property was slight. Only the 182 lawyers obtained even 10% of their income from urban real estate—which suggests that the understatement of income inherent in the sources may not be great. The landed and business groups were numerically about the same; and although business income was overshadowed by the total income of the rentiers, the business sector controlled a larger share of intracity income. Since this wealth was less likely to be committed to long-term obligations, the importance of the business sector in urban society was greater than the adjusted figures in Table 4.4 indicate.

Below the commercial and professional groups, income disparities rapidly

12. Earl J. Hamilton, *War and Prices in Spain, 1651–1800* (1947), app. 5, "Money Wages in New Castile, 1737–1800," pp. 268–269, gives average daily rates for construction labor. Yearly totals conventionally credited an urban worker with 180 days of earnings, and domestics with 250; see Pierre Vilar, "Estructures de la societat espanyola cap al 1750," and *La Renta Nacional,* p. 129. The official instructions for the *Catastro* give 180 days for artisans, 120 for *jornaleros,* and 250 for servants and lackeys (AVM, Secretaría, sig. 2–359-17, fol. 10 ff.). The one noble family whose income can be checked (the Infantados) appears accurately registered (Archives Nationales, Paris, IV-1608B/2II 46–1, courtesy Prof. Richard Herr; AHN, *Osuna,* leg. 1570-A, accounts from the Infantado holdings). The accuracy of recording in the professional, commercial, and artisan-cum-retailer groups cannot be tested.

13. The economic weight of the clergy is understated. Clerical landholdings accounted for about a third of the net agricultural product of Castile and 17% of Castile's national income as of 1750; see *La Renta Nacional,* pp. 189–203.

become extreme. Artisans and food suppliers were as numerous as clerical, titled, business, and professional elements combined; but while the latter enjoyed 75% of total urban income, they got only 13.5%. Furthermore, many crafts included individuals of substantial wealth, indicating even greater disparity within the poorer sectors. This part of society had virtually no income from urban real estate, and is unlikely to have had extra-urban rents. Manufacturing may have produced extra-urban earnings through commerce—and to the extent that Madrid profitably exported its products, industrial income is understated. The distortion is minor, however, since as late as 1789 only 6,500,000 *reales* worth of goods left the city, and the profit from that volume of sales was too small to have much effect on the distribution of income.[14] Construction and personal service were at the bottom of the income structure; most people in these categories were at best semi-skilled and easily replaceable. With 46% of the total work force, these groups shared only 11% of adjusted urban income. Thus the distribution of urban income by occupational sector clearly reveals the dependence of the urban economy on political and residential functions.

If the sectoral distribution of income documents the relationship of the city's political and aristocratic functions to its economic structure, the overall distribution of income defines the city as a market for external suppliers and links its economic structure with its demographic patterns. These points are illustrated by the distribution of income in each occupation, as given in Table 4.5, and by Table 4.6, which cross-tabulates income levels with numbers of recipients. Both tables use the adjustments for extra-urban rents of the landed elite, but exclude the arbitrary estimate of extra-urban clerical income.

While the mean recorded income was about 6,300 *reales*, the median income was about 1,450. Nearly 70% of the population had incomes below 2,000 *reales*, accounting for less than 13% of the total, while about 1% of incomes exceeded 40,000 *reales* and comprised more than 40% of the total. These disparities have little meaning out of context, and the one useful comparison comes from England. English income distribution is considered to have been very uneven in the eighteenth century, and that inequality remained constant until after World War I. Figure 4.1 compares income distribution in pre-industrial and modern England with that of eighteenth-century Madrid, where the disparities emerge as far more extreme.[15] Figure

14. The one private-sector export industry was publishing, which developed after the 1750's; see Diana Margaret Thomas, "The Royal Company of Printers and Booksellers of Spain, 1763–1794 (Ph.D. diss., 1974). The charter of the *Compañía de Libreros y Impresores* (1764) is in AHN, *Consejos,* leg. 51634–13.

15. The English figures are from Lee Soltow, "Long-run Changes in British Income Inequality" (1968). While the comparison between a national estimate and one for a city within

4.1 is really an abstract portrait of a small, well-defined elite which created a narrow market for luxury goods and specially made items and supported a large service class with very little buying power.[16]

This abstract picture can be given some quantitative substance by combining data from the *Catastro* with prices and wages for the 1750's and various accounts of daily diets to estimate plausible annual food budgets (see Table 4.7).[17] The basic daily diet included a pound of bread, 60 to 100 grams of meat, a small quantity of chickpeas or dried beans, a little salt pork, and an ounce or two of olive oil.[18] While wine was a popular beverage, contemporary accounts do not list it among the basic essentials, and there was great variation in the quality and combination of even the most basic items. Eaten as bread at breakfast and bread stew *(puchero)* for lunch and dinner, this dreary diet cost 920 *reales* yearly for two adults in mid-eighteenth-century Madrid.

To food we can add 60–70 *reales* per year for a single tenement room.[19] Ramón de la Cruz presents these quarters in detail, describing a two-story building with a small patio and a fountain for water and laundry. With seven rooms on each floor and two more in the attic, this tenement housed 13 households and 23 persons. The depiction includes only one child; but even at

---

another society is of course imperfect, it provides a helpful illustration. Soltow focuses on the degree to which income inequality aided development and was reinforced by industrialization. Our comparison suggests that what is important about Soltow's figures is the relative breadth of income distribution, not its extremes. Soltow's estimates are based on figures compiled by Gregory King in the 1690's. Recent work by Peter Lindert shows important omissions in King's work and, among other things, enlarges the size of the middle-income groups prior to 1750. This makes the Madrid-England contrast even more pronounced. See Peter Lindert, "English Occupations, 1670–1811" (1980), and his "Working Paper no. 144" (1980), Dept. of Economics, University of California, Davis.

16. Carlo M. Cipolla, *Before the Industrial Revolution: European Society and Economy, 1000–1750* (1976), pp. 8–14, discusses income distribution in pre-industrial Europe. He includes a table based on the well-known compilations made by Gregory King in the 1690's. It shows an income distribution in England in 1688 that was considerably more equitable than that of eighteenth-century Madrid. Cipolla quotes Francesco Guiciardini, who noted that in sixteenth-century Spain "except for a few grandees of the kingdom who live with great sumptuousness, one gathers that the others live in great poverty" (p. 14).

17. Earl Hamilton has been criticized for the use of wholesale prices, which imply a downward bias in price averages. If true, poverty incomes bought even less than assumed here. In practice, Hamilton's prices—upon which Table 4.7 depends—match those of other sources. Compare Hamilton, *War and Prices,* app. 1, "Commodity Prices in New Castile, 1751–1800," and app. 5, "Money Wages in New Castile, 1737–1800," with Gonzalo Anes Álvarez, *Las crises agrarias en la España moderna,* graphs of commodity prices; and the *Correo Mercantil* (Madrid) for 1792–94, passim, in Bancroft Library.

18. Earl Hamilton, *War and Prices,* pp. 251–255; Manuel Espadas Burgos, "Abasto y hábitos alimenticios en el Madrid de Fernando VII" (1973), pp. 258–263, 267–277; Vicente Palacio Atard, *Los españoles de la Ilustración* (1964), pp. 300–305. See also Antonio Fernández García, *El abastecimiento de Madrid en el reinado de Isabel II,* pp. x-xv.

19. William J. Callahan, "Corporate Charity in Spain: The Hermandad del Refugio of Madrid, 1618–1814," p. 165; Callahan also gives a good sketch of life at this income level.

Table 4.5. *Distribution of Income by Occupational Sectors in Madrid, 1757*

Sector	Income Level (in *reales*)								
	0-1,000	1,001-1,500	1,501-2,000	2,001-3,000	3,001-4,000	4,001-5,000	5,001-7,500	7,501-10,000	10,001-15,000
Propertied and titled persons(a)	—	—	—	645	137	—	—	357	—
Government(b)	—	450	—	250	—	450	—	225	600
Legal, medical, etc., professions	24	498	45	100	—	381	499	—	149
Church and monastic persons, excl. servants	2	46	2,617	100	109	759	16	13	10
Business and mercantile, incl. servants	688	189	—	95	—	180	11	92	245
Crafts: precious metals	178	57	234	31	4	8	103	107	75
mechanical and metallurgical	539	270	201	16	21	103	135	127	22
textiles and leather, finished and lux.	442	1,089	793	225	167	1	476	6	75
textiles and leather, intermediate	346	333	40	100	26	17	146	183	89
miscellaneous	144	115	13	—	—	15	98	63	8
Food: basic foodstuffs	537	398	—	242	108	—	224	—	26
luxury foods, spices, etc.	129	88	148	25	68	—	36	17	128
Construction	4,630	712	751	10	166	5	205	117	9
Skilled services, entertainment	245	44	—	275	289	37	46	5	11
Unskilled and day labor, servants	2,851	8,363	306	347	—	12	—	—	—
Totals	10,755	12,652	5,148	2,413	1,095	1,968	1,995	1,312	1,447

(Table 4.5. cont.)

Sector	Income Level (in reales)							Total
	15,001-20,000	20,001-40,000	40,001-60,000	60,001-175,000	175,000-350,000	350,000-3,500,000	Over 3,500,000	
Propertied and titled persons(a)	20	–	38	76	32	39	7	1,351
Government(b)	330	635	60	–	–	–	–	3,000
Legal, medical, etc., professions	23	50	2	–	–	–	–	1,771
Church and monastic persons, excl. servants	2	–	2	–	–	–	–	3,628
Business and mercantile, incl. servants	137	264	25	–	–	–	–	1,926
Crafts: precious metals	–	–	22	–	–	–	–	819
mechanical and metallurgical	–	39	–	–	–	–	–	1,473
textiles and leather, finished and lux.	16	–	–	–	–	–	–	3,290
textiles and leather, intermediate	2	10	–	–	–	–	–	1,292
miscellaneous	10	36	–	–	–	–	–	502
Food: basic foodstuffs	160	8	–	–	–	–	–	1,703
luxury foods, spices, etc.	14	134	–	–	–	–	–	787
Construction	103	10	–	–	–	–	–	6,718
Skilled services, entertainment	60	40	3	–	–	–	–	1,055
Unskilled and day labor, servants	–	–	–	–	–	–	–	11,879
Totals	877	1,226	152	76	32	39	7	41,194

a. Propertied and titled persons distributed as per adjustments to the *Catastro* for total rent figures of 1808, discounted 30% as per first adjustment in Table 4.4.

b. Distribution of governmental incomes represents a tentative estimate, excluding the immediate royal household.

Table 4.6. *Distribution of Recipients and Income by Income Level, Madrid, ca. 1757(a)*

Income Level (in reales)	Recipients No.	Recipients %	City Income	% of Recipients	Cumulative Income
0-1,000	10,755	26.1%	3.11%	26.1%	3.11%
1,001-1,500	12,652	30.7	6.09	56.8	9.20
1,501-2,000	5,148	12.5	3.47	69.3	12.67
2,001-3,000	2,413	5.9	2.33	75.2	15.00
3,001-4,000	1,095	2.7	1.48	77.9	16.48
4,001-5,000	1,968	4.8	3.41	82.7	19.89
5,001-7,500	1,995	4.8	4.88	87.5	24.77
7,501-10,000	1,312	3.2	4.17	90.7	28.94
10,001-15,000	1,447	3.5	7.02	94.2	35.96
15,001-20,000	877	2.1	5.92	96.3	41.88
20,001-40,000	1,226	3.0	14.17	99.3	56.05
40,001-60,000	152	0.5	3.78	99.8	59.83
60,001-175,000	76	0.2	3.44	100.0	63.27
175,001-350,000	32	0.1	3.24	100.1	66.51
350,001-3,500,000	39	0.1	20.02	100.2	86.53
Over 3,500,000	7	0.02	13.49	100.22	100.02
Totals	41,194	100.22%	100.02%		

a. Incorporates the suggested adjustments in the text, including the hypothetical distribution of government employees and adjusted incomes of titled nobility. Additional adjustments for extra-urban rents would no doubt increase the proportion of the middle ranges (5-40,000 *reales*) and reduce somewhat the proportion attributed to the very wealthy, but would still serve primarily to illustrate the extremes of income distribution which characterized the city. By these figures, the mean income of the city was about 6,300 *reales*, while the median income was slightly under 1,500 *reales*. The percentages do not total exactly 100% because of the need to round off decimals in the calculations.

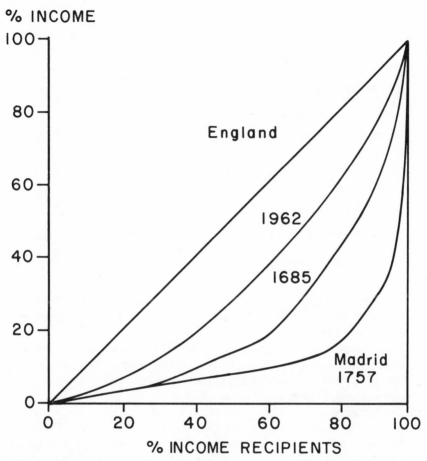

Figure 4.1 *Distribution of Income and Recipients in England (1688 and 1962) and Madrid (1757)**
*English figures from Lee Soltow, "Long-run Changes in British Income Inequality," *Economic History Review*, 2nd series, 21 (1968), 12–29.

that low economic level, three households had servants.[20] An eyewitness description from 1836 presents a four-story tenement with a wide range of rents, temporary living stalls in the hallways, and 62 households in one building.[21] Allowing for food, housing, wine, clothing, and miscellaneous items,

20. Taken from Ramón de la Cruz, *La Petre y la Juana,* as cited by Arthur Hamilton, "A Study of Spanish Manners, 1750–1800: From the Plays of Ramón de la Cruz." Writing in the twentieth century, Arturo Barea describes what could almost be the same building in *The Forge* (1944), pp. 127–130.
21. Mesonero Romanos, *Obras,* vol. 2, pp. 113–114.

Table 4.7 *Estimated Annual Food Costs per Person in Madrid, 1750s*

Example	Cost of Basic Diet	Cost of Diet with Wine, Fruit, Spices, Vegetables
Moderately affluent household, 7-10 persons, incl. children and servants	797 rs.	920 rs.
Bakery, 10 adult working men	806	1,117(a)
Bakery, 6 working men and boys	280	590(a)
Typical diet of the 1820s at 1750s prices	460	770(a)

Sources: Food prices and descriptions of diets taken from the citations in note 19.
a. Based on per-capita wine consumption, as calculated in Chapter 6.

the median income of 1,450 *reales* barely supported two adults and left little leeway for temporary unemployment or unstable food prices—no strangers to the poor of the city.[22]

This rough estimate of the cost of survival provides a yardstick that gives some meaning to the income of more affluent groups. It indicates that a family of four or five required 3,000 to 4,000 *reales* yearly to enjoy more than minimal food, housing, and clothes, and 5,000 *reales* to achieve a measure of "bourgeois" comfort. In the professions, the 381 surgeon-barbers averaged about 4,800 *reales* per year; the 182 lawyers 5,900; and the 85 medical doctors 13,500, as did business agents. Wholesale merchants and the 278 members of the Five Greater Guilds ranged from 17,500 to 37,000 *reales* per year, the latter being the average of the 28 members of the *Gremio de la Seda* (Silk Merchants Guild). The 129 bakery owners and 28 wine wholesalers averaged 18,000 per year, and the 22 jewelers in the Silversmiths' Guild more than 50,000 *reales* per year. Among the artisans, a few trades show a considerable concentration of wealth—the 15 brass and bell casters, 24 wrought-iron suppliers, 22 wax and candle sellers, and 14 dyers averaged 25,000 to 35,000 *reales*. In most guilds, masters with their own shops had comfortable but more modest incomes of 6,000 to 12,000 *reales* per year. In contrast, masters without shops and working for wages were credited with 1,200 to 2,200 *reales*, depending on the trade. Journeymen were paid somewhat less, giving

22. The rough clothing provided in the *asilio de méndigos* would alone have absorbed much of the margin (ibid., p. 42).

them incomes that put a family at the subsistence level. The tradition that journeymen were unmarried was due to more than guild regulation.[23]

That is the context in which 645 propertied widows averaged 2,900 *reales* yearly, and 357 owners of urban *mayorazgos* received around 9,200. At midcentury the salary of a royal councilor was 40,000 *reales*, reaching 90,000 by 1790.[24] The 120 resident titled nobles averaged 44,000 *reales* in city-derived income, while the comparable figure for the 53 resident grandees was 140,000 *reales* per year. With adjustments for extra-urban land rents, 46 grandees had annual incomes over 350,000 *reales*, and 7 of them exceeded ten times that figure. Roughly 300 families, 0.8% of income recipients, enjoyed incomes over 40,000 *reales* and accounted for 40% of all income received in the city. Below this extremely wealthy group was a "middling class" of about 3,600 families with incomes between 10,000 and 40,000 *reales*; some 3,300 families with between 5,000 and 10,000 *reales*; and about 3,000 with between 3,000 and 5,000. Thus the "middling class" of the largest city in Spain at best included no more than 10,000 households. This class formed the demographic core able to sustain households and reproduce in the urban context, in contrast to the young, single, or childless immigrants entering low-income niches in the service sector and unskilled occupations. The result is in sharp contrast with the growing market at the "middling class" level in England, and a very small arena for the producer using capital-intensive mass production.

III. Consumption

Eighteenth-century Madrid thus constituted a market in which at least 70% of incomes hovered around the subsistence level. Judging by the percentage of the population that was economically active and the high proportion of young adults, the poor survived because they were single or because more than one member of the household worked.[25] These were the apprentices, day laborers, *gente de librea*, water carriers, sweepers, rag collectors, porters, refuse movers, washerwomen, and peddlers who appear in the poor relief records, in the *Catastro*, and in the depictions of the playwrights.[26] They were also those immigrants who entered the urban workforce because there was

23. Kany, *Life and Manners*, pp. 161–163.

24. In 1799, 22 members of the *Consejo de Estado* averaged 147,000 *reales* per year, while members of the *Consejo de Castilla* got 106,000 and members of the *Sala de Alcaldes y Corte* 36,000 *reales* (Jose Canga Argüelles, *Diccionario de Hacienda* (1834), vol. 2, p. 533).

25. The immigration by single adults from rural areas and the low marriage rates and small childhood cohorts shown in Chapter 3 all confirm this pattern.

26. William J. Callahan, "Corporate Charity," p. 162, and *La Santa y Real Hermandad del Refugio y Piedad de Madrid, 1618–1832* (1980), p. 14.

even less room for them in the countryside. This segment of society consumed most of the basic supplies entering the city, and a decline in their real wages or employment meant forgoing all other commodities in the search for food.

At the other extreme, perhaps 7,000 incomes permitted the bourgeois comforts of an apartment with several rooms; a diet including fruit, vegetables, and sweets; and a cook, a houseboy, and two maids. Such a life-style implied a budget of 2,000 to 3,000 *reales* just for food, and another 1,000 for servants, plus the cost of clothes, transport, tutors, and other accoutrements of respectability.[27] Moreover, a large share of urban income went to families so wealthy that basic needs represented a small share of their expenses, leaving them insulated from fluctuating food prices. This explains why, as noted in Chapter 3, the core of the urban population appeared demographically stable in the face of crises that caused serious distress in the economically marginal "envelope" of urban society.

Thus Madrid's occupational and income structures point to an urban market with definite characteristics. They imply consumption of large quantities of a few basic commodities—wheat, meat, fuel, wine—and small but stable amounts of higher-priced foodstuffs, such as condiments, fish, fresh vegetables, and fruit. The low incomes of most inhabitants, and the sharp disparities in income distribution, also suggest that the demand for semi-luxuries and low-quality manufactures fluctuated greatly with real income. Such a market was extremely sensitive to the interplay of harvest yields in supply zones, the size of the city relative to the supply system, and the ability of the urban elite to pay their bills and support marginally useful domestics.

Although they are often hard to disentangle, the city was susceptible to two types of economic crisis. When events reduced elite income, incomes dependent on elite demand also declined; thus a crisis in the political and economic systems of the monarchy affected all levels of urban society. Regional subsistence crises, on the other hand, affected primarily the food supply, driving up prices and drawing disposable income to essential commodities with little impact on the habits of the wealthy. Thus regional subsistence crises aggravated disparities in income, since the living standards of the wealthy were less affected. Despite their interaction, the two patterns must be kept in mind, since they reflect Madrid's position in Spain's dualized economy.

The actual structure of urban demand is documented by a resumé of 1789.[28] Imports ranged from 1,500,000 bushels of wheat and 38,000 tons of

27. Arthur Hamilton, "Manners," pp. 35–36, 64–65.
28. AVM, *Secretaria,* sig. 4–5–67. One need not go far to find defects in such official resumés, especially when related to taxes; see Stanley J. Stein, "Reality in Microcosm: The Debate Over Trade with America, 1785–1789" (1973). Any built-in bias in reporting worked to understate reality. Where the reported volume of imports can be compared with other official sources, they are consistent. Thus the figures may be understated, but they are of similar magnitude and reflect the relative importance of items.

charcoal to 105 silk petticoats and 103 bushels of rye. There are many omnibus headings such as "spices," "munitions," and "trinkets and costume jewelry of little value" registered in bales, boxes, casks, dozens, and pounds. Only 14 items are recorded as exports or re-exports, 11 of them in small quantities (e.g., 1,860 sheets of painted wallpaper; 326 pounds of lacquer). Two of the larger exports were 335,000 decks of playing cards and 112 tons of saltpeter, both from royal monopolies. Books were the only private-sector export of consequence, destined for the protected market for religious tracts and prayer-books in Spanish America. The internal orientation of Madrid's industries is shown here by the fact that printing and playing cards involved only 700 out of 12,000 artisans.

The significance of this emerges when imports are linked with prices to create an approximation of their relative importance in the market. The results indicate an overwhelming urban trade deficit in which an estimated 433 million *reales* worth of imports was offset by only about 6–7 million *reales* worth of exports.

To obtain this estimate, imports were grouped as (1) basic subsistence commodities (wheat, barley, wine, meat, fuel); (2) other foods and beverages, colonial products, and raw materials; and (3) semi-finished products and manufactures. Various sources were checked for prices to attach to commodities.[29] Prices were found for about 100 items that were on the imports list or were close substitutes. The goods that could be priced cost urban consumers a minimum of 325,000,000 *reales*. If this represents 75% of the value of all imports, the minimum total paid for imports was 433,000,000 *reales* for the year.[30] By contrast, urban exports amounted to only 6–7 million *reales*. This omits unrecorded goods exported by villagers and transporters, but evidence indicates that these were negligible.[31]

The massive trade deficit was financed not by providing commercial and industrial services, but by the power of the city's elites to transfer rents, taxes, and tithes for dispersal in the capital. Government salaries and pensions

29. See note 17 above, and also Antonio Matilla Tascón, ed., *Balanza de comercio exterior de España en el año 1795* (1965). Some items are underpriced; if there was a risk of overpricing an item, it was omitted. Those that could not be priced included many luxury items that were traded in small volume and left no quotations. This is offset by the absence of raw and construction materials. When several prices were available, low quality was assumed, producing a consistent downward bias. The distortions generally minimize the importance of manufactures and imports from outside of Castile.

30. An independent estimate by Napoleonic authorities in 1811 suggests a "normal" yield of 100,000 *reales* daily from a 10% entry duty and implies an annual volume of 365 million *reales*, excluding bread and bread-grains. Given the reduction of trade due to the war, this fits with our estimate. See Geoffroy de Grandmaison, ed., *Correspondence du Comte de la Forest, ambassadeur de France en Espagne, 1808–1813* (1906–1913), vol. 4, p. 499.

31. Of 800 complete commodity transfers by such people, 50% involved delivery of goods to Madrid, but exactly two describe goods leaving the capital. David R. Ringrose, *Los transportes* (1972), maps and appendix.

totaled 45 million *reales* in 1757, and 100 million by 1790, not including the expenses of a garrison of 7,000 to 10,000 soldiers. The 192 titled families in the city in 1757 received 100–110 million *reales* in income from extra-urban sources.[32] The Duke of Osuna offers a typical example of private revenue transfers: During 1650–1700, one-third to one-half of his expenditures were in Madrid, approaching 400,000 *reales* annually and including 3 million *reales* for a new palace. Typical of the blurring of public and private income, the palace was reputedly paid for with "profits" from the Duke's service as Viceroy in Milan.[33] With over 3,000 religious personnel and dozens of en-dowed institutions, the clerical contribution to the city's deficit of payments was also considerable.[34] These fragmentary figures demonstrate the depen-dence of the urban economy on the state and on the private and clerical rentier elements in the capital.

This massive imbalance in Madrid's trade highlights an important aspect of the city's failure to stimulate economic change in its hinterland. Unlike Barcelona or London, which imported, processed, repackaged, and re-ex-ported many goods for both hinterland and long-distance markets, Madrid simply imported from both for internal consumption. The capital provided few goods and commercial services that might have induced rural Castile to intensify and specialize so as to add variety to its standard of living. Location and urban taxes made Madrid the most unlikely of entrepôts. Thus Madrid itself provided few affordable inducements to rural productivity and was unable to create links between maritime demand and the products of the interior. Lest the importance of this be missed, Madrid's consumption in 1789 exceeded half the value of Spain's import, export, and bullion trade at Cádiz, making it a centerpiece of the country's nonsubsistence economy.

If the one-sided nature of Madrid's trade reveals something of the city's association with its hinterland, the nature of urban imports provides addi-tional insights. In Table 4.8 the imports of 1789 that could be assigned prices have been classified as subsistence commodities, non-subsistence foods, raw materials and semi-finished products, and manufactures. The value of goods that could be priced in each category is shown as a percentage of the value of all imports that could be given prices. The results reinforce the findings in the earlier sections of this chapter. Despite the high proportion of low incomes,

32. AVM, *Secretaria*, sig. 2–360–5; Antonio Matilla Tascón, "El primer catastro de la villa de Madrid"; Canga Argüelles, *Diccionario,* vol. 2, p. 184; Archives Nacionales, Paris, IV-1608B/2II 46–1. (Courtesy Prof. Richard Herr.)

33. Lorna Jury Gladstone, "Aristocratic Landholding and Finances in Seventeenth-Century Castile: The Case of Gaspar Téllez Girón, Duke of Osuna (1656–1694)" (Ph.D. diss., 1977), pp. 146–154, 156–184.

34. Given the size of clerical landholdings (see note 13) and the fact that Madrid accounted for over 6% of ecclesiastical personnel in Castile, and an even larger share of endowed religious institutions, the Church's contribution to the urban economic base was very large.

Table 4.8. *Distribution of the Value of Madrid Imports by Type of Commodity, 1789*

Category(a)	
Subsistence commodities	40.1%
Nonsubsistence foodstuffs	16.2
Raw and semi-finished materials	6.4
Manufactures	37.1

Source: Based on AVM, *Secretaría*, sig. 4-5-67, and the sources in note 17.
a. Subsistence commodities = wheat, meat, wine, charcoal, and olive oil. Nonsubsistence foodstuffs = sugar, chocolate, fruit, etc. Raw and semi-finished materials = silk, wool, yarn, iron, etc. Manufactures = textiles, hardware, shoes, etc.

the economic importance of nonessential goods is striking, and reflects the extreme concentration of wealth. This again highlights another of Madrid's structural traits: the orientation of manufacturing and commerce to the city's internal market. Unable to export, and having an urban market with only a few thousand affluent households, Madrid could absorb only a small volume of any given product. Hence manufacturing and marketing were locked into the handicraft stage. By the later eighteenth century, it was precisely such handicraft production that was becoming vulnerable to European competitors who, because they enjoyed expansive markets, were able to experiment with new industrial techniques that lowered production costs and allowed penetration into markets which, like Madrid, were serviced by high-cost producers.

IV. Implications

In a narrow market with few affluent customers, the final cost of a good is frequently less important than its uniqueness, variety, and style. This context emphasizes profit per unit sold, rather than profit through volume sales.[35] The type of elite that Madrid exemplifies has little concern for the geographic origin of the goods it fancies—distant origin is often part of the intangible uniqueness of a costly item important to the externalities of status. Thus Madrid's market absorbed a large volume of a few basic commodities required by virtually all inhabitants, and a remarkable variety of luxuries, textiles, and manufactures sought by the narrow middle- and high-income market. The relative unimportance of raw materials and semi-finished prod-

35. Sjoberg, *The Pre-Industrial City*, pp. 196–199, 204–209, gives a good description of this market structure.

ucts reflects both the weak urban demand for industrial products and the dependent position of the craft sector in the urban economy.

This interaction of consumer and producer afflicted Spain beyond Madrid and shaped the industry of the interior from the sixteenth century onward. It became even more striking as Madrid did, in fact, become a major industrial center of pre-industrial Spain.[36] It was, however, an industrial community in an environment unlikely to stimulate structural change in production or alter the mentality of producers and distributors. Madrid's dominant urban functions and concentration of income created a pattern of consumption in which demand for imported luxuries remained inelastic unless there were major problems in the monarchy itself. The extensive fields of influence created by political power and aristocratic social integration produced an urban elite which was largely immune to economic distress in the Castilian interior. Indeed, crop shortages generated high grain prices that tended to enhance the situation of a rentier class with stocks of grain to sell. At the same time, the demand for basic foodstuffs remained inelastic because most of the population was so near the subsistence level that it could not reduce consumption without serious results.

Income distribution and urban function thus interacted with fluctuations in food supply and the effectiveness of political authority to create a market with inelastic demand for a few agricultural commodities and a great many luxury products. The segment of urban demand that was highly elastic involved the lower-quality manufactures of the interior and less essential foodstuffs.[37] Consequently, the structure of the urban economy left the craft industries and specialized agriculture of the hinterland vulnerable to the changing fortunes of the city.

The stultifying effect of concentrating so much buying power in a market so constructed marks a strong contrast with seventeenth- and eighteenth-century England and London. Residence for a rising "pseudo-gentry," London's very size implied returns to scale in distribution and a volume of demand that stimulated significant productivity increases in agriculture. As F. J. Fisher comments: "Had the consumption of imports and city-made goods been confined to the upper classes, it is doubtful whether much weight could reasonably be attached to them as a spur to production."[38] In Madrid, not only was wealth concentrated among the upper classes, but within the elite there were disparities that rendered buying power even more concentrated than it first appears.

36. *La Renta Nacional,* pp. 46–47, 152–153.

37. As Chapter 6 will show, wine was the most important commodity of this type.

38. F. J. Fisher, "London as an 'Engine of Economic Growth' " (1976), pp. 205–215, esp. p. 211. See also Wrigley, "A Simple Model"; and Robert Brenner's comments on this theme in "The Origins of Capitalist Development: A Critique of Neo-Smithian Marxism," pp. 45–47. A more recent summary is in John Patten, *English Towns, 1500–1700* (1978), p. 87.

The perennial reliance of Madrid on distant suppliers also meant that, despite a rudimentary regional economy, long-distance commerce was well developed. Beginning in the later eighteenth century, accelerating European industrialization set the stage for a progressive shift in urban preferences toward imported goods. By the second quarter of the nineteenth century, the dependence on imports involved the purchasing patterns of the poor as well. These trends spelled trouble for the craft industries of Castile and for the manufacturing sector of Madrid. This is hardly a surprising result of the industrial revolution, and the Spanish preference for imports is a cliche. But the economic structure that Madrid's *raison d'être* imposed upon its urban economy, and the narrow market structure that resulted, suggest that the capital transmitted economic forces into the Castilian hinterland in ways that reinforced its economic stagnation. To verify that, we must next examine some of the long-term changes in the structure of the urban economy.

5. Changes in the Urban Economy, Seventeenth Through Nineteenth Centuries

The patterns of population, income, occupations, and urban consumption just presented permit several insights into the interaction of city and country as the fortunes of Madrid changed. The eighteenth-century cross-section and the long-term trends outlined in Chapter 2 provide a structural context for a variety of evidence on changes in the urban economy from the seventeenth through the early nineteenth centuries.[1] This chapter presents evidence on changes in occupation, income, and trade structures, while in Chapter 6 we will examine the evolution of the city as a market.

I. The Seventeenth Century

Between 1560 and 1630, Madrid evolved from a second- or third-order place in an urban hierarchy oriented to Toledo into a position of urban dominance as the largest city in Spain. In the process, her urban functions and fields of influence changed radically, as politically sustained growth overwhelmed the sixteenth-century town and created an economic pattern that persisted through the nineteenth century. We have seen that by 1630 a demographic pattern of few children, low marriage ratios, a stable core, and a large population of young adult immigrants was well established. Simultaneously,

---

1. Only a few aspects of this have been examined thus far. A study of seventeenth-century Madrid is being done by Claude Larquié; see his "Quartiers et paroisses urbaines: L'exemple de Madrid au XVIIIe siècle" (1974); "Etude de démographie madrilene: la paroisse de San Ginés de 1650 a 1700" (1966); and "Les esclaves de Madrid a l'époque de la decadence, 1650–1700" (1970); and with J. Fayard, "Hôtels madrilènes et démographie urbaine au XVIIe siècle" (1968), p. 234. William Callahan has studied poor relief in Madrid; see his "Corporate Charity in Spain" (1976), pp. 159–171 and *La Santa y Real Hermandad del Refugio y Piedad de Madrid, 1618–1832* (1980). Also see Charles Carlson, "The Vulgar Sort in *Siglo de Oro* Madrid."

the city developed the large service class and internal, elite orientation of industry and trade characteristic of the eighteenth century.

The evolution of this occupational structure dates from the early seventeenth century and can be glimpsed in 527 *peticiones de vecindad* preserved from the period 1600–1663.[2] Despite the lag between immigration and eligibility for citizenship, the pattern of immigration implied from Table 5.1 reflects the economic structure that was emerging. Women, servants, and unskilled workers were either ineligible or had little to gain from formal citizenship and are absent from the sample. Consequently, the artisan, construction, and service sectors are seriously under-represented here, compared with the *Catastro* data, while the food and government sectors are correspondingly overstated. Nevertheless, the occupational structure of recorded immigration for the first two-thirds of the century shows the same emphasis on craft, food, and service industries and on state-related professions apparent in the workforce of the eighteenth century.

Table 5.1. *Occupational Distribution of 527 Requests for Citizenship in Madrid, 1600-1663*

Occupation	1600-63	1600-30	1631-63
Government, royal service	9.1%	4.9%	16.7%
Títulos and *caballeros*	3.4	0.3	9.4
Business and professions	9.5	8.6	5.8
Service industries(a)	13.3	13.2	15.2
Food industries and trades	17.3	20.6	11.6
Artisans and skilled labor	25.6	34.0	9.4
Miscellaneous	5.3	5.8	1.5
Unstated	16.5	12.6	30.5

Source: AVM, Secretaría, sigs. 2-347 and 2-348.
a. Includes barbers, surgeons, innkeepers, etc.

There is also evidence illustrating the adaptation of the occupational structure to the growing predominance of the city's political and aristocratic functions. There was a sharp reduction in business and artisan requests for citizenship, and a marked increase in noble and bureaucratic applications, after 1630. While the sample for 1631–63 is probably too small to be valid on its own, the changes in the distribution of occupations are suggestive and fit well with other indications of a transition in the city's evolution during the

2. AVM, *Secretaria,* sigs. 2–347 and 2–348. The statistical validity of the sample is debatable, since we have no knowledge of the relationship between the number of surviving petitions and the number granted, or of the reasons why this particular selection survived. The sample averages 10 cases per year for 1600–1620, 23 per year in 1621–30, and only 7 per year after 1630.

1620's. Population trends show that Madrid grew rapidly from the late sixteenth century until 1630. Even with unskilled laborers unrepresented, the occupational picture for the petitioners between 1600 and 1630 confirms the image of a rapidly growing city building up its handicraft, food supply, and construction industries. It coincides with the collapse of Toledo as the primary center of Castile, and supports contemporary concern over the flight of Toledo's industrial and commercial population to the new capital.[3] After 1630 the applications suggest the stagnation of the urban economy and confirm both the city's role as political and residential center for the governing elites and the structure of its future economy.[4]

This coincides with other evidence of transition around 1625–30. We have seen that the revenue from the *peso mayor* in the central market rose until 1620, was very unstable in the decade after 1625, and dropped quickly thereafter. The behavior of the *peso* series reflects a rise in real wages through 1620, and coincides with evidence of rapid population growth.[5] Concurrently, artisans, food processors, merchants, and professionals made up over 60% of the requests for citizenship, and the era was one of heavy investment in the physical infrastructure of the capital.[6] The growing importance of Madrid as a central place is reflected in tolls collected on long-distance trade into the city, which rose even faster than population prior to 1625.

After 1625 the trend changed, and the traits of the eighteenth century emerge more clearly. Population continued to grow for a decade, but real wages declined and *peso mayor* revenues ceased to expand. Tolls collected on trade reflecting the city's political and aristocratic functions continued to grow, while requests for citizenship increasingly mentioned service and governmental occupations. The occupational structure, demographic charac-

3. See Michael Weisser, "Les marchands de Tolède dans l'économie castillane, 1565–1635" (1971).

4. The influx of notables to the court is discussed at length by the *arbitristas;* see Thomas K. Niehaus, "Population Problems and Land Use in the Writings of the Spanish Arbitristas, 1600–1650" (Ph.D. diss., 1976). Niehaus quotes Saavedra Fajardo as saying ". . .just as the burning liver attracts to itself the body's heat and leaves the rest of the body weak and spiritless, so the pomp of the court, its comforts, its delights, the advantages of the arts, and the opportunity for rewards attracts people to it . . ." taken from Saavedra Fajardo, *Idea de un principe politico-cristiano* (1640), in *Biblioteca de autores españoles* (1947), vol. 25, p. 182. The general impression of a city consisting largely of retainers, bureaucrats, poor, and service personnel is apparent in Carmelo Viñas y Mey, "Notas sobre la estructura socio-demográfica del Madrid de los Austrias" (1955).

5. The applicability to Madrid of Earl Hamilton's figures in *American Treasure*, pp. 262–281, is debatable, since his wage figures combined data from all over Spain. Much of the increase in real wages reflects an easing of inflationary pressure in the first two decades of the century, paralleled by regional population loss due to plague, famine, and emigration. The wage pattern fits with the sustained rise of urban imports of basic commodities until around 1625 and a noticeable decline after 1630.

6. Larquié, "Quartiers," pp. 167–168; and Ruth Lee Kennedy, "The New Plaza Mayor of 1620," p. 49.

teristics, and income inequality that later marked Madrid were emerging, and were to prove remarkably durable.

II. Eighteenth- and Nineteenth-Century Changes

A. The Lower Classes in the Workforce, 1757–1857

Beginning with the 1750's, we can develop some idea of the proportion of the population that was economically active and of the distribution of that workforce between occupational sectors. Relying on the three most credible tabulations (1757, 1804, and 1857), we find that the relative size of the workforce was almost constant for a century, despite a near-doubling of total population (see Table 5.2).[7] It was also relatively large, reflecting the high proportion of immigrant adults and small number of children. In view of the prosperity of the later eighteenth century, the upheavals of the early nineteenth century, and the cost to Spain of the loss of the American empire, the figures show remarkable consistency. They identify a long-run structural trait of Madrid's economy linked with the wasp-waisted, immigrant-dominated structure that appeared in the seventeenth century and persisted as late as 1900.[8]

Within that stable framework, the same sources suggest various shifts in occupational distribution that point to growing inequality in the distribution of income and a decline in overall urban per-capita income. There is no source comparable with the rich *Catastro* of 1757, but comparisons across various time spans are possible for several categories. While few of these comparisons bear much scrutiny alone, several together lend support to our perception of a trend within the urban economy.

Domestics, day workers, and artisans were especially difficult to count accurately, in part because they were inconsistently classified. Artisans appear undercounted or redefined in the census of 1787, as do servants and day laborers in 1799, while the censuses of 1757 and 1804 appear more complete and consistent (see Table 5.3). By 1857, definitions of shopkeeper, craftsman, laborer, and domestic had clearly changed, and there is a pervasive vagueness

7. In addition to the *Catastro*, there are five detailed censuses of Madrid (1757, 1787, 1797, 1804, and 1857), of which 1757, 1804, and 1857 are the most useful. The commonly cited censuses of 1787 and 1797 appear to have been less inclusive of economic activity and used varying criteria for classification. (For citations to census sources, see Table 3.6.) With respect to Castile as a whole, it now appears that the census of 1787 was about 5% low, and that of 1797 at least 10% below the actuality. See *La Renta Nacional,* pp. 62–70, 76–77; and Francisco Bustelo García del Real, "Algunos reflexiones sobre la población española de principios del siglo XVIII" (1972), and "La población española en la segunda mitad del siglo XVIII" (1972). The census of 1857 suffers from the problem of changing categorical definitions, but tax registers from 1841 and 1848 allow adjustment for the effect of these nineteenth-century occupational redefinitions.

8. Carmen del Moral, *La sociedad madrileña de fin de siglo* (1974), p. 46.

Table 5.2. *Total and Economically Active Populations
of Madrid, 1757-1857*

Year	Total Population (est.)(a)	Economically Active(b)	
1757	142,000	44,611(c)	31.4%
1787	175,000	53,394	30.5
1797	195,000	57,709	29.6
1804	190,000	59,325	31.2
1857	275,000	80,338	29.2

a. Estimated population totals are from Chapter 2.

b. Includes clergy, nobles, and property owners.

c. This conflicts with *La Renta Nacional*, pp. 76-77, because of differing definitions of "economically active" and differing estimates of total population. The figure there, 35.8%, is midway between our estimate and the 40.9% obtained from the unadjusted figures for the domiciled population in 1757.

about the boundaries between domestic and day worker and between day worker and artisan.[9] In the later eighteenth century the guild system came under considerable pressure from the Crown for its exclusiveness and monopolistic tendencies, and during the first half of the nineteenth century it was abolished. Thus many shopworkers and artisans of the eighteenth century were classified as day laborers in the nineteenth; skilled laborers previously outside the guilds may have been reclassified as artisans; and many who were domestics by eighteenth-century definition became artisans or day laborers by nineteenth-century standards. Similarly, guild-masters with shops, classed as artisans in the eighteenth century, were now placed in the mercantile category.[10]

Despite their problematic accuracy, certain impressions emerge from these figures. The least ambiguous development is the growth of the servant class. Domestics increased from 20% of the workforce in 1757 to about 30% at the turn of the century—and despite the vicissitudes of the city's economy, included well over a third of the workforce by 1857. Given nineteenth-century customs favoring women as servants and celibacy in service, this trend helps explain both the increasing preponderance of women in the urban population and the declining marriage rate noted in Chapter 3—trends already apparent in late eighteenth-century Madrid.[11]

9. On this problem, refer to Michael Katz, "Occupational Classification in History."

10. The confusion is more understandable when one realizes that a journeyman *(oficial)* in the eighteenth century guilds was also referred to as either a *jornalero* or an *añero*, depending on whether his contract called for pay calculated on a daily or yearly basis. See Charles Kany, *Life and Manners in Madrid, 1750–1800*, p. 162.

11. Theresa McBride comments on this, in "Traditional Socialization for Women," for nineteenth-century Paris, and it was already a well-defined pattern for house servants in Madrid

Table 5.3. *Domestics, Artisans, and Day Workers in the Economically Active Population of Madrid, 1757-1857*

Year	Economically Active Pop.	Domestics	Artisans	Day Laborers	Total for All Three Groups
1757	44,611	19.9%	32.3%	18.5%	70.7%
1787(a)	53,395	32.4	13.4	16.7	62.5
1799(a)	57,709	19.4	23.0	13.4	55.8
1804	59,325	30.7	23.0	17.4	71.1
1857	80,338	34.0(b)	27.1	16.2	77.3

a. These censuses present the most problems for analysis; 1787 raises concerns about definitions of categories, and 1799 is generally regarded as not very reliable.

b. This estimate of domestics is based on a partial census of 1845. If the number of domestics rose proportionately with the population, there were 27,000 by 1857, or 34% of the workforce. This coincides with the increased proportion of females and unmarried adults.

The artisans and day laborers are harder to follow through time because of the problems of enumeration and classification. Ignoring the questionable censuses of 1787 and 1799, it appears that the artisan sector declined from 32% to 23% of the workforce in the second half of the eighteenth century, but then rose somewhat by 1857. The relative eighteenth-century decline is consistent with population growth which featured expansion of the marginal "envelope" of new and unskilled immigrants compared with a more stable urban core. The later expansion suggests either an artisan sector growing faster than the city's population or a problem of occupational definition; the second hypothesis seems more credible. The proportion defined as day laborers is more consistent, drifting slightly downward from 18.5% in 1757 to 16% in 1857. While apparent trends in the artisan and day-labor sectors say less about the workforce than about changing definitions, the growth of the servant class is confirmed.

B. Industry and the Urban Economy, 1757–1789

General censuses provide few reliable insights into development in the industrial sector, but other sources offer indications of its evolution in the late eighteenth century. It was possible to compare the number of masters in 32 guilds for 1757 and 1775, and to develop a separate but overlapping comparison of the number of operatives and degree of concentration in 21 industries between 1757 and 1789. While the two lists are an incomplete reflection of the city's industrial sector, they are suggestive of the way it was changing.

Some aspects of these trends are documented by comparison of the num-

---

in the later eighteenth century. Kany, in *Life and Manners*, pp. 252–261, develops a good picture of this out of the stereotypes in the comedies of Ramón de la Cruz.

Table 5.4. *Guild Members in 32 Guilds, Madrid, 1757
and 1775*

Guild	1757	1775	Change
Glove makers	6	19	217%
Iced refreshment sellers	14	29	107
Basket, wood utensil makers	8	16	100
Hatters	22	38	73
Brass casters	15	25	67
Esparto workers	22	31	41
Heavy-ironwork makers	24	32	33
Coppersmiths, pot makers	25	33	32
Jacket and doublet makers	11	14	27
Candle makers, wax dealers	22	27	23
New-shoe makers	200	242	21
Carpenters	159	189	19
Shoe repairers and cobblers	33	38	15
Silversmiths	212	287	12
Light-ironwork makers	13	14	8
Plaster and cement makers	19	20	5
Locksmiths	69	70	2
Cart makers	9	9	0
Candy makers, confectioners	98	91	−7
Coach makers	85	78	−8
Pastry makers	24	22	−8
Hair and wig dressers	194	177	−9
Winesellers	108	95	−12
Glaziers	57	44	−23
Mead makers	36	27	−25
Knife makers	38	28	−26
Clothing dealers	43	30	−30
Harness makers	25	15	−40
Tailors	420	250	−40
Woolen workers	27	15	−44
Tanners	16	8	−50
Wine-container makers	8	4	−50
Totals	2,062	2,017	−2%

Sources: Antonio Matilla Tascón, "El primer catastro de la villa de
Madrid;" *Archivo del Real Sociedad Económica de Madrid*, leg. 3-4, "Lista
de las ordenanzas y individuales gremiales" (1775).

ber of guild-masters in 1757 and 1775. These figures indicate that the number
of recognized masters stayed almost constant for over two decades, but say
nothing about the scale of enterprise within the guild system. What does
emerge is a surprising amount of change in individual guild-master lists, as
some doubled in size while others declined by half (see Table 5.4).

Of 15 "growth" industries in Table 5.4, 12 produced high-value finished
products, luxuries, and metal goods oriented to the elite market. Among the

more plebian crafts, only basket-making and esparto-working showed significant increases in the number of masters. The declining guilds involved products that could readily be imported or industries that were either moving out of the city or escaping the guild system. The most striking decline is in the Tailors' Guild, which lost 40% of its masters—a figure that conflicts with our image of tailoring as a major industry. Except for identifying certain growth areas, Table 5.4 tells us relatively little; but coupled with a second comparison it is much more enlightening.

Two trends emerge from these sources: increased economic concentration in many trades, and a weighting of industrial expansion toward wealthy, elite markets. Compiled without reference to guild organization, the figures in Table 5.5 show a trebling of the number of workers in 21 activities between 1757 and 1789. They also indicate an increase in average size of enterprise. The number of workers in these activities rose from 1,591 to 4,683, while the number of establishments fell 20%, from 624 to 499. As a consequence, the number of persons per shop rose from 2.55 to 9.38. Most of the change in scale was concentrated in a limited number of areas, while most growth was concentrated in 10 of the 21 activities. Of 8 industries with shops averaging over 10 persons in 1789, the 6 that were privately owned accounted for 70% of the 3,100 new workers. Three private industries where shops remained small—silversmithing, silk-working, and tanning—also showed substantial growth and accounted for most of the remaining new workers. The concentration of growth in the quality-goods industries—silks, linens, woolens, embroidery, lace, hats, jewelry, tapestries—that is suggested from Table 5.4 is even more evident in Table 5.5. The largest single industry continued to be precious-metal working, and only the printing industry had significant markets outside of Madrid itself.[12]

Thus we have clear evidence that the number of masters and shops was declining, while the size of the individual enterprise was growing. Moreover, comparison of Tables 5.4 and 5.5 indicates a rapid shift of some activities out of the guild system. Growth and concentration were not distributed evenly, and industries producing valuable products for final consumption—in particular, textiles and metal products—were most affected. The case of the woolen industry, where shops and masterships declined drastically while the number of workers grew by 1,151%, implies a tantalizing structural transformation of unknown nature. Food-handling trades and lesser traditional activities stagnated or lost ground. Given that the city was growing rapidly during this period, the unequal development of craft industry is suggestive. It coincides with both the growing importance of the servant class and the deterioration of

12. See n. 14, ch. 4.

Table 5.5. *Change in 21 Industrial Activities in Madrid, 1757 and 1789*

Activity	Workers in 1789	Average no. of Workers per Shop		Increase
		in 1757	in 1789	
Woolens	588	1.7	118.0	1,151%
Pottery	27	3.0	5.4	800
Linen-working	338	2.5	19.9	590
Tapestries	118	18.0	118.0	555
Tanning	211	2.1	3.7	521
Lace and ribbons	932	2.9	11.0	501
Playing cards	84	20.0	84.0	320
Wrapping paper	30	4.0	4.7	275
Printing	598	6.9	23.9	222
Hat-making	96	2.0	13.7	129
Embroideries	158	1.3	7.9	108
Silversmithing	977	2.3	6.4	104
Silk-working	316	2.6	6.9	98
Windscreens (lamps)	24	1.9	3.4	60
Harness-making	109	2.8	15.6	58
Blanket-making	28	2.7	2.5	47
Dyeing	59	2.9	5.4	44
Wax and candles	69	2.6	3.3	21
Glove-making	16	2.5	8.0	7
Plaster and cement	43	2.8	4.8	−20
Turning and lathing	14	2.8	4.7	−67

Sources: For 1757: Antonio Matilla Tascón, "El primer catastro"; for 1789: AVM, *Secretaría*, sig. 4-5-67.

general living standards dramatized by the declines in marriages and births and the increases in deaths and foundlings (see Chapter 3).

It also reflects the decline in real wages of low-income groups, the growing wealth of the urban elite, and growing inequality in the distribution of income. Thus the evolution of the industrial sector conforms to the pattern predicted by the general structure of occupations, income, and urban function. While the late eighteenth century saw imperial prosperity and urban growth, there is no doubt that real wages in Madrid fell—between 1750 and 1790, money wages declined 30% relative to the general price index. The income distribution documented in Chapter 4 shows that in 1757, 70% of incomes were low enough to seriously expose a childless couple to the trend, and 80% were low enough to leave a small family vulnerable. By the later 1780's, urban poverty was prompting official concern, and the Crown began to subsidize the production of cheap *pan de pobres* at the city grain depot.[13] One indication that real wages had been depressed to the subsistence level

13. AHN, *Consejos*, leg. 6780, *Pósito* regulations dated 1791.

was the general increase in money wages whenever bread prices rose for any length of time.[14]

Under such circumstances, urban prosperity and growth were unlikely to increase the complexity of the economic relationship between Madrid and its hinterland. Once again the contrast with Barcelona is instructive. There wage earners experienced only a 10% decline of real income from 1750 to 1800, most of which coincided with the disruption of trade in the 1790's. Prior to that, real wages may well have been rising.[15] As Barcelona doubled and trebled in size, relations with its hinterland were conditioned not only by urban demand for food and exports but also by a demand for popular manufactures and luxuries that at the least kept pace with the growth of population.

In Madrid, the aggregate wealth of the city clearly increased during the last half of the century, but the collective buying power of the lower four-fifths of the economically active population grew much more slowly as real wages fell. This implies different rates of growth in demand for various commodities, and even the possibility of declining demand in some cases. In the early seventeenth century, under similar conditions, Madrid's consumption pattern showed an increasing preference for wheat relative to wine or meat, and for wine or meat as opposed to olive oil.[16]

Poor families with declining purchasing power discriminate not only among foodstuffs, but between food and fuel on the one hand and manufactures and luxuries on the other. Given the limitations of available transport, the poor of the capital constituted the only concentrated source of potential demand for the crude products of the rural industry of the interior. Thus, increasing inequality in the distribution of income, and the evolution of industry to meet elite demand in the city, worked not only against the diversification of regional agriculture but also against the development of regional industry. Elsewhere in seventeenth- and eighteenth-century Europe, rural crafts developed to compensate for economic pressures in agriculture. This response was not absent in Castile; but lacking an urban hierarchy capable of coordinating regional exchanges of the sort that marked the sixteenth century, it apparently made little headway.[17] The market situation, dominated by Madrid, mitigated against diversification of the rural economy.

14. The wage pattern is very similar to that of sixteenth-century Belgium, where real income fell to basic subsistence levels, after which money wages followed the rising price of subsistence commodities closely; see Charles Verlinden, J. Craeybeck, and E. Scholliers, "Price and Wage Movements in Belgium in the Sixteenth Century" (1972).

15. Earl Hamilton, *War and Prices* pp. 250–257, 268–271; Pierre Vilar, *Catalunya dins l'Espanya moderna* (1966), vol. 3, pp. 68, 369–438.

16. David R. Ringrose, "The Impact of a New Capital City," pp. 772–779.

17. José Gentil da Silva, *En Espagne*, pp. 28–31. The drift into handicraft industry in rural England in the eighteenth century is a well-known phenomenon.

C. Industry and the Urban Economy, 1789–1857

While Madrid obviously did not lose its function as political and residential center, the monarchy passed through a massive crisis in the early nineteenth century, necessitating painful readjustment to a more limited sphere of influence. These readjustments were heralded and accompanied by demographic changes in the city that suggest a greater degree of urban poverty, and by growth in the importance of personal service as an occupation. The impact of these realities on urban industry is apparent in a comparison of Madrid's imports in 1789 with those of 1847. Table 5.6 gives an indirect reflection of the evolution of urban industry, but it points to a number of important changes.

Table 5.6 indicates that metal-working was the only urban industry which expanded between 1789 and 1847. Most of the metal was iron, and total metal imports amounted to less than 1,900 tons. While changing technology may have increased demand for finished metal goods, most of the material was probably destined for construction. The same sources indicate that consumption of hides and leather by the urban leather-working trades fell more than 90%, indicating that the entire industry either moved out of the city or gave way to competition from more distant suppliers.

The most significant change, however, was in textiles, where the volume of raw material for urban manufacture fell by half. Simultaneously, the consumption of imported textiles altered dramatically. Although population had risen at least 20% while local production declined, the volume of textiles imported fell 6%. Moreover, consumption of woolens dropped more than 50% and that of linen and silk fell by nearly 80%. Cottons, meanwhile, jumped from 5.7% to 71.7% of the market. Thus Madrid shifted away from textiles produced locally and from the textiles typically produced by Spain's rural industry, and favored cloth from Barcelona or foreign sources.

Less dramatic changes in demand for luxury goods reinforce the sense of growing income disparity. In 1789, 62% of the fish consumed was salt cod. By 1847, cod accounted for only 46%, and the favored varieties were the more expensive *besugo, merluza*, and preserved fish.[18]

Thus, while in the late eighteenth century urban manufacturing may have grown along with concentration of ownership and weakening of guilds, the nineteenth century saw the end of the guilds and, despite the stable relative size of the industrial workforce, the collapse of important local industries. The city was becoming increasingly dependent on distant sources of finished goods, with a corresponding decline in the importance of urban manufacturing and finishing and in demand for the medium-quality commodities of its

18. AVM, *Secretaria,* sig. 4–5–67; Pascual Madoz, *Diccionario geográfico de España* (1847), vol. 10, pp. 1020–1035.

Table 5.6. *Comparison of Imports of Selected Commodities into Madrid, 1789 and 1847*(a)

Category/Commodity	1789	1847	Change
Metals	75,578 ar	151,262 ar	+100.1%
Hides and pigskin	772,684 lbs	50,207 lbs	−93.5
Skins and furs	395,437 pcs	87,346 pcs	−77.9
Cured leather	423,933 lbs	50,562 pcs	
Textile fibers, all	1,014,021 lbs	550,030 lbs	−45.8
Textiles, all	6,021,206 va	5,643,716 va	−6.3
Woolens	996,323 va	469,215 va	−52.9
Cottons	341,768 va	4,044,828 va	+1,083.5
Silks	1,375,114 va	283,285 va	−79.4
Linens	3,308,000 va	731,572 va	−77.9
Unidentified types		114,816 va	

Sources: For 1789: AVM, *Secretaría*, sig. 4-5-67; for 1847: Madoz, *Diccionario geográfico*, vol. 10, pp. 1037-1059.
   a. Units: ar = *arrobas*; va = *varas*; lbs = *libras*; pcs = pieces.

hinterland. This conclusion, combined with the rough data on the working classes during 1757–1857, allows us to make some further inferences about the increasing inequality in the distribution of income. Between 1757 and 1857, laborers, artisans, and domestics increased from 70.7% to 77.3% of the active population (see Table 5.3). Given the quality of our sources, this by itself is slender evidence for a trend—but two points are worth making: The slight trend that *is* apparent runs directly counter to the downward drift in the relative size of the economically active population. This means that while the active share of the population decreased, those who did find work were increasingly relegated to low-income occupations. Since the industrial base of the city was deteriorating as the servant element grew steadily, the logic, if not all the data, support an impression of growing impoverishment.

More and more of the manufactures used in Madrid came from elsewhere. The city itself, never industrial beyond the needs of its own narrow market, was becoming ever more service-oriented and acquiring more nonworking dependents. With the collapse of empire and exposure to European industrialization, Madrid's economy and income structure became more directly dependent on its role as capital, and Madrid's market continued to offer little stimulus to its Castilian hinterland.

D. The Professional and Commercial Sector, 1757–1857

Further support for these hypotheses is found in the available data on the size of the professional and commercial groups in Madrid. It is commonly assumed that with the 50% growth of Madrid between 1800 and 1857, the business and professional groups expanded as well. An often-cited summary of the census of 1857 has encouraged this assumption, since it not only indicates a surprising 4,308 persons in the "professions," but lists 3,723 *comerciantes,* implying a healthy and disproportionate expansion of the business middle class compared with 898 *comerciantes* in 1787 and 1,442 in 1804.[19] The apparent growth of the professions is even more impressive. As we have seen, however, the census of 1857 marked important changes in the way occupations were classified, and this somewhat specious embourgeoisement of Madrid is belied by comparison of eighteenth-century sources with tax rolls from the 1840's.[20]

Using this approach, almost every middle-class category saw a notable increase in numbers from the mid to late eighteenth century, followed by stagnation or decline lasting until as late as 1848 (see Tables 5.7 and 5.8). The nineteenth-century decline in the numbers of lawyers and surgeons, and the modest increase in medical doctors relative to population growth, suggest that fewer people could afford professional services and that business and earnings were concentrated in fewer hands. This approach obviously misses the increase in the number of people recognized by society as professionals during the nineteenth century. Most of that growth, however, was the result of redefinition of guild occupations as professions. Master builders became architects or contractors, while painters, musicians, and sculptors ceased to be artisans and became professional artists in the modern sense. When this is allowed for, the stagnation of the traditional professions in the nineteenth century identifies an area that was declining in size within the economically active population.

Similarly, while the nineteenth century is characterized as a bourgeois era in Spain as elsewhere, the number of persons identified as merchants, businessmen, and financiers belies the parallel assumption that the business class grew. If one uses eighteenth-century definitions to select people from the tax rolls of 1841 and 1848, the results are interesting (see Table 5.8). In the century of the "bourgeois revolution," Madrid apparently experienced an absolute as well as relative stagnation of its business middle class. The wholesale merchant community, which remained static through the late eighteenth century, appears even smaller in 1841. The specifically financial sector of the commercial class also showed remarkable changes in numbers between 1757 and 1857. Eighteenth-century criteria yielded 274 finance-related persons in 1757, 319 in 1841, and 144 in 1848. This does not speak to changes in mode of thought, organization, behavior—but if change was involved, it was contained within the existing economic structures.

19. AVM, *Secretaría,* sig. 6–61–47.
20. AVM, *Contaduría,* sig. 3–410–1; Madoz, *Diccionario geográfico,* vol. 10, pp. 973–979.

Table 5.7. *Selected Professional Groups in Madrid, 1757-1848*

Year	Lawyers	Scribes	Medical Doctors	Surgeon- Barbers	Druggists	Veterin- arians
1757	182	269	85	381	71	84
1787	595	259				
1799	671	268	123	614	82	129
1804	568	244				
1841	261	116	125	448	77	77
1848	379		154	304	84	

Sources: All figures are taken from the *Catastro* and census sources cited elsewhere, except for 1841 and 1848. For 1757: Matilla Tascón, "Primer Catastro"; for 1787: RAH, *Censo de Floridablanca*, leg. 9-6235; for 1799: Canga Argüelles, *Diccionario de hacienda* (1834), vol. 2, pp. 67-69; for 1804: AVM, *Secretaría*, sig. 4-4-37; for 1841: AVM, *Contaduría*, sig. 3-410-1; for 1848: Madoz, *Diccionario geográfico*, vol. 10, pp. 973-979.

Table 5.8. *Mercantile Groups in Madrid, 1757-1857*

Year	Wholesale Merchants	Retail Merchants	Business and Finance	Official Total, Mercantile
1757	335	278	274	887
1787				898
1799	351	1,091		1,442
1804	365	999		1,364
1841	194	669	319	1,182
1848			244	—
1857				3,723

Sources: See Table 5; for 1857, AVM, *Secretaría*, sig. 6-61-49.

One is prompted to recall Hexter's comment that a class is like a bus through time—people get on and off, but the bus doesn't change much.[21] The collapse of imperial trade and the depreciation of the government paper to which everyone was committed during the Napoleonic crisis must have hurt the Madrid business world. On the other hand, capital and personnel from Cádiz, Barcelona, and America probably migrated to Madrid as a replacement. Almost nothing is known about this process, but stagnation makes more sense than the bland assumption that the "middle class" of Madrid grew because the city grew, when in fact apparent structural change really reflected new census definitions.

The retail business sector is harder to measure, because its lower boundary is blurred. The eighteenth-century definition was narrow, excluding artisan

21. Jack H. Hexter, *Reappraisals in History* (1961).

shops and distributors of food and fuel. By 1804, and more clearly in 1857, retail outlets for food, fuel, and feed were being defined as mercantile enterprises, along with many artisan shops. Thus the reported number of retailers could jump from 278 in 1757 to 1,091 in 1799, and the number of mercantile people reach 3,723 in 1857. The tax roll for 1841 offers a better comparison, since it is possible to count small food and fuel vendors separately. Using the eighteenth-century's narrow definition results in a retailing class in 1841 no larger relative to the population than in 1757.[22] Conversely, if every wine, vinegar, oil, charcoal, egg, and sausage seller is considered a merchant, there were around 3,000 "merchants" in 1841—a total that is in line with the 3,723 reported for 1857. Similar treatment of the *Catastro* of 1757 in fact produced 2,000 such "merchants"—roughly the same proportion of the population as in 1857. What this *petite bourgeoisie* may have thought of itself individually or collectively in one period or another still represents a problem, but again the change was qualitative, not structural.

In general, the professional and mercantile elites increased with imperial prosperity in the late eighteenth century but declined in numerical importance in the first half of the nineteenth, as urban expansion outpaced the resources brought to Madrid through the functions it performed. This conveys the impression of redistribution of wealth in a static society, not a process of basic economic change.[23]

III. The Government and the Urban Economy

Aside from domestic service, the one part of the active population that grew consistently was the bureaucracy. The census of 1787 shows 5,575 people paid by the Crown, including 499 with military status *(con fuero militar)* and about 1,800 workers in royal factories and monopolies. In 1857, despite the sale of government factories, the figure reached 7,332, to which were added over 3,000 *cesantes*, furloughed or semi-employed personnel on partial pay (see Table 5.9). Thus the bureaucracy grew from 7.1% of the economically active population in 1757 to 12.5% in 1857, and the number of persons paid by the state trebled.

The long-term growth of the government sector is also suggested by various estimates of the expenses of government and the Court in Madrid. From 1561, when Philip II established Madrid as his capital, the Court disbursed a growing stream of money into the urban economy. Under Philip II the figure

22. The liberal government of Madrid in 1821 had information that the official resident population of the city had declined from 156,339 in 1797 to only 135,629 in 1821, and assumed a corresponding reduction in the business and artisan community. See Manuel Cristobal y Mañas, *La hacienda municipal de la villa de Madrid* (1901), p. 39.

23. Nicolás Sánchez-Albornoz, *Jalones en la modernización de España* (1975), pp. 62–79.

Table 5.9. *State-Supported Personnel in the Economically Active Population of Madrid, 1757-1857*

Year	No. of Persons Supported by State	Percentage of Economically Active Population
1757	3,000 (est.)	7.1%
1787	5,576	10.4
1799	6,482	11.2
1857	10,423	12.5

Sources: See Tables 5.7 and 5.8.

was a modest 4,500,000 *reales* per year, but under Philip III it reached 14,300,000 annually. In the first years of Philip IV, wartime necessity and reform reduced the figure to 12 million *reales*—a reversal that coincides with the beginning of Madrid's seventeenth-century decline. But after the failure of the Count-Duke of Olivares' effort to reform government finances in the 1630's, and despite the revolt in Catalonia, the loss of Portugal, and the dilapidated condition of the empire, the expenditures of the Court rose steadily, and by 1691 they had reached 36 million reales.[24] Even adjusted for inflation, such numbers identify a principal function of the capital and explain how the city survived despite the economic crises of seventeenth-century Castile. Inevitably, the Court and its capital received priority over foreign policy, army, and navy in the allocation of resources.

Analogous figures for the eighteenth century indicate the same drift of government resources toward the capital. Before 1750, state expenditures were stable, coinciding with the relatively slow growth of the capital. Urban growth and the expenditures of the Court subsequently increased. In 1757 the Crown dispersed 45 million *reales* in wages, salaries, and pensions within Madrid;[25] by 1800 the figure had reached an estimated 100 million *reales*,[26] and neither total includes the cost of the 7,000- to 10,000-man garrison.

There are no comparable figures for nineteenth-century Madrid, but the evolution of the national budget suggests the continuation of priorities that favored the capital. In the 1780's royal revenues were about 700 million *reales* per year, half of which was remittances from America, customs duties, and taxes collected in Andalucía, where the American trade was based.[27]

24. Antonio Domínguez Ortiz, *Crisis y decadencia de la España de los Austrias* (1969), pp. 73–96.

25. See the analysis in Chapter 4 of the *Catastro;* and José Canga Argüelles, *Diccionario de Hacienda* (1834), vol. 2, p. 70, for figures based on 1770 revisions of the 1757 figures.

26. Canga Argüelles, *Diccionario,* vol. 2, p. 184.

27. On the significance of America for the royal treasury at the close of the century, see Jacques Barbier, "Peninsular Finance and Colonial Trade: The Dilemma of Charles IV's Spain" (paper given at American Historical Association, 1978).

That revenue base had been destroyed by the 1820's, and total revenues declined to 450 million *reales*. With great difficulty, the peninsular economy was forced to provide 550 million *reales* in revenue by 1830. In adjusting to this crisis, the budget allocated a growing share of surviving revenue to support of government operations in Madrid. The continued subsidy for the Court and growing administrative costs, particularly in the treasury, were counterpoints to the massive decline of naval outlays and heavy reliance on deficit financing. All suggest the continued significance of the government in Madrid's economy and Madrid's growing importance for the state.

With relative political and fiscal stability after 1839, the identification of the urban economy with the state became even more apparent, and there is a close correlation between the economic boom of the capital and the growth of the national budget to 1,200 million *reales* by 1845.[28] Admittedly, much of the increase involved commitments outside of Madrid, but support for the central bureaucracy and the Court also increased as the treasury was strengthened by the tax reforms of 1845. The fortunes of individual officials may have declined in the nineteenth century, as salaries and pensions were neglected, and resources may not have kept pace with the size of the bureaucracy—but over the long run, both continued to grow. The renewed expansion of the capital after 1840 is clearly linked with the reconstruction of Spanish politics after the warfare of 1808–1839.

Many kinds of evidence from three centuries document the basic relationship between the Spanish state and Madrid's importance and economic structure. The relationship appears in the evolution of government outlays and in the growing importance of government employment for the city's economically active population. It provided a stable core for the socio-demographic structure outlined in Chapter 3. When the empire was prosperous, the government supported the central bureaucracy (and its capital), imperial reform, and active foreign policy. When crisis came, the reflex was to protect the center of the system. In the seventeenth and again in the early nineteenth centuries, the army and navy were neglected. In the first case the market economy of Castile was sacrificed,[29] while in the second the patrimony of the Church was seized.[30] Deficit financing perennially diverted savings and capital throughout the economy. This power of the state to allocate resources encouraged a concentration of landed and educated elements seeking income and prestige, reinforcing the constant growth of the bureaucracy that staffed

28. Josep Fontana Lázaro, *La quiebra de la monarquía absoluta,* pp. 57–63, and *Hacienda y Estado, 1823–1833* (1973), p. 144; Fabian Estapé y Rodriguez, *La reforma tributaria de 1845* (1971), pp. 230, 243.

29. See Chapters 11 and 12 below.

30. Brenner, "The Origins of Capitalist Development," p. 45.

the state. Thus Madrid and its resident elites were insulated from difficulties elsewhere in the economy.

IV. Conclusion

Several types of evidence thus support the trends in Madrid's development which were suggested by the logic inherent in the economic structure outlined in Chapter 4. After becoming the capital of Spain, Madrid grew at an accelerating rate, and by the early seventeenth century its economy was being transformed by the requirements of the political and residential functions imposed on it. The salient feature was an extremely unequal distribution of income, which produced a very narrow market and drew urban industry toward specialized products hard to sell outside the city. The landed and bureaucratic elements attracted an immense and poorly paid service class and encouraged an age-sex structure in which thousands of immigrant adults and few children existed alongside a smaller core of stable citizens. Renewed expansion in the eighteenth century brought growth of the bureaucracy, the servant class, and industries oriented to the elite market. Meanwhile, the poor experienced a prolonged decline of real wages, and there are demographic signs of growing misery after 1780. There was more wealth, but it was distributed with increasing inequality in an urban economy that exported its demands for all but basic agricultural supplies to distant producers. In the nineteenth century, population growth combined with a decline in urban resources. There are signs of greater urban distress and indications that the elites were static or shrinking in numbers. Consumption turned away even more from domestically produced goods, and the urban economy became less varied and less capable of providing economic stimulus to Castile.[31]

Taxes and rents flowed from countryside and empire into the hands of the wealthy of the city, thence to administrators and lawyers, to merchants for imported products, to artisans, and to domestics.[32] They then flowed out of

31. No better illustration of this can be cited than the results of bank development in the 1850's and 1860's. Considerable capital was mobilized, but most of it was invested in land or railroads. The railroads locked up capital because they were overbuilt and unprofitable, at the same time facilitating the dependence of the Madrid market on imports; the economics of railroading simply were not understood by the mercantile community of Madrid. See Sánchez-Albornoz, *Jalones*, pp. 62–79; and Ringrose, "España en el siglo XIX." The process represents an interesting extension of Robert Brenner's comments in "Origins," pp. 45–47, on the role of urban centers in "serf societies" in which urban development is oriented to the land-owners only, and thus creates few urban-rural interactions.

32. For a clear statement of the preferences of the Madrid market and its strong orientation to imported, especially French customs and luxuries, see J. F. Bourgoing, *The Modern State of Spain* (1808), vol. 2, pp. 308–309. See also the vignette of Ramón Mesonero Romanos, "El extranjero en su patria" (1970; written in 1833), pp. 61–68.

the city in payment for the food, manufactures, and raw materials used in the city. Internal income distribution and market structure focused part of the demand on the city's hinterland, but this emphasized the few basic agricultural commodities which the poor could afford. An ever larger share of income, however, was spent on the luxury products of the craft guilds and on imports from the periphery or overseas.

This is extremely important, because by mid-seventeenth century Madrid was the dominant economic and urban center of Spain. Its fields of influence, reflecting its predominant functions, placed Madrid at the head of an urban hierarchy that linked it with Sevilla, Cádiz, Mexico City, and Lima. Simultaneously, the capital reached beyond Castile to the coasts and to Europe for the luxuries and manufactures consumed by the urban elites. Madrid also needed supplies and simple manufactures for the bulk of its population, and this required a huge tributary zone that brought the city's needs into conflict with any other economic activity competing for the sparse agrarian resources of Old and New Castile. Inevitably, Madrid was a city in which commercial life consisted of collection and final distribution rather than industry or entrepôt services.

In the nineteenth century, when the loss of empire and its trade crippled government finance and the great port cities, the rentier elite of Madrid and its commercial adjunct became relatively more important within the political and economic framework of the capital and country. A greater share of government revenue had to come from peninsular sources, and the agricultural sector became relatively more important as a source of wealth. With the mid-century land sales, agriculture did become more responsive to market pressures. But the pattern of urban dependence and exploitation was unchanged, and therefore little happened to alter the basic interactions between capital and country. This weak interaction was not because Madrid lacked commercial significance—at the middle of the eighteenth century the commercial and industrial income attributed to the capital matched that of the entire province of Sevilla, including the cities of Sevilla and Cádiz.[33] The reasons lie in the structure which urban function imposed on the city's economy, coupled with the accidents of geography.

In effect, Madrid presented Spain with an urban center very different from the "motor for economic growth" which Wrigley suggests for seventeenth- and eighteenth-century London. Madrid could provide little stimulus for interior Spain, and may have functioned as a motor for regional economic stagnation. It concentrated the wealth, disposable income, and commercial activity of the country on a narrow market with a few thousand affluent families—only a few hundred of them really wealthy—and on a mass of

33. Vilar, "Estructures," p. 28.

urban poor with extremely low incomes and low productivity. This produced a consuming elite whose basic needs cost only a small part of their income, even during subsistence crises, and whose demand for quality imports was surprisingly constant despite the state of the urban economy. Moreover, the range of imported commodities they came to expect expanded continually. At the same time, the huge population on the edge of subsistence was constantly forced to choose between food and the amenities of life. Whenever food became dear or real wages fell, they were forced to limit their purchases to food. Consequently, urban demand for domestic manufactures and agricultural specialties was extremely variable.

6. The City as Market:
The Evolution of Consumption

Madrid's political and residential functions produced well-defined demographic, occupational, and income structures in the early seventeenth century. Once established, these structures governed the city's internal economy and the dynamic relationship between Madrid and the rest of Spain.

A city consumes products from its tributary hinterland and from more distant sources in exchange for goods and services. Madrid increasingly consumed a distinctive mix of commodities and provided few commercial or manufacturing services in return. Unequal income distribution heightened the effect of urban elasticities of demand and limited the incentives the city offered to its hinterland, despite the growth of population. Such growth aggravated recurrent subsistence crises and shortages and raised supply costs and food prices, forcing the poor to forgo other regional products for basic foodstuffs. For different reasons, the small elite maintained a similarly inelastic demand for imports. Demand for middling-quality farm products and manufactures from the hinterland was thus vulnerable to economic change and was correspondingly unstable. The urban market also changed as the fortunes of the monarchy altered the city's economic base. Finally, the geographic scope of the city-oriented market depended on relative transport costs and on the willingness of the authorities to coerce commodity movements.

Generally speaking, the commodities that are best documented are the basic staples drawn from the agricultural hinterland of Old and New Castile, some of which can be traced from the late sixteenth century. Not until the eighteenth century do we have data on the luxury goods and colonial products consumed by the city's elite market.

I. Consumption of Basic Staples, Sixteenth Through Nineteenth Centuries

A. Wheat

Wheat was not only the largest item in the budget of three-fourths of Madrid's population, but represented 30% of the value of imports from the city's hinterland and over 10% of all urban imports. Consequently, its price and availability played a major role in shaping demand for other commodities.[1] Unfortunately, there are few concrete figures for annual consumption before the nineteenth century. Those that we do have are given in Table 6.1, with indications of the relative quality of the harvests.[2] The growth of demand before 1630 is clear, although the decline of the mid-seventeenth century is less well documented. The eighteenth-century expansion is well defined, as is the contraction of Madrid in the early nineteenth century.

We get a fuller picture of the actual consumption levels from Figure 6.1, which extrapolates from reported crisis consumption to suggest the scope of the market under normal supply conditions. Demand for wheat and population were closely connected and reinforced each other. Consequently, the population estimates from Chapter 2 have been superimposed on Figure 6.1. The range of variation of total consumption in response to harvest quality is based on eighteenth- and nineteenth-century sources. In 1767 officials reported that a 20% decline below normal supply was enough to cause starvation, while demand in a bountiful year might exceed normal levels by 30%.[3] Similarly, annual totals in the 1820's and 1840's show bad years that were 23% and 30% below the prevailing average.[4] Thus crisis-level consumption was about 75% of normal, and the band reflecting normal to minimal wheat consumption on Figure 6.1 is based on that assumption.

The results mesh with the figures from sixteenth-century Valladolid, where 40,000 people consumed 146,000 *fanegas* of wheat in a normal year.[5] That indicates that the Madrid of 1599, with 65,000 people, normally used 237,250 *fanegas* a year. A 25% reduction of supply would have cut that to

1. The classic example of this analysis is in Emmanuel Le Roy Ladurie, *The Peasants of Languedoc*, pp. 98–110.

2. There was no tax on wheat or bread and thus there are no fiscal records that reflect consumption. Moreover, the topic was rarely discussed in its totality before 1760, and the problem was handled in a unified way only in time of crisis. Early totals are thus minima. Only later eighteenth-century sources estimate normal needs. Pascual Madoz published a number of nineteenth-century totals, giving us the range of consumption for the 1820's and 1840's, in his *Diccionario geográfico* (16 vols.; Madrid, 1847).

3. AVM, *Secretaría*, sig. 2–122–1.

4. The years of shortage and high prices coincide with consumption lows. Nicolás Sánchez-Albornoz, *Las crisis de subsistencias en España en el siglo XIX* (1963), p. 8.

5. Bartolomé Bennassar, *Valladolid au siècle d'or* (1967), pp. 71–76.

Table 6.1. *Wheat Consumption in Madrid*

Year	Wheat(a)	Harvest Quality
1561	(36,500)	?
1599	180,000	Poor
1608	(292,000)	Poor
1614	(365,000)	Poor
1628	(438,000)	Poor
1630-31	517,051	Poor
1667	(414,185)	Normal-Poor
1767	(438,000)	Poor
1767	(547,000)	Normal
1767	(730,000)	Very good
1779	648,579	?
1780	730,000	?
1784	730,000	Normal
1784	821,000	Very good
1789	782,874	Fair
1792	741,315	Poor
1797	(937,050)	Good
1812	(400,000)	Poor-Famine
1815	619,222	?
1818	389,915	?
1820	385,693	?
1824	511,999	Poor ?
1825	758,727	Good ?
1826	760,164	Good ?
1827	630,698	Fair ?
1828	661,668	Fair ?
1829	759,494	Good?
1839	744,272	Good-Normal ?
1842	678,862	Fair ?
1844	783,594	Good ?
1845	791,275	Good ?
1846	755,464	Normal ?
1847	491,453	Poor

Sources: See Appendix D, section I.A.
   a. Figures in parentheses are extrapolations from daily totals to annual ones.

178,000 *fanegas*, remarkably close to the 180,000 *fanegas* that officials considered an absolute minimum.[6] The estimated minimum for 1630 is probably low, thanks to a conservative interpretation of the supply accounts.[7] The source for 1667 estimates baking capacity in the context of crop failure and allows extrapolation of a consumption level that fits well with population estimates for 1657 and 1684.[8] The supply crisis of 1812 was the worst in the

6. AVM, *Secretaria*, sig. 2–96–1.
7. AVM, *Secretaria*, sigs. 2–99–4, 2–102–8, 2–140–6.
8. AVM, *Secretaria*, sig. 2–190–5.

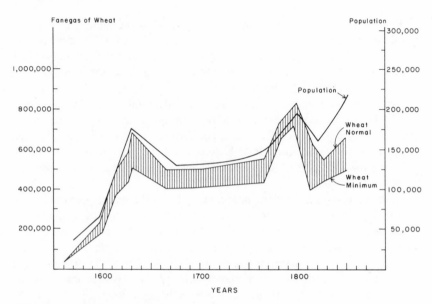

Figure 6.1 *Population and Wheat Consumption in Madrid*

history of the city,[9] while in the 1820's consumption appears as low as in the 1770's.

With certain exceptions, fluctuations in wheat consumption coincide with long-term trends in wheat prices, an important link between urban and regional economies. In the late sixteenth century, nine-year wheat prices rose steadily to a peak in 1595–1600, eased off, then hit a higher peak in 1606–10. Thereafter, despite rapid growth in Madrid's wheat consumption, the trends diverged for the next fifteen years and wheat prices drifted downward until the bad weather of 1626–31 produced the highest averages in the first half of the century. The price then drifted downward until 1642 as urban growth slackened, followed by a rise due to political and fiscal conditions in the 1640's. The latter period experienced the highest single-year prices before 1650, but the sharpest short-run fluctuations came in 1598, 1607–08, and 1626–31.[10] The early seventeenth century saw a break in the long sixteenth-century trend toward a tighter grain market in New Castile that requires examination. As we will see in Chapter 10, that break was connected with the collapse of Toledo as a competing market.

9. Manuel Espadas Burgos, "El hambre de 1812."

10. This follows the trends in Castilian grain prices shown in Ural A. Pérez, "El precio de los granos en la península ibérica, 1585–1650" (1965), p. 128. It corresponds with prosperity and a building boom between 1610 and 1625; see Kennedy, "The New Plaza Mayor," pp. 49–53.

Population and wheat consumption stagnated in the 1630's, and the 75 years after 1650 saw a downward trend in the price of wheat despite economic and political instability. Falling to the level of 1601–20 after 1650, prices fluctuated violently around that trend during the crises of 1664, 1668, 1677–78, and 1683–84, and the recurrent monetary manipulations. In the background, however, the basic level of urban demand declined with population.[11] The deflation of 1680 reduced nominal prices sharply and, except for brief shortages in the 1690's, prices, population, and consumption changed little for a quarter-century. Poor harvests and the Succession War forced prices up for a few years, but thereafter wheat prices reached remarkably low levels in the 1720's.

In the second quarter of the new century Madrid began to expand slowly, and by 1740 an upward trend in wheat prices had developed that continued throughout the eighteenth century.[12] With accelerating population growth and wheat consumption, wheat prices exhibited a series of plateaus separated by increases in the basic price level in 1730–36, 1762–66, 1781–83, and 1799–1803. As in the early seventeenth century, the averages obscure year-to-year fluctuations, and there were extremely high prices in 1753, 1766, 1780, 1794–95, and 1803–04.[13] The tendency for fluctuations to become more extreme is apparent, suggesting that once more consumption was reaching the limits of available supplies.[14]

B. Wine

Because it was regularly taxed, evidence for trends and volume in wine consumption is much fuller than for wheat. Figures for the volume of wine entering the city were found for the 1630's, 1698–99, 1730–40, 1757, 1770–80, and 1789, and for 17 years between 1824 and 1847. Other sixteenth- and seventeenth-century figures are based on the *sisa del vino,* imposed in 1582 at

11. This manipulation involved repeated doubling and halving of the face value of copper coinage, plus massive emissions of copper in the 1670's. It reflected juggling of debt servicing and extraction of silver from the economy for foreign exchange. The process ended with the deflationary reform of 1680, which stopped the use of monetary instability as an instrument of policy. Earl Hamilton, *War and Prices,* pp. 13–23.

12. This echoes favorable conditions elsewhere in early eighteenth-century Europe. See A. H. John, "Aspects of English Economic Growth in the First Half of the Eighteenth Century" (1961 and 1962); and Le Roy Ladurie, *Peasants,* p. 310.

13. Wheat prices follow Hamilton's index of agricultural prices—*War and Prices,* pp. 172–173—fairly well, except that in the 1780's our nine-year average anticipates the general increase after 1785.

14. This is also suggested by Pedro Romero de Solis, in *La población española,* p. 186, who projects growing instability through the first restoration. It is also suggested in the unstable grain prices quoted by Sánchez-Albornoz, *Las crises,* p. 8.

the rate of 16 *maravedises* per *arroba*.[15] Comparable estimates for the eighteenth century are derived from the revenues of the *primer cuartillo en arroba de vino*.[16]

Figure 6.2 shows rapid growth in wine consumption before 1630, a gradual decline in the next decade, and an abrupt drop by midcentury. Consumption leveled off between 1655 and the crises of 1677–85, then dropped even further. After 1730 it fluctuated around a gradual upward trend until 1790, when consumption stagnated. After the French occupation (1808–13) it rose for a decade, then declined in 1825–40, before it began a more sustained expansion.

While wine consumption was affected by population, the correlation was weak. It rose almost as quickly as population until 1630, but then declined more sharply than population.[17] After 1730 consumption responded more weakly to population change than it had a century before. In the 1730's Madrid consumed 475,000 *arrobas* per year, and about 10% less in the 1750's. From that point consumption climbed to 550,000 *arrobas* in 1789, then dropped back to 500,000 by 1807—only 10% greater than in the 1730's, even though the population was 40% larger. After a high in 1814–20, the figures ran around 550,000 *arrobas* in the 1820's, fell dramatically during the

15. Where it was possible to compare estimates with recorded consumption, the margin of error was small enough to allow the assumption that the composite series reflects trends accurately (see Appendix D).

16. Multiplying revenue figures by the number of *cuartillos* per *real* produced estimates of the volume of wine. Where they could be checked with recorded consumption, the discrepancy was stable. There are risks in relying on tax revenues for estimates of consumption: evasion was common, privately produced wine owned by residents was tax-exempt, and tax farming implies that city revenue was less than actual receipts. On evasion, AHN, *Consejos,* leg. 7168, exp. 87 (1650's), and leg. 7221 (1770's); on evasions and exemptions in the eighteenth and nineteenth centuries, Madoz, *Diccionario,* vol. 10, pp. 988–989, 1016. Predictably, evasion means that official figures are low; but evasion was probably within customary limits in the short run. Supervision was close in the early seventeenth century, with annual contracts. By 1650, contracts ran four years, leaving room for unregistered change in volume. The eighteenth century saw a return to annual contracts, consolidation of taxes, and regulation of exemptions. The reign of Ferdinand VII saw the breakdown of administration, and Madoz assumed substantial evasion in the 1840's. Nevertheless, the series documents consumption with greater reliability than comparable French sources; see Monique Gebhart and Claude Mercadier, *L'octroi de Toulouse a la veille de la Révolution* (1967).

17. In part the decline is exaggerated, since rising taxes encouraged evasion and, after 1650, the *sisa del vino* was rented on four-year contracts, weakening the correlation between revenue and volume of wine entering the city. We cannot follow the wine market through the middle seventeenth century, because the wild price fluctuations due to monetary manipulation, epidemics, and weather are further complicated by the fact that Hamilton changed his sources after 1650. While the shift to Madrid sources makes the later series more relevant to this study, the post- and pre-1650 series cannot be joined.

Carlist War, then rose steadily during the next decade.[18] The long-term trend suggests that two factors were affecting total consumption: the level of population and a decline in per-capita use of wine.

C. Olive Oil

Madrid's consumption of olive oil also reflects population change, but suggests an increase in individual usage over 250 years. The sixteenth and seventeenth century figures in Figure 6.3 are based on the *sisa del aceite* established in 1582 at the rate of 100 *marevedises* per *arroba*. Later eighteenth-century estimates are calculated from oil-tax revenues and the ratio between revenue and known consumption.

Most olive oil came from Andalucía, and was produced under regional conditions different from those of Castile. Thus short-term changes in consumption do not always coincide with those of wine, as when plague struck Andalucía in 1590, 1626–27, 1635, and 1647–50, curtailing supply and forcing up oil prices in New Castile.[19] Similarly, there was an increase in oil consumption around 1640, even though the demand for wine fell rapidly. Apparently the olive groves planted when demand was strong began to produce just as war restricted exports.[20] The decline of 1602–06, however, reflects the Court's absence from Madrid.[21] Underlying these variations is an upward trend in consumption from 1590 to 1620 that was reversed between 1625 and 1650, despite the brief upsurge in the early 1640's.

Eighteenth-century figures show a similar cycle of expansion and contraction, but much higher total consumption. By the 1750's, volume was double the seventeenth-century maximum and rose faster than population until 1792–98. With the subsistence crisis of 1799, oil consumption began to decline as population fell, and by 1807 had dropped to the level of the 1760's. It remained low until the 1830's despite population recovery, but after 1840 expansion was dramatic and in 1848 it was 50% above any previous maximum.

D. Meat

Meat includes several commodities, the most important being beef, mutton, and pork, but they cannot be sorted out before the eighteenth century. Pork is documented only after 1740, and beef and mutton were taxed to-

18. This is the point at which Madoz is explicit about fraud and, without evidence, estimates an annual total of 800,000 *arrobas*. This is well above eighteenth-century levels, but only 60% of the official peak of the seventeenth century.

19. Earl Hamilton, *American Treasure*, pp. 346–347, 370–375.

20. It took about ten years for olive trees to yield a significant crop, and by 1640 the Thirty Years War had disrupted many trades. See René Baehrel, *Une croissance, la Basse-Provence rural* (1961), p. 157.

21. The decline is evident in all of the commodity taxes.

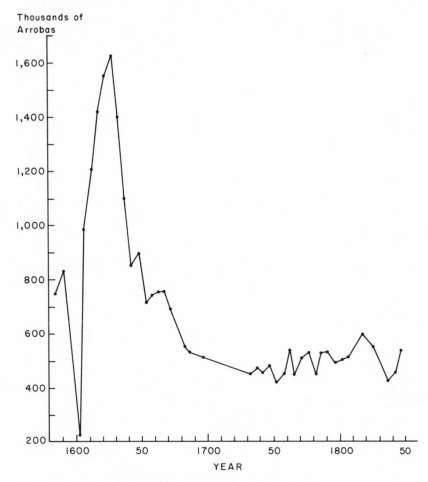

Figure 6.2 *Wine Consumption in Madrid, 1584–1847**
*Averages of five-year periods or nearest approximation.

gether at different rates. Without knowing the ratio between the two, revenue figures cannot be converted to estimates of consumption. A few figures for beef and mutton consumption were developed from fragmentary seventeenth-century sources, and official totals exist for the eighteenth and nineteenth centuries (see Table 6.2 and Appendix D). In conjunction with revenue trends, they provide a profile of the volume and evolution of urban meat consumption.[22]

22. The sources are the *sisa del rastro,* imposed in the 1590's with three tariffs, and the *sisa del carne mayor* on beef and mutton for 1741 to 1808. Both were assessed at fixed monetary rates and thus immune to inflation.

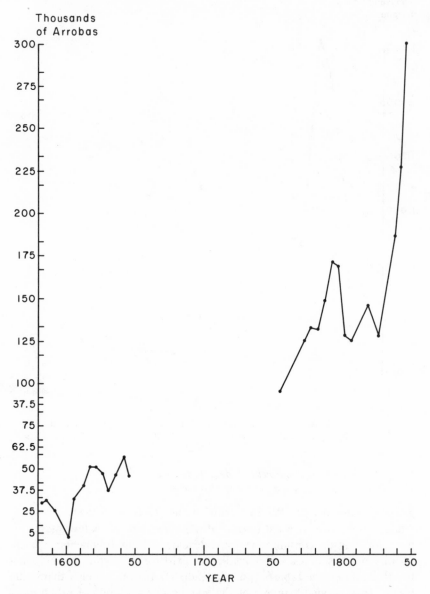

Figure 6.3 *Olive Oil Consumption in Madrid, 1584–1647 and 1757–1847**
*Averages of five-year periods or nearest approximation.

Table 6.2. *Estimates of Annual Consumption of Beef and Mutton in Madrid*

Date	Castilian Pounds
1601	2,542,904
1607-08	5,616,708
1632	8,210,630
1630's	9,500,000
1743	8,253,952
1751	10,641,232
1757	8,625,000
1763-64	10,172,142
1766	10,300,000
1789	12,757,674
1796-1801 (av.)	14,990,048
1824	10,710,439
1825	10,865,935
1826	10,158,375
1827	10,178,096
1828	10,350,051
1829	10,874,660
1838	10,167,941
1839	10,215,385
1840	10,154,892
1841	10,982,514
1842	11,189,279
1844	13,678,012
1845	14,461,522
1846	15,981,607
1847	16,566,420
1848	14,553,027

Sources: See Appendix D, Section II, C.

Urban consumption of meat rose rapidly in the early seventeenth century, and the data suggest that consumption and population rose together. The consumption estimate for 1632 coincides with an annual meat tax revenue 15% less than average revenue in the 1630's, indicating that consumption of beef and mutton was about 9.5 million pounds yearly in that decade, three and a half times that of 1601. Tax revenues imply that consumption declined rapidly between 1640 and 1650 and remained low in the later seventeenth century (see Appendix D). By the 1750's consumption had reached 10 million pounds and, except for a slump in the early 1780's, the increase kept pace with population until 1800, when it began a pronounced decline. Consumption remained low until the end of the Carlist War, and only in the 1840's did it surpass the high of the 1790's, reaching 150% of the seventeenth-century peak.

Pork consumption is documented for the later eighteenth century, and the expansion from 2.2 to 4.2 million pounds per year between 1740 and 1800 presents an exaggerated version of the concurrent cycle for beef and mutton. Annual fluctuations were sharper, and the trend clearly outpaced that of beef and mutton in the 1760's and '70's. The relative change is greater, as the quantity of pork consumed rose 75% between the 1760's and 1790's, and the subsequent decline is more precipitous. Apparently the rural economy could respond faster to the demand for pork, and for the urban consumer pork was cheaper if less desirable than mutton and beef.

E. Charcoal

The fifth mass-consumption commodity was charcoal, and the available annual figures are presented in Table 6.3. Consumption grew with population, but the timing suggests a supply problem and declining per-capita consumption during the 1790's. Annual consumption in the mid-1760's was 40% higher than the isolated estimate of 1695, and by 1789 it had doubled that of the 1760's—a rate of growth considerably greater than that of the population. Consumption then experienced an equally abrupt 30% decline in the 1790's.

Table 6.3. *Charcoal Consumed in Eighteenth-Century Madrid*

Year	Castilian Arrobas(a)
1695	1,200,000
1766	1,701,182
1767	1,739,755
1769	1,263,505
1771-72	1,932,469
1781	1,987,304
1789	3,579,977
1796-97	2,332,758
1800-01	2,307,052
1801-02	1,984,258
1802-03	2,055,042
1803-04	1,930,447

Sources: AVM, *Secretaría*, sigs. 1-92-19 and 4-5-67; AHN, *Consejos*, leg. 6790-8, 29; AHN, *Sala de Alcaldes*, libro for 1695, fols. 362-363.

a. One *arroba* is approximately 25 U.S. pounds.

II. Per-Capita Consumption and Evolution of the Market for Agricultural Commodities

The preceding supply history allows a profile of urban consumption over time that is unique in urban history and permits a rough picture of overall market development in the course of 250 years. Using population estimates from Chapter 2, Table 6.4 presents the evolution of the city's per-capita consumption of agricultural staples. Where possible, consumption estimates are based on averages of adjacent years to minimize the effects of short-term shortage. The results are not directly comparable to the diets presented in Chapter 4, but they are remarkably close to those diet figures.

Table 6.4. *Per-Capita Annual Consumption of Basic Staples in Madrid*

Year	Wheat (bu.)	Wine (lit.)	Olive Oil (lit.)	Beef, Mutton (lbs.)	Pork (lbs.)	Char- coal (lbs.)
1597	5.0	207	8.4	38.5	—	—
1630	5.3	156	5.3	47.5	—	—
1685	5.7	66	—	—	—	—
1757	—	64	12.2	63.1	18.9	—
1769	5.5	55	16.2	68.7	20.0	282.5
1787	6.5	57	15.6	72.9	22.9	500.0
1799	7.2	46	15.8	64.6	17.9	295.0
1821-24	5.9	65	12.4	66.9	—	—
1842	5.3	41	17.8	55.0	—	—
1850	5.5	45	24.7	70.5	—	—
1850(a)	—	65				

Sources: Based on data in Chapter 6, Part I; Appendix D; and the population figures developed in Chapter 2.
   a. Personal estimate by Pascual Madoz.

With two exceptions, average bread consumption fluctuated between 5.3 and 5.9 bushels per capita per year for two and a half centuries;[23] the principal deviations from the norm appear in 1597 and in 1787–99.[24] As bread was

23. This figure is confirmed in Bennassar, *Valladolid,* pp. 71–76, for sixteenth-century Valladolid, where 40,000 people consumed 220,000 bushels of wheat yearly, just under 5.5 bushels per inhabitant.
   24. The variables that might explain them are inaccurate figures on consumption, inaccurate estimates of population, or change in consumer preferences. Charles Carlson indicates, in "The Vulgar Sort," pp. 85–92, that early seventeenth-century diets in Madrid contained more bread and less meat than these averages suggest. This may reflect the sources used, but it does not conflict with the lower meat consumption that the above figures attribute to the seventeenth century. Jacques Soubeyroux, *Pauperisme et rapports sociaux à Madrid au XVIIIème siècle*

the basic foodstuff of any poor European population, it was the last thing sacrificed in times of dearth. Hungry people sought cheaper substitutes where they could, but in the city there were few alternatives. Thus it is not surprising that wheat was the single most important commodity in Madrid's economy, that per-capita consumption changed little, and that total consumption reflected population trends.[25] The best explanation for the low figure in 1597 is that consumption was depressed by shortage, while population may be overestimated; but the discrepancy is not enough to affect the analysis. The more substantial anomaly comes around 1800, when average wheat consumption had risen 30% in a quarter-century. Since consumption and population data are relatively good, the best explanation is that per-capita consumption of bread really did rise. This is consistent with market conditions that combined falling real wages with a decline in the price of wheat relative to other commodities. It is also reflected in the fact that per-capita consumption of four of the other five commodities in Table 6.4 declined in the last decade of the century. The drift to the cheapest forms of food is consonant with the demographic trends discussed in Chapter 3.

The evolution of wine consumption shows surprising elasticity of demand, given the conventional image of wine as a basic beverage, and also indicates the inability of wine-producing areas to supply large quantities at stable prices. The figure of 207 liters annually per inhabitant for the late 1590's is extremely high, but we must remember that most of the population was adult. The same is true for 1630, although by then average consumption is much closer to the 109 liters Bennassar found for Valladolid. These figures are easier to accept when compared to the 250 liters per-capita of Calvinist Geneva in the eighteenth century.[26] Prior to 1610, wages in Madrid fell behind the price of wheat, and wine consumption grew more slowly than population or wheat consumption, as declining real income made it difficult for the poor to buy wine even at lower prices. After 1610 the situation changed as real wages rose—and even though the price of wine rose, that of wheat drifted downward and wine consumption soared. This coincides with the rise of the market-tax revenues shown in Chapter 2, a further indication of demand for less essential goods.

Thus wheat and wine consumption and population growth demonstrate the growing wealth of the early seventeenth-century capital. They also imply changes in the relationship of the Castilian hinterland to urban demand.

(1978), gives figures for the population that produce a somewhat lower per-capita figure at the end of the century; but his century-long population trend produces the same trend in per-capita figures.

25. Thus far, at the risk of circular analysis, we have assumed that individual consumption of wheat was stable. Now we can check that assumption.

26. Anne-Marie Piuz, *Recherches sur le commerce de Genève au XVIIe siècle* (1964), p. 86.

Wheat clearly became more available to Madrid after 1610, allowing the increase in real wages and in demand for other commodities. This is a significant rural response to urban demand, and as we will see, it reflects a restructuring of the regional economy. By 1630 the trends had reversed: inflation returned, real wages were declining, taxes were being increased, and bread prices were climbing. Wine prices, which declined in 1588–1611, soared to a high plateau that ended in a new upsurge in the 1640's, suggesting permanently higher costs in the industry. Individual wine consumption reacted to wine prices and began to decline as soon as the cost of a basic diet without wine began to rise faster than wages, after the prosperity of 1609–22.[27] In the eighteenth century, wine prices began to rise sooner than those of wheat; but in the early decades, wine consumption may have benefited from the cheapness of wheat. As wheat became more expensive relative to wages, however, wine became less of a bargain. Around 1735 a worker could get seven pounds of bread by giving up an *azumbre* of wine, but by the 1790's he could get only four. Consequently, wine consumption rose slowly and erratically compared with population. Relatively high in the 1720's and early '30's, it fell as wheat prices jumped during the erratic harvests of the early 1750's. Wine consumption then oscillated around 500,000 *arrobas* per year to the end of the century, despite the addition of 40–50,000 people to the city. Along with relatively rapid increases in the price of wine, this explains the decline in per-capita consumption after 1757. If we accept Madoz' estimate of consumption in 1850,[28] the highest comparable figure for the 1840's is 65 liters annually per person, close to eighteenth-century averages.

Thus per-capita consumption of wine dropped sharply in the seventeenth century, hovered at 60 liters in the eighteenth century, with a decline at the end, and barely reached eighteenth-century levels by 1850. Compared with wheat, wine consumption was very sensitive to economic conditions. Whenever bread became expensive relative to wages, per-capita consumption of wine dropped. Urban population and aggregate wealth were thus less relevant to the wine market than were real wages and consumer preferences, and there was little in the structure of Madrid's market that allowed urban growth to encourage Castilian viticulture. It is a cliché that rigid and uneconomic land-owning arrangements stifled Castilian agriculture, but in this instance the nature of the market is an equally good explanation.

Consumption of olive oil did not react to the conditions that influenced wheat and wine, suggesting that its urban market was different. In the early seventeenth century, consumption grew regardless of changes in wheat and wine prices, and even despite increases in the price of oil, and demand re-

27. Carlson, "The Vulgar Sort," pp. 85–92.
28. Madoz, *Diccionario*, pp. 988–989.

mained strong in the crisis-ridden 1640's and 1790's. This identifies olive oil as a commodity used primarily by the affluent, who were not forced by high price to surrender amenities from their diet. At the same time, olive oil shows a long-term trend the reverse for that of wine. From 5.3 liters per capita in 1630, consumption had tripled by 1769 and remained at 16 liters annually per inhabitant for the rest of the century. After a decline in the 1820's, it reached 25 liters per inhabitant in the 1840's, five times the seventeenth-century average. This does not mean that oil was widely used by the poor, since much of what entered the city was destined for street lighting and industrial use. The immunity of oil consumption to changes in the real wages of the poor reflects the fact that the poor could hardly stop using something that they made little use of anyway. Consequently, Madrid provided a sustained and growing demand for olive oil in contrast to viticulture. This represents an inducement to agricultural specialization derived from urban demand, but one that affected distant Andalucía far more than the Castilian interior.

Our calculations indicate that per-capita annual consumption of beef and mutton was relatively low at the end of the sixteenth century and had doubled by 1787. It declined subsequently, and as of 1850 had not exceeded the level of the eighteenth century. Use of pork followed the pattern of beef and mutton in the eighteenth century, but with higher rates of increase and decrease. At its peak, consumption of beef, mutton, and pork was about 4.2 ounces per day per person, a third of which was probably fat. This is a high figure for a pre-industrial city,[29] but is not far from that Bennassar gives for Valladolid in the 1590's.[30]

If we accept that Spain was inherently better suited for livestock than other European countries,[31] the relative importance of meat in the diet is not an issue, and the trend of consumption is more significant. Since we cannot separate beef and mutton consumption, analysis of meat consumption is restricted. Its increasing availability in the urban diet is a clear reflection of the growing importance of stock-raising in seventeenth-century Castile. By the same token, the economic crisis of the late eighteenth century signaled a shift away from livestock, and per-capita meat consumption between 1787 and 1842 fell significantly before recovering its eighteenth-century level around 1850. The decline coincides with a steady expansion of rural population and agriculture.[32] It is also interesting that the urban crisis in 1793–1807

29. Slicher van Bath, *Agrarian History,* pp. 85–87.
30. Bennassar, *Valladolid,* p. 72.
31. Carmelo Viñas y Mey, "Apuntes sobre historia social y económica de España" (1965), pp. 75–79.
32. Gonzalo Anes Álvarez, "La agricultura española desde comienzos del siglo XIX hasta 1968" (1971), pp. 256–263; Romero de Solis, La población, pp. 159–172; Miguel Artola, *La burguesia revolucionaria, 1808–1869* (1973), pp. 109–111.

marked the beginning of a massive shift from mutton to beef in the diet. In 1796–99, beef represented 30% of the total of beef and mutton. By 1825, beef accounted for 60% of the total, and by 1847 it accounted for 77%.[33] The recovery of per-capita meat consumption in nineteenth-century Madrid was clearly associated with a major shift in the nature of Spanish stock-raising.

The series on consumption of charcoal is consonant with other developments in the eighteenth century, although it is too short to provide much perspective.[34] The high per-capita figure for 1789 is from a good source, and the decline in the 1790's is not an illusion caused by the documents. Charcoal was the household fuel, but it was also the source of industrial energy in the city. Bakeries, breweries, distilleries, chocolate makers, and metal foundries all used it extensively. In Chapter 5 we showed that Madrid saw a degree of elite-oriented industrial expansion in the 1770's and 1780's, and this accounts for the apparent increase in per-capita use of fuel. The economic difficulties that began in the 1790's curtailed development, as trade was disrupted and inflation caused the more affluent to cut back on marginal luxuries. At the same time, the drop in wages was bound to curtail household use of fuel.

Total and per-capita consumption of wheat, wine, and olive oil thus provide insights into three important elements of the Madrid market and show us how they changed with urban prosperity and growth. Wheat was essential to the poor at any price; hence urban growth brought increased demand, supply difficulties, rising prices in the city, and pressure on the real incomes of the poorer three-fourths of the population. Nevertheless, wheat consumption grew with the city, and sometimes faster, and every effort was made to mobilize supplies for the urban market. Wine was also a commodity of mass consumption, but was not essential in a supply crisis. As the real income of the poor declined, per-capita use declined, even though wine prices fell behind those of wheat. Thus Madrid's growth offered few market opportunities to viticulture and similar industries. Wine was a major agricultural commodity in the interior, but imperial and urban prosperity could not stimulate this important aspect of the rural economy. The urban elite used olive oil in increasing amounts, since they could afford any reasonable price without much concern for the cost of other staples. Since oil came from Andalucía, the stimulus of increased urban demand was transferred to suppliers outside of Old and New Castile.

Meat is usually presented as a commodity with an elastic demand curve similar to that of wine, and in some cases the two were affected by the same urban conditions. But in the Spanish context, the structure of the rural econ-

33. See Appendix D.
34. Carlson, in "The Vulgar Sort," pp. 102–120, gives 350 pounds per household per year as typical of the seventeenth century. This is plausible, but it is not clear where this figure comes from, and it is only an indication of the order of magnitude.

omy was probably more important in determining levels of meat consumption. Despite widespread poverty, economic conditions allowed a level of consumption that was high for a pre-industrial city. Thus we see in urban meat consumption a reflection of the shift in Castilian agriculture toward higher-value commodities and reduced labor requirements that marked seventeenth-century Spain, as well as a reverse trend in the early nineteenth century.

III. Structure of the Urban Market

A. Agricultural Commodities, 1601–1800

The preceding discussion traced the evolution of effective demand in Madrid for basic commodities and showed that both urban income and rural conditions affected price and consumption patterns. The next step is to estimate the changing economic significance of the pattern of consumption for the rural economy and its elites. Our estimates of consumption and Earl Hamilton's prices provide an approximation of the annual value of each commodity, and thus a rough index of the gross return to suppliers. We can follow the relative significance of each commodity by comparing benchmark cross-sections. Figure 6.4 illustrates the relative importance of wheat, wine, olive oil, and meat in each of five periods, while Table 6.5 details the changes in volume and price in the early seventeenth century.

Expressed as five-year averages, the prices of these four commodities rose 30% to 79% between 1600 and 1631. After adjustment for the 31.2% increase in the price index, however, there was no increase in the real prices of wine and olive oil. Consequently, the gross return from those commodities could increase only as fast as consumption itself. To the extent that prices hid new taxes, the actual return to the producer rose more slowly than total consumption. Consequently, real increases in revenue in those trades could only come from greatly expanded volume or lower production costs. Given the decline of rural demand after 1610 and evidence of rising real wages in 1610–25, neither alternative is very plausible. Thus the fact that the consumption of wine and olive oil did increase in Madrid implies the decline of alternative markets and reflects the stagnation of trade at Sevilla and the collapse of Toledo and other interior cities.[35]

The contrast between the wine and olive oil markets and those for meat and wheat echoes the urban shift to more basic foodstuffs. It is worth noting that while meat consumption rose with population, mutton consumption appar-

35. See Domínguez Ortiz, *La sociedad española en el siglo XVII*, vol. 1, pp. 115–160; John Lynch, *Spain Under the Hapsburgs*, vol. 2 (1969), pp. 126–130, 137–153; Gentil da Silva, *En Espagne*, pp. 104–120, 151–160; and Bennassar, *Recherches*, pp. 60–68. Domínguez Ortiz' account has yet to be superseded.

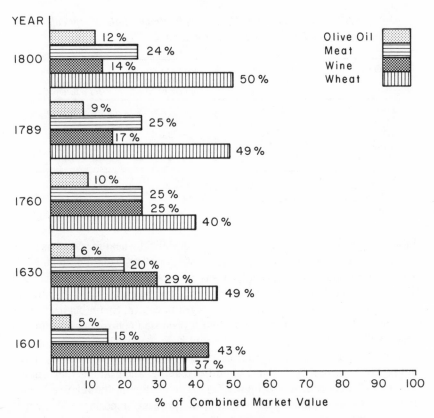

Figure 6.4 *Structure of the Market for Basic Agricultural Commodities in Madrid**
*Value of Wheat, Meat, Olive Oil, and Wine marketed relative to the combined value of all four.

ently rose faster than beef, reflecting a slower price rise. A declining Castilian labor force encouraged grazing, even as the difficulties of the European wool industry in the early seventeenth century sped more sheep to the slaughter-yards. Thus, even though its real price was static, selling mutton to the Madrid market remained a logical alternative for some land-owners, and the "decline" of Castile made another brief contribution to the general prosperity of early seventeenth-century Madrid.

Wheat, of course, was the most important commodity. The volume of sales increased with the population, while its price outpaced the general price index by 23%. The importance of this commodity in the Castilian economy is suggested by the fact that in 1601 the retail value of the wheat sold in Madrid equaled one-third of government remittances from America and 12% of all

Table 6.5. *Changes in Price, Volume, and Value of Basic Agricultural Commodities in Madrid Between 1601 and 1632*

Commodity	Change in Consumption (a)	Change in Price (adjusted for inflation) (b)	Change in Sale Value (adjusted for inflation) (b)
Beef (est.)	+ 222.9% (c)	+ 47.4%	+ 375.8%
Mutton		− 0.6	+ 221.0
Wheat	+ 173.9	+ 23.5	+ 238.4
Wine	+ 76.5	+ 0.9	+ 77.3
Olive Oil	+ 60.0	+ 4.7	+ 67.6

a. Increase in population: + 169.2%
b. Increase in quinquennial price index: + 31.2%
c. Includes both beef and mutton.

bullion registered. By 1632, the value of the Madrid wheat market was three times those government remittances and 80% of all registered bullion, while wheat consumption in Madrid alone was 50% more than that of Madrid and Toledo combined in 1595. In this context, the interest of the nobility in acquiring jurisdictional control over villages in central Spain begins to look economically rational, to the extent that it promised control over communal lands, tithes, and taxes collectable in grain.[36]

The significance of this pattern is better appreciated if we look at the aggregate value of these four commodities together and examine their changing relative importance (see Figure 6.4). The decline in the relative importance of the wine industry is dramatic, the growing importance of meat is notable, and wheat came to represent nearly half of the value of the four basic staples. The real value of wine and olive oil sales increased by only two-thirds, while that of wheat and meat nearly trebled. Landed elements that could channel meat or wheat to Madrid apparently fared better than those providing wine or oil.

We cannot construct a similar cross-section of the commodities market for the later seventeenth century, but there is evidence for the direction of change. Wine continued to lose its share of what had become a generally contracting market as consumption continued to decline after the population stabilized. Wheat remained the most important commodity, and shortages were chronic despite the reduced urban market. Mutton had increased its share of the market in 1601–32, but as the wool market improved it became

36. These sales involved local jurisdictions, offices, *alcabalas*, and the royal share of the tithe. They provided leverage in determining use of communally owned lands. The greatest volume of sales is precisely in the period before the urban market declined, and many of the towns were within the zone supplying Madrid. See Antonio Domínguez Ortiz, "Ventas y exenciones de lugares durante el reinado de Felipe IV" (1964).

more expensive relative to bread.[37] Thus the poverty of most of Madrid's population continued to encourage the drift of Castilian agriculture toward wheat production and sheep, despite the decline of the overall market. The recurrent wheat shortages suggest that as urban demand fell, rural society moved toward local self-sufficiency and withdrew from distant markets.[38] At the same time, the Madrid market supported grazing by providing an alternate source of income for sheep-raisers. By the late seventeenth century, the price of mutton in Madrid reflected conditions in international trade. When war disrupted the wool trade, the price of mutton fell in Madrid, suggesting a partial remedy for loss of access to wool markets. To the extent that Madrid thus encouraged export of raw materials, it reinforced the drift of the national economy toward dependence on European markets.[39]

The structure of the basic commodities market in the eighteenth century verifies and extends the declining relative importance of wine. From 30% of the basic commodities by value in 1632, wine fell to 25% in 1766 and less than 15% by 1800. Meanwhile, the volume of olive oil sales rose and its value increased from 2.8% of the commodities market to 10.5% by the end of the eighteenth century. Thanks to reduced urban demand, better crops, and lower prices, the relative importance of wheat declined in the early eighteenth century. By 1750, however, wheat consumption and prices were rising, and by 1800 wheat alone accounted for half of the market value of basic staples. Despite this growing emphasis on bread, the relative importance of meat remained much greater than in the early seventeenth century, reflecting the place of grazing in the structure of the regional economy.

The evolution of Madrid's market for agricultural staples reveals part of the urban-rural interaction centered on the city. As the city grew and acquired its distinctive economic structure, it reinforced seventeenth-century trends toward cereal monoculture, grazing, and local self-sufficiency in the interior, encouraging the separation of interior and peripheral economic life. Urban demand for wheat encouraged the search for new *señorios* despite the rural crisis, while mutton consumption gave sheep-raisers an alternative source of income when the wool trade was disrupted. Viticulture became unprofitable as weak demand and scarce labor reversed the favorable condi-

37. For the concordance between mutton consumption, prices, and wool, see Jean Paul LeFlem, "Las cuentas de la Mesta, 1510–1709" (1972); and Carla Rahn Phillips, "Spanish Wool Exports in the Sixteenth and Seventeenth Centuries" (paper given at American Historical Association, 1978).

38. Carla Rahn Phillips, *Ciudad Real, 1500–1750* (1979), pp. 115–116, shows how this isolation dominated a small city.

39. This alternation depended on the ability of the flocks to recover from the effects of sending sheep to the slaughteryard and on the marketability of mutton from wool sheep. As will be shown in Chapter 10, the wool and mutton patterns are so clearly interlocked from year to year that the connection is hard to deny.

tions of the sixteenth century, resulting in a long-term decline. As Madrid contracted after 1640, these processes did not simply go into reverse. Without the developed urban network of the sixteenth century, the simplification that marked the Castilian economy continued, and the emphasis on self-sufficiency, grazing, and grain was strengthened.

When Madrid began to grow again in the eighteenth century, it exerted the same pressures as in the seventeenth century, but was acting upon an economy already shaped by the first episode. Thus viticulture remained a stagnant industry, expanding slightly in the 1770's but faced with a static or declining market. Because of different market and production conditions, olive oil became substantially more important. Wheat consumption rose faster than population, as bread supplanted other foods in the popular diet because of declining real wages. By the last decade of the century, even meat, a basic staple in Madrid, was losing ground as a source of income for market-oriented agriculture. Thus as the city grew, the structure of income and demand in Madrid created a market for the hinterland that encouraged a limited range of market crops, especially wheat; while the growing demand for oil exemplifies the tendency of Madrid to transfer urban demand out of the city's Castilian hinterland altogether.

B. The Late Eighteenth Century: Staples and Other Commodities

If urban demand shifted toward one or two Castilian monocultures, it also gravitated toward more expensive commodities of distant origin, further contributing to Spain's economic dualism. This polarization of demand is apparent at the end of the eighteenth century, when we can document consumption, market shares, and geographic origin for a larger group of commodities. A detailed breakdown is presented in Appendix D, but the pertinent trends are summarized in Tables 6.6 and 6.7.

Table 6.6. *Market Shares of Staple and Semi-Luxury Commodities in Madrid, 1766-1800*

Period	Wheat, Wine, Mutton, Beef, Pork, Charcoal(a)	Olive Oil, Wax, Sugar, Fish, Soap(a)
1766-70	74.9%	25.1%
1786-90	75.3	24.7
1796-1800	72.0	28.0

Sources: See Appendix D, Section IV; Tables D.1, D.2, D.7, 6.1, 6.2, and 6.3; and prices from Hamilton, *War and Prices*.
a. Percentages are for estimated total retail value of all 11 commodities in the sample for the period indicated.

Table 6.7. *Market Shares of Interior and Periphery/Overseas Commodities in Madrid, 1766-1800*

Period	From the Interior(a)	From the Periphery and Overseas(a)
1766-70	78.0%	22.0%
1786-90	79.6	21.4
1796-1800	74.5	25.5

Sources: See Table 6.6.
a. Percentages are for estimated total retail value of all 11 in the sample for the period indicated.

As we might expect with inflation and the prevailing income structure, the portion of urban income devoted to staples fell, while the share committed to semi-luxuries rose. Simultaneously, the share of purchasing power linked to distant sources of supply rose from 21.4% to 25.5% as purchasing power shifted to elite consumers. In addition to the growing importance of wheat, the decline of mutton and wine, and the rise of olive oil, there was a shift to pork as a cheaper meat and also a notable increase in the value of imports of fish, a sharp jump in the importance of sugar, and a drop in the relative importance of wax, one of the few domestic luxury commodities. Thus there was a distinct shift in urban demand—especially during the 1790's, when other indicators reveal economic and social stress.

This information also allows us to refine the established simplifications about real wages in Madrid in the late eighteenth century by clarifying the sources of inflationary pressure. In the twenty years before 1789, the price increases were strongest among staples from the interior, but thereafter imports registered the fastest increases. Comparing money wages with general prices, Earl Hamilton suggests that real wages fell 13% from 1766 to 1789 and another 15% between 1786–90 and 1796–1800. In fact, during the first period the price of wheat rose 13% faster than the general index, that of charcoal 45%, and beef 20%. Pork, however, did not keep up with the general index, hence the relatively rapid increase in its consumption. Since these basic staples accounted for 70% of the budget of the poor, the deterioration of real wages prior to 1789 was far more serious than Hamilton implies. This makes the rapid deterioration of urban demographic conditions shown in Chapter 3 much more logical.

For the last decade of the century, Hamilton's figures show a 28% rise in the general price index and a 15% fall in real wages, but the impact of prices on wages is overstated. Semi-luxuries like soap, cacao, and sugar, which had barely kept pace with the general index before 1789, rapidly became more expensive. The most notable increases were logged by overseas products and by olive oil, which outpaced the general index all through the last third of the century. By contrast, wheat prices rose 20% less than the general index, and the same was true of charcoal. Beef also fell behind the general index, while mutton followed it closely, and wine continued its long-term decline relative to general price levels.

This confirms that even before 1789 the economic position of the poor had reached a point at which whatever happened to general prices, money wages followed bread prices because people were at the edge of subsistence. The misery this entailed is spelled out in the vital statistics of the 1790's, the subsequent decline of total population, and an urban market in which consumption of the cheapest staples (wheat and pork) rose faster than the population, while demand for other commodities used by the poor stagnated or declined.

In the third quarter of the eighteenth century, therefore, urban growth brought greater demand for staples from the Spanish interior, even though it did not create a diversified market for that hinterland. Charcoal, pork, beef, wheat, and wax registered 25% to 90% increases in volume and 45% to 175% increases in market value when adjusted for inflation. Around 1789, however, urban demand shifted to the cheapest staples on one side and semi-luxuries on the other. In the last years of the eighteenth century, therefore, Madrid bought a static or declining volume of hinterland products, except for wheat and pork. Adjusted for inflation, the market value of hinterland commodities consumed in Madrid fell anywhere from 40% in the case of charcoal to 5.5% in the case of wheat. By contrast, consumption of sugar, olive oil, fish, and cacao all rose noticeably, and their adjusted retail values climbed even more. Despite higher international prices, the city increased its consumption of these semi-luxuries, a sure indication of an increased polarization of urban incomes and of the dualized structure of the urban economy. The implications of this for a landed elite with urban habits are obvious.[40]

C. Structural Trends from Eighteenth to Nineteenth Centuries

Fragmentary sources make it difficult to follow these trends into the nineteenth century, but some changes are apparent (see Table 6.8). The first section of this chapter and Table 6.4 on per-capita annual consumption offer figures that provide a starting point.

40. To the extent that taxes and rents supporting Madrid depended on the sale of agricultural products to the capital, feeble leadership is not the only explanation for the increased political activism of the landed element at court in the 1790's. On the nobility's resentment of fiscal policy, see M. E. Martínez Quintero, "Descontento y actitudes políticas de la alta nobleza en los orígenes de la Edad Contemporánea" (1977).

Table 6.8. *Madrid: Consumption Trends of Ten Major Commodities, 1779-1847*
(Index: 1789 = 100)(a)

Year	Wheat	Meat	Wine	Cod	Fish	Soap	Oil	Sugar	Cacao	Wax
1779				84		67	89	75	78	90
1789	100	100	100	100	100	100	100	100	100	100
1794									112	
1798	127	119	96	131		114	109	88	92	89
1817	64	86	118		66		98			
1828-31		85	108	63	79	94	88	78-102	63-82	58-60
1839-40	100	83	84		72	117	126	119	58	45
1847	105	112	101	80	150	156	197	157	86	58

a. See Tables D.8 and D.9 for base consumption levels, more detailed indices, and sources.

Per-capita consumption of meat, already declining in the 1790's, continued to drop until the 1830's, and by 1817 had contracted 30% compared with a 20% reduction of population. Only in the 1840's did total and individual consumption begin to recover, but in 1848 it was still no higher than in 1800. Thus, despite a larger base population, it took half a century for meat consumption in Madrid to return to the level of the 1790's, indicating a long period of poor urban living conditions. When volume did recover, beef consumption rose 115% while mutton declined 60%, indicating that the grazing industry had been reorganized.[41]

The trend in wheat consumption also implies periods of prolonged distress and a general recovery after 1840. Between 1810 and 1820 consumption fell below that of the 1750's, and only in 1840 did it reach the volume of 1789. Thereafter wheat prices declined and consumption drifted upward, suggesting an easing of the domestic grain market.[42] It also implies a modest increase in lower-class real income and helps explain both the increase in per-capita meat consumption and renewed demand for less essential commodities.

The latter point is confirmed by the wine and olive oil markets. In the late eighteenth century, oil prices rose rapidly without preventing a rise in demand; and when consumption did decline, the drop was small. By the 1820's oil prices had declined farther than those of other commodities, yet consumption in Madrid remained 15% below that of 1789. Clearly the city's industrial and elite markets had contracted. Beginning in the 1830's, olive oil prices began a rise that outstripped other commodities, yet consumption developed at an even faster rate. By the 1840's Madrid was once again a strong and growing market for the olive oil producers of the south, encouraging specialization in that area and reflecting the improved economic situation of the urban elites.

The change in the wine market is even more interesting, since it reverses a decline that dated from the 1630's. In the eighteenth century, urban wine consumption fell despite low prices. After 1814, when population and consumption of other basic staples were low, wine consumption was 20% greater than in 1789. Thereafter it dropped rapidly, and in the late 1830's was 15% lower than in 1789. In the 1840's wine consumption recovered despite rising wine prices, and by 1850 volume had surpassed the eighteenth-century peak and was still climbing. This parallel increase in consumption and price of a commodity that was readily expendable in the diet is another indication of improved living standards and implies new incentives for viticulture.

The trends of these four staples have been supplemented on Table 6.8 with

41. See Appendix D.
42. Vicens Vives, *Manual de Historia económica,* p. 632; Raymond Carr, *Spain, 1808–1939,* pp. 197–199; Miguel de Terán, "Santander, puerto de embarque por las harinas de Castilla" (1947).

consumption data on wax, fresh fish, salt cod, cacao, soap, and sugar. Before 1789, consumption of all commodities increased strongly, with semi-luxuries showing the fastest expansion and staples other than wheat the slowest. The 1790's marked a shift in which wheat, meat, and dried cod consumption continued to expand, while the volume of other commodities experienced relative and even absolute decline. Neither trend, however, should be confused with change in the value of commodities at current prices. After 1800, all commodities except wine declined in volume for two to three decades. By 1820 wheat consumption was recovering and the demand for meat had stabilized, but otherwise the decline was not reversed until the later 1820's. Consumption of some commodities began to rise in the 1830's, and by 1840 a general trend was established.

Examined more closely, this trend of expansion, contraction, and recovery offers some implications about the urban economy and its market in the nineteenth century. Except for the sharp drop in wheat demand for 1815–18, the consumption of basic staples (wheat, wine, and meat) remained more stable than demand for less essential commodities and imports. This is not a surprising pattern, but we have seen that in the eighteenth century both key staples *and* luxury goods had inelastic demand curves, testifying to the buying power of the more affluent strata. In the 1790's, while demand for wheat and meat continued to grow, imports of overseas products except salt cod tapered off, although the amount of elite income devoted to those products continued to increase. After 1800 the decline of demand for luxuries accelerated, and did not reverse until around 1825. By 1840, sugar from the Antilles, olive oil from Andalucía, soap from regional industry, and fresh ocean fish had returned to eighteenth-century levels. Consumption of cacao and salt cod, however, remained well below eighteenth-century levels as late as 1850.

Among other things, this implies a generation-long impoverishment of the urban elite. The collapse of the monarchy imposed a change in the economic and social structure of the country and exposed many elements of the eighteenth-century elite to economic distress. The element in the best long-term position was the landed class. The city's demand for what they could bring to market was inelastic and relatively stable. The poor of Madrid had to eat or they would (and did) revolt. The parallel with early seventeenth-century Spain is close, and the strengthening of elite control over agricultural resources that marked the nineteenth century gained much of its impetus from post-Napoleonic economic realities.

Madrid's renewed prosperity in the 1840's resembled the market expansion of the late eighteenth century, but with differences. The easing of grain supplies allowed an increase in demand for other staples, but this growth of the staples market fell behind the growth of demand for sugar, oil, soap, cacao, and fish. Thus much of the market growth implied by political stability and urban prosperity benefited Andalusian, coastal, and overseas producers rather than those of Castile. By 1850, Madrid's population had surpassed that of the eighteenth century and was absorbing a growing volume of agricultural staples. But it was a prosperity in which per-capita consumption of staples had changed little since the eighteenth century, while income distribution had become more uneven. At the same time, demand for less essential commodities from distant areas had increased.

The limited scope of nineteenth-century renewal of urban demand is suggested not only by Table 6.8, but by consumption of a wider range of commodities in 1789 and 1847 (see Table 6.9). As a market for Castile, Madrid was not much different in 1850 from what it had been 60 years earlier, and had experienced several decades when it was much less. There were changes: the shift from mutton to beef, expanded olive oil consumption, increased consumption of dairy products, and a decline in domestic sweets that coincides with increased sugar imports. The new sources of both sugar and fat (oil) represent transfers of demand out of the Castilian hinterland, a counterpoint to the renewed demand for wheat, meat, and wine. Thus, while Madrid renewed its aggregate demand for agricultural products, there are new indications of a narrowing of the market that the capital presented to the interior. These shifts are not in themselves striking, but they are part of the ongoing transference of growth-inducing linkages away from the city's hinterland.

IV. Urban Trade and Economic Dualism

The continuing weakness of Madrid's impact on its Castilian hinterland emerges more clearly when we examine urban consumption of manufactures and related commodities. We have already seen indications of a shift of demand toward imported agricultural commodities. The eighteenth and nineteenth centuries also saw consumer preferences undercutting many of Madrid's craft industries and the three traditional industries of the Castilian countryside—wool, linen, and silk textiles. This emerges if we classify imports as recorded in 1789 in two ways: first as staples, other foods and beverages, raw and semi-finished materials, and manufactures; and second as being of interior, coastal or maritime, or uncertain origin.[43] Table 6.10 shows the approximate distribution of the value of urban imports type of commodity. As the city's income distribution indicates, the bulk of wealth went to nonsubsistence goods. The difficulty of finding prices for manufactures, and

43. The estimate of the value of urban imports in 1789 is 425 million *reales* (see Chapters 4 and 5). A separate estimate by Napoleonic authorities in 1811 suggests a "normal" daily yield of 100,000 *reales* from a 10% entry duty. This suggests an annual volume of 365 million *reales*, exclusive of bread and bread-grains (Grandmaison, ed., *Correspondence du Comte de la Forest*, vol. 4, p. 499).

Table 6.9. *Castilian Products Entering Madrid, 1789 and 1847*

Commodity(a)	1789	1847
Wheat and flour	773,639 fn	541,885 fn
Beans, peas, etc.	231,880 fn	203,080 fn
Barley, etc.	236,223 fn	195,994 fn
Freshwater fish	5,943 ar	5,366 ar
Meat	22,125,073 lb	21,684,306 lb
Olive oil	126,189 ar	289,819 ar
Lard	17,865 ar	8,500 ar
Tallow	14,007 fn	5,729 fn
Alcoholic beverages	688,550 ar	618,249 ar
Eggs	1,045,680 dz	1,707,678 dz
Milk	10,515 ca	36,745 ca
Cheese	9,227 ar	17,000 ar
Honey	9,383 ar	3,557 ar
Sweets, turron	276,450 lb	77,655 lb

Abbreviations: fn = *fanega*; ar = *arroba*; lb = *libra*; dz = dozen; ca = *cántara*.
a. See Tables D.10 and D.11 for more detailed listings and sources.

Table 6.10. *Structure of Consumption by Type of Commodity, Madrid, 1789*

Type of Commodity	
Subsistence: wheat, wine, meat, fish, barley, olive oil, charcoal	40.1%
Other foods and beverages	16.2
Raw materials, semi-finished products	6.4
Manufactured goods	37.2

the inclusion of fish and olive oil among the subsistence staples, probably overstates the economic weight of basic staples.

The geographic dualism of this commerce appears when each commodity is first classified by origin and then by type (see Table 6.11). The contrast between the two market profiles is striking. By value, about 85% of the goods from the hinterland were destined for direct consumption, while about 80% of the products from distant sources were manufactures or supplies for the finishing industries in the city.[44] Madrid emerges as the focal point of two

44. This is reflected in Spain's import-export trades. Exports featured wool, olive oil, *barilla* for soap, sherry, and Malaga wine—many of these being luxuries that the periphery also

Table 6.11. *Structure of Imports, Madrid, 1789: Interior and Distant Trade Calculated Separately*

Type of Commodity	Interior Trade	Distant Trade	Uncertain(a)
All types	100.0%	100.0%	100.0%
Subsistence(b)	64.4	6.2	20.2
Other food and beverages	19.7	13.4	7.6
Raw materials and semi-finished goods	6.8	15.9	0.8
Manufactures	9.1	64.4	71.4

a. The high proportion of manufactures in the unknown category suggests that most of these goods were of distant origin. Only domestic wool cloth is pointed to as being of high quality and value. See *Manual de España*, pp. 189-190, 392.
b. Includes the same commodities as Table 6.9.

distinctive trades, one extending over a tributary field of influence in the two Castiles, the other linking the elites to the outside world. Both were financed entirely by the power of the state, Church, and landed class to collect taxes, rents, and income from the Spanish world and convert them into purchasing power in the capital.

It would be surprising if the trade structure of any major pre-industrial city did not include this pattern, but Madrid's failure to draw manufactures from its hinterland is striking. Moreover, there are signs of a progressive sharpening of this commercial duality. This is the opposite of what happened around cities like Barcelona, London, or Amsterdam. From its emergence as capital, Madrid drew to itself the skilled crafts of the interior and developed elite tastes and an income structure that restricted urban-rural economic interaction of the sort that stimulated complex hinterland economies elsewhere.

Thus far, most of the evidence for this trend has involved the impact of urban growth on demand for foreign or domestic agricultural commodities. Comparison of urban imports in 1780 and 1847 illustrates the same shift in the origin of industrial products and raw materials. Demand for nonessential goods from distant suppliers substantially surpassed eighteenth-century levels and rose faster than at any previous time (see Table 6.12).

In the context of a 20% increase in the city's population, these figures reflect the decline of many urban industries and the shift of economic stimuli inherent in urban wealth to the coast and beyond. The volume of textile fibers fell almost 50% by 1847, documenting a decline in spinning, weaving, and

"exported" to Madrid. Imports included quality cloth, salt cod, lead, tin, stockings, ginger, and wax—commodities that were imports for the peripheral provinces and "re-exports" to Madrid. See Jean O. Maclachlan, *Trade and Peace with Old Spain* (1974), pp. 6–17; and Matilla Tascón, ed., *Balanza de comercio exterior en 1795*.

Table 6.12. *Raw Materials and Textile Products Imported into Madrid, 1789 and 1847*

Commodity(a)	1789	1847
Metals, total	75,578 ar	151,262 ar
Steel	692	875
Nails	4,698	8,860
Iron hardware	1,606	3,961
Iron	56,358	75,698
Lead	11,712	58,000
Tin	—	2,153
Copper and brass	512	1,715
Textile fibers, total	1,014,021 lbs	550,939 lbs
Cotton	43,484	24,500
Hemp	237,620	150,000
Esparto	180,750	136,500
Yarn (*hilaza*)	26,616	10,000
Linen thread and yarn	109,134	12,000
Wool and worsted	326,986	174,439
Flax	31,456	5,500
Silk	57,975	38,000
Hides and leather		
Hides and pigskin	772,684 lbs	50,207 lbs
Skins and furs	395,437 pcs	87,346 pcs
Cured shoe leather	423,933 pcs	50,562 lbs
Textiles, total	5,991,206 va	5,643,716 va
Wool cloth	966,323	469,215
Cotton cloth	341,768	4,044,828
Silk cloth	1,375,115	283,285
Linen cloth	3,308,000	731,572
Unidentified	—	114,816
Stockings, total	171,775 pr	104,913 pr
Cotton	107,817	72,978
Worsted	16,632	31,800
Silk	47,326	135
Handkerchiefs, total	107,197 pcs	301,500 pcs
Cotton	97,846	292,800
Silk	9,351	8,700

Abbreviations: ar = *arrobas*; lbs = *libras* (pounds); pcs = pieces or units; va = *varas*; pr = pair.

a. See also Table D.11 for more detail and sources.

textile-finishing in the city. Moreover, raw materials from the Castilian hinter-land—hemp, linen, flax, and wool and worsted yarn—experienced the worst decline. The decline reflects a contraction of urban industry and consequently of the raw materials market that the city offered the Spanish interior. The pattern is repeated in the collapse of the city's imports of hides and leather. Essential for footwear, harnesses, containers, and a host of everyday articles, the volume of cowhides and pigskins plummeted to 6% of the 1789 level, and that of skins and furs to 22%. Moreover, these materials were not replaced with semi-finished leather and pigskin, which declined at the same rate.

Among the imports destined for urban manufacturing, only metals in-creased. Their volume doubled in the 60-year interval, but the amounts remained small: 9 tons of steel, 18 tons of copper and brass, 22 tons of tin. The two largest items were iron and lead, and the volume of iron suggests the eighteenth-century pattern of demand for iron tools, fixtures, locks, and win-dow grills, rather than use for construction and machines. At the same time, the quintupling of the use of lead coincides with an urban building boom that used lead roofing and incorporated indoor plumbing as a staple of well-to-do living.

The same picture is apparent in the changing demand for consumer goods. Demand for stockings fell by a third, and silk stockings were completely replaced by worsted and cotton ones. Obviously this reflects changing fash-ion, and fashion is often presented as a stimulus for diversification in an economy. As in Spain's past, however, fashion came from abroad, with the result that a larger share of a reduced volume of manufactures and raw materials came from outside the interior. This is further illustrated by a minor item like handkerchiefs, where volume trebled, but growth took the form of cottons from Catalonia or Europe.[45]

The most sweeping change took place in the urban market for textiles. Despite the 20% increase in population, the volume of textiles entering Madrid fell 5%, implying a decline in per-capita use. This has little force without information about contraband and the quality and durability of the textiles involved, but changes within the totals are compelling and reflect the industrialization of the European textile industry. In 1789 linens accounted for 55% of total yardage and constituted the fabric of the poor—sheets, shirts, underwear, canvas, etc. By 1847 only 12% of all yardage was linen. Moreover, woolens had fallen to 7% of the market, having declined by 53%,

45. A more subtle but equally symptomatic shift involved chocolate. As late as 1830, only 4% of all chocolate and cacao reached Madrid as processed chocolate. By 1845 this had reached 15% and local processing showed a significant decline (Madoz, *Diccionario,* vol. 10, pp. 1020–1035).

while silk contributed only 5% of all textiles—an 80% decline from eighteenth-century yardage. By contrast, cotton goods, which commanded only 5% of the market in 1789, represented 70% of Madrid's textile market 60 years later. Catalonian penetration was apparently rapid, and by 1831 Catalan cotton production far exceeded any eighteenth-century figures.[46] Catalonián industry was developing by displacing traditional textiles, not by opening new markets, and the habits of the Madrid market were central to the process.[47]

46. Jordi Nadal Oller, *El fracaso de la revolución industrial en España* (1975), pp. 189–211; see also José Félix de Lequerica, *La actividad económica de Vizcaya en la vida nacional* (1956), pp. 56–57.

47. On traditional industries, see *Manual de España* (1810), pp. 289–290, 392. On import climate, see José María Tallada Buli, "La política comercial y arancelaria española en el siglo XIX" (1943), p. 49. For regional examples, see Eusebio García Manrique, *Borja y Tarazona y el Somontano del Moncayo* (1960), pp. 11–19; and Valentín Cabero Dieguez, *Evolución y estructura urbana de Astorga* (1973), pp. 38–39.

Part Two
Madrid and Rural Castile

7. Markets, Merchants, Bureaucrats: The Organization of Supply

As a major political capital, Madrid was the center of a variety of fields of influence that linked the city to both interior and maritime economic worlds. Madrid contained an important nucleus of demand consisting of a large population of poor and unskilled people and a small wealthy elite. The poor could buy only a limited range of staples, the wealthy tended to enrich their life-style by importing goods from afar. Elite prosperity brought expansion which, because of the nature of the rural economy, meant increasingly unstable urban food supplies, declining urban real wages, and a narrowing of the range of goods that the poor could buy from the hinterland. At the same time, the wealth of the elite that was not used to acquire services and palaces was used to buy luxuries from distant sources. This situation contributed to the collapse of Castile's sixteenth-century market economy after 1600 and helped lock the interior into a rigid pattern of subsistence farming, wool production, and the wheat-wine-meat triad of monocultures. This structure was little affected by urban growth in the eighteenth century; and the process went a step further when, in the nineteenth century, the capital shifted its demand for cheaper textiles to distant suppliers, undermining the textile industry that had been part of the rural economy for centuries.

Behind this dynamic relationship is the constant reality that Madrid did supply itself on a large scale from its Castilian hinterland. Having summarized the evolution of Madrid as a market, we must now examine the ways in which the capital city interacted with the rural world despite the lack of change that resulted. This implies a Castilian version of the urban "conquest of the soil" characteristic of other European cities.[1] These "conquests" in-

1. Marc Venard, *Bourgeois et paysans au XVIIe siècle, Recherche sur le rôle des bourgeois parisiens dans la vie agricole au Sud de Paris au XVIIe siècle* (1957), pp. 17, 31–33, and esp. ch. 8, pp. 93–107; Gaston Roupnel, *La ville et la campagne au XVIIe siècle, Étude sur les*

volved control of the collection and sometimes the production of rural surpluses for the urban market. They included various combinations of
regulation, reorganization of land use, and changes in land ownership. In
Spain, this "conquest" oriented rural economic interests to affairs in Madrid
without greatly altering the structure of landowning and rural power.[2] This
may reflect the fact that while the urban bourgeoisie bought into the rural
economies surrounding many urban centers, there is not much evidence for it
in Castile. There are some indications of the process around Ciudad Real, but
urban life there was more an extension of rural society than the source of
potentially significant change.[3]

Nevertheless, links between urban supply and rural surpluses encouraged
the interpenetration of rural and urban elites. Landed families that accumulated marketable commodities were drawn into urban supply, while the functionaries, contractors, and wholesalers who mobilized supplies were not
averse to a "vertical integration" of their activities that extended their influence into rural life. Not until the nineteenth century did Castile witness the
kind of large-scale transfer of land to ostensibly bourgeois hands that marked
the seventeenth-century Venetian Terrafirma or the Parisian hinterland. Even
then, it is an open question whether in the process the city conquered the
countryside or the Castilian countryside confirmed its conquest of the Spanish capital.[4] Whatever the relationship of urban supply agents to the land, the
elaboration of the supply system brought about a long-term restructuring of
the urban network of Castile and of associated long-distance trade. In Part
Two we will examine Madrid's conquest of the Castilian commodities trade
and try to help explain why Madrid's impact on its hinterland did so little to
orient agriculture to the market, compared with that of London or Barcelona.[5]

I. Wheat and Bread

In common with most larger towns, Hapsburg Madrid possessed medieval
señorial privileges that obligated the towns in its jurisdiction to provide bread
to the city at regulated prices. The system was so detailed that quotas were

populations du pays dijonnais (1955), pp. 199, 229–231, quotation from pp. 248–249; Daniele
Beltrami, *La penetrazione economica dei veneziani in Terraferma, Forze di lavoro e proprietà
fondiaria nelle campagne venete dei secoli XVII e XVIII* (1961), passim, esp. pp. 57–81 and
101–112.

2. On the *politica de abastos,* see Manuel Colmeiro, *Historia de la economia politica de
España* (1965), vol. 2, pp. 863 ff.

3. Carla Rahn Phillips, *Ciudad Real, 1500–1750,* ch. 5, pp. 65–75, and app. C, pp. 129–134.

4. See Richard Herr's discussion of the Castilian landed elite in the nineteenth century in
"Spain" (1978).

5. Stanley J. and Barbara H. Stein, in *The Colonial Heritage of Latin America,* pp. 85–196,
discuss this pattern of dependence in Spain.

assigned to individual residents in each town,[6] and in the early eighteenth century this service obligation extended to towns 40–50 miles away.[7] Even so, it quickly became a minor part of the bread supply, and in the 1660's this *pan de obligación* provided only a tenth of Madrid's annual consumption.[8] The regulations of 1660 were still in force in 1739, however, and in 1765 the amount of bread provided was about the same, even though the system had supposedly been dismantled after the crisis of 1753.[9] When the system finally disappeared, after the grain trade was deregulated in 1765, it was succeeded by a dispute over access to the urban market—an indication that the system of *obligación* had created a permanent baking industry in several communities.

The early seventeenth century saw administered production supplemented by regulation of the price and transfer of both bread and wheat. The area of control varied with the quality of the harvest, but it tended to grow with the city. In the 1580's, bread and wheat embargoes occasionally extended as far as 45 miles; but after 1598, distances of 60–70 miles were common—in 1608 and 1631, the distances reached 80 and even 120 miles.[10] Authorities also began to set the price of bread in the villages at a lower level than in the capital. The distorting effects of these measures are clearly present in the co-variations of regional price trends between 1590 and 1640.[11] The towns of the region continually resisted this expansion of control, and by the 1630's deterioration of the regional economy had led to the exemption of many communities, and the system was becoming ineffective.[12]

Meanwhile, Madrid developed an urban baking industry, capable by 1667 of producing over 1,000 *fanegas* of bread daily.[13] As the industry grew, authorities shifted attention to the wheat market and improvised a structure of

6. E.g., the *reparto* of 832 *fanegas* of bread in Leganes in 1644: AHN, *Alcaldes*, libro for 1644, fol. 681.

7. The system is described as of 1600 in AVM, *Secretaria*, sig. 2–140–5; quota lists for towns for 1600 and 1608 are in sig. 1–445–2.

8. Ibid., sigs. 2–109–5, 14, 15.

9. AHN, *Alcaldes*, libro for 1739, fol. 186, and *Consejos*, leg. 6780; AVM, *Secretaria*, sig. 2–122–2.

10. AHN, *Alcaldes*, libros for 1583, fol. 78; 1606, fol. 26; 1610, fols. 570–572; 1614, fol. 241; 1618, fol. 234; 1631, fol. 118; AVM, *Secretaria*, sigs. 1–455–2, 2–95–23, 2–96–2, 2–98–11, 2–447–26; F. Pérez de Castro, "El abasto de pan de la Corte madrileña en 1630," p. 131. Only large-scale transactions were regulated at 120 miles.

11. Wheat prices rose faster in New Castile than in Old Castile before 1600. Old Castile prices fell faster between 1600 and 1620 as Toledo's collapse eased pressure in New Castile. Thereafter there came a sharp rise in New Castile as Madrid exhausted the regional market, but the Old Castile parallel was milder, reflecting the city's weaker impact. See Ural A. Pérez, "El precio de los granos en la península ibérica, 1585–1650," pp. 128–134.

12. AVM, *Secretaria*, sig. 1–455–2; AHN, *Alcaldes*, libros for 1630, fols. 12, 64, 49, 151, 340, 422; 1631, fol. 196; 1632, fols. 134, 398; 1635, fols. 35, 95.

13. AVM, *Secretaria*, sig. 2–109–5.

transportation controls and purchasing agents. The first third of the seventeenth century saw the rapid development of judicial protection for long-haul transport, combined with renewal of government power to preempt transport services.[14] In 1600 the city council, concerned about extreme price fluctuations and rural speculation in grain, also discussed using a single broker to coordinate purchases from various supply areas.[15] The proposal was not adopted, but private brokers were increasingly used to acquire grain for the Madrid *Pósito*, laying the basis for an expanded role by that institution. As wheat controls evolved, the detailed regulation of regional bread prices fell into disuse.[16] When supplies were adequate, the grain administration remained in the background and bakers bought their wheat privately from suppliers in the provinces of Madrid, Guadalajara, and Toledo. This private grain market remains shadowy, although there are eighteenth-century references to grain markets in Arévalo, Guadalajara, Talavera, Alcalá de Henares, Illescas, and Guadarrama.[17]

Crops in New Castile were sensitive to the weather, and supplies disappeared quickly after a poor harvest. Consequently, as the city grew, the supply of *pan de obligación* and the private wheat market used by bakers were increasingly supplemented by the municipal grain depot, the *Pósito*. This climaxed in the crisis of 1630–31, when the *Pósito* handled over 1.5 million bushels of wheat, a two-year supply.[18] The *Pósito* obtained the grain through private contractors backed by a *juez protector*. The costs were initially subsidized by assessments and forced loans from the city's guilds, but by the 1660's they were a regular part of the fiscal structure of Crown and city.[19]

Headed by a member of the city council, the *Pósito* in 1748 came under supervision of a new *Junta de Abastos,* which also acquired jurisdiction over beef, mutton, pork, olive oil, candles, fish, and charcoal. After the riots of 1766, the *Junta* was replaced by the *Real Dirección de Abastos,* supervised by the city government.[20] Between 1774 and 1799, this agency was run by Don

---

14. On the development of purchasing: AVM, *Contaduría,* sigs. 2–103–1 and 3–580–1; and Pérez de Castro, "El abasto de pan," pp. 117–150. On carters: David R. Ringrose, "The Government and the Carters in Spain, 1476–1700" (1969).

15. AVM, *Secretaría,* sig. 2–140–5.

16. AHN, *Alcaldes,* libros for 1595, fol. 400; 1605, fols. 295–298, 305; 1606, fol. 41; 1610, fol. 72.

17. AVM, *Secretaría,* sig. 2–122–1; AHN, *Consejos,* leg. 6774–30, *memoria* by Pablo de Olavide.

18. AVM, *Secretaría,* sig. 2–102–8.

19. On no-interest forced loans to the *Pósito* in 1630, 1637, and 1647: AVM, *Secretaría,* sig. 2–434–2. This is a larger if more haphazard version of the municipal takeover of grain supplies of Geneva, where the city created a municipal monopoly in the early seventeenth century. Although it involved a much smaller population (15,000 to 17,000 people), Geneva's political context created supply problems requiring official intervention in the grain market. See Anne-Marie Piuz, *Recherches sur le commerce de Genève au XVIIe siècle,* pp. 44–66.

20. Maria Carmen García Monerris and José Luis Peset, "Los gremios menores y el abastecimiento de Madrid durante la Ilustración" (1977), p. 77.

Manuel de Santa Clara, simultaneously a *regidor* of the *Ayuntamiento* and director of the *Pósito*. A good example of eighteenth-century bureaucracy, the *Pósito* now included a five-man *Junta de Dirección,* a five-man accounting office, three administrators, four receiving and dispatching officers, two measurers, and a corps of laborers to handle the grain. There was also an assortment of guards, messengers, chaplains, a surgeon, and four bakery inspectors. It supervised a baking industry that had 129 bakers and over 900 employees in 1757, and had by the 1780's developed a well-organized producers' guild.[21]

The relative importance of public and private supply is apparent in a report from 1779 summarized in Table 7.1. The *Pósito* supplied 19% of the city's grain through its own roving agents and another 7% through purchase of shipments brought to the city by small vendors. The city's bakers obtained 57% of the total through their own regional market network and another 13% from small vendors who brought their grain to the public grain exchange, the *Alhóndiga*.

It became increasingly difficult to maintain the stability of supply and price after 1750,[22] and the government simultaneously expanded its own activities and experimented with freer grain and bread markets. The wheat administration became more complex and extended farther and farther across the interior (Map 7.1). In 1753 the network of over 100 mini-depots, part of the system of *pan de obligación,* was abandoned in favor of large outlying granaries on major supply routes.[23] By 1790 the system included resident commissioners in Arévalo, Salamanca, Toro, and Córdoba. There were five supplementary depots (two in Arévalo, two in Navas de San Antonio, and one at Guadarrama), with a capacity of 300,000 bushels, a combined staff of 12, and a complete flour mill. In 1785, concerned over the condition of the poor in the capital, the Crown opened a large bakery in the *Pósito* itself to produce 5,000 loaves of *pan de pobres* daily from cheaper flour produced at the administration's Guadarrama mill.[24]

While hardly a novel institution, the *Pósito* of eighteenth-century Madrid acquired a noteworthy importance within existing market and supply structures. It routinely bought sizable quantities of grain from the market created by small suppliers near the city and from sources outside the bakers' market area. Distant purchases were made at current local prices after the harvest, and as private supplies were used or hoarded, this wheat was sold to bakers in quantities designed to dampen price fluctuations.[25] When crops were poor,

21. AHN, *Consejos,* leg. 6780; AVM, *Secretaría,* sig. 2–126–7.
22. David R. Ringrose, "Madrid y Castilla, 1560–1850," p. 95; Gonzalo Anes Alvarez, *Las crises agrarias en la España moderna,* pp. 401–422.
23. AHN, *Consejos,* leg. 6780.
24. Ibid., *Pósito* regulations dated 1791.
25. Contemporaries were explicit about this policy. AVM, *Secretaría,* sigs. 2–122–1 (1767) and 2–126–7 (1784); AHN, *Alcaldes,* libro for 1734, fols. 670–672. It is illustrated in

Table 7.1. *Wheat Entering Madrid in 1779*

Type of Purchase	Amount(a)	Subtotals
Pósito (total)		176,359 fn.
Bought at door	47,264 fn.	
Bought by agents	129,095	
Bakers (total)		484,374
Bought at *Alhóndiga* in Madrid	95,968	
Bought in the country	388,406	
Convents	15,662	15,662
Private residents	1,170	1,170
Total		677,565

Source: AHN, *Consejos*, leg. 6776-3.
a. Quantities in Castilian *fanegas*; one *fanega* = 1.5 bushels. The total does not include a possible 120,000 *fanegas* of bread from nearby towns: AHN, *Hacienda*, leg. 3713.

the *Pósito* mobilized supplies throughout Old and New Castile and sometimes acted as the sole agent for the city's wheat supply. In the last two decades of the eighteenth century, the *Pósito* handled 30% of annual supply even when the harvests were good, often providing over half the daily supply in the months before the next harvest.[26] As supply became more precarious, the *Pósito* claimed to need at least a third of the market in order to remain financially stable.[27]

Not surprisingly, the *Pósito* became very protective of the thinly spread supply of movable surpluses upon which it depended. In 1779 the director expressed concern over the proposed military purchase of 150,000 bushels of wheat in the Toro-Salamanca-Zamora region and the risk of disrupting the grain market. Six years later, efforts to mobilize Castilian grain in order to supply peninsular naval bases created a confrontation between military supply contractors and *Pósito* authorities.[28] All of this is a clear indication of the degree to which the city had outgrown the market-oriented mobilization of surpluses at politically acceptable prices.

---

the operations of the *Pósito* during the crisis of 1765–66; see Gonzalo Anes Álvarez, "Antecedentes próximos del motín contra Esquilache" (1974).
26. In 1783 and 1791, for example, the *Pósito* supplied half the city's grain in May, June, July, and August until the new crop was available: AVM, *Secretaría,* sig. 2–126–22; and AHN, *Consejos,* leg. 6780.
27. AHN, *Consejos,* leg. 6780.
28. Ibid., legs. 6775–2 and 6777–15. The latter shows that important figures in the Madrid grain supply—Pedro Casamayor & Company, and the merchant house of Cabarrús & Lalonne—were also contracting to supply the military.

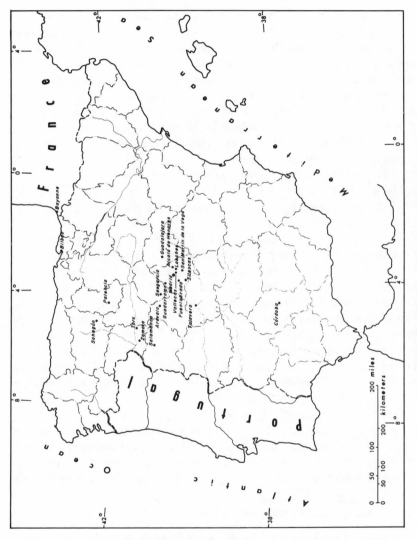

Map 7.1 *Locations Supplying Wheat to Madrid, 18th Century*

To accomplish its task, the *Pósito* of the late eighteenth century regularly purchased 200–300,000 bushels of wheat from as far away as Palencia, Sahagún, and Zamora—200 miles by oxcart or muleback. Agents then contracted with transporters for delivery to Madrid, using royal authority to preempt their services. The cost of this grain delivered in Madrid often exceeded the price at which it was distributed, representing a direct subsidy of the food supply. Less obvious subsidies were also involved. To hold down the cost of transport and assure its availability, the government strongly supported the transporters' access to common and winter pastures, despite local resistance. Moreover, the frequent commandeering of transport to move grain interfered with commerce, even when it was otherwise encouraged.[29] The government also interfered with grain exports in quite distant areas for the sake of Madrid. In 1789, for example, export of Andalusian wheat was prevented on the grounds that Andalucía was an area that often supplied Madrid, even though the regional contribution was quite small.[30]

Meanwhile, the supply of bread itself continued to arouse discussion. By 1765 the old system of *pan de obligación* and related *positillos* had disappeared, but it left in a number of communities a developed baking industry that was dependent on access to Madrid. At least six towns possessed authorized flour scales, and in 1771 nine communities were providing over 300 *fanegas* of bread daily to the Plaza Mayor. The Bakers' Guild successfully expelled this competition between 1771 and 1791, but in 1790 residents of ten towns still sold 85 *fanegas* of bread daily outside the city gates. In 1791, *pan de fuera* was readmitted on the grounds that "a free commerce" would bring "the best results at the best price," but on the condition that participants also sell to the *Pósito* the equivalent in wheat of one-third of their bread. Complaints over this liberalization appeared in 1794, and in 1801 the Crown rejected a Bakers' Guild proposal for a joint-stock company with a complete monopoly of the urban bread supply.[31]

While participating directly in the wheat and bread trades on a large scale, the government assumed the presence of private grain markets and was laying the basis for their increased prominence in the nineteenth century. Hapsburg Spain is notorious in the textbooks for its use of a *tasa* (price ceiling) to hold down prices as grain left the farm.[32] In fact, this ceiling was

29. Ringrose, *Transportation and Economic Stagnation in Spain, 1750–1850*, pp. 116–117 on regulation, 104–112 on pasture and privileges, and 123–124 on disruption of economic activities.

30. Miguel Capella Martínez and Antonio Matilla Tascón, *Los Cinco Gremios Mayores de Madrid* (1957), p. 248.

31. On bread-producing towns in the area: AHN, *Alcaldes*, libro for 1768; and AHN, *Hacienda*, leg. 3713. On sales outside the gates and readmission to the city: AHN, *Consejos*, leg. 6780. On subsequent disputes: AHN, *Hacienda*, legs. 1608-C, 4608-C, and 2235. There were 3,000 two-pound loaves in 85 *fanegas*.

32. For the standard example, see Vicens Vives, *Manual de historia económica de España*, pp. 314–315.

periodically adjusted,[33] and by the later seventeenth century was widely ignored.[34] In 1755, movement of grain to Madrid was deregulated, allowing grain merchants, bakers, transporters, and private individuals to bring in grain freely.[35] In 1765 the entire Castilian grain trade was freed from price regulation, although import and export controls soon reappeared. One of the preliminary reports on the reform contains a classic statement of faith in the free market:

> In this manner, with the modifications indicated, the supply of Madrid would be assured, since the bakers cannot run short of grain as long as any is available in Spain. It might be expensive, but this would attract more to the market and thus its very expensiveness, attracting competition, will produce cheapness. The only additional requirement is that the bakers, even though wheat is very expensive, be required to continue producing bread.[36]

The same report assumes the need for continued regulation of bread prices. The decrees freeing the internal grain trade also required grain merchants to register with the authorities and report all transactions.[37]

It is possible to quote provincial officials to the effect that there was no Castilian grain market in the eighteenth century, but such sources were biased toward protecting local economies, and the elements of a Castilian commercial network were appearing.[38] The *Cinco Gremios Mayores* were active in the Castilian grain trade in 1737 and 1753,[39] while the regulations of 1755 and 1765 clearly assume the presence of a market network. The *Pósito's* use of roving agents offered a model for private traders, and it is suggestive that some of its purchases were made through established local brokers. The muleteers of Sangarcía in Segovia offer an example of private enterprise building upon commercialization developed by the state. Starting as transporters for the *Pósito*, after 1770 they developed a private supply link be-

---

33. AHN, *Alcaldes*, libro for 1628, fol. 474.

34. Gonzalo Anes Álvarez and Jean-Paul LeFlem, "Las crises del siglo XVII: producción agrícola, precios e ingresos en tierras de Segovia" (1965), pp. 63–65; and Anes, *Las crises agrarias*, pp. 337–338.

35. Capella Martínez and Matilla Tascón, *Los Cinco Gremios*, p. 253.

36. *Memoria* by Pablo de Olavide in AHN, *Consejos*, leg. 6774–30. In the original it reads: *Parece que de este modo, y con los auxilios indicados, se asegurá la subsistencia de Madrid, pues a los panaderos no les puede faltar trigo si lo hay en España. Podía ser caro, pero siendolo, vendrá a los mercados, y su misma carestia, trayendo la concurrencia, producirá la barratez. Sola resta, que a los panaderos aun que [sic] este el trigo muy caro, les tenga siempre cuenta panaderalo . . . .*

37. Some of these lists have been found: AHN, *Consejos*, leg. 6774–30; *Alcaldes*, libros for 1768, fols. 404–411, and 1790, fols. 1125–1135. The major list is in AHN, *Consejos*, leg. 6777–21.

38. Anes, *Las crises agrarias*, pp. 329–336.

39. Capella and Matilla, *Los Cinco Gremios*, p. 253.

tween Old Castile and the market in Madrid. The eighteenth century also brought a growing number of local fairs and markets, many of which were in grain-exporting regions. While these fairs were dominated by local subsistence exchanges, they could be used to consolidate stocks for long-distance commerce.[40]

Not surprisingly, most private grain merchants were clustered around Madrid, and the official register contains 230 entries between 1768 and 1785. Of these, 178 represent neighborhood stalls retailing fodder, including 23 connected with taverns and various other retail enterprises;[41] 31 merchants ran wholesale-retail outlets within the city, while 26 wholesalers maintained warehouses in 15 outlying towns. Several of the latter were owned by residents of Madrid, and some combined rural storehouses with outlets in the city. The most intriguing figures are Antonio Corte, who had warehouses in Loeches and San Martín de la Vega; Manuel Angulo, with warehouses in Vallecas and Fuenlabrada; Don Juan Angel de San Pelayo, with warehouses in Madrid and Vicalvaro; and Francisco Cabarrús, who registered in 1776 as owner of grain warehouses in five different towns, making him the city's biggest private grain speculator well before his emergence as a financier in the 1780's.[42]

The location of outlying wholesalers matches the geography of the grain markets proposed in 1765 for Arévalo, Guadalajara, Talavera, Alcalá de Henares, Illescas, and Guadarrama (Map 7.1). Given capital, provincial brokers, and transporters like those of Sangarcía, these businesses were equipped to enter the Old Castile market at times when regional price differentials were great enough. The private system thus imitated and built upon that of the *Pósito*, with its roving agents, secondary granaries along the highways, and provincial commission agents. Here we have an important link in the chain of connections between the bakers of the city and their suppliers, and a glimpse of the increasingly sophisticated system that channeled grain to the urban market.

Another link in this system was the *Alhóndiga*, Madrid's commodity exchange for private grain transactions. This was an old institution that increased in prominence whenever government intervention in the grain supply

40. Angel Garcia Sanz, *Desarrollo y crisis del Antiguo Régimen en Castilla la Vieja: Economia y sociedad en tierras de Segovia de 1500 a 1814*; Anes, *Las crises agrarias*, pp. 321–325; Martiniano Peña Sánchez, *Crisis rural y transformaciones recientes en Tierra de Campos* (1975).

41. AHN, *Consejos*, leg. 6777–21, "Lista de comerciantes en granos, 1768–85."

42. Born of a merchant family in Bayonne, Francisco Cabarrús served a commercial apprenticeship in Valencia and married his employer's daughter. He was sent to manage a soapworks owned by her family in Carabanchel Alto near Madrid, and appears as a grain speculator on a large scale in 1776 at the age of 24. See Antonio Elorza, *La ideologia liberal en la Ilustración española* (1970), pp. 139–140.

was reduced. It was the place where bakers bought or registered wheat they did not get from the *Pósito*. In 1755 it became the sole municipal exchange for wheat, barley, rye, oats, and carob beans. By 1790, very few staples actually passed through the *Alhóndiga* except for luxury-grade flour. This reflects the increased role of the *Pósito* and the bakers' use of grain dealers outside the city. Additional exchanges were created in 1806, and the *Alhóndiga* continued to register grain imports and provide monthly reports of grain movements.[43]

In the ideological climate of the nineteenth century, the emphasis shifted from the *Pósito* to the *Alhóndiga*, but the government was unable to withdraw from direct intervention. Napoleonic authorities abolished transport controls and preemptive bidding for grain shipments,[44] and in 1814 Ferdinand VII renewed the legislation of 1765 freeing the grain trade. Wheat remained scarce, however, with a long period of disorganized supply;[45] and in 1820, despite the Liberal premises of the new regime, the *Alhóndiga* was intervening to stabilize prices as the *Pósito* had done earlier. In 1824–25 the restored monarchy went to great lengths to bring state- and Church-owned wheat to the city, but sold it at the *Alhóndiga* rather than at the *Pósito*.[46] In 1832–34, the *Alhóndiga* was still submitting reports of grain flows in conformance with the regulations of 1790.[47] The markets for all foodstuffs were freed of regulation in 1836, but the *Alhóndiga* continued to figure in the documents, while in 1837–38 and again in 1847 the *Pósito* was subsidized to provide supplements to the grain supply. As of 1852–54, the city still provided 15% of annual consumption and spent another 450,000 *reales* on subsidizing bread prices for the poor.[48]

It does not appear that increased emphasis on market institutions in grain made much difference in supply conditions. The wheat supply does appear more stable in the 1840's as grain farming expanded, but severe shortages reappeared in 1847, 1853, 1857, and 1867–68, and New Castile remained the focus of the most severe price fluctuations in Spain.[49] The persistent tension

43. AHN, *Alcaldes*, libros for 1734, fols. 692–93; 1755, fols. 235–238; and 1806, fol. 244; AHN, *Consejos*, leg. 6780, *Ordenanzas* for 1790, part 4; AHN, *Hacienda*, leg. 2235 (1801). The new posts were in the Plaza de Góngora and the Plaza de la Cebada.

44. Geoffroy de Grandmaison, ed., *Correspondence du Comte de la Forest*, vol. 1, p. 423, and vol. 2, p. 108.

45. Maria Concepción Alfaya L., "Datos para la historia económica y social de España" (1926).

46. Manuel Espadas Burgos, "Abasto y hábitos alimenticios en el Madrid de Fernando VII," pp. 244–253.

47. There are two years of monthly summaries giving daily volume and price for wheat and barley in AHN, *Consejos*, legs. 9381–5 and 9378–1.

48. Antonio Fernández García, *El abastecimiento de Madrid en el reinado de Isabel II*, pp. 35–38, 67–75.

49. Nicolás Sánchez-Albornoz, *Las crisis de subsistencias en España en el siglo XIX*, pp. 62–65.

between free market, speculation, and public order maintained government intervention and encouraged opposition to the tariff barriers sought by agricultural interests.[50] Thus the institutional framework of the wheat supply may have changed over the generations, but the fundamental reality of a politically subsidized market remained part of the urban-rural relationship from Madrid's rise to prominence through the mid-nineteenth century.[51] Without cheap transportation, a true market could not function beyond a radius of 50–75 miles. The alternatives were administrative organization of grain movements or subsidization of the consuming market so that it could pay a market price high enough to absorb the costs of an extended supply network. The outcome was a combination of open market exchanges, administered transfers of supplies, and a subsidized urban market structure staffed by a cadre of functionaries and merchants. The system was superficially becoming market-driven, but it still depended on the ability of the state's "revenue economy" to maintain the economic base of the consuming market. In any case, the system operated to draw producers and owners of surplus grain over a wide region into regular commercial relationship with the capital city.

II. Other Staple Commodities

No other commodity was as basic to public order as wheat, and government supervision of other supply trades involved less direct intervention.[52] The system that evolved in the seventeenth century covered seven commodities: meat, pork (which was administered separately), olive oil, fish, charcoal, soap, and candles. The government used a pattern of annual contracts or concessions of the sort seen in various forms throughout Europe. Contracts were let in competitive bidding, sometimes to one individual who supplied two or three commodities, sometimes to a consortium of investors and suppliers providing a single staple. The successful bidder *(obligado)* negotiated retail prices, market guarantees, control of supplies, and access to transport. The commodities were then retailed through private stalls and vendors in the city. Some contracts included advances from the government,

---

50. The protective controls that guaranteed the domestic market to Castilian producers were established by the Cortes of 1820 and received only minor adjustments until 1869; see Nicolás Sánchez-Albornoz, *España hace un siglo, una economia dual*, pp. 45–51, 63, 70, 73–74, 110–113; and *Las crises de subsistencias*, pp. 16–20.

51. Fermín Caballero—in *Fomento de la población rural* (1863), p. 82—speaks of the free trade in grain allowing New and Old Castile to "compete" for the Madrid market, but does not give details, and also implies that only railroads changed the market of the interior.

52. A distinction noted by Jean-François Bergier in *Genève et l'économie européenne de la Renaissance* (1963), pp. 100–116. Wine was regulated for purposes of morality or taxation, but not as a commodity essential to urban subsistence.

but ultimately the contractor paid the government for the concession. With occasional exceptions, the government relied on private contractors until 1786, experimented with a combined contract with the Five Major Guilds until 1794, and thereafter used various forms of provisional administration.[53]

The center of this system of concessions was another old institution, the administration of the *peso real*, where commodities other than grain had to be weighed and registered before sale.[54] In the eighteenth century, this agency complemented the *Pósito* and *Alhóndiga*, administering controls at the city gates, monitoring the contracts negotiated by the *Junta de Abastos* and its successor agencies, and adjusting retail prices of commodities to market conditions.[55] Through this institution, the food and merchandise of daily life flowed out to the stalls of the *rastro*, which serviced the poor, and the *Plaza Mayor*, central market for household supplies for more affluent families.[56]

In the late eighteenth century, joint-stock companies organized by merchant guilds and the *Cinco Gremios Mayores* became active in supply contracting as an urban business elite developed. The supply business became risky after 1785, as supply fell behind demand, and many concessions became losing propositions, forcing the authorities into administrative improvisation.[57] The state's obligation to maintain stable supplies and "just" prices was challenged as the fiscal desperation of the government of Charles IV (1788–1808) coincided with pressure from speculators and landowners to hasten experiments with freer markets. The pressure for access to the Madrid market had already been reflected in a reluctance to concede true supply monopolies. The hostility to supply monopolies appeared as early as 1766, and the admitted difficulty of making *peso* controls actually work is indicative of the problem.[58] Since each commodity involved a different network of urban-rural connections, it is worth our while to examine them individually.

---

53. García Monerris and Peset, "Los gremios menores," p. 80; Vicente Palacio Atard, "Problemas de abastecimiento en Madrid a finales del siglo XVIII" (1969), p. 284.

54. The sources refer to *mantenimientos y especias, y herrage, acero, lavor, lienzos, cera, seda, pez, resena, cueros y ganados*. With some exceptions, the fees were 0.5% on sales brokered and 3 *maravedises* per *arroba* for certifying weight. This complex of *peso real, correduria*, and *repeso* was remarkably durable. AHN, *Alcaldes*, libro for 1623, fol. 545 (a contract); *Consejos*, leg. 511–5, fols. 21–25, 58 (regulations of 1563); AVM, *Secretaria*, sigs. 2–307–9 (regulations of 1615) and 2–487–28 (renewal of regulations of 1563, with modifications of 1756, reiterated in 1810). Annual revenue figures for the *peso* begin in the mid-sixteenth century (see Chapter 2).

55. García Monerris and Peset, "Los gremios menores," pp. 81–86.

56. Arthur Hamilton, "A Study of Spanish Manners, 1750–1800," pp. 56–58.

57. By 1809 the fish supply owed 100,000 *reales,* the meat supply 400,000, and the *Posito* 7 million. On the difficulties in 1791–1810: Archivo del Banco de España, legs. 562 and 716. Palacio Atard, in "Problemas del abastecimiento," p. 284, states that the seven supply branches lost 80 million *reales* under the Five Major Guilds in 1786–94, 22 million *reales* in 1796–98, and 11,500,000 in 1799–1801.

58. García Monerris and Peset, "Los gremios menores," p. 85; Anes, "Antecedentes."

A. Wine

By 1600, city authorities were granting annual concessions to groups of suppliers who agreed to obtain and retail wine at prices regulated by the city. The concessionaires in the seventeenth and early eighteenth centuries were the *Gremio de Herederos Cosecheros de Madrid* and the *Gremio de Taberneros*. The first began as a guild of the vintners in the jurisdiction of Madrid, with privileged access to the market. As the city grew, they had become middlemen for wine from more distant sources. The second competitor was the Guild of Wine-sellers within the city, which also was involved in wholesale trading. The guild that held the contract negotiated for a set price to the rural supplier and a radius of control within which wine had to be marketed in Madrid.

The price and area of control reflected both the grape harvest and estimated urban demand, and were intended to forestall sale to other markets. The embargo zone grew from 8 leagues before 1586 to 15–20 leagues during the first half of the seventeenth century.[59] Unlike the *tasa* on wheat, the farm price of wine was adjusted every year, while retail prices were changed every few weeks. By the 1620's, the *tasa* or maximum price allowed producers was scaled to compensate for the supply contractor's transport costs from more distant sources. Thus when the price was 7.5 *reales* an *arroba* within 5 leagues, it was only 6.25 *reales* for wine originating from beyond 10 leagues. Producers complained that they were forced to accept legal prices when crops were short, but that the contractors were not held to them if the supply was more plentiful than expected, nor would they buy wine that had been stored from the previous year. The supply contractor, meanwhile, constantly dickered with the government for higher retail prices and complained because wine was sold in Madrid for less than it brought in Toledo.[60]

In 1650 we see the *Herederos* providing not only their own wine but large quantities from the region around Toledo. By 1678 they held a six-year concession for the entire wine supply, except for a few specified exclusions. The inclusion of the contract to farm the substantial wine taxes was attractive, and the competition with the *Taberneros* was intense. By 1683 the contract had passed to the *Taberneros*, who in any case controlled the final retailing of the commodity.[61]

In the eighteenth century, official attention shifted to taxes and away from actual supply, leaving the wine market relatively free. Annual summaries of taxable and nontaxable wine appear,[62] along with more careful regulation of

59. AHN, *Alcaldes,* libros for 1586, fol. 194; 1595, fol. 69; 1598, fols. 157–171; 1599, fol. 224; 1613, fol. 112; 1628, fol. 176.
60. For examples: ibid., libros for 1623, fol. 520; 1625, fols. 11, 49, 73; 1628, fols. 10, 12, 175–176.
61. Ibid., libros for 1650, fol. 132; 1678, fols. 346–347; 1683, fols. 70 and 128.
62. AHN, *Consejos,* leg. 7222.

the wine that religious communities sold to the public at their wine-shops.[63] By midcentury the authorities farmed the taxes for collection at the city gates, and there are no further mentions of wine price controls in the countryside, although the *peso* continued to set retail wine prices. There is no indication of a monopoly concession, and the government used a system of vending licenses available to *Herederos, Taberneros,* religious communities, and out-of-town suppliers.[64] Once taxes were paid on entry, the wine market was surprisingly free and involved wholesalers, the retailers' guild, and rural producers seeking direct access to the urban market. This clearly represents a functioning regional market that provided the basis for nineteenth-century supply.[65]

B. Olive Oil and Soap

The city's olive oil supply contracts were similar to those for wine in the seventeenth century; but while the wine concession was deregulated after 1700, the olive oil supply remained highly monopolistic. The contracting broker provided a guarantor *(abonador)* for the contract and supplied oil at negotiated prices that varied with the season and proximity of the new crop. In the 1740's the contract specified two warehouses in the city, 12 wholesale outlets with a staff of 24, and a minimum of 130 retail stalls *(tiendas)*. Retailers could not deal with other suppliers, while the contractor could deal with carriers arriving with oil and with producers in Andalucía.[66] The monopoly was often violated, and in 1734 the concessionaire complained bitterly about nonresidents selling oil in the streets at less than the negotiated price.[67] Officials became convinced that important amounts of oil were escaping taxes and, after an investigation in 1745, temporarily placed the oil supply under municipal administration.[68]

Judging from the tenor of the documents, the oil monopoly was one of the most difficult for contractors and administrators to enforce. In part this was because olive oil was a major raw material for the soap industry. Soap manufacturers were forbidden to sell oil in the city; and when the two were controlled by the same concessionaire, conflict was minimized.[69] Between 1780

---

63. In 1739 there were 14 of these, and they were accused of selling wine that had evaded taxation and keeping the extra profits that resulted: AHN, *Alcaldes,* libro for 1739, fols. 8–9, 48. By 1772 there was a system of rebates for tax-exempt institutions, which taxed wine on entering and returned the taxes on wine used for institutional purposes: Madoz, *Diccionario geográfico,* vol. 10, p. 1002.

64. AHN, *Alcaldes,* libros for 1742, fols. 261–264, and 1743, fols. 60–62.

65. Fernández García, *El abastecimiento,* p. 120.

66. AHN, *Consejos,* leg. 6733–2; *Alcaldes,* libros for 1739, fols. 75–80; 1741, fols. 7, 28; 1742, fols. 54–58, 187; 1743, fols. 73–76.

67. AHN, *Alcaldes,* libro for 1734, fols. 326, 332.

68. Ibid., libro for 1745, fol. 3.

69. Ibid., libros for 1734, fol. 321, and 1742, fol. 188. In 1768 both were provided by the same individual on a month-to-month arrangement, pending review of the joint contract. The

and 1785, the oil supply was taken under direct administration. The concession was sought by the *Compañia de Longistas* (mercantile wholesalers), who had other interests in the supply system, but it ultimately passed to the *Cinco Gremios Mayores*. They agreed to a stipulated price, provided 240 retail shops, and paid rent for city-owned facilities. Responding to objections to the monopoly, the government authorized producers and transporters to sell their own oil in their own shops. The concessionaire, meanwhile, got permission to send itinerant retailers through the city streets, and obtained the contract to supply oil for the city's streetlights. The *Cinco Gremios* also got a parallel concession for the soap supply that included control of the city's retail outlets and the right to distribute soap to neighboring towns. Here, too, they had to accept the presence of wholesale outlets belonging to independent producers, but the latter had to obtain licenses for their stores.[70]

The contract was not a success, and three years later, agents of the *Cinco Gremios* were complaining that the concessions were ignored by many towns and urban wholesalers, and that they could not find transport for oil purchased in Andalucía. Transporters apparently preferred to work for producers and urban distributors outside the concession. Consequently, the *Cinco Gremios Mayores* had trouble meeting contract terms and were losing money.[71] The licensing of supplementary vendors and the persisting evasion of regulations suggest the elements of a more flexible distribution resembling that for the wine supply. Thus the nineteenth-century abolition of the government's role in coordinating oil supply did not disrupt the market, and coincides with rising demand.[72] Oil producers and transporters, regional soap manufacturers, and urban distributors had developed a web of contacts which supplanted monopolistic concessions.

C. Fish

The arrangements for supplying fish, particularly the widely used dried cod, paralleled those for olive oil and soap. The commodity came from a distant source, there were few intermediate suppliers, and regulation was relatively easy. Consequently, we see an exclusive concession to a contractor who provided a guarantor and made the commercial arrangements with the suppliers in Bilbao.[73] This particular supply trade was part of the commerce

---

next year a contract was granted with little change in the terms. AHN, *Alcaldes*, libro for 1768, fols. 10, 3, 9; *Consejos*, libro 2703.

70. This is not surprising, considering that powerful nobles like the Marques de Mondéjar long operated sizable soap factories in New Castile. See Helen Nader, "Nobility as Borrowers and Lenders" (paper given at American Historical Association, 1976), p. 13. Also AHN, *Alcaldes*, libro for 1787, fols. 1376–1446.

71. AHN, *Consejos*, leg. 6791–14.

72. Fernández García, *El abastecimiento*, p. 125.

73. AHN, *Alcaldes*, libros for 1739, fol. 94; 1741, fols. 7–28; 1742, fol. 187; and 1743, fol. 79.

between Madrid and the periphery of the peninsula, and in 1768 the contractor had a Catalán name and the guarantor was a French commercial house with contacts in Bilbao and Bayonne.[74] Here, too, there was little real reason for control once supply was separated from taxation, and nineteenth-century governments did little to regulate the fish supply. By that time the trade showed a reduced volume and a greater variety in what was basically a luxury food.[75]

D. Pork and Pork Products

The supply of fresh and preserved pork followed the same pattern as olive oil and soap. In the 1730's and 1740's, there was an exclusive concession which gave the contractor a monopoly on sausage as well as fresh pork sold. The contractor had access to salt pans, got a ban on street vendors, and was protected from competitive bidding in the first two days of regional livestock fairs. The contract also precluded competition in the city from other suppliers.

There were a number of supplements to the main concession that suggest that a true monopoly of this trade was hard to enforce. Hogs were raised in the mountains, fattened on barley, and brought to the livestock fairs in Talavera, Medellín, and Trujillo. Bakers and millers in the city customarily bought hogs to be fattened on waste materials from the bakeries, and they were suspected of selling pork below the established price. Stockmen, like the organized group at Talavera, also sought access to the city market independent of the concessionaire. To prevent interloping, the contractor obtained a ruling that hogs had to be in the sellers' possession for six months and properly fattened on barley. City residents could buy whole carcasses outside the walls, but the stock-owners were prevented from making sales inside the gates.[76]

These regulations changed little in the course of the eighteenth century, although, as with other commodities, the pork supply passed for a time under contract with the *Cinco Gremios Mayores*.[77] The decreased regulation of supply that marked the nineteenth century was less complete in this case, but coordination of supply gave way to regulation of the quality and cleanliness of the product. The government-contracted supplier of the eighteenth century was replaced in the nineteenth century by a number of private slaughterhouses and purveyors. In 1841 the government established a municipal slaughterhouse and sought to impose tighter quality controls.[78] There is no

74. Ibid., libro for 1768, fol. 5.
75. Espadas Burgos, "Abasto y hábitos alimenticios," p. 267.
76. AHN, *Alcaldes,* libros for 1734, fols. 319–320; 1739, fols. 81, 90; 1741, fols. 7–28; 1742, fols. 174–186; and 1743, fol. 81.
77. Ibid., libro for 1791, fol. 726. See also Capella and Matilla, *Los Cinco Gremios,* p. 251.
78. Fernández García, *El abastecimiento,* p. 83.

evidence that the authorities assisted in financing the pork supply after the mid-1830's, and market-oriented supply systems that can be glimpsed in the eighteenth-century sources became the central feature of the trade.

E. Beef and Mutton

Beef and mutton were the most important of the supply trades after wheat, and their administration was correspondingly complex. As with other commodities, the basic mechanism was a concession granted to a contractor who undertook to provide meat at stipulated prices under defined conditions. The prices fluctuated within limits designed to protect the consumer from sharp changes caused by weather and speculation. Prices were scaled in advance to allow for seasonal availability, with beef being about 10% more expensive in December, January, and February. Retailers in the *rastro* (slaughteryard) got an established mark-up, and those in other markets around the city were allowed a slightly larger margin to cover distribution costs. More than in the other commodity trades, contracts often involved government loans for initial purchases at the livestock fairs. Agents of the concessionaire could buy cattle and sheep in Extremadura, Andalucía, Galicia, Asturias, La Mancha, and throughout the two Castiles. They had precedence over buyers from other towns, and could make preemptive matching bids within eight days of any sale, while purchasing agents from Aragón, Valencia, and Catalonia were forbidden to compete for Castilian cattle.[79] The supply contractor also had the right to pasture cattle en route to Madrid in any common or council-owned pastures within 20 miles of the capital, and was guaranteed rental of pastures for cattle in transit.[80] In the late 1780's, the concession was held by the *Cinco Gremios Mayores,* which channeled part of the business out of Castile to Portugal and Morocco.[81]

The presence of interlopers on the concession, suggested by various special regulations, is confirmed by a proposal made in 1805–06 by graziers and brokers from outlying towns. They sought the right to maintain their own urban outlets outside the official concession, offering a kind of market-sharing agreement in which they would agree to fixed quotas on the amounts sold. The proposal confirms the presence of developed market structures and shows the same tendency for the supply to become more open which we have seen in the wine, olive oil, and pork trades.[82]

The Napoleonic wars created a livestock shortage in Spain, and after 1814

---

79. This is particularly interesting, given the dependence of Valencia on Castilian mutton; see James Casey, *The Kingdom of Valencia in the Seventeenth Century.*
80. AHN, *Alcaldes,* libro for 1741, fols. 427–436; *Consejos,* leg. 11463; and *Clero, Jesuitas,* leg. 27–5.
81. This was done as early as 1789–91: Capella and Matilla, *Los Cinco Gremios,* p. 251.
82. AHN, *Consejos,* leg. 6785.

meat was again brought from France, Portugal, and North Africa.[83] In the 1820's the government stopped granting concessions, and meat was provided by a group of private suppliers. Actual processing of meat was done at a municipal slaughterhouse, with a staff of 21 employees and numerous casual laborers, but government intervention was confined to quality rather than market control.[84] Once again, a nineteenth-century "free market" was peopled by purveyors who appeared as organized interlopers in the eighteenth-century system of monopolistic concession.

F. Charcoal

The organization of the charcoal supply was basically similar to that of other concessions, but the nature of the commodity imposed important differences. Charcoal is a bulky commodity and needed substantial storage facilities and transport services. The industry also required extensive forest tracts that were harvested every 15–20 years. Of necessity, the concession involved owners of large tracts of land.

With the exception of mandatory firewood supplies for royal palaces around Madrid, there is little mention of fuel in the seventeenth-century sources until the severe winter of 1694–95. At that time, the *Alcaldes* ordered registration of all supplies warehoused in the city, and authorized anyone paying the appropriate taxes to sell fuel, regardless of the existing concession.[85] Similar shortages in 1715 led to attacks upon shipments brought in by the supply contractor. By the 1730's the position of the contractors had been strengthened by delegation of the Crown's right to preempt transport services. This was made more specific in 1739, when complaints that construction of the royal palace was monopolizing transport resulted in the allocation of 4,000 carts to the charcoal suppliers.[86]

The form of the charcoal supply contract in the eighteenth century is exemplified by the multiple partnership that undertook a two-year concession in 1745. Only the concessionaires could buy timber for charcoal from *montes* within 40 miles of Madrid. They were authorized to force landowners to sell timber, given general access to transport, allocated full use of carters from 11 mountain towns near charcoal-processing sites, and received exclusive access to several pastures on supply routes. The contract stipulated two wholesale warehouses and 16 retail outlets within Madrid. It allowed for vendors outside the concession, but they were restricted to wholesale transactions, limited to one outlet each, and required to maintain a minimum volume of sales;

83. Espadas Burgos, "Abasto," pp. 259–263.
84. Fernández García, *El abastecimiento,* pp. 85–103.
85. AHN, *Alcaldes,* libros for 1648, fol. 230, and 1695, fols. 17, 30, and 362–363.
86. AHN, *Consejos,* legs. 6772 and 51375.

these exceptions were restricted to charcoal producers marketing their own product.

Noble participation in this supply trade is documented by a clause near the end of the charcoal concession:

> With the condition that, should some of those entering in this contract as partneřs be *"Hijosdalgo de sangre notoria,"* as it seems unjust that there should be any derogation of their nobility for entering the agreement, the *Consejo* has ordered that, despite their being such contractors, the agreement cannot embarrass them during its duration, or afterwards, and they will continue to be able to have coaches and sedan chairs, regardless of any regulations to the contrary.[87]

This is confirmed by sources which show the Dukes of Medinaceli and Infantado routinely selling charcoal to the city.[88]

Charcoal appears to have been more closely supervised in the eighteenth century than any other commodity except wheat. Government involvement in the supply was substantial, and the city maintained warehouses, equipment, and other facilities that were leased to the contractor. In 1766 the bureaucracy included a central staff of 13, plus 16 supervisors and assistants in 4 district warehouses in the city, and 4 commissioners with 8 assistants who canvassed woodlots and contracted for charcoal production.[89] In the last decades, charcoal provision aroused serious concern and passed through various management arrangements. In the ten years after 1794, the charcoal supply accumulated a deficit of 18 million *reales*, with debts outstanding to the *Pósito*, the Bank of San Carlos, the Countess of La Coruña, the *Cinco Gremios Mayores,* and various agencies of the Crown. Ultimately, the fiscal crisis of the wars with France and England forced the government to accept the proposals of economists who favored the end of government intervention. In 1805 the state abandoned the charcoal supply and sold the system—

---

87. This contract is in AHN, *Alcaldes,* libro for 1745, fols. 15–23. The quotation, from clause 27, fol. 21, reads: *Con condición, que respecto de ser algunos de los que entramos en esta obligación, y fueren nuestros Partices Hijosdalgo de sangre notoria, y no parece justo que por entrar a ser obligados, les obste para poder gozar de su Nobleza: el Consejo se ha servido mandar, que sin embargo de ser tales obligados, no se les pueda embarazar el tiempo de la obligación, ni para en adelante, el que pudiesse* [sic] *tenga coche, silla-volante, no obstante qualesquiera órdenes que haya en contraria.*

88. For charcoal sales by the Infantados: AHN, *Osuna,* leg. 70 (accounts from 1775–1808); for the Medinacelis: *Archivo del Duque de Medinaceli* (Sevilla), estado de Medinaceli, legs. 60–82, 83. William J. Callahan's discussion of noble business activity—in *Honor, Commerce, and Industry in Eighteenth-Century Spain* (1972), pp. 15–20, 27—ignores urban supply, emphasizing that land precluded other investments. But land had to yield income, which meant commercializing its products, and charcoal supply was an obvious option for those who controlled forested land. The dichotomy between commercial and landed interests is too sharply drawn, and this is but one example of noble involvement in urban supply (see Chapter 8).

89. García Monerris and Peset, "Los gremios menores," p. 78.

warehouses, equipment, existing inventories, and purchase contracts—at auction.[90]

There is little subsequent reference to regulation of fuel, and reliance on private suppliers, combined with land sales, precipitated much of the deforestation apparent in modern Spain. Traditional charcoal-harvesting cut the trees and left the stumps. The commonly harvested tree species regrew from the stumps, leaving the soil-holding root system intact. The landowners and purveyors of the nineteenth century not only harvested the trees, but pulled up the stumps to get a larger immediate return on their investment. The result was erosion and deforestation of hill areas within the urban supply network.[91]

III. Conclusion

The bureaucratic systems of the seventeenth and eighteenth centuries grew out of very old traditions of municipal government supplemented by improvisations during Madrid's first phase of rapid growth. The second period of urban growth, in the eighteenth century, found those arrangements inadequate and produced another set of expedients, foreshadowing the more overtly market-driven supply structures of the nineteenth and twentieth centuries. A close examination of the regulatory arrangements of the eighteenth century reveals that the "freeing" of trade in agricultural staples in the nineteenth century was but one step in a long process through which administered economic flows were supplanted by a market network and a community of commercial intermediaries with agricultural connections. Eighteenth-century administrative expedients often involved recognition of this structure, and verify national adaptation to Madrid as the permanent economic reference point for the interior.

This did not necessarily change the underlying relationship of the landlord to the countryside or the state, nor the state-supported nature of the market in Madrid. In Chapter 8 we will look at the regional and rural markets from which supplies were drawn, and document the ways in which urban supply connected with the people who had stocks of commodities that the government hoped to mobilize for its capital city.

90. AHN, *Consejos,* leg. 6790–19, 24, 26, 29.
91. Eusebio García Manrique, S.J., *Borja y Tarazona y el Somontaño del Moncayo* (1960), pp. 161–168; Vicens Vives, *Manual de historia económica,* p. 613; and Raymond Carr, *Spain, 1808–1939,* p. 273.

8. The Countryside and the City: Context and Contact in the Rural Economy

I. The Rural Context

In this study we assume a peninsular economic dualism in which the coastal provinces could look to the sea for economic opportunities, while the interior had no choice but to turn in on itself and make do with limited resources, poor transport, and unreliable harvests. Such circumstances restricted market-oriented agriculture and encouraged regional self-sufficiency.[1] Thus historians who comment on the lack of an interior market in Spain are partly correct, but they are also guilty of oversimplification. At the level of local, intraregional life, there were durable, functioning markets and money economies.[2] In the fifteenth and sixteenth centuries, these exchanges were integrated into a long-distance commercial network centered in Toledo and Valladolid. In the early seventeenth century this integration of local and long-distance economies broke down, and regional isolation was intensified. Meanwhile, a politically supported network of supply arrangements evolved around Madrid. Extending throughout central Spain, this system gradually came to be regarded as a functioning market by its participants.

---

1. The limits are inherent in the light seasonal rainfall. To avoid summer dessication, crops in Old Castile had to be sown in late fall, but only after the autumn rains. If the rains were late, the growing season extended into hot, dry weather and crops were poor. The long-term Malthusian cycle is typified by Segovia, which expanded 1530–1580, stagnated 1580–1600, declined 1600–1650, stagnated 1650–1700, expanded 1700–1760, and stagnated 1760–1814. Total production in the late sixteenth and late eighteenth centuries was remarkably similar. See Angel García Sanz, *Desarollo y crisis del Antiguo Régimen en Castilla la Vieja: Economia y sociedad en tierras de Segovia de 1500 a 1814,* pp. 24, 75.

2. E.g., the lists of local markets and fairs in the *Guía de Forasteros* for any year after 1740.

Central Spain was inherently an isolated, regionally self-sufficient agricultural society.[3] Most production (livestock excepted) occurred on peasant farms, sometimes owned but more often rented, with rents and other obligations commonly paid in kind.[4] The farther south one went in the Castiles, the more likely it was that the peasant was a tenant, and the greater the dependence on day wages. Self-sufficiency was based on overlapping regional commodity exchanges that were sometimes not far from barter.[5] Thus the villages of the mountains exchanged wood, fuel, and cattle for the cereals and wine of the plains.[6] In the small cities and towns there were potters, weavers, shoemakers, harness-makers, and blacksmiths who provided the necessary rough manufactures for the region.[7] Exchanges rarely transcended a 50 to 75-mile radius created by terrain and transport that could double the price of wheat within 100 miles.[8]

This indicates that a lack of concentrated markets was a basic aspect of the economy of the interior. Coastal areas could meet local agricultural food shortages from cheaper maritime sources before prices got high enough to cover transport from inland suppliers.[9] After the de-urbanization of the seventeenth century, interior markets were limited to a few cities of under 25,000 inhabitants, reducing internal trade to export-oriented grazing and "the exchange of domestic products and merchandise from one region to another in the interior."[10] The Castilian rentier class was thus confronted with limited possibilities for transforming agricultural products into other forms of wealth. The physical isolation of interior Castile made it difficult to reach extraregional markets with agricultural staples that could be exchanged for

3. José Luis L. Arangurén comments in *Moral y sociedad: La moral social española en el siglo XIX* (1970), p. 40, on the profound isolation of the peasantry. Antonio Flores, in *Ayer, hoy y mañana*, vol. 1: *Ayer, o la sociedad de la fe en 1800* (1892), pp. 175–184, describes a trip from Madrid to Salamanca: it was distasteful, uncomfortable, slow, and dangerous and required armed escorts.

4. Pedro Romero de Solis, in *La población española*, pp. 27–28, summarizes this pattern in the seventeenth century, as part of a strongly Marxist analysis.

5. Edward W. Fox, in *History in Geographic Perspective*, p. 29, discusses this kind of monetized regional self-sufficiency.

6. David R. Ringrose, *Transportation*, maps.

7. A quick review of any of the 45 volumes of Eugenio Larruga's *Memorias políticas y económicas sobre los frutos, comercio, fábricas y minas de España* (1787–1800) confirms this dispersion of regionally oriented handicrafts. In the words of Nicolás Sánchez-Albornoz, in *España hace un siglo*, pp. 8–11: *"La mayor parte de la producción agraria tenía por destino la satisfacción del consumo de la gran masa rural, en tanto que solo una proporción pequeña entraba en el mercado."*

8. Ringrose, *Transportation*, p. 85.

9. Gaspar Melchor de Jovellanos, *Informe de ley agraria* (1968), pp. 176–177; Pablo Fernández Albaladejo, *El crisis del Antiguo Régimen en Guipúzcoa* (1976), pp. 41–51.

10. The mechanisms are illustrated by several writers, notably Sánchez-Albornoz, in *Los precios agrícolas,* vol. 1, pp. 35, 39–59, who documents recurrences as late as 1882.

imports.[11] Such exchanges encourage regional specialization and greater productivity, but interior conditions favored commodities too bulky to absorb the cost of primitive transport and remain competitive beyond the local context.[12] The same conditions limited the import of staples when crops failed. The result was economic self-sufficiency, a lack of specialization, low productivity, and vulnerability to unstable weather.[13]

These difficulties did not prevent the Old Regime from mobilizing agricultural staples for use as exchange for imports to some extent. Church, state, and landlords used taxes, tithes, señorial obligations, jurisdictional authority, restrictions on access to land,[14] and rural indebtedness to create a maze of nonmarket mechanisms through which a small elite accumulated agricultural products to use as payments for imports into an otherwise regionally self-sufficient agriculture.[15] A large part of the output collected by rentiers was received as tithes, *tercias reales,* and *alcabalas* that had been ceded to the nobility by the Crown. Consequently, the landed elite was often unable to control the way in which the land that supported them was actually used.[16] The perennial indictment of the system is that it prevented the conversion of land to more productive uses—although without markets and transport the complaint seems hypothetical. It also leaves out another actor—the small-

11. Writing in 1927, long after completion of the Liberal reforms, José Ortega y Gasset—in *La redención de las provincias,* pp. 25, 48—still saw isolation as the basic problem of the countryside, commenting: *"Hay que remozar a España. En todos sentidos. Hay que hacer caminitos relucientes por todas las glebas, hay que hacer que se afeitar los curas y que los radicales de pueblo digan menos palabras inanes, hay que hacer innumerables cosas mas."* See also Álvaro Flórez Estrada's complaints a century earlier in Luis Alfonso Martínez Cachero, *Álvaro Flórez Estrada* (1961), p. 30.

12. See Manuel Colmeiro's comments in *Historia de la economia política en España,* vol. 2, pp. 846–847.

13. Romero de Solis, *La población,* pp. 111–112, describes this dependence upon local production and high transport costs. Valentín Cabero Diéguez, in *Evolución y estructura urbana de Astorga* (1973), pp. 44–45, shows the limited ability of transport to stimulate a regional economy. García Sanz, in *Desarrollo y crisis,* pp. 24, 177, gives a succinct statement of this situation.

14. Aranguren, in *Moral y sociedad,* p. 40, comments that land was as much an instrument of power as of wealth.

15. The classic statement on land control is in Carmelo Viñas y Mey, *El problema de la tierra en la España de los siglos XVI-XVII* (1941). See also Helen Nader, "Nobility as Borrowers and Lenders," p. 14, and the comments on absenteeism, *tierras de propios,* etc., in Colmeiro, *Historia,* vol. 2, pp. 683–685, 713. For a detailed case study, see *La economia del Antiguo Régimen: El Señorío de Buitrago* (1974), esp. pp. 143–181. Also see Helen Nader, "Nobility," p. 8, and her "Noble Income in Sixteenth-Century Castile: The Case of the Marquises of Mondéjar, 1480–1580" (1977).

There is controversy over the collection of land rents. Pastures and vineyards were usually rented for money, farmland for part of the commodity produced. Given the interaction of prices and control of marketable supplies in directing the benefits implied by conjunctural trends, this point needs more study. For apparently typical rental patterns in Old and New Castile: AHN, *Clero, Jesuitas,* legs. 27–1, 2, 3, 4; 38–6, 7; 67–1–10; and 215–3.

16. García Sanz, *Desarrollo y crisis,* pp. 347–356.

town *labrador rico* who produced marketable surpluses. These local notables, powerful in decisions about village land-use, not only were part of the system that collected rents and tithes for absentee rentiers but were involved in market-oriented agriculture. They emerge as important in nineteenth-century politics, but were present much earlier.

The landed elites apparently collected 30–50% of agricultural output, and, depending on the balance between grazing and farming, 20–80% of that revenue was in the form of wheat, barley, rye, wine, and wool—some of which were commodities difficult to exchange for other forms of wealth.[17] Where direct control of the land was possible, managerial solutions included the diversion of land to grazing, which produced salable wool and hides; storage of grain until crops were poor and local prices rose, and dependence on markets created by the revenue economy of the state.[18] Exploitation of periodic shortage is hardly novel. Castilian harvests were sensitive to the weather, and a decline of only 15% in supplies reaching Madrid spelled hardship.[19] Under such conditions, local bread prices fluctuated as much as 400% in a single year. Able to store grain from harvest to harvest, rentiers loaned or sold it when supplies ran short. The small farmer, unable to store reserves, had to accept low prices after good harvests and had no salable surplus after a bad harvest, when he might have gotten a higher price. Consequently, he was increasingly bound to the landlord who provided credit, seed grain, or rent deferrals.[20] The rentier also took advantage of high food prices to transport commodities to otherwise unprofitable markets. Thus the landed elites strengthened their control of rural society while turning some of their stock into cash.[21]

In practice, the isolation and self-sufficiency of Castilian agriculture varied considerably and became more pronounced as Madrid grew to dominate the regional urban network. During the sixteenth century, while plague, war, and Turkish expansion sapped the vitality of the Mediterranean provinces, the interior experienced a prosperity based on favorable land/labor ratios, stable

17. In eighteenth-century Segovia, the take was about 30% of agricultural output, 80% of that in commodities. In sixteenth-century New Castile, it was somewhat higher, but the role of money was greater: ibid., pp. 383–385.

18. The terminology is that of Sir John Hicks, in his discussion of "revenue economies" in *A Theory of Economic History,* pp. 9–24 and 81–100.

19. AVM, *Secretaría,* sig. 2-122-1. See also Ringrose, "Madrid y Castilla, 1560–1850," p. 95.

20. Nader, "Nobility," pp. 14–15.

21. Romero de Solís, in *La población,* pp. 113–115, comments on the increasing use of such accumulations for speculation during the later eighteenth and nineteenth centuries. For a contemporaneous assumption about its prevalence, see Jovellanos, *Informe de ley agraria,* p. 124. The definition of landed elites used here is that suggested by Richard Herr in "Spain," pp. 98–102. It was not just the rural elite which took advantage of such speculation, since the controlling elite of seventeenth-century Valencia exploited the city granary in the same manner; see James Casey, *The Kingdom of Valencia,* p. 172.

government, and craft industries with both European and Arabic techniques at their command. Population growth stimulated regional industries which in turn participated in the maritime market system. Textiles in Segovia, Guadalajara, Cuenca, and Ávila, ceramics at Talavera, wool at Valladolid and Burgos—all fed a market network based on Toledo, with its own woolens, silks, and weapons industries and active entrepôt trade. Stimulated by European economic expansion, the prosperity of this complex was reinforced by the wealth of the American empire until after 1575.[22] Castile's population expanded from 3.1 to 5.9 million between 1530 and 1591, with the most rapid increases in the earlier decades.[23] The relationship of population to market development in New Castile is apparent in the concentration of population growth near Toledo and Madrid which is shown in Table 8.1.

Not surprisingly, serious stresses soon appeared in the Castilian economy as population and urban development outstripped its economic potential.[24] The smaller cities of the interior were already declining in the 1590's, undermined by the fiscal policies of the Crown, the Dutch wars, and disruption of international commerce and credit. Rising taxes and prices, diversion of domestic buying power to foodstuffs, and lower production costs abroad undermined the textile markets of Segovia, Cuenca, and Toledo. In the last decades of the sixteenth century, inflation and the acceptance of new varieties of cloth worked to the disadvantage of Castilian woolens. After 1610 the international market for woolens collapsed, and all the major producers— Venice, England, the Low Countries—experienced difficulties. Under these circumstances, Spanish woolens not only lost their foreign markets but were displaced from domestic markets by cheaper imports.[25]

García Sanz shows how, as the rural population of Segovia grew, it released less and less grain to the market, urban supply became erratic, and regional

22. See José Gentil da Silva, *En Espagne*, pp. 1–57; Fernand Braudel, *The Mediterranean and the Mediterranean World in the Age of Philip II*, vol. 1, pp. 293–294, 404–408; Noël Salomon, *La campagne de Nouvelle Castile à la fin du XVIe siècle*.

23. Braudel, *La Méditerranée*, vol. 1, pp. 370–371; Vicens Vives, *Manual*, pp. 301–302. Credible estimates for the 1590's run as high as 6.5 million: Domínguez Ortiz, *La sociedad española del siglo XVII*, p. 113. The presence of the trend, whatever the absolute figures, is documented by the *Relaciones Topográficas* of the 1570's, in which 234 of 370 villages responding in New Castile indicated noticeable population growth. See Gentil da Silva, *En Espagne*, pp. 21–22; Salomon, *La campagne de Nouvelle Castille*, p. 44.

24. On population density, see José Gentil da Silva, pp. 19–26, and Salomon, pp. 42–49. On reduction of the growing season, see Bennassar, *Valladolid;* and Braudel, *La Méditerranée*, vol. 1, pp. 245–252. Degradation of the soil has been suggested as a cause of decline. In the fifteenth and early sixteenth centuries the areas near Madrid were described as having good ground water, truck gardening, and forest cover. By mid-seventeenth century, the area was described as wretched, barren, and dusty. See Jose Deleito y Piñuelo, *Solo Madrid es Corte*, pp. 69–70. On forests, see J. M. Houston, *The Western Mediterranean World* (1964), pp. 114–115; and H. Hopfner, "La evolución de los bosques de Castilla la Vieja en tiempos históricos" (1954).

25. Jean Vilar, *Literatura y economía* (1973).

Table 8.1. *Population of Castilian Provinces Near Madrid, 1541 and 1591*

Province	1541	1591	Increase
Segovia (a)	33,795	41,413	23%
Guadalajara	16,157	39,901	52
Cuenca	33,341	65,368	97
Avila	31,153	37,758	21
Toledo (total)	80,957	147,549	82
Toledo (less city)	73,957	135,549	83
Madrid (total)	13,312	31,932	140
Madrid (less city)	7,312	22,391	206
Totals	208,715	363,921	66.3
Totals (less cities)	195,715	342,380	66.0

Source: Fernand Braudel, *La Méditerranée,* vol. 1, p. 370.

a. García Sanz, in *Desarrollo y crisis,* pp. 45-46, gives different estimated populations, but they are derived from the same *vecino* counts and show the same percentage of change.

markets for non-food products weakened. The smaller towns succumbed to pressure from the larger cities, which in turn were undermined by the same conditions.[26] The economies of the provincial cities were further weakened as the nobility shifted investments to government offices and annuities and to real estate in the growing capital, ultimately moving their households there.

At best the population of Castile reached a precarious equilibrium by the turn of the seventeenth century, and had declined 25% by 1646.[27] Beginning with an epidemic that killed over 500,000 people in 1596–1602, the rural population was under heavy pressure.[28] Castile lost 4,000 people yearly to America and, after 1635, as many as 12,000 men to the military, while Madrid absorbed over 4,000 young adults every year.[29] There were severe

26. García Sanz, *Desarrollo,* pp. 58–59.

27. Gonzalo Anes, *Las crises agrarias,* p. 116; Valentina Fernández Vargas—in *La población de León en el siglo XVI* (1968), pp. 135, 163—shows that León declined 30% between 1591 and 1646; Gentil da Silva, p. 110; Domínguez Ortiz, *La sociedad del siglo XVII,* p. 113.

28. On the general situation: Braudel, *La Méditerranée,* vol. 1, p. 370; Vicens Vives, *Manual,* p. 301; Gentil da Silva, pp. 106–111. Bartolomé Bennassar, *Recherches sur les grandes épidemies dans le nord de l'Espagne à la fin du XVIe siècle,* pp. 62–63, and Domínguez Ortiz, *Siglo XVII,* pp. 69, and 81, consider that the plague was serious. On the other hand, a contemporary chronicler, Antonio Rodríguez León Pinelo, in *Anales de Madrid, 1598–1621,* passes it off with the comment that *"Este año* [1599] *pico algo la peste in Castilla y en esta villa. . ."* with brief descriptions of precautions used.

29. Domínguez Ortiz, *Siglo XVII,* pp. 90–95; see also Chapter 3 above.

Table 8.2. *Estimated Population*(a) *of Castilian Towns, Sixteenth and Seventeenth Centuries*

City	1530	1594	1646	1694
Toledo	28	65	15	23
Valladolid	30	45	13.5	16.5
Salamanca	12	22	13	11
Burgos	7	12	3	8
Palencia	6	13	4	4
Avila	7	13	5	4
Medina	19	12	3	4
Segovia	14	25	(10?)	7
Totals	123	207	66.5	77.5
Madrid	20	65	150	120

Sources: Niehaus, "Population Problems," p. 44; Domínguez Ortiz, *Siglo XVII*, pp. 137-140; José Larraz López, *La época del mercantilismo en Castilla, 1500-1700* (1943), pp. 94-95; and Juan Plaza Prieto, *Estructura económica de España en el siglo XVIII* (1975), pp. 100-101.

a. Expressed in thousands. Excluding some Madrid and Valladolid figures, the estimates are based on *vecinos* multiplied by 4.5.

subsistence crises in 1606–07, the late 1620's, and the 1640's, the last two accompanied by plague in southern and possibly central Spain.[30]

Whatever the mixture of negative forces, the decline of the urban network around Madrid is apparent in the population figures for Castilian cities in Table 8.2. In the 1590's, the Castilian urban system contained 200,000 consumers in addition to the 65,000 in Madrid. A century later, the same system included only 78,000 people in addition to Madrid's population of 120,000.[31] Serious rural depopulation hit eastern Toledo and western Guadalajara provinces, although the mountain villages suffered smaller losses because of their isolation.[32] A survey of 31 towns in south-central Toledo found a total of 9,588 *vecinos* in 1590, 5,033 in 1646, and only 3,435 in 1715.[33] As urban

30. Carla Rahn Philips, "Ciudad Real in the Seventeenth Century" (paper presented to the Society for Spanish and Portuguese Historical Studies, 1972).

31. Thomas K. Niehaus, "Population Problems and Land Use in the Writings of the Spanish Arbitristas," p. 44. See also Ramón Carande, *Carlos V y sus banqueros*, vol. 1 (1965), p. 60; Anes, *Las crises agrarias*, p. 459.

32. Domínguez Ortiz, *Siglo XVII*, pp. 124–126.

33. Michael Weisser, "Crime and Subsistence: The Peasants of the *Tierra* of Toledo" (Ph. D. diss., 1972), p. 53, and "The Demography of the Heartland of New Castile, 1550–1700" (manuscript, 1974), p. 6.

demand declined and labor became scarce, agriculture shifted to crops that required less labor or were better suited to local conditions, and landlords favored livestock in the search for products that could be used or exchanged under the new situation.[34]

By 1700 the low point had been passed, and the rural population was drifting upward. The 1760's saw concern over landless transients, evidence of land hunger and enclosures in the villages, and competition for communal grazing land.[35] This was accompanied by greater vulnerability to food shortages and expansion of grain farming under traditional patterns of tenure.[36] This gave individual farmers little reason to produce beyond immediate needs, since in a landlord's rental market the landlord soon captured the benefits. If anything, productivity per acre fell as less fertile land came into use, farmsteads were fragmented, and older land was farmed more intensively. Some communities were having difficulty producing surpluses for regional markets as early as the 1750's. As a measure of the demand for farmland, pasture rents rose 150% between 1710–39 and the 1790's, while the price of the wool produced on them rose only 82%.[37] As early as 1739, townspeople near Madrid were protesting enclosure of *montes y baldíos* because it reduced pasturage for the animals used to connect their sizable bread industry with its market in Madrid.[38]

Evidence of wheat production in the provinces of Sevilla, Segovia, and Zamora shows good yields until the 1750's, a drop in the 1760's, a peak in the early 1780's, and then a pronounced decline accompanied by subsistence crises.[39] At the same time, the seed/yield ratios on the fertile and well-watered bottomland around Aranjuez fell from 1:10 in the 1770's to 1:7.5 in 1782–95. This, too, suggests expansion of cultivation onto poorer land without improvement in technique.[40] These indicators are supported by changes in production reflected in tithe returns (see Table 8.3). Cereal production rose in only 5 of the 14 areas documented. The three examples of stagnation are

---

34. Segovia is a good example; see García Sanz, *Desarrollo,* pp. 63–64.

35. Vicente Llombart Rosa, " 'Ley agraria' and 'Sociedades de agricultura' " (1976), p. 62; *La Renta Nacional,* pp. 47–48; Francisco Bustelo García del Real, "Algunos reflexiones sobre la población española de principios del siglo XVIII" and "La población española en la segunda mitad del siglo XVIII."

36. In Segovia province, the output of bread-grains per capita declined 40% from 1600 to 1800. This was partly compensated for by increases in livestock and lesser grains, but the decline is striking; see García Sanz, *Desarrollo,* pp. 84–85, 110–115.

37. Ibid., pp. 63–64, 169.

38. AHN, *Consejos,* leg. 11463.

39. Anes, *Las crises agrarias,* pp. 155–160, 430–431, 465–466.

40. Ibid., pp. 193–198, 480–481. A second example, the town of La Solana, saw its seed/yield ratio fall from 1/6 in 1720–1765 to only 1/4.5 in 1765–1807. Similar trends are documented by García Sanz, pp. 156–159, for Segovia, where late eighteenth-century yields were not different from those of the late sixteenth century.

Table 8.3. *Change in Average Annual Wheat Production in Various Locations Between 1726-41 and 1790-1808*(a)

Town	Province	Change
Granja	Zamora	−42%
Riego	Zamora	−16
Zarza	Salamanca	+92
Toro	Toro	+67
Paredes de Nava	Valladolid	+88
Villarramiel	Valladolid	+33
Valbuena de Duero	Valladolid	−17
Arévalo(b)	Segovia	+30
Bocequillas	Segovia	−9
Ajalvir	Madrid	−16
Alcalá de Henares(c)	Madrid	−12
	Palencia (a,d)	+ 4
	Toledo(d)	−1
	Sevilla(d)	−4

Source: Anes, *Las crises agrarias*, pp. 151-157.
   a. Periods averaged for Palencia, Paredes de Nava, and Villarramiel, 1728-32 and 1787-97.
   b. Terminal period for Arévalo: 1771-89.
   c. This district, now in Madrid province, was part of Toledo before 1835.
   d. Provincial averages based on scattered episcopal holdings.

composites of tithes collected throughout large dioceses. All indications of increases in output are confined to the central "breadbasket" areas of Old Castile and León.

Described as "static expansion," this situation saw population and production growth tightly linked, but neither provoked structural change.[41] The growth of rural population and diminishing returns in agriculture threatened a reduction of marketable surpluses, even as the authorities sought to increase their mobility. Thus it is not surprising that, despite slow population growth, fragmentary statistical and literary evidence shows rural stagnation lasting well past the middle of the eighteenth century.[42]

41. Llombart Rosa, "Ley agraria," p. 62. On productivity, see Anes, *Las crises agrarias,* pp. 151–157. Similar observations have been made about the Tierra de Campos in the late eighteenth century; see Peña Sánchez, *Crisis Rural,* p. 95. In Segovia, fallows were allowed to stand longer to increase grazing, even though it reduced absorption of moisture. The two-field pattern was sometimes broken with a quick-growing fodder crop. This allowed some growth in total output, but did not prevent the decline in per-capita output; see García Sanz, pp. 25–27, 218.

42. There are reports of persistent depopulation near Salamanca and Ciudad Rodrigo, and in Extremadura and Soria. Many compare the situation in the 1760's and 1770's with that of

This "static expansion" without structural change is supported by the pattern of authorized enclosures between 1755 and 1773. Of 200 permits, 183 involved conversion of forest and pasture to cultivation, while only a handful mentioned grazing or vineyards. A third of the permits requested division of the land among the *vecinos* because of local shortage of farmland. Much of the land was described as mediocre, and the process resembles that stimulated by late sixteenth-century land shortage.[43]

The static aspect of the eighteenth-century countryside should not be overstated, and it is apparent that not all enclosure was a response to local land hunger. In 17 towns the councils were changing the rental status of their *propios* to pay for public works or tax obligations.[44] Even more intriguing are the enclosures leased as large open fields. This suggests capitalist farming, as do 21 enclosures by religious institutions, wealthy *labradores,* and titled nobles. These cases hardly offset the volume of conversions that simply extended village subsistence economies, and clearly the rural situation was complex. In particular, the enclosures by nobles sometimes involved over 2,000 *fanegas* of land in two or three communities. It is hard to escape the conclusion that these were management decisions reflecting a changing grain market.[45]

This is also suggested by the geographic distribution of enclosure, which was concentrated in regions linked to Madrid's supply system. The 142 enclosures that could be located produced the regional distribution given in Table 8.4. Nevertheless, it appears a weak response to the progressively more intense supply crises in the capital and an ever-widening search for rural surpluses that could be channeled toward urban consumption.[46]

---

the late seventeenth century; see Anes, *Las crises agrarias,* pp. 142–144, 166–185, 462. Birth and death trends for 8 towns, 2 in New Castile and 6 in Old Castile, suggest an increasing population base in one town for each region, a decreasing base in one for each region, and no discernible change in the remaining 4.

43. Already in 1750, beginning date of the preceding sample, there were numerous complaints by graziers about these enclosures: AHN, *Consejos,* leg. 11450; García Sanz, pp. 148–154.

44. This is a little-studied topic, and may be another aspect of subsistence enclosure. In the 1750's, intermittent rural food shortages become noticeable, forcing towns to buy grain, committing income from their *propios* to pay the necessary loans. One source names 33 towns, many quite substantial, forced to this by the crisis of 1753: AHN, *Consejos,* leg. 11489.

45. Based on Anes, *Las crises agrarias,* p. 459; the actual registers in AHN, *Consejos,* leg. 4184; and personal notes from that source provided by Professor Anes. The problem of landlord adjustment to the market needs more study—since, while it may have been marginal income for most, examples keep appearing. Conversely, in Segovia, rental terms were unchanged through all the conjunctural shifts between 1500 and 1800. Moreover, the government of the eighteenth century tended to protect the peasants in the courts, while landlords complained of fragmentation of leaseholds and the difficulty of collecting rent; see García Sanz, pp. 296, 308–309, 319.

46. Anes, *Las crises agrarias,* pp. 401–422.

Table 8.4. *Regional Distribution of 142 Enclosures, 1755-1773*

Region	No. of Enclosures	Percentage of Total
Crown of Aragón	18	12.5%
Andalucía	16	11.5
Extremadura	33	23.0
Madrid hinterland (New Castile and Segovia)	53	37.0
Remaining provinces	22	16.0
Totals	142	100.0%

Source: Based on Anes, *Las crises agrarias*, p. 459.

II. Regional Market Structures

Contrary to the strong impression that the Castilian interior was characterized by structural rigidity and local isolation, the preceding section indicates the presence of numerous links with the urban market. Those links were part of an institutional structure sustained by the need to provide an adequate urban supply and to prevent urban unrest. They provided the context for evolution of a Madrid-oriented supply system driven by market forces. By the end of the eighteenth century, Liberal economics, the rising cost of administrated supply, and massive war debts were pushing the monarchy toward abandonment of all government subsidies and administered commodity flows.[47]

Despite the static appearance of the rural economy, the urban supply network could not have functioned without mechanisms for exchanging and accumulating commodities in the countryside. In practice, the interior combined local and long-distance markets with various nonmarket arrangements that consolidated supplies which then became potentially marketable. The principal channels for consolidation of stocks were tithe collections, including the share owned by the Crown; rents in kind from land; and accumulation by religious communities and farmers working the soil themselves.[48] Purchases for military supply reflected local market prices, but were the result of political rather than market-inspired decisions. In the early phases of Madrid's growth particularly, the city's recurrent forays into more distant markets had

47. Jacques Barbier, "Peninsular Finance and Colonial Trade: The Dilemma of Charles IV's Spain," pp. 4–8.

48. These are part of a six-item list in Anes' discussion of the grain trade in *Las crises agrarias*, pp. 340–350.

the same quality. Tithes, rents, and direct exploitation provided the basic stock of commodities available outside rural households and transferable outside local communities.

Working at odds with the accumulation of staples for regional exchange and export were the local granaries and charitable agencies that attempted to insure peasant communities against recurrent crop failure. Spain had a tradition of municipal grain depots endowed as charitable public services. These *pósitos* held capital assets, maintained stocks of grain that they loaned to farmers, and charged a nominal interest to cover their costs. The Crown encouraged these depots during the eighteenth century, creating a *Superintendencia de Pósitos*. This system expanded rapidly after 1750, as benefactors endowed a truly impressive policy of organized grain-hoarding.[49] Designed to help the small farmer, these agencies tied up substantial assets and large inventories of wheat. By 1800, many smallholders were dependent on these agencies. Between 1751 and 1793, while the population of Castile rose 25%, granary reserves almost doubled—from 5,400,000 bushels to 9,300,000 bushels—and reached 15%-20% of annual consumption.[50] This development helps explain the relative tranquility of the countryside that Callahan finds so striking in eighteenth-century Spain.[51]

The *pósitos* were thus a major part of the grain market, absorbing ever more of the yield of good harvests and buffering the countryside against bad ones. While this stabilization of rural grain supplies helps explain rural stability, it also meant that the countryside competed with Madrid for available supplies and cut into the stocks available for commercialization. To the extent that they moderated price fluctuations, granary reserves also reduced the rentier's ability to profit from his accumulated stocks. This no doubt contributed to contemporary criticism that rentier ownership contributed little to the development of an agricultural sector that could export to the cities and to distant markets in return for goods and services. It has even been suggested that the deregulation of the grain trade after 1765 encouraged this hoarding, because speculative grain accumulation, an aspect of market development, aggravated price instability and encouraged protective accumulation.[52] Thus, while the *pósitos* absorbed a growing volume of rural surpluses, they were part of the pattern of regional self-sufficiency and mitigated against the development of a national market.

49. Gonzalo Anes Álvarez, "Los pósitos en la España del siglo XVIII" (1968), pp. 50–54.
50. Peña Sánchez, *Crisis rural*, p. 91.
51. Consumption was 50–60,000,000 bushels, assuming 5 bushels per capita per year. Madrid itself consumed around 1.1 million bushels annually. William J. Callahan, in "Caridad, sociedad y economía en el siglo XVIII" (1978), suggests that the urban unrest of the early nineteenth century is connected with the dismantling of this welfare system.
52. Romero de Solis, *La población*, pp. 111–115.

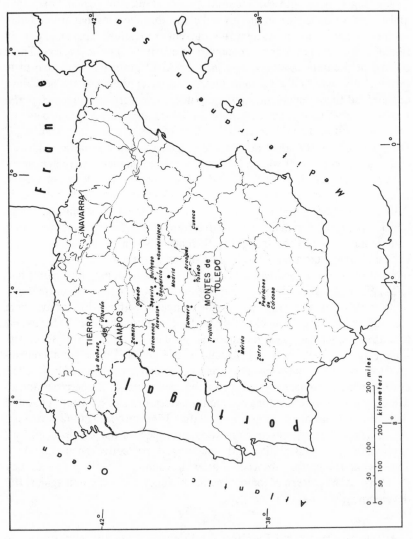

Map 8.1 *Locations Cited in Chapter 8*

Operating alongside the redistributive agencies of society and the state, two genuine market structures persisted. One, based on fairs and clearing centers such as Trujillo, Arévalo, Sangarcía, Villalón, La Bañeza, and Illescas, concentrated surpluses for sale to the world of urban demand and exports (for geographic detail, see Map 8.1 and Chapter 9, Section II). Most of these goods traveled to complementary interior regions or to the modest provincial cities, and they rarely moved more than 50–75 miles. Overall, however, the network produced limited exports to the coast to pay for a modest flow of luxuries and manufactures for distribution at interior fairs. The second market network took the form of numerous weekly *mercados* and facilitated local and district self-sufficiency. This pattern has been documented for the Tierra de Campos, in the province of Segovia, the *señorío* of Buitrago, and elsewhere. The conflict of interests between local residents benefiting from one or another level of transaction is an important part of the problem of rural response to urban demand.[53]

This tension is most clearcut in the case of the much-maligned wool industry. Since wool was the most easily marketable commodity of the interior, it was a perennially important factor in the behavior of people able to divert land to grazing. For centuries, wool was Spain's principal export and source of foreign exchange. Thus it is hardly surprising that much of the interior was committed to pastures by the landed elite. Wool production was highly monetized, with money rentals for pasture, money wages for the labor force, and profits in hard currency. Wool exports rose during the eighteenth century, and in 1795 two-thirds went to England. To keep things in perspective, we should note that the 277,000 *arrobas* of wool exported in 1795 brought a return of 80 million *reales*.[54] While this is barely half the value of agricultural commodities consumed by Madrid each year, it explains why even modest landowners and tenants maintained surprisingly large flocks despite scarce grazing. It was the best way of participating in the regional and long-distance economy.[55]

Compared with the wool trade or the Madrid supply market, exports of staples like wheat and wine were modest. Quantities were traded between complementary locales within Castile, and some reached the Cantabrian

53. Peña Sánchez, *Crisis rural*, p. 88; García Sanz, p. 177; Artola, *El Señorío de Buitrago*, pp. 117–123.
54. Phillips, "Spanish Wool Exports," table; Antonio Matilla Tascón, ed., *Balanza de comercio exterior en 1795*, pp. 7, 89.
55. Peña Sánchez, *Crisis rural*, p. 79. Helen Nader made the same comments about the province of Guadalajara at a seminar at the University of California, San Diego, in 1979. Another little-explored aspect is the seaport demand for meat. Grain was readily imported by sea, but livestock came from the interior. Seventeenth-century Valencia, for example, consumed 80,000 sheep from the *meseta* every year; see Casey, *The Kingdom of Valencia*, p. 79.

Mountains in the north,[56] but the coasts of Asturias and Galicia made up deficits in local production with wine imported from Catalonia, Andalucía, or France. In Galicia, outside of the most localized exchanges, only cattle were traded (to Madrid and Castile) for a few Palencian and Segovian textiles.[57]

The wheat trade was slightly more important, especially in the nineteenth century. A modest export of wheat and flour from Old Castile developed at the end of the eighteenth century, involving 100–150,000 *fanegas* yearly destined for the military, but this clearly taxed the market for disposable supplies.[58] The north coast towns sometimes used Castilian wheat, but their deficits were greatest when Castile had the least grain to spare and everyone was importing from abroad.[59] A flour-milling industry and export trade appeared around Santander, but late eighteenth-century exports accounted for only 10–20,000 *fanegas* of Castilian wheat yearly, in contrast to the 750,000–1,000,000 consumed by Madrid. Even this trade decayed after the Restoration in 1814, as grain producers and merchants in Palencia complained about the decay of the Reinosa highway to Santander.[60] Grain exports were briefly important in the nineteenth century as the Canal of Castile cheapened transport and grazing land was put under cultivation.[61] But this hardly compensated for the decline of wool as a cash crop,[62] and it can be argued that the interior was becoming even more isolated.

Thus Madrid loomed very large in Castilian exchanges outside the context of regional self-sufficiency, and only the wool trade offered much alternative. Exports of wheat and wool from Castile to the outside world were really adjuncts to a Madrid-based network for turning agricultural commodities into disposable wealth.

Both regional and long-distance trade depended heavily on the politically

56. Ringrose, *Transportation,* map 3.

57. Antonio Mejide Pardo, *Economía marítima de la Galicia cantábrica en el siglo XVIII* (1971), pp. 103–104; Pedro Antonio Sánchez, *La economía gallega* (1973, written in the 1790's), pp. 24, 127–142.

58. In 1786, military contractors relied on the yield to the government of the *gracia y escusado,* a resource that had often been a back-up reserve for the Madrid bread supply. The contract for 1786 involved 200–240,000 *fanegas* of wheat (14.5 million daily rations of bread) and 340,000 *fanegas* of barley. Only a part of this was to be drawn from Castile: Archivo del Banco de España, *Memorias de la Quinta Junta General* of the Bank of San Carlos, December 1786, leg. 454. See also Capella and Matilla, *Los Cinco Gremios,* pp. 56, 197–201.

59. Mejide Pardo, *Economía marítima de Galicia,* p. 106. Essentially the same pattern appears in seventeenth-century Valencia; see Casey, p. 79.

60. Vicente Palacio Atard, *El comercio de Castilla y el puerto de Santander en el siglo XVIII* (1959), p. 149; Archivo de la Sociedad Económica de Madrid, leg. 247–16.

61. Peña Sánchez, *Crisis rural,* pp. 102–103. Miguel de Terán, in "Santander," pp. 746–757, indicates that flour exports ran 12,250–25,000 tons between 1818 and the 1840's.

62. The late eighteenth century saw the merino strain acclimatized in France, Germany, and England. England cut its demand by two-thirds in the 30 years after 1795; see Jordi Nadal Oller, *El fracaso de la revolución industrial en España* (1975), pp. 78–79.

created wealth of the capital city. By the nineteenth century, the disparity between Madrid and the other urban markets of the interior had become even more pronounced. The combined population of 15 Castilian cities and towns increased by 40,000 between 1797 and 1860 (from 123,300 to 163,900), but virtually all of the growth was confined to Valladolid and Burgos. Valladolid developed as Old Castile's regional market center, Burgos as the transit point between Castile and Vizcaya. In the same period, Madrid alone added 100,-000 people, reaching 300,000 inhabitants in 1860.[63]

Within this amalgam of nonmarket transfers, local exchanges, limited exports, and a politically supported market for staples, we can see the basis for a mercantile community. Many urban residents extended their investments from various mercantile occupations to the urban supply trade. Francisco Cabarrús is but the most spectacular example of activities long dominated by the retail merchants of the Five Major Guilds *(Cinco Gremios Mayores)*. As individuals, through guild-based companies, and through the *Compañia General de Comercio* sponsored jointly by the *Cinco Gremios*, these merchants enlarged their activities far beyond their origins. They formed numerous partnerships; they held deposits at interest; they farmed municipal taxes; and they extended credit to private borrowers, the city, and the Crown. They had a long-standing interest in urban supply, and in the 1780's undertook management of the whole municipal supply system. The merchants of the *Cinco Gremios* were part of a community of supply contractors, grain merchants, wealthy brokers, and business agents at the center of a web of fiscal, credit, and commercial links with the agricultural interior and the maritime world. One of the ironies of this growing sophistication is that the *Cinco Gremios,* involved in both commercial circuits, were instrumental in shifting urban demand from interior to distant suppliers, providing one of the mechanisms that precluded urban growth from stimulating the economy of the Castilian hinterland.[64]

The *Cinco Gremios* were but part of a community of wholesalers, administrators, business agents, and contractors in the city—a community that was extended across the countryside and its regional exchange systems by the government system of purchasing agents, transport controls, and pasture allocations. Reaching beyond the readily commercialized areas within 75 miles of the city, this system drew in wheat, hogs, cattle, sheep, and charcoal while creating a pool of men informed about market and supply conditions from Córdoba to Palencia to Galicia. This expertise was easily transferred to

63. F. Garrido, *España contemporánea* (1865), vol. 1, pp. 490–491.

64. Capella and Matilla, in *Los Cinco Gremios Mayores,* summarize their early development and commercial interests on pp. 42–43 and document their growing sophistication on pp. 210–215.

private entrepreneurs, and government agents sometimes entered trade on their own. The muleteers of Sangarcía in Segovia long provided transport for the Castilian wheat owned by the Madrid *Pósito,* but after the liberalization of the grain trade they went into business on their own. They evolved a tight local association that included 20 sedentary merchants who used their own capital and hired local carriers and Castilian agents. By the end of the century, they handled 30,000 *fanegas* of wheat annually and were accused of speculation and manipulating prices in Madrid. They signify an important extension of Madrid's private grain market into northern supply areas, one made possible by government initiatives.[65]

Developments like this: the Galician cattle trade; the Andalusian oil trade; the livestock fairs at Mérida, Trujillo, La Bañeza, and Talavera; the grain markets at Villalón, Olmedo, Arévalo, Navalcarnero, Guadalajara, and Illescas; the wholesale grain dealers in towns around the capital; and the efforts of livestock, olive oil, soap, and charcoal producers to penetrate the urban market, all point to the evolution of a network of commercial arrangements focused on Madrid (Map 8.1). Thus it was that the long-term maintenance of Madrid as capital and the administrative diversion of Castilian commodities to the city encouraged a self-propelled market network that required only consistent support for the economy of the city.[66]

An outstanding example of someone who emerged from the Old Regime blend of public and private commercial life is Juan de Álvarez y Mendizabal, Prime Minister in 1836 and sponsor of the disentailment of monastic lands. Born of a Cádiz merchant family, he was involved in contracting military supplies for the Cádiz government of 1808–12, and by 1819 was partner with the Valencian supply contractor Vicente Bertrán de Lis in supplying Ferdinand VII's army of Andalucía. In the 1830's he emerged as a leading Liberal politician and financier, providing a choice example of how the internal supply network of the eighteenth century produced important elements of Spain's nineteenth-century leadership.[67]

Under men like Mendizábal, nineteenth-century Spain saw the wholesale abolition of institutions they considered obsolete. The process had begun much earlier, and its acceleration was partly due to an internal power vacuum. This left the field open to potential and actual participants who had

65. García Sanz, pp. 72–73, 182–184; see also Anes, *Las crises agrarias,* pp. 340–350. This parallels the development, after 1750, of peninsula-wide luxury trade by the *arrieros* of León; see José Luis Martín Galindo, "Evolución agrícola y ganadería en Maragatería" (1957), p. 118.

66. García Sanz says something like this, on pp. 191–193 and 326, in attempting to show the presence of a Castilian bourgeoisie which could help explain the "bourgeois revolution" of the nineteenth century. He comes closer than most to grasping the evolution of the Madrid-based network of relationships involved, but is hampered by his focus on events in the provinces.

67. Peter Janke, *Mendizábal y la instauración de la monarquía constitucional en España* (1974), pp. 5–9.

found the system of concessions discriminatory and uncomfortable. Favoring an unregulated market, they endorsed ideological and institutional arrangements that implied deregulation. A symptom of this change is seen in the fact that beginning as early as 1803, state sales of land authorized the new owners to expel tenants or raise rents. The new nineteenth-century proprietors thus threatened the isolation of rural communities, while the sale of municipal land weakened the autonomy of local government and pushed many small farmers toward dependence on day-labor.[68] Despite these hints of change, the underlying structures that tied city and hinterland together were little affected. They reflect the dominance of Madrid as consumer of the disposable surpluses of the entire interior from the Cantabrian Mountains to the Sierra Morena and from the Portuguese border to the Kingdom of Aragón.

III. The Producers in the Market Network

Our final step in tracing the urban market system back to the rural society that supplied it requires a look at the people who had surpluses to sell. The sellers are easy to identify, at least in general terms; how they acquired their surpluses is a much more complicated problem. The documents contain several accounts listing people who sold wheat and livestock to the city market. The livestock transactions have a relatively modern air, but this is because distance and geography did not hamper long-distance livestock marketing as much as transfers of less mobile commodities. It is important to recall the relative importance of the commodities in Madrid's supply trade. Around 1800, beef and mutton sales reached 30 million *reales* and charcoal about 6 million, but a conservative estimate would put the grain trade at well over 60 million *reales*.

The meat supply was the center of two distinct markets. As of 1797–98, 45% of sheep and 39% of cattle were sold directly to the Madrid stockyards by private parties, indicating a sizable direct-market response. The remainder were purchased by government agents at regional livestock fairs.[69] Direct sales to the slaughteryards were dominated by a few large suppliers. A typical monthly account in 1798 shows that 31 vendors provided 902 cattle, but 55% of that total came from a single source in the form of four weekly consignments—and because of the high prices his stock commanded, that purveyor captured a considerably larger share of the sale revenue. Seven others supplied more than ten cattle each, some appearing as regular participants in the market; the other 23 individuals in the sample, many from carting communities around the country, supplied 9% of the total, usually at

68. Nadal Oller, *El fracaso,* pp. 57–67 and 84; the evidence on this is sketchy.
69. There are detailed accounts of purchases of the total supply for the year running from mid-1797 to mid-1789 in AHN, *Consejos,* leg. 6785.

lower prices. Clearly they were disposing of worn-out or surplus draft animals while in the city. Sheep sales show a similar pattern, with one of 12 vendors providing 36% of 9,236 animals, again in weekly shipments. Six other individuals sold more than 500 sheep each and provided 49% of the total; the remaining 15% came from smaller shipments, one being only 98 head.[70]

This reveals a private market serving a supply concession that, while dominated by two large vendors who were probably brokers, did not exclude smaller participants. The two major purveyors were doing business at the rate of 250–400,000 *reales* monthly, a very substantial business for the time. It is worth noting that the last name of the major cattle supplier—Aguirre—is the same as that of the treasurer of the municipal supply office of the *Cinco Gremios Mayores,* the meat-supply contractor at the time. The summary account of the previous year also shows three entries, totaling over 1,000 cattle, from two Basque firms importing similarly expensive cattle from Navarra and France.

Meanwhile, 55% of sheep and 61% of cattle were purchased by meat-supply agents visiting regional livestock fairs in Trujillo, Salamanca, Zamora, Pedroches de Córdoba, Torremocha, Zafra, and La Bañeza. A detailed account of the purchase of 2,276 cattle at the Trujillo fair in 1798 (see Table 8.5) provides an idea of the types of suppliers participating in such local markets. Sales ranged from 5 to 183 head, the latter a transaction of 125,000 *reales*. There were more than 75 head of cattle involved in 9 out of 45 sales, and the sellers included three titled nobles and the monastery at Guadalupe; they provided 44% of the cattle bought at the fair and, because of the quality of their livestock, received nearly half of the proceeds.

The fairs, and the government supply agents using them, obviously were a conduit between urban demand and provincial landed elites. The entire livestock business was within a cash context that involved even small stockraisers and thus provided a common orientation for both landed nobility and the lesser landed elements in this segment of the economy. It also fits with the widespread prevalence of livestock even in farming areas such as the Tierra de Campos and Segovia.[71]

There is, however, a suggestive contrast between the regional fairs and the sales at Madrid. The fairs brought relatively modest vendors into contact with official buyers who directed stock to Madrid. This provided provincial elites with an economic link to Madrid that also had a political component, one which took responsibility for risks and costs on the long trip to the final

70. Ibid., leg. 6786.
71. In Buitrago, for example, aside from the absentee Infantados, 17 stock-raisers shared 600,000 *reales* from the sale of meat and wool outside the district: Artola, *El Señorío de Buitrago,* pp. 134–137. For another impressive list of flocks, see Marqués del Saltillo, "Ganaderos sorianos del siglo XVIII" (1952), pp. 387–389.

Table 8.5. *Sales of Cattle at Trujillo Fair,
1798*

No. of Cattle Sold	No. of Sellers
1-20	10
21-40	16
41-75	10
76 and above	9
Total no. of sellers	45

destination. The transactions at Madrid were dominated by commercial middlemen who consolidated and directed livestock privately. Either arrangement was probably viable, but they posed different conditions. Private brokering needed private capital and required rural vendors to adjust to dependence on market arrangements that they were less able to influence, weakening one of the subtle links between provincial elite and traditional government.

Scattered granary accounts provide similar valuable information about the people who had wheat to sell and the nature of the wheat market that was within reasonable transport distance from the city. Other accounts document the types of suppliers participating in a long-distance supply network where transfer costs required political intervention to establish the flow of commodities to the urban consumer. Together they provide some insights into the supply milieu of the inner and outer of the three wheat-market zones identified in Chapter 7. Illescas, south of Madrid, has been identified as a grain-marketing center in this study, and we have an account by the agent of the *Pósito* based in neighboring Getafe in 1785 of purchases in the nearby towns of Villamanrique, Estremera, Fuentidueña, and Belinchón (see Table 8.6).[72] The size distribution of these transactions confirms that many peasants made occasional small grain sales, but that otherwise the grain trade was concentrated in the hands of a few landlords and *labradores ricos*.

These figures show an extremely high degree of concentration of disposable surpluses. This concentration is probably much higher than the concentration of landholding, since the small landholders required all but a minuscule share of their crop for their own use, plus tithes, taxes, and rent, and were less likely to be in the market at all. The average sale was 98 *fanegas*, worth about 4,000 *reales* at current prices, but half the actual transactions were 30 *fanegas* or less. At the other extreme, 10% of the transactions, ranging from 10,000 to 80,000 *reales*, accounted for half the total.

72. AHN, *Consejos*, leg. 11470.

Table 8.6. *Grain Sales in Four Towns of New Castile, 1785*

Size of Transaction	No. of Sellers
0-20 *fanegas*	25
21-50	25
51-100	11
101-150	4
151-250	3
251-500	3
2000	1
Total no. of sellers	72

Source: AHN, *Consejos*, leg. 11470.

This reveals a hierarchy similar to those found in peasant villages every-where in western Europe.[73] The most immediate examples are the sixteenth-century villages of the Montes de Toledo 50 miles south of Madrid, where the wealthiest 20% of landholders controlled almost 50% of the land and over 50% of the harvest.[74] The distribution in the sixteenth century appears less extreme than the cases we are considering, but by the end of the seventeenth century the inequalities in land distribution had become more extreme and thus more closely approximate our eighteenth-century example.

In the two largest villages, the economic hierarchy appears to parallel a social one. In Fuentidueña, where sales totaled 1,310 *fanegas*, seven of the eight largest sales were by people with the same patronym (Sánchez) and totaled 958 *fanegas*. Moreover, they were linked with two matronyms to additional vendors accounting for another 157 *fanegas*. The situation was similar in Belinchón, where sales totaled 2,779 *fanegas:* five residents with the patronym Salazar were the five largest vendors and sold a total of 1,500 *fanegas.* While we cannot know the degree to which these wealthier *la-bradores ricos* were really farmers or rentiers, it is probable that they domi-nated village politics and the management of communal properties. A number of these large vendors merited the honorific *Don*, but only in the case

73. Spanish variants include seventeenth-century Valencia, where, beneath the señorial elite, villages were controlled by a few *labradores* with relatively large holdings. There the tendency had been enhanced by sale of *morisco* lands. In livestock-oriented Buitrago, 5% of resident families received half of all income; see Casey, pp. 44–45, and Artola, *El Señorío de Buitrago,* pp. 134–141. And in a transaction involving wine, a single *labrador* paid 10,000 *reales* per year to rent sequestered Jesuit vineyards near Alcalá de Henares: AHN, *Clero, Jesuitas,* leg. 215–3.

74. Michael R. Weisser, *The Peasants of the Montes* (1976), pp. 37–53, and personal letters. The parallel is close, since 70–80% of harvest value was in grain in this area.

of Doña Teresa Estebán Martínez, with 2,000 *fanegas* of wheat at her disposal, can we be reasonably sure of dealing with a rentier landlord.

This pattern of sales suggests that a sizable number of farmers on occasion participated in the market, but that in any given town a slight decline in the quality of the crop restricted potential vendors to a very short list. As the distance to market became greater, the costs inherent in dealing in small quantities restricted the trade to larger producers, leaving the others out of the market.

The above picture is modified slightly by a second set of *Pósito* accounts. Between January 1 and 15, 1785, the *Pósito* purchased at its doors 229 shipments of wheat totaling 11,371 *fanegas* (see Table 8.7). As the maps in Chapter 9 show, most of these came from within 50 miles of the capital, although some of the largest originated in the southeast, where a number of professional transporters resided. The average shipment here was about 50 *fanegas*, half that of the preceding account, while half of the shipments were less than 41 *fanegas*. The upper limit reflects the nature of professional transport, which restricted such transactions to the cargo of a large *recua* (70 mules) or a *cuadrilla* of 30 *carretas*.[75] The number of small shipments suggests villagers with small surpluses taking advantage of slack time in the crop cycle to bring grain (or send it with neighbors) to market. Such small and dispersed quantities and short distances were not interesting to professional transporters; but as an activity marginal to agriculture, it yielded a net benefit to a household as long as the return exceeded the extra costs of travel to market.[76]

These examples suggest that agriculture around Madrid was linked to the urban market in ways that, given the structure of that market, were not conducive to rural change. As every essay on the Spanish countryside (and on peasant villages in most of western Europe) asserts, much of the land was exploited in small plots that gave the peasant only occasional surpluses. Thus a large part of the land and rural population were locked into subsistence farming. The producer most likely to respond to new market incentives was the wealthy peasant who, even in a poor crop year, had a few hundred, or even just a few dozen, bushels of grain to sell. The incentive to expand this part of his economy was, however, limited by the nature of the Madrid market. Moreover, the eighteenth century saw rural population growth that encouraged regional subsistence economies, and was abetted in this by the Crown's encouragement of supply stability via village granaries. The logical outcome was the withdrawal of smaller producers from the market. This also helps

75. Such convoys were common, but the upper limit of a shipment was 250–300 *fanegas:* Ringrose, *Transportation,* pp. 58–68.
76. Ibid., p. 122.

Table 8.7. *Grain Purchases by the Grain Depot of Madrid, January 1785*

Size of Purchase	No. of Sellers
0-20 *fanegas*	55
21-50	95
51-100	63
101-150	7
151-250	7
251-500	1
Total no. of sellers	228

Source: AHN, *Consejos*, leg. 11470.

explain much of the enclosure we have observed, and possibly also declining yields, as measured by tithes.

As we have seen, because of the structure of Madrid's economy and distribution of income, even among the Castilian monocultures the choices for profit-motivated response narrowed whenever maritime Spain prospered and the capital grew. Thus, while the English landlord and his tenant farmers could introduce convertible husbandry, forage crops, and new rotations, because their market absorbed the produce, their Castilian counterparts had little option but to extend existing monocultures and stock-raising. Even that response brought tension between the two, and stagnation of alternatives such as viticulture.

At the same time, the *labradores ricos* could at best follow the Prussian rather than the English model. This implied accumulating grain using the traditional techniques of renting out pastures to farmers, raising rents, manipulating communal lands, and using señorial prerogatives to strengthen rural authority. This attempt to create marketable stocks thus interacted with the development of minifundia as population growth brought division of leaseholds among heirs, further increasing the polarization of village economies.[77] The village oligarchs of the eighteenth century were obvious participants in this structure of local power, and became more prominent as the landed elite reintegrated in the nineteenth century.[78] In the region within 75–100 miles of the city, supply commerce was dominated by a private-sector network, and the link between these prosperous *labradores* and the middlemen of the capital formed another part of the evolving agro-commercial oligarchy of nineteenth-century Spain.

77. García Sanz, p. 262.
78. Richard Herr, "Spain."

What then of the perennial connections between Madrid and Old Castile? While there are important similarities, individual sales were typically much larger and the sellers more prominent in the Castilian elite. The earliest details come from an account of 1630–31 that combines the activity of a number of purchasing agents with varying degrees of detail. A full third of the 77,624 *fanegas* of wheat accounted for was bought from the traditional rentier elite: eight titled nobles, two bishoprics, and parts of the Crown's share of Church tithes.[79] A second account, from 1665, details the purchase of 30,490 *fanegas* well enough to reveal the size distribution of the transactions. While confined to a smaller area, the Tierra de Campos, it appears to reflect the same pattern as the accounts of 35 years earlier (see Table 8.8).

Excluding two entries that appear to refer to middlemen, 30 vendors provided an average of 872 *fanegas* of wheat each, while the 5 largest sold half the total, or 15,000 *fanegas*. More than half of all transactions exceeded 400 *fanegas*, more than ten times the average size of agent purchases near Madrid. The prominence of señorial and clerical sellers in these two accounts indicates an important link between the señorial regime and urban supply in the seventeenth century.

Accounts from the late eighteenth century indicate that authorities had broadened and deepened their penetration of regional markets. From Olmedo, midway between Valladolid and Segovia, we have a list of transactions dated 1767. The scale of transaction in this case was similar to those of Belinchón and Fuentidueña, although the distance to Madrid was considerably greater. One of the 12 vendors was an untitled absentee, the first and third largest appear to be *labradores* of the village, four were convents, and two were titled nobles, while only three vendors, including the two smallest, were simply farmers. This was a bad crop year, and the smaller producers have disappeared from the market, leaving only rent recipients and operators of larger farms with marketable surpluses.

The seventeenth-century link between urban supply and landed aristocracy reappears in a fragmentary account extending from 1766 to 1770. The documents record 100–200,000 *fanegas* of wheat a year, and separately cite large purchases negotiated directly with rentiers who appear to live in Madrid. These transactions include the purchase of 13,370 *fanegas* of wheat from the Countess of Campo Alange and 5,273 from the Duke of Alba from two harvests; 1,878 *fanegas* from the Count of Cifuentes in 1770; 3,766 from the Cathedral Chapter of Toledo; and 11,576 from the sequestered Jesuit

79. Because of the aggregate nature of many of the account entries, this is only a minimum figure for participation by rentier landowners and institutions: derived from AVM, *Contaduria,* sigs. 2–103–1 and 3–580–1. Among the key figures were the Count of Grajal, the Marquis of Bayona, the Count of Villanueva de la Cañada, and the Bishoprics of Palencia and Valladolid.

Table 8.8. *Grain Sales in Tierra
de Campos, 1665*

Size of Transaction	No. of Sellers
0-250 *fanegas*	9
251-500	9
501-1000	7
1001-2500	4
4000	1
Total no. of sellers	30

Source: AVM, *Secretaria*, sig. 2-106-28.

properties in Old and New Castile.[80] These are not insignificant transactions, since, at prevailing prices, 13,000 *fanegas* of wheat were worth over 600,000 *reales*, more than the annual income of many Spanish grandees.

The link between urban supply and the señorial regime is further documented in an account of 140,000 *fanegas* purchased in 1779–81; 90,000 *fanegas* came from the *escusados* (ecclesiastical income reserved for the Crown), and 30,000 were sold by 13 titled nobles including the Count of Altamira, the Duke of Abrantes, the Marquis of Almarza, the Duke of Osma, and the king's brother, the Infante Don Luis. Six of the sales were between 2,000–7,800 *fanegas*, the latter representing 400,000 *reales* at prevailing prices. It is interesting to note that by the fall of 1781 the price had fallen from 50 to 35 *reales* per *fanega*, and there is not a trace of these public-spirited citizens in the accounts.[81]

Taken together, this handful of accounts shows the *Pósito* involved in several exchange networks. The granary itself was a center of a local market for surpluses from the surrounding region, and occasionally used agents to draw upon that source more directly. The central granary purchased ecclesiastic and royal stocks accumulated as tithes and *escusados*, and negotiated purchases from individual aristocrats resident in Madrid. Finally, the *Pósito* penetrated the grain market of Old Castile through the use of buying agents who consolidated local supplies and arranged for their shipment to Madrid at government cost. In the 1760's and 1770's, as in the seventeenth century, the larger religious, royal, and noble reserves became prominent whenever grain became scarce.

Judging from surviving accounts, by the end of the 1780's the purchasing system had penetrated more deeply into the rural economy of Old Castile.

80. AHN, *Consejos*, leg. 6775–26, 52, 58; see also Anes, *Las crises agrarias*, p. 362.
81. AHN, *Consejos*, leg. 6775–3.

This is exemplified by the Olmedo account of 1766, but is better illustrated by one final example, an account that details the purchase of 31,800 *fanegas* by a single agent in the Tierra de Campos in 1788 (see Table 8.9). It includes no titled nobility or absentees, but the 60 vendors included 6 priests and vicars and 35 persons with the honorific *Don*. The average sale was 530 *fanegas*, and 50% of sales were larger than 330, implying a sizable farmstead or estate; 14 of the 60 vendors provided 51% of the total, in quantities matching those of all but three or four of the previously cited aristocrats. Only three sales were smaller than 100 *fanegas*, omitting small farmers like those who reached the Madrid market from its nearby hinterland. A comparison with the accounts from Belinchón and Fuentidueña indicates that the purchasing network in Old Castile touched only those rentiers and farmers who were the economic equivalent of the few *labradores ricos* at the top of the local hierarchies in our New Castilian examples. Even in the Tierra de Campos, granary of Old Castile, only 4 of 27 towns produced more than three transactions on that scale, and one of those was Villalón, a regional market where 20% of all the transactions in the account took place.

This pattern is verified by the economic structure of the villages in the area. In five villages near Villalón, the distribution of sales is clearly reflected in the distribution of access to land: 37% of the land was actually owned by farmers, 75% of all farms had less than 5 hectares, and 88% less than 10. A family of five, allowing for seed, tithes, rent, and bread-grain, required about 25 hectares to be self-sufficient in grain and 30 to supply other necessities as well. Only one in ten farms actually exceeded 20 hectares, and only a few—typically one per village—could yield 300 *fanegas* for the market in an ordinary crop year. Under these conditions, small farms were forced into a marginal viticulture to generate cash income. The larger grain sales inevitably

Table 8.9. *Grain Sales in Old Castile, 1788*

Size of Transaction	No. of Sellers
0-100 *fanegas*	3
101-200	13
201-500	23
501-1000	11
1001-1500	9
1900	1
Total no. of sellers	60

Source: AHN, *Consejos*, leg. 11470.

represent not only the crop of the seller himself but grain acquired as rents, tithes, and privately owned *tercias* ceded by the Crown.[82]

IV. Conclusion

With these findings, we get not only a confirmation of our general perception of wealth and land distribution of Castilian villages, and of the relationship of the rentier elements to the countryside, but also an idea of the specific mechanisms that channeled rural surpluses into urban markets, particularly that of Madrid. For livestock, two parallel systems had evolved, one in which private middlemen used their own networks to deliver meat animals directly to the city, another in which public authorities (often the same purveyors operating with government concessions) linked regional livestock fairs with urban demand. Under these arrangements, the herds and flocks of graziers of all sizes were integrated into a Madrid-oriented market network.

For wheat, transport difficulties created a more complex hierarchy of networks. Within economically feasible distances of Madrid, very small to very large producers routinely brought their surpluses to market themselves, with the help of neighbors, or by hiring professional transporters. Any given town, however, contained only a handful of farmers with farms large enough to allow regular participation on a scale that made the returns an important part of the household or village economy. The structure of surviving accounts and the discussions surrounding the deregulation of the grain trade make it clear that the bakers and millers of the city obtained a large share of their supplies from a private network that tapped these sources inside a radius of 75–100 miles of Madrid.

To attract supplies from beyond that radius, other arrangements were needed. A corps of purchasing agents, similar to those for the meat supply, traveled throughout Castile buying up the output of the two or three major farmers and rentiers in each village and dealing with resident brokers in the principal market towns. There is little evidence that this interregional system touched the small peasant who, if he entered a market, contributed to a local network analogous to the one around Madrid. Some of the participants in the government's system, like the *arrieros* of Sangarcía, used the connections they had discovered in government service to develop private channels for bringing grain from Old Castile to the Madrid market. At the same time, the *Pósito* dealt directly with important rentiers to mobilize the supplies they had accumulated.

The wheat and cattle transactions we have outlined were part of a complex

82. Peña Sánchez, *Crisis rural,* pp. 39, 48, 52–56, 66–68, 70–71.

economic network, some of which was market-driven, some of which had important political components. In the nineteenth century, many of the overtly political components were eliminated, allowing greater latitude for market response and price speculation. In practice, this process was well under way in the last half of the eighteenth century and did not represent a sudden and arbitrary change. The "liberalization" of the interior market shifted risks and costs from the government to the consumer, and depersonalized the relationship of the rural elite to the urban market and the state, but did not modify the underlying economic structure of the interior.

The effect of the mid-nineteenth-century land sales on this economy has been the subject of much discussion. Some new landowners from the towns did appear in the countryside. The degree to which this is seen to represent a revolutionary insertion of capitalism into agriculture reflects the inclinations of the researcher. In the Tierra de Campos, about 28% of all land changed hands, creating a new group of absentee landlords and a few large *fincas* that were connected with the evolution of *caciquismo*. In the district of Olmedo, northwest of Segovia, 25% of the land changed hands between 1820 and 1891. A third of that was acquired by absentee rentiers or speculators, but 55% was bought by the better-off *labradores* in the area. The actual cultivated plots were seldom reorganized and averaged one acre in size in 1750, again in 1879, and even in 1950. In the province of Valladolid the pattern was similar, and the purchasers of land were either the peasants themselves or the rentiers, large farmers, or businessmen already involved with agriculturally oriented commerce. Very few new fortunes and only a handful of major new landlords appeared.[83]

Seen in a broader context, some old absentees were replaced by other new ones, who restructured some farms and forced up some rents. Yet absenteeism was already common, and rural labor and potential tenants were plentiful anyway, so the only real result was a marginally different matrix for the rural elite and a modest increase in familiar forms of rural misery.[84] It is a choice example of how profit-maximizing attitudes can lead to a freezing of rural production because of the nature of the overall market.[85] The situation favored the few who controlled farms of significant size and those who could increase rents and control tithes and commons land. The process may even have been more pronounced before the disentailment of the 1830's, since

83. Germán Rueda Hernánz, *La desamortización de Mendizábal en Valladolid, 1836–1853* (1980), pp. xlv, 60, 204, 219–220, and 229, and "La desamortización del siglo XIX en una zona de Castilla la Vieja" (1976), pp. 206, 227; see also Richard Herr, "La vente des propriétés de mainmorte en Espagne, 1798–1808" (1974).
84. Peña Sánchez, *Crisis rural,* pp. 99–101.
85. Robert Brenner, "The Origins of Capitalist Development," pp. 45–46.

under Ferdinand VII (1808–33) enclosures continued apace, but it favored those who controlled traditional señorial power in the countryside.[86]

Subsequently, the competing rentiers and *labradores ricos*, having shared out the lands of the churches and municipalities, merged into an integrated rural hierarchy that dominated Castilian politics.[87] This is reflected in the underlying consistency of policy on agricultural tariffs—the Liberals of 1820, Ferdinand VII, the *Moderados*, and the Restoration of the 1870's all used tariffs to protect Castilian agriculture at the expense of the towns.[88] This landed class participated in the urban supply system in various ways, even as the middlemen of the supply system developed rural assets and connections. The evolving landed class drifted steadily into the cities and absenteeism, but the shift to Liberal economics and property law did not make landowners bourgeois or capitalist—that process had long since begun. The "bourgeois revolution" is a concept that stands for the rationalization of the marketing of surpluses extracted from the countryside. The economic life of the countryside itself resisted more than marginal modifications through much of the nineteenth century.[89]

All of these processes explain the eternal lament that there was no domestic market in Castile and that wrong-headed policies prevented one from developing. In fact, the liberalization of landholding and control served initially to aggravate the narrowness of the market-oriented segment of each village by keeping the poor out of the market altogether, encouraging a concentration of landholding. This facilitated the movement of the families able to participate in a national market to the very city that restricted such a national market as it grew and prospered. The rentiers and *labradores ricos* who entered the long-distance market under the Old Regime were also drawn into nineteenth-century politics and into a milieu in which their prosperity depended on Madrid both as consumer and as maker of economic policy. The liberalization of property was a prerequisite for rural economic change, but until transport was modernized the structure of the rural economy remained that of the Old Regime.

86. See Pierre Ponsot, "Revolution dans les campagnes espagnoles au XIXe siècle: Les désamortissements" (1972), pp. 107, 114; and Sánchez-Albornoz, *España hace un siglo,* pp. 18–19.

87. Richard Herr, "Spain"; and Miguel Artola, *Antiguo Régimen y revolución liberal* (1978), pp. 117–118, 151, 199–305.

88. Sánchez-Albornoz, *Los precios agrícolas,* vol. 1, pp. 35–59; Anes, *Las crises agrarias,* pp. 434–448.

89. Herr, "Spain," pp. 108–111.

9. The Geography of Urban Influence in Castile

In Chapter 8 we offered some generalizations about the nature of the links between urban supply and rural elites. While conforming to other things we know about the countryside, those generalizations are based on a limited number of supply accounts and a few districts, and thus leave open to question the geographic scope of the orientation to Madrid that they imply. Consequently, definition of the fields of influence created by the urban supply trades provides an important key in demonstrating the capital city's influence. Since a city lives from the tributary areas that develop around it, the geographic scope of its influence is a function of the size and power of the central place.

Normally, poor transport limits the market for bulky commodities unless some additional factor intervenes. The limiting effect of transport on urban size has a compelling logic which prompts one scholar to comment: "Until the railroads reduced long-distance land transport costs, the needs of 10,000 or more city dwellers could only be met through waterborne commerce."[1] Madrid, with twenty times that number and an overland supply system, is thus a rather remarkable artifact. It is already apparent that the city's supply systems reached far beyond the 50–75-mile range of private grain marketing apparent in the eighteenth century, and established far-reaching influence. In charting the areas the city drew upon, therefore, we can define another dimension of urban influence. At the same time, it is important to the discussion in Chapters 11 and 12 to relate the geographic incidence of Madrid's growing demands to the region that supplied Toledo and the other cities of the interior. Obviously, we will not be able to establish a sharp boundary and say "Here stops the influence of Madrid," but we can identify the regions that regularly interacted with the capital in an economic way.

1. Josef W. Konvitz, *Cities and the Sea, Port City Planning in Early Modern Europe* (1978), p. xi.

I. Sixteenth- and Seventeenth-Century Expansion of Influence

A. Wheat

As we have seen, the earliest regulation of wheat supplies took the form of embargoes on all grain traded within a specified radius of the capital. As a complement to the long-established price ceiling *(tasa)* on wheat leaving the farm, this was an administrative redefinition of urban demand in an existing market. As the area of embargo was increased, it meant that Madrid pre-empted supplies customarily used by Toledo. Some embargoes directed the movement of all salable grain to the capital, others established price differentials that made Madrid a more attractive market. As the sixteenth century drew to a close, control zones with radii of 5 and 8 leagues gave way to a 12-league radius during the supply crises of 1583 and 1591, and the first 18-league radius appeared in the crisis of 1598–99. In the first quarter of the seventeenth century, 12 leagues became the minimum, 16- and 20-league radii appeared frequently, and in 1631 the city regulated wheat for a 32-league radius and bread-baking within 20 leagues.[2]

The significance of these ever-expanding control areas is apparent when they are illustrated as on Map 9.1, which shows 8-, 18-, and 32-league limits. Beginning with the crisis of 1598–99, Madrid's supply zone frequently enveloped that of Toledo, as well as those of Ávila, Guadalajara, and Segovia. The 18-league radius, used or exceeded at least six times between 1598 and 1630, not only surrounded Toledo but included the best farming areas of New Castile.

As we have seen, this embargo system proved inadequate for the city's growing needs as the rural economy deteriorated. Specific references to grain sources are scanty before the supply crisis of 1630–31, but as late as 1614 officials of the *Sala de Alcaldes y Corte* still relied heavily in time of shortage upon La Mancha, Guadalajara, and the Bishoprics of Osma and Sigüenza north and east of Guadalajara. Of these, only La Mancha was outside the largest embargo radius, and recourse to Old Castile is mentioned only as an afterthought.[3]

After two decades of rapid urban growth, the pestilence, cold weather, and crop failures of the late 1620's forced authorities to increase the scope of the supply system in order to maintain Madrid's grain supply. This is illustrated by three complementary accounts from 1630–31 which detail the purchase of 175,000 *fanegas* of wheat, a third of the annual supply. Two of the documents

2. AHN, *Alcaldes,* libros for 1583, fol. 78; 1591, fol. 400; 1599, fol. 224; 1605, fols. 293–298, 305; 1606, fols. 37, 41; 1607, fols. 37, 41; 1610, fols. 570–572; 1613, fol. 110; 1614, fol. 241; 1616, fol. 327; 1631, fol. 118; and 1641, fols. 1, 152; AVM, *Secretaria,* sigs. 2–95–23 (1598), 2–96–2 (1599), 1–455–2 (1608), and 2–447–26 (1609); F. Pérez de Castro, "El abasto de pan," p. 131.

3. AHN, *Alcaldes,* libros for 1606, fol. 41, and 1614, fol. 241.

are summary accounts of wheat purchased by agents who ranged from Andalucía to Palencia, while the third details purchases by an agent who acquired 55,000 *fanegas* of wheat in the provinces of Segovia, Ávila, Valladolid, and eastern Zamora and Salamanca.[4]

The two general accounts list points of purchase throughout Old and New Castile and Andalucía (see Map 9.1), and represent the geographic range of the city's wheat purchases in the seventeenth century, 53% of which came from the Tierra de Campos between León, Palencia, Valladolid, and Zamora, while an additional 13% came from other parts of Old Castile and León. A fourth of the total came from Andalucía and La Mancha; and of the areas cited as sources in 1614, only Osma and La Mancha are mentioned in this crisis.[5]

A third of the 175,000 *fanegas* in all three accounts came from the Tierra de Campos, and the number and density of the towns mentioned suggests that the area was thoroughly canvassed. Some 70% of the grain purchased by these roving agents came from beyond the 32-league control zone of 1630-31,[6] and virtually all of it came from beyond the 18-league radius of previous crises, prefiguring the three-tiered grain market outlined earlier. Madrid was now reaching to the extremes of the peninsula for supplies and making major intrusions into the wheat markets of Old Castile. The capital was clearly capable of disrupting the regional grain markets crucial to the Castilian urban network.

Purchasing records from 1664-65 document Madrid's continued reliance on this Old Castilian supply system, despite a decline in the size of the city.[7] An area that includes 31 towns where an agent of the *Pósito* purchased 31,000 *fanegas* of wheat from the 1664-65 crop is shown on Map 9.1. While this is less than 10% of the city's consumption, it shows that even after its decline Madrid continued to reach as far as 200 miles into Old Castile for its grain: 70% of these purchases came from the Tierra de Campos, more than 125 miles from Madrid.

The sweeping nature of the capital's effort to attract grain supplies in years of dearth is evident. While the city may not have disturbed the affected areas in most years, it exacerbated the effects of periodic crop failure across a considerable distance. This mechanism helps to account for the extremely wide price fluctuations in market centers when the crop was poor, and thus for the parallelism of regional price trends noted by Earl Hamilton. Under the

4. It also refers to 42,000 *fanegas* purchased by the *Corregidor* of Zamora on a similar commission in the Zamora-Salamanca area: based on AVM, *Contaduria*, sigs. 2–580–1 and 2–103–1; and Pérez de Castro, "El abasto de pan, " which is based on AVM, *Estadística*, sig. 3–284–3.

5. Antonio Domínguez Ortiz, *La sociedad del siglo XVII*, vol. 1, pp. 124–126.

6. Pérez de Castro, "El abasto de pan," p. 131.

7. AVM, *Contaduria*, sig. 3–641–2, and *Secretaria*, sig. 2–106–28.

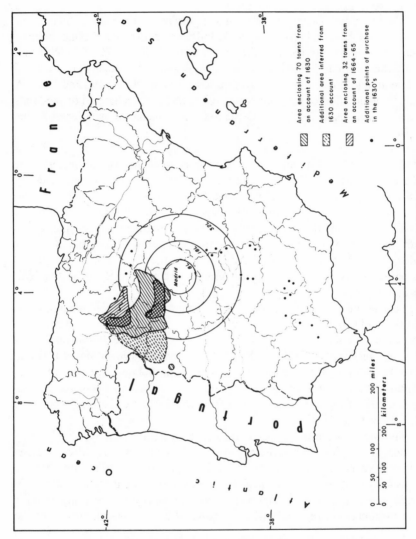

Map 9.1 *Areas Supplying Wheat to Madrid, 17th Century*

circumstances, surprisingly small purchases could be very disturbing to the local market.[8]

B. Bread

The expansion of control closer to the capital is illustrated by the developing system of *pan de obligación*. Towns near the capital were required to prepare bread for sale in the city, often with grain supplies organized by the *Pósito*. Two surviving lists of contributor communities illustrate the evolution of this aspect of the supply system. Map 9.2 shows the area that includes 39 of the 44 towns so obligated in 1599.[9] Most were within 10 leagues of the city, but almost all were northeast of Madrid—the quadrant of the city's hinterland farthest from Toledo. A comparable list for 1739 gives a different picture.[10] This second area, also shown on Map 9.2, is not only larger, but its geography has shifted remarkably. Many of the northeastern towns on the earlier register have disappeared, half of the towns now listed are between Madrid and Toledo, two or three literally within sight of Toledo.

C. Wine

The evolution of the geography of Madrid's wine supply in the seventeenth century is even more striking, since the area to the north, east, and south of Toledo was the heart of the Castilian wine industry in the sixteenth century (see Map 9.3).[11] To follow this development, references to towns selling to the Madrid market were taken from entries regarding wine supply in the *libros de año* of the *Sala de Alcaldes y Corte* of Madrid.[12] The citations were grouped as pre-1601 sources, sources for 1601–30, and sources for 1631–1700. As Map 9.3 shows, before 1600 Madrid drew its wine from several districts, but left most of the wine regions of New Castile to Toledo. Some wine came from central areas that were long-established producers, but Madrid drew heavily on Old Castile, especially the province of Valladolid.[13] The city also relied on wine from its hinterland to the northeast, and from towns immediately to the south; but references to the great wine-producing regions around Yepes,

8. Earl Hamilton, *American Treasure,* pp. 203–221.
9. The *libros* of the *Sala de Alcaldes y Corte* contain numerous lists, but most are of towns that had not met their obligations. The lists cited here enumerate the towns that actually participated. On 1599: AVM, *Secretaría,* sig. 2–95–28.
10. AHN, *Alcaldes,* libro for 1739, fol. 182.
11. José Gentil da Silva's figures for village wine sales from *En Espagne,* pp. 36–38, and Hamilton's prices for wine in Toledo.
12. Additional citations come from Miguel Herrero García, *Las bebidas* (1933), pp. 5–55.
13. In addition, see Alain Huetz de Lemps, "Le vignoble de la Tierra de Medina aux XVIIe et XVIIIe siècles " (1957), pp. 410–411; he refers to Alaejos, Medina del Campo, Coca, and Nava de Medina.

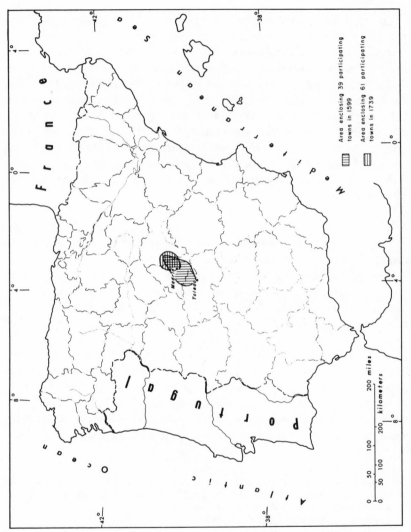

Map 9.2 *Areas Supplying* Pan de Registro *to Madrid*

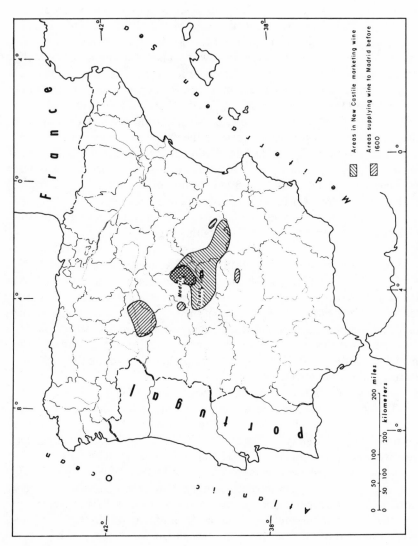

Map 9.3 *Areas Marketing Wine in the 16th Century*

Orgaz, Ocaña, Lillo, and Tarrancón are sparse, and they are mentioned only as emergency sources.

From 1601 to 1630, when the capital was expanding rapidly, there was a distinct geographic shift in wine sources (see Map 9.4). The same distant suppliers in Cuenca and La Mancha reappear, but Old Castile has virtually disappeared. While Madrid continued to draw from the towns to the northeast and immediate south, this period saw the supply net extend deep into the wine-producing regions around Toledo—the districts of Casarrubios del Monte, Ocaña, and Lillo in Toledo province, Tarrancón in Cuenca, and most notably the Orgaz district south of Toledo. This shift coincides with the unprecedented volume of wine entering Madrid at the time, and it is evident that the capital was coming to dominate the producing regions of New Castile. At the same time, the decline of wine prices between 1590 and 1615 explains the disappearance of Old Castilian wine from the market. The cost of transport from Old Castile and the collapse of demand in Toledo meant that wine from New Castile reached Madrid more cheaply.[14]

As with wheat and bread, the late sixteenth and early seventeenth centuries saw recurrent regional embargoes that regulated the price and movement of wine within various distances from the capital. In the later sixteenth century, the control area was typically 8 or 12 leagues, and exceptionally 15. From 1599 it was normally 15 leagues and on occasion was extended to 20. At the same time, the city applied a two- and three-tiered price structure to wine leaving the vineyards. The farther from the capital, the lower the price the producer was permitted to charge, thus compensating middlemen and supply contractors for transport costs. In this way the retail price in the city could be held down without reducing a contractor's profit as he drew in supplies from farther and farther afield.[15]

The geography of the capital's wine supply shifted farther south in 1631–1700, even as consumption in Madrid declined rapidly. Old Castile disappeared completely, as did most of the towns northeast of the capital that had been Madrid's wine suppliers for 50 years before 1630. The Casarrubios and Tarrancón districts also disappeared, calling to mind Domínguez Ortiz' observation about the decline of western Guadalajara and eastern Toledo provinces in the early seventeenth century. These were some of the same districts that also faded from the bread and wheat supply.[16] What remained was the cluster of communities between Madrid and Toledo that had been prominent in 1601–30, and the areas around Ocaña, Orgaz, and Lillo that

14. Ibid., pp. 411–412.

15. AHN, *Alcaldes,* libros for 1586, fol. 194; 1595, fol. 69; 1598, fols. 157, 166, 178; 1599, fol. 224; 1613, fol. 110; 1623, fol. 520; and 1628, fols. 110, 176; Herrero Garcia, *Las bebidas,* p. 37.

16. Domínguez Ortiz, *Siglo XVII,* pp. 124–126.

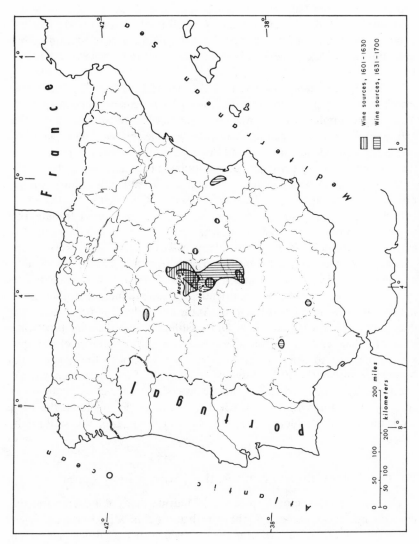

Map 9.4 *Areas Supplying Wine to Madrid, 17th Century*

now appear as regular, rather than occasional, contributors to the Madrid wine supply. Another aspect of the evolving wine market is the growing frequency of references to quality wines from long distances—Sevilla, Córdoba, and Valencia—and the growing prominence of La Mancha, including the regions of Madridejos, Consuegra, Ciudad Real, Daimiel, and Mebrilla. In more recent times, La Mancha has been the main source of Madrid's table wine, but references to the area became prominent in the sources only after 1650.

Thus the wine-supply system of Madrid shifted south during the seventeenth century, first as a response to growing total demand, then in a search for alternate suppliers as the towns of central New Castile dropped out of the market and regional demographic decline became serious.[17] This period of increasing dependence on newer and more distant suppliers coincides with the marked decline of per-capita consumption in the city.

In mapping the development of Madrid's seventeenth-century wheat, bread, and wine supplies, we have defined some of the fields of urban influence that the growing capital city created in the Spanish interior. Initially, the city relied on nearby parts of New Castile or its hinterland to the north and east, where Toledo's influence was relatively weak. Those sources were supplemented as necessary with wheat and wine from Old Castile. As the city grew, however, the Crown expanded its zones of wheat and wine control to include most of New Castile, reorienting bread production in the region between the two cities toward Madrid. At the same time, Madrid thrust more deeply into the wheat markets of Old Castile and into the wine-producing areas of Toledo and La Mancha. The result was the appearance of a supply system oriented to Madrid that stretched from León in the north to La Mancha in the south. Without details on meat and fuel, the evidence is not complete, but the redirection of those commodity trades certainly followed suit. By the eighteenth century, when they can be documented, the wide scope of Madrid's influence in the economy of the interior was well established.

II. The Eighteenth- and Nineteenth-Century Supply Zones

The seventeenth-century expansion of Madrid's fields of influence was the consequence of two processes—the growth and stabilization of the city itself and a decline of agriculture near the city which increased dependence on more distant suppliers, even though the size of the capital shrank consider-

17. Michael M. Weisser, "The Decline of Castile Revisited: The Case of Toledo" (1973), pp. 638–640. This is discussed in detail in Weisser's manuscript, "The Demography of the Heartland of New Castile, 1550–1700," pp. 5–7; he shows the population of Toledo's hinterland declining by two thirds in the seventeenth century.

ably. The eighteenth- and nineteenth-century sources are more complete; they allow us to map in detail the origins of wheat, charcoal, and meat, and offer other indications of the regional orientation to urban requirements.

A. Wheat

Several accounts have been combined to create a representative sample of 262,595 *fanegas* of wheat purchased by the *Pósito* in the late 1760's. Modest quantities of grain came from the nearby districts of Guadalajara, Madrid, and Toledo, significant amounts from La Mancha, and a sizable quantity from the Sigüenza-Osma area in southern Soria and northern Guadalajara provinces. The combined volume of all those sources, however, did not match the quantities brought from just the Tierra de Campos in Old Castile, not to mention the quantities from Salamanca, Ávila, and southern Valladolid. This pattern is supported by records from 1779 that indicate weekly grain arrivals at the *Pósito* by the region of origin.[18] These reiterate the dependence of the city on Old Castile and the thinness of supplies in the region near the city. They also add an element that is harder to document, the use of Andalucía to supply 10% of the total delivered to the *Pósito*. The region is treated as a routine source, and the Crown expressed concern about exports from the area; so it appears that by the late eighteenth century Madrid regularly bought grain from that far away.

The composite of supply accounts illustrated on Map 9.5 for 1785–90 is incomplete in that there are no eighteenth-century references to Soria-Guadalajara, La Mancha, or Andalucía, but it does reveal another aspect of the urban wheat supply. The *Pósito* did not normally supply all of the city's wheat, and with one exception its agents are seen operating at considerable distance from the capital. In Chapter 8 we showed that quantities of grain did come from nearby as small shipments brought by owners or transporters directly to the *Pósito*. The latter type of transaction is shown separately, indicating that the two mechanisms were geographically distinct. Moreover, considerable territory in Segovia, Ávila, and New Castile is not covered by either, despite the fact that those areas are known to have produced grain. These are the supply areas which were organized by the exchange centers considered as sites for grain fairs, and which supported the market network of Madrid's bakers and grain merchants. Since this grain was registered at the *Alhóndiga* without control as long as prices were stable, it represents an area of market influence which is hard for us to document directly.

In general, nearby producers with small surpluses could reach either the *Pósito* or *Alhóndiga* directly and avoid middlemen—the arrangement favored by official attitudes. Direct government purchases, for which au-

18. AHN, *Consejos*, leg. 6775-3.

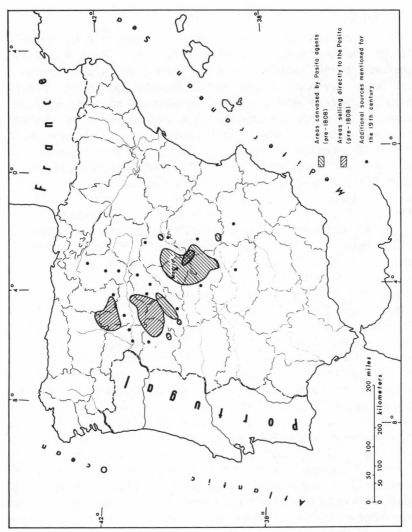

Map 9.5 *Sources of Wheat for Madrid, 1775–1850*

thorities arranged transport, were usually in zones where the cost of delivery to Madrid was high and stocks had to be diverted from alternative uses. Larger private sales included areas in the nearby New Castile provinces of Guadalajara, Cuenca, Toledo, and La Mancha. Thus Madrid was the focal point of three overlapping market systems: one organized by the government beyond a radius of 100 miles; the private-sector grain market extending out about that distance; and the third, with a much smaller radius, based on the direct sale of small shipments in the capital itself. The additional wheat sources shown on Map 9.5 for the early nineteenth century serve to illustrate the continued growth of the city's grain supply area. All of the previously mentioned areas appear except Andalucía, while Albacete, Burgos, and parts of Zamora provinces appear for the first time.

Thus the eighteenth- and nineteenth-century wheat supply involved fields of influence that drew modest amounts of grain from La Mancha and Cuenca, and important quantities from Madrid, Guadalajara, and Toledo provinces, but also relied heavily on Old Castile and León for supplies. Government intervention, which created most of our documentation, assumed a self-operating market in nearby regions, but organized purchase and delivery from more distant sources. The latter oriented the Old Castilian grain trade to Madrid and created a system that could then be copied by private traders as they acquired the connections and capital needed to hold stocks in anticipation of price changes. Thus it was that distant sources remained linked to Madrid after government intervention became less systematic. We glimpse here the development of entrepreneurs ready to take advantage of government withdrawal from management of the grain market. Regardless of the balance of public and private organization, the geographic scope of this aspect of Madrid's demands on Castile is well established.

B. Fuel, Lumber, and Transport

One of the important staples of any large city is fuel, and in pre-industrial Madrid this was primarily charcoal. By the end of the eighteenth century, the city used over 25,000 tons of charcoal yearly, with a market value in the capital reaching 10 million *reales*. Map 9.6 illustrates the geography of fuel supply, indicating the areas where the charcoal administration contracted for its fuel for the fiscal year 1803–04, and the districts that supplied 700 tons of firewood annually to the royal palaces in the 1640's. Madrid obtained over half of its charcoal from two districts: the belt of mountain country north and west of the city (the Guadarrama and Gredos Mountains), and the hill country known as the Alcarría in south-central Guadalajara and northern Cuenca. Sizable amounts also came from much farther afield—the Montes de Toledo, the rugged country of northwestern La Mancha, and the hill country along

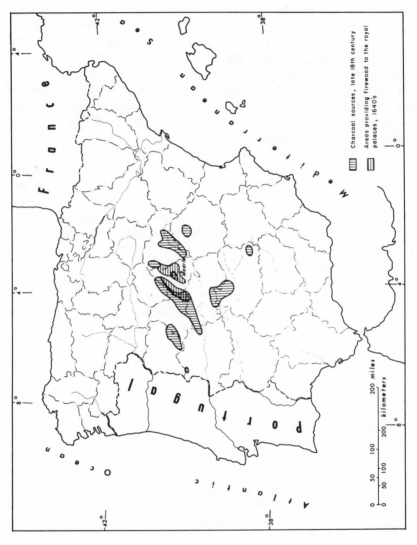

Map 9.6 *Sources of Charcoal and Firewood for Madrid*

the Salamanca-Ávila border north of Bejar. Both are areas separated from Madrid by over 100 miles of rugged terrain. Smaller amounts arrived from as far as the extreme southeast of La Mancha and the Sierra de Gata in the northwest corner of Extremadura.

If Maps 9.5 and 9.6, on wheat and charcoal supply, are superimposed, the second fills in many of the geographic spaces on the first, showing Madrid's widespread influence on commodity flows in the interior. The dominance was even more pervasive than this observation suggests. Certain commodities and services were closely linked within the pre-industrial economy. One of the most important of these complexes was charcoal, lumber, transport, and grazing—all of which involved the same basic resources and regions. Thus Maps 9.5 and 9.6 must be viewed in conjunction with Map 9.7, which locates a number of other supply activities. Madrid used about 1,600 *carros* of lumber yearly for construction, cabinetry, and wood-working. Not surprisingly, many of the areas producing fuel also provided lumber. The most significant exception is the hill country of Soria, which supplied lumber, but not fuel; this was the major source of the pine which constituted half of all the lumber used in Madrid.

Moreover, both charcoal and lumber were linked with transportation—in particular the long-haul carters, equipped to carry large, heavy cargoes, who frequently came from villages in the forest districts. These carters, in turn, employed transhumant cattle-grazing as an integral part of their economic activities, requiring the rental of winter pasture throughout the Spanish interior.[19] To illustrate the many points at which Madrid touched the economy of the interior, therefore, Map 9.7 indicates lumber sources, home towns of the professional carters, and the areas where they regularly rented winter pastures. The result is a complex of supply activities that ranged over most of the interior provinces of the old Crown of Castile.

C. Other Products and Raw Materials

Map 9.7 also shows details on some less well-documented trades. These include *yeso* or gypsum, soap, and raw materials for soap. A cluster of several *yeso* factories appears near Madrid, as well as a group of soap cauldrons around the city and others scattered as far south as Toledo and La Mancha. Soap in turn was linked with raw materials such as soda, *barrilla*, and olive oil from Murcia, Albacete, Toledo, La Mancha, and Andalucía. Finally, Map 9.7 locates the few specific sources of wine mentioned in the eighteenth-century documents, which suggest a continuation of the southward drift of Madrid's wine-supply zone. The older wine areas around Toledo still participated, but

19. David R. Ringrose, *Transportation,* pp. 43–57 and map 14.

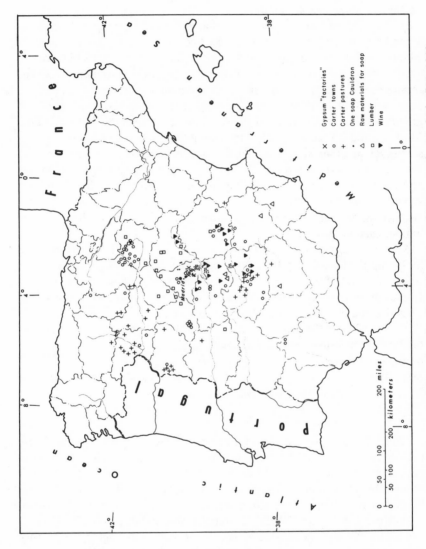

Map 9.7 *Sources of Wine, Lumber, Soap, Gypsum, and Transport for Madrid, 1750–1808*

south-central Cuenca and La Mancha, particularly the Valdepeñas district, have become much more important.[20]

D. Meat

After wheat, the most important commodity was meat, and the meat supply drew upon parts of the interior that thus far have not appeared on our supply maps. Almost half of all meat animals appear to have originated near Madrid, but this reflects their sale at the city stockyards without clear indication of point of origin. The rest of the livestock was purchased by supply agents at provincial livestock fairs, and some of their accounts indicate origins in detail. Large numbers of sheep came from the modern province of Badajoz, site of winter grazing for many Mesta flocks, and from northern Córdoba. Cáceres also made major contributions to the mutton and beef supplies, as did Salamanca. Quantities of mutton animals came from Zamora and the Tierra de Campos, while thousands of beef cattle were bought in the Leonese fair town of La Bañeza.

The geographic significance of this is apparent when we look at Map 9.8. The cattle traded at Trujillo came from as far as 70 miles away, and the area thus reached by the agent at the Trujillo fair is shown on the map. If we infer the same pattern for the La Bañeza cattle fair, it would have reached the hills of northwest León and the mountains of Galicia.[21]

The registers of sales transacted at Madrid provide incomplete data on the origins of that part of the livestock supply. Large numbers of cattle were sold by brokers or owners of feed-lots near the city, and we have no clues to where those animals originated. There were also numerous small sales of cattle from Burgos, Soria, Cuenca, Toledo, and La Mancha—frequently the home regions and towns of long-haul carters. Since the latter used oxen as draft animals, the overlap into the meat supply was logical. A sizable number of high-quality beef cattle came from Navarra and southern France. The sheep purchased in the city did not come from as far afield, originating in La Mancha, Toledo, Ávila, and Segovia provinces. For the most part, this in-

20. Here we see overlapping fields of influence. Madrid ceased to draw wine from Old Castile, but the areas that had supplied her in the sixteenth century continued to export wine, having reoriented themselves to an interregional exchange with the Cantabrian Mountains: Ringrose, *Transportation,* p. 20. In the nineteenth century, Medina, Alaejos, and Nava del Rey declined, although Rueda and La Seca continued as important wine centers. As transport improved, competition from La Mancha affected the region; see Huetz de Lemps, "Le vignoble," p. 414.

21. The significance of the fair at La Bañeza is suggested by the fact that villagers from as far away as the Tierra de Campos routinely used it to buy cattle, wood, charcoal, and other mountain products from the northwest; see Peña Sánchez, *Crisis rural,* pp. 87–88. José Lucas Labrada—in *Descripción económica del Reino de Galicia* (1971, first published in 1804), pp. 130, 143, 200—makes several references to Galician trade with Castile.

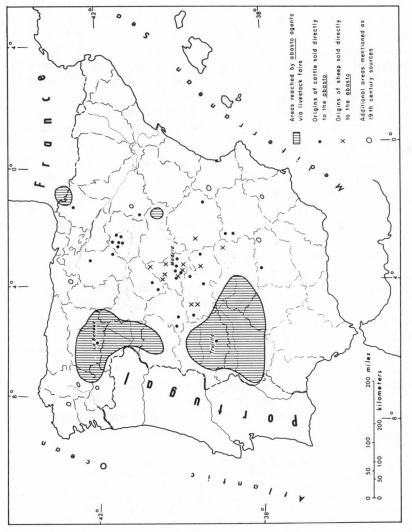

Map 9.8 *Sources of Meat for Madrid, 1790–1850*

volved districts between Madrid and the areas served by the western livestock fairs.

The most direct impact of the meat supply was upon the graziers who marketed livestock, but it also touched communities nearer the capital. Meat was a commodity that walked to market instead of being transported, and this required grazing along the way. A group of disputes from the mid-eighteenth century provides several specific references to the location of such grazing, and these have also been plotted on Map 9.8. The sites are located along the main routes to the city: Extremadura-Talavera-Navalcarnero-Madrid; La Mancha-Toledo-Getafe-Madrid; Soria-Madrid; and Old Castile-Real de Manzanares-Madrid. In addition, the government maintained a blanket privilege that allowed meat cattle in transit to graze freely on town commons land anywhere within 7 leagues (25 miles) of the city.[22]

The composite of the eighteenth-century meat sources provides an example of a nearly peninsula-wide network focused on Madrid. It reached from Navarra and France in the north to Galicia in the northwest, to the *sierras* along the north edge of Andalucía. It touched eastern Cuenca and Guadalajara, and even reached into the Aragonese province of Teruel. While many of the more distant transactions were not very significant in the economies of the producing districts, the meat trade drew into Madrid's orbit areas not involved in supplying other commodities—in particular Córdoba, Badajoz, Zamora, and León-Galicia. By mid-nineteenth century, minor changes had taken place in this network, but the effect was to increase even further the geographic scope of the city's influence. Navarra and France are no longer mentioned, but Galicia is mentioned specifically, and all of the central and western provinces participated. In addition, there are references to pork coming from Jaén, Murcia, Valencia, and Aragón, and to beef cattle from the Cantabrian Mountains of Santander province.

III. General Observations

It would be foolish to assert that Madrid controlled the market economy of every area from which she drew some supplies, and many supplying areas participated in trade with other regions as well. Wine moved north through Old Castile to the mountains; meat and fish traveled the reverse route into Old Castile; and grain was hauled north to Cantabria and Santander from the Tierra de Campos. Wool and some wheat were exported. Valencia and Andalucía maintained a separate interregional exchange of wheat and rice, and Valencia bought its mutton from Castilian graziers. Wood and building mate-

22. AHN, *Consejos,* leg. 11463, mentions several towns and districts affected.

rials moved from Soria to Old Castile and the north coast.[23] Yet if we super-impose the fields of influence represented by the various commodities markets onto a single map, and remember our earlier estimates of the quantities and values involved, Madrid emerges as the market *par excellence* for the interior. The city's effective hinterland stretched from the Cantabrian Mountains to the Sierra Morena, and from the Portuguese to the Aragonese borders, while several of the connections reached beyond into Andalucía, Galicia, Valencia, and Aragón.

This may not have represented a "market economy" in the sense used by Fontana Lázaro,[24] but it represents a pattern of established economic activity of great permanence that linked the fortunes of the interior with those of the capital city. Taken together with the urban institutions of supply, the examples of how urban supply touched rural life, and the underlying patterns of interregional trade, this evidence for the geographic scope and complexity of Madrid's supply system offers a convincing picture of the structural patterns that oriented rural elites to affairs in the capital. The "bourgeois" oligarchy of Castile is not so much the product of economic change involving capitalist attitudes as the consolidation of a complex continuum of urban-rural relations.

23. Ringrose, *Transportation,* maps.
24. Josep Fontana Lázaro, *La quiebra de la monarquia absoluta, 1814–1820* (1971), pp. 47–57, and *Cambio económico y actitudes politicas en la España del siglo XIX* (1973), pp. 17–37.

Part Three
Madrid and the Spanish Economy

10. Between Castile and the Sea: The Coastal Fringe

One of the major points of this study is that Madrid created a community of interests in Spain that transcended regional boundaries. As part of a dynamic relationship between Madrid and Castile that precluded a reversion to the economic life of the sixteenth century, that community of interests nurtured historical structures that have made Spain resistant to modernization. Recent scholarship has shown the basic differences between the Spanish coastal and inland economies in many ways. In English, the best-known work is Earl J. Hamilton's; although he does not address regional contrasts directly, Hamilton's price data extending from 1350 to 1800 repeatedly demonstrate the vulnerability of the Spanish interior to subsistence crises. The coastal provinces, with access to maritime trade, were relatively safe from such crises and could adjust their agriculture to incentives offered by external markets. Catalonia and Valencia also had separate monetary systems which afforded some protection from the manipulations of the Castilian coinage.[1]

Pierre Vilar has documented both the sluggishness of the Catalán economy and the expansiveness of Castile's in the sixteenth century, and the reversal of the situation in the eighteenth.[2] Vicens Vives notes the close interaction of the two economies in the sixteenth century. The woolens crisis of 1548–58 and price rises later in the century were felt with comparable intensity in both regions; but unlike Castile, Catalán prosperity was not the result of domestic development—indeed, Catalonia's late sixteenth-century expansion was externally induced by diversion of traffic from the Sevilla-Castile-Burgos cir-

1. Earl J. Hamilton, *Money, Prices, and Wages in Valencia, Aragon, and Navarre, 1351–1500* (1936); *American Treasure and the Price Revolution in Spain, 1501–1650* (1934); and *War and Prices in Spain, 1651–1800* (1947), p. 121.
2. Pierre Vilar, *Catalunya dins l'Espanya moderna* (1968), vol. 2, pp. 216–224, 247–253, 254, 268–270; vol. 3, pp. 439–443; vol. 4, pp. 27–66.

cuit into the Mediterranean because of hostilities in the Atlantic. The seventeenth century saw depression in both areas, with only Catalonia showing much sign of recovery before 1700. By the eighteenth century, population, commercial, and wage trends in Madrid and Barcelona diverged in a manner that clearly identifies Catalonia as a much more dynamic region.[3]

Historians often refer to the coastal periphery of Spain as though it were a unified economic system providing convenient contrast with a static, homogeneous, and isolated interior. In fact, of course, neither the interior nor the coastal fringe was as homogeneous as our framework in Chapter 1 suggested, and some aspects of the dualism are as well explained by the differing social structures of Castile, Aragón, and Portugal as by geography. Nevertheless, to understand how Madrid affected the course of events we must have a clear perception of the economic evolution of both the peninsular interior and its maritime periphery.

Sixteenth-century Castile proved that a narrow base of movable surpluses could be used to create an urban network, an industrial sector, and a mercantile system capable of linking regional economic life to external markets. The domestic components of this commercial system were vulnerable to population growth, diminishing returns, and international price differences; but the factor that most precisely paralleled the actual breakdown of this fragile economic structure was the emergence of Madrid. Sustained by rents, taxes, and commodities drawn from a worldwide political empire, Madrid reoriented the limited marketable supplies in Castile. The impact on the regional urban network resulted in Toledo's fall from primate city to provincial backwater and can be seen in the history of commercial activity in other interior cities.

The coastal areas had no such common point of reference, though they all shared access to the sea. Some regions became involved in long-distance maritime exchange, Barcelona and Sevilla-Cádiz being the preeminent examples. Others, like the northern coastal districts from San Sebastián to Vigo, developed a self-sufficiency analogous to, but qualitatively different from, that of interior areas. Coastal trade meant that Galicia sometimes ate French wheat and Vizcaya sometimes used Gallego wine. Despite its inward orientation, Guipúzcoa, for example, was constantly preoccupied with supply by sea, and never experienced the supply crises that crippled seventeenth-century Castile.[4]

While the coastal regions had in common the economic possibilities inherent in access to the sea, the varied fortunes of Vizcaya, Galicia, Sevilla, and

3. Jaime Vicens Vives, *Manual de historia económica de España* (1967), pp. 330–546; Vilar, *Catalunya*, vol. 2, pp. 262–267; vol. 3, p. 68.

4. Pablo Fernández Albaladejo, *El crisis del Antiguo Régimen in Guipúzcoa, 1700–1833*, pp. 41–51.

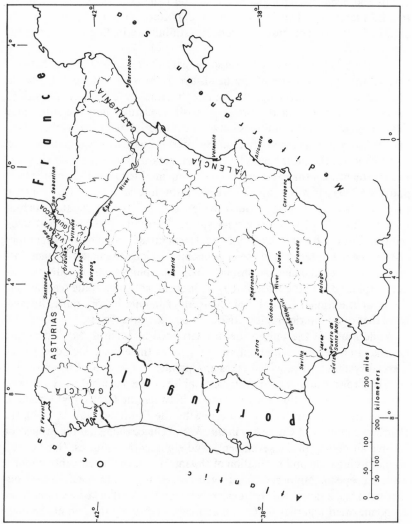

Map 10.1 *Locations Cited in Chapter 10*

Catalonia attest that they were not able to exploit them to the same degree, or in the same ways. These differences were more pronounced in the sixteenth century than later. By the eighteenth century, the maritime commercial trends and economic changes of the coastal fringe exhibited two important trends: increasing divergence from the pattern of the interior, and increasingly similar responses to economic stimuli originating in northern Europe.

Whatever linkages and common social patterns may have existed between coastal and interior parts of the peninsula in the sixteenth century, by the eighteenth they clearly operated under distinctive economic conditions. Provincial variations in the prices of basic foodstuffs indicate substantial differences in market conditions between the interior and the periphery. During subsistence crises, food prices in the interior fluctuated two to three times as much as on the periphery.[5] This pattern persisted into the second half of the nineteenth century and has been documented for the crises of 1856–57 and 1866–69, when the price of wheat in the interior rose to four times as much as in coastal towns.[6] Such evidence is not the entire story behind regional differences, and we must not succumb entirely to geographical determinism. But the fact remains that social structures limited by the geography of the Spanish interior had fewer economic options than similar ones with access to the sea and cheap transport. Their possibilities may not always have been exploited, and the reasons may lie in social not geographic realities, but the most traditional coastal region has an economic history quite different from that of an interior region organized by the same society.

While much of the interior became oriented to Madrid, Madrid in turn depended on periphery and empire. So long as the empire included a commercial system that provided taxes and private fortunes, Madrid prospered and the Crown could mediate between empire on the one hand and interior on the other. Centralization caused tensions between the Crown and Catalonia and the Basque provinces, as witnessed by the Catalán revolt of 1640, the Bourbon conquest of Catalonia in the War of Succession, and the attacks on Basque autonomy in the seventeenth and eighteenth centuries. But the economic subjugation and stagnation of the interior in the seventeenth century, while European commerce encouraged coastal regions to specialize for distant markets, aggravated the tension between the landlocked and maritime economies tied together by Crown and capital city. By the end of the eighteenth century, though ostensibly successful, the peninsular system had become extremely fragile. Since Madrid lived in two economic worlds, we must

5. Anes, *Las crises agrarias en la España moderna,* pp. 217–269, 495.
6. Sánchez-Albornoz, *España hace un siglo: una economia dual,* pp. 31–118.

trace the chronologies of both to perceive how the capital followed the trends of the larger world while reshaping the urban system of Castile.

Three Spanish coastal centers were perennially linked with the maritime world of Europe—Barcelona, Cádiz/Sevilla, and the Basque provinces—and each had a different relationship with its peninsular hinterland. At Barcelona, overseas commerce interacted with the Catalán hinterland and the economy of the port itself. Barcelona functioned as an entrepôt between the international market and a regional economy featuring specialized agriculture and craft industries that were moving toward industrial development on the English pattern by the end of the eighteenth century. Sevilla and Cádiz were entrepôts for European goods on the way to America and colonial products on the way to Europe. In the mid-sixteenth century, Sevilla served as an entrepôt like Barcelona, linking Indies trade with Andalusian agriculture and the Castilian textile industry. But by the seventeenth century, Sevilla and Cádiz were little more than clearinghouses for trade between the Spanish empire and Europe. Except for export of wool, sherry, and olive oil, the links between seaport and hinterland were confined to urban supply and provision of the mercantile fleet.

The third maritime center was in the Basque provinces, part of the maritime fringe of the northern coast. Vizcaya became the transit area for departing Castilian wool and incoming European manufactures destined for the Spanish interior—a trade that involved Castilian markets but had few links with the Basque hinterland. Associated with these three areas were the coastal trading circuits of the Mediterranean and northern littorals, also part of what we have referred to as the "periphery."

I. From Barcelona to Sevilla

A. Catalonia

Thanks to Pierre Vilar, we can construct a profile of commercial trends in Catalonia based on port duties in Barcelona and in the smaller ports of the Catalán littoral (see Tables 10.1 and 10.2). These figures verify that in the first two-thirds of the sixteenth century Barcelona recovered very slowly from its medieval depression. Adjusted for changes in the composite Spanish price indices, the value of traffic at Barcelona appears static until 1578, and only in the last quarter of the century did it increase significantly.[7] This reflects the

7. Since the series is based on an *ad valorem* port duty, it was undoubtedly affected by prices. The price index is not a very direct reflection of the situation in Barcelona, and the real trend was probably somewhere between the nominal and adjusted index numbers. These Barcelona series present a problem which affects this entire chapter. Some taxes were levied on the quantity of traffic, some were assessed *ad valorem*, and some combined both. To follow actual

Table 10.1. *Port Traffic in Barcelona Sixteenth and Seventeenth Centuries*(a)

Sixteenth Century

Period	Index of Nominal Value (1572-82 = 100)	Index Adjusted for Spanish Price Changes
1502-03	39.3	112.5
1521-27	46.0	96.5
1546-60(b)	66.6	92.0
1572-78	94.6	96.0
1579-86	151.6	107.2
1605-06	190.1	131.3

Seventeenth Century(c)

Period	Index of Nominal Value (1679-82 = 100)	Index Adjusted for Barcelona Prices
1664-74	69.7	—
1679-82	100.0	100.0
1686-87	52.3	65.9
1693-99	99.0	89.7

Source: Based on Vilar, *Catalunya*, vol. 2, pp. 245, 384. See also Robert S. Smith, *The Spanish Guild Merchants*, p. 140.

    a. Sixteenth-century values ranged from 133,000 to 645,000 Catalán *llures*.

    b. Includes 1548-54, 1557-58, 1559-60.

    c. The highest totals for this period, in 1697 and 1699, were well over 1,000,000 *llures*, the lowest, in 1686-87, was 500,000.

diversion of Italian capital that had financed the medieval Italy-Barcelona-Valencia-Balearics trade circuit to the Italy-Sevilla-Lisbon-Bruges circuit. In the late sixteenth century, however, the situation in northern Europe disrupted that trade, diverting Spanish wool to Mediterranean ports and causing a shift of Spain's European commerce to the Barcelona-Genoa-Austria route.[8] The induced nature of Barcelona's revival is attested by the tendency for prices there to follow those of Sevilla, indicating that Barcelona was exposed to inflationary pressures originating in America.[9]

    Barcelona lost considerable ground in the first half of the seventeenth

trends in traffic, tax revenues must be adjusted for inflation where possible, although the price series are often inadequate. Where possible, indices will show both nominal change and change adjusted by the nearest plausible price series. This provides a range of possibilities within which the actual trend probably existed. Even this has risks, because the *ad valorem* tax was probably collected on a mix of commodities different from that on which the price index was based. There were also occasional reforms of these minor taxes. Examination of annual municipal accounts suggests that these are usually reflected in breaks between coherent series. On the serial data not taken from secondary sources, see Appendix E.

    8. Federigo Melis, *Mercaderes italianos en España, siglos XIV-XVI* (1976), pp. 195-198; Geoffrey Parker, *The Army of Flanders and the Spanish Road, 1567-1659* (1972), pp. 50-62.

    9. Vilar, *Catalunya*, vol. 2, pp. 262-268, 274-275.

Table 10.2. *Port Duty Revenues in Eighteenth-Century Catalonia*(a)

Period	Index of Port Duty(b) Revenues in Barcelona	Index of *Lleuda* of Other Ports
1751-59		86.3
1760-68	111.7	136.3
1769-77	175.3	188.3
1778-89	223.8	240.3
1790-98	478.2	287.7
1799-1807	260.6	366.3

Source: Vilar, *Catalunya*, vol. 4, pp. 28, 35.
a. Index bases: port duty, 1760-64 = 100; *Lleuda*, 1751-65 = 100.
b. The *periatge* of Barcelona.

century, but by the third quarter of the century there was a substantial recovery that survived the deflation and subsistence crises of 1677–85. When adjusted for Barcelona prices, the average yield in 1693–99 was 10% below that of 1679–82, but the level of traffic sustained through the fourth quarter remained high. The recovery in Barcelona may have begun during the French occupation in the 1640's, and was furthered by the penetration of French capital into the Mediterranean and Cádiz trades.[10]

The growth of Barcelona and its hinterland was more apparent in the eighteenth century, as reflected in the indices of port duty yields (Table 10.2). Port duty revenues rose 378% between 1760–64 and 1790–98, and it is unlikely that adjustment for inflation could change this impression of spectacular growth.[11] Moreover, the port duties (*lleuda*) in the outlying ports of the Catalán coast, collected as fixed fees and therefore immune to inflation, increased an impressive 188% by 1790–98. If the Barcelona series could be accurately deflated, it would still show a similar rate of growth. The indicators for both the region and the capital show steady expansion of commercial activity in the first half of the eighteenth century, extending the trend of the late seventeenth. Growth accelerated after 1750 as the city's population rose from 30,000 inhabitants early in the century to 100,000 by 1800.[12]

From the mid-seventeenth century, Barcelona was becoming a center of Mediterranean trade and an intermediate stop between Marseilles and Cádiz, as French activity at Cádiz created a flow of traffic along Spain's Medi-

10. Robert S. Smith, *The Spanish Guild Merchant: A History of the Consulado, 1200–1700* (1940), p. 140. Albert Girard, *Le commerce français à Séville et Cádix au temps des Habsbourg* (1932; reprinted 1967).

11. There is no appropriate price index to let us adjust the *periatge* (an *ad valorem* tax) for inflation, but between 1742–59 and 1790–1800 wheat prices in Barcelona rose 140%, meat 9%, olive oil 126%, and wine 18%: Vilar, *Catalunya*, vol. 3, pp. 386, 396, 419, 425.

12. Ibid., vol. 2, p. 240, and vol. 3, pp. 59–60; Josep Iglesias, ed., *El cens de Comte de Floridablanca, 1787*, pp. 51–52.

terranean coast. The parallel expansion of traffic in Barcelona and the smaller regional ports indicates that economic expansion took place in the context of a network of ports, rather than at a single convenient stopping place.[13] This commercial growth reflected the development of domestic industry and intensive agriculture in Catalonia; a re-export trade giving Spanish-American sugar-growing importance in the Mediterranean; and a growing stream of Catalán and French manufactures destined for Málaga, Cádiz, and America.[14] The expansion of commercial activity at Barcelona after 1796, however, is an illusion reflecting the impact of price inflation on *ad valorem* duties. But if the real value of traffic at Barcelona stagnated or declined, it rose in the outports as the regional market system adjusted to disruption of commerce in its major port.

Even this sophisticated regional economy, however, was limited by geographic realities. Its direct connections with the Castilian interior were few, and its economic activities did not penetrate very far inland. Economic change remained slow in the mountain and inland regions of Catalonia and, while rents rose rapidly along the coast, they remained much lower inland. The impressive investments in drainage and irrigation were concentrated near the coast or the Ebro River, and most of it was within 30 miles of Barcelona itself.[15] The peripheral nature of this development is documented by its location on the coastal fringe and by its orientation to Spain's maritime economy.[16]

B. Sevilla-Cádiz

Spain's second major link with the maritime world was the Indies trade, first at Sevilla and later at Cádiz. Whether measured by the tonnage of trade with the Indies in the sixteenth century or by its contribution to national income as measured by the *Catastro* of 1750, the importance of this port complex is manifest.[17] Between colonial remittances, customs duties, *alcabalas*, and tobacco monopoly revenues, the old province of Sevilla (modern Sevilla, Huelva, and Cádiz) provided nearly half of royal revenues in the late eighteenth century. Its network of merchant families, Andalusian nobles, and

13. Vilar, *Catalunya*, vol. 4, pp. 35–36, 40, 51, 67–72.
14. Luis José Navarro Miralles, "Contactos comerciales entre el litoral catalán y puertos de Andalucía, 1799–1808"; and José María Delgado Ribas, "Cádiz y Málaga en el comercio colonial catalán posterior a 1778," p. 127.
15. Vilar, *Catalunya*, vol. 3, pp. 141–181, 259–367, 528–537.
16. Delgado Ribas, "Cádiz y Málaga," p. 127. At the end of the century, 56.7% of littoral exports went to Cádiz, 37.8% to Málaga: Navarro Miralles, "Contactos comerciales."
17. Vilar, "Estructures de la societat espanyola cap al 1750," pp. 9–22. This *Catastro*, or national economic survey, recorded the property and earnings of every household in the Kingdom of Castile for 1750. The portion compiled for Madrid in 1757 was used heavily in Chapters 4 and 5.

privileged guilds formed an integral part of the imperial power structure, reflecting the interpenetration of public and private interests and providing the Crown with a major source of credit.

1. Maritime Activity

Four indicators provide a long-term profile of overseas commerce in this port complex—the familiar figures on the tonnage of Indies trade to 1650, a small *ad valorem* tax on goods handled by the *Consulado* of Sevilla (1551–1700), a 0.5% *aduanilla* collected *ad valorem* by the city of Cádiz (1656–1800), and the estimates of Indies tonnage developed by García-Baquero for the eighteenth century. These are presented as index numbers in Tables 10.3, 10.4, and 10.5, indicating where appropriate both nominal and price-adjusted levels of tax revenue.

These figures suggest that the recovery of Andalusian commerce, so apparent in the eighteenth century, actually began between 1650 and 1700, and that it was in the later seventeenth century that the drastic decline of the official American trade monopoly was reversed. The transition is obscured by evidence of contraband, monetary instability, and the fact that García-Baquero's tonnage estimates only begin in 1680. Without a longer perspective,

Table 10.3. *Tonnage of American Trade and the* Blanca al Millar *of the* Consulado *of Sevilla (1621-1630 — 100)* (a)

Period	Index of Indies Tonnage	Index of *Blanca* (adjusted)	Index of *Blanca* (nominal)
1551-60	31.8	274.2	131.7
1561-70	43.7	286.8	174.8
1571-80	57.8	276.5	179.0
1581-90	78.0	324.7	235.8
1591-1600	83.4	224.1	176.7
1601-10	108.5	192.3	177.7
1611-20	106.6	128.1	107.7
1621-30	100.0	100.0	100.0
1631-40	70.5	63.6	65.7
1641-50	53.9	37.6	46.8

Source: Huguette and Pierre Chaunu, *Seville et Atlantique*, vol. 7, pp. 46-47; and Smith, *The Spanish Guild Merchants*, pp. 140-141, totals adjusted to compensate for the doubling of the tariff in 1603 (Smith, p. 105).

a. This base period is the decade for which the greatest number of indexed comparisons are possible. Adjustment for prices is based on Hamilton's Andalusian series, adjusted to 1621-30 — 100. To the extent that the mix of goods taxed *ad valorem* matched the composition of the Andalusian indices, our adjusted and unadjusted indices provide the range of trends within which change took place. Tonnages varied from 82,500 in 1551-60 to 281,500 in 1601-20. Maximum nominal *blanca* revenue was 13,895 *reales* in 1581-90.

Table 10.4. *Indices of Commercial Activity at Sevilla and Cádiz,*
1651-1700(a)
(1681-80 = 100)

Period	Indies Tonnage	Sevilla *Blanca* (adj.)	(nom.)	Cádiz *Aduanilla* (adj.)	(nom.)
1651-60		100.0	125.2	52.0	65.0
1661-70		77.3	118.6	51.2	78.5
1671-80		84.6	135.3	55.7	89.2
1681-90	100.0	100.0	100.0	100.0	100.0
1691-1700	80.3	149.0	134.2	247.9	223.4

Sources: Same as for Table 10.3, plus annual accounts of the city of Cádiz in
the municipal archives, 1656-1800, and García-Baquero, *Cádiz y el Atlantico*,
vol. 2, pp. 126-128.
    a. All figures are adjusted to base 1681-90 to allow inclusion of tonnage
data. Adjustments for prices are based on Hamilton's five-year indices for
Andalucía, 1651-1700.

they suggest an end-of-century decline prolonged by the War of Spanish
Succession. Table 10.4 contradicts this trend and, even when adjusted for
price fluctuations, shows a substantial recovery of port activity after a low
point in the 1660's. The most pronounced change coincides with the official
transfer of Indies trade to Cádiz, but the concurrent doubling of port duty
revenue at Sevilla is noteworthy. The volume of trade in question was undeni-
ably small, but the trend is similar to that in Barcelona—recovery in the third
quarter of the century, with a mild setback in the final decade.

The principal link between this port activity and the peninsular interior
was the resource base of revenue and credit that Andalusian commerce
produced for the government in Madrid. Sevilla's maritime commerce had
been separated from the economy of the Spanish interior by the early seventeenth century. At the end of the century, even the immediate Andalusian
hinterland of the two major ports was but lightly involved with the imperial
monopoly, exporting a modest 40,000 *arrobas* of wine and 6,000 *arrobas* of
olive oil yearly.[18]

Table 10.4 gives the real and nominal index values for the *blanca* of Sevilla
and the *aduanilla* of Cádiz, both of which were minor *ad valorem* taxes
similar to the port duty (*periatge*) of Barcelona, and the index of Indies
tonnage as offered by García-Baquero. The *ad valorem* indicators are presented with index numbers for both their nominal value and their value
adjusted for Andalusian price levels. Since both port duties were collected *ad*

18. Lutgarda García Fuentes, "Sevilla y Cádiz en los exportaciones de productos agrarios a
Indias en la segunda mitad del siglo XVII." Neither amount was more than a tenth the annual
consumption of Madrid at the time.

Table 10.5. *Index Numbers of Indies Tonnage,* Aduanilla *Revenue, and Ferry Revenue at Cádiz, 1656-1800*(a)
(1721-30 = 100)

Period	Tonnage to Indies	*Aduanilla* (adjusted)	*Aduanilla* (nominal)	Sancti Petri Ferry
1656-60	—	22.0	29.8	76.1
1661-70	—	21.7	36.0	139.5
1671-80	—	23.9	40.9	167.3
1681-90	82.6	42.2	45.9	80.8
1691-1700	66.4	105.2	102.5	69.3
1701-10	35.3	74.5	83.1	110.9
1711-20	51.6	74.9	80.1	43.2
1721-30	100.0	100.0	100.0	100.0
1731-40	107.8	101.6	110.4	161.0
1741-50	133.0	96.7	102.2	235.0
1751-60	211.8	93.9	118.2	264.5
1761-70	264.3	122.8	159.4	174.0
1771-80	269.3	138.4	194.1	131.7
1781-90	—	142.0	235.6	149.2
1791-1800	—	67.0	143.3	267.6

Sources: García-Baquero, *Cádiz y el Atlantico*, vol. 2, pp. 126-128; Municipal Archives, Cádiz, annual account books, 1656-1800.
a. Price indices are derived from Hamilton and adjusted to base 1721-30 = 100.

valorem, the adjusted figures are likely to be more accurate, and conflict with the trend of Indies tonnage, which drifts downward until 1709.[19] It can be argued that regionally based commerce, illicit American trade, and general port activity rose during 1675-1700 outside the legal Indies monopoly. This would be consistent with the revival of commerce in Barcelona and with the growth of trade all around the Atlantic. It also coincides with indications of a substantial increase in the flow of American silver through private channels. The scale of fraud in the official Indies monopoly was large enough to suggest that the official tonnages may reflect aspects of Atlantic trade that had little to do with Andalucía.[20] Thus it is plausible to suggest a modest reversal of the seventeenth-century trade decline in coastal Andalucía after 1670, even while the interior went through the prolonged crisis of 1677-85.

The magnitude of this recovery after the 1660's should not be overstated. Hamilton's silver prices indicate that the silver equivalent of the Sevilla *Consulado* tax in the 1690's was only about 12.5% of that for 1601-10, but

19. Antonio García-Baquero González, *Cádiz y el Atlántico, 1717-1778: El comercio colonial español bajo el monopolio gaditano* (1976), vol. 2, pp. 126-128.
20. Henry Kamen, in *Spain in the Later Seventeenth Century* (1980), pp. 133-140, indicates that the flow of bullion at the height of the legal monopoly may have exceeded anything found by Hamilton in the official sources. See also Barbara and Stanley Stein, *The Colonial Heritage of Latin America*, p. 94.

the proportionate drop in Indies tonnage was far greater.[21] Nevertheless, the seventeenth-century decline had been reversed. The fact that port duties in both Andalusian ports follow the same chronology indicates a quickening of regional commercial life only partly connected with the American trade.[22] This is reinforced by the trend of traffic on the ferry from Cádiz to Puerto Santa María, outport for the Jérez district. Revenue from this ferry rose 150% from the late 1650's to the 1680's and remained fairly high in the 1690's. Since the fare was not an *ad valorem* tax, revenues were not affected by prices.

The eighteenth century saw an expansion of commerce at Cádiz that can now be seen as a continuation of the modest expansion of the last quarter of the seventeenth (see Table 10.5). Indies tonnage, the *aduanilla* of Cádiz, and the cross-bay ferry all show a recession during the War of Spanish Succession. This began in the 1690's for the Indies monopoly; but in the years from 1709 to 1720, all of these trends were sharply reversed. Indies tonnage rose 175% between the 1720's and the 1770's, as did the nominal value of the port tax in Cádiz. Adjusted for Andalusian prices, however, the value of that revenue rose much more slowly. The price-adjusted *aduanilla* suggests a long-term increase in port activity from 1680 to about 1725. Then, while the volume of Indies tonnage rose, the port revenue drifted downward until 1760, followed by a sustained increase in real value until 1792. Traffic in the bay area, as shown by revenue from the *barca de Sancti Petri*, rose sharply after the succession war. In part this reflects suppression of the Puerto Real and Puerto Santa María ferries; and when the royal highway to Cádiz was completed, ferry revenues dropped substantially.

Tonnage data is not available after 1778, but following the reforms of that year the official value of legal Indies trade rose dramatically, and in 1792 it was five times that of 1778.[23] This is an increase far in excess of the unadjusted *aduanilla* revenue, indicating a trend independent of the regional economy served by Cádiz. After 1797 the Indies trade was subjected to violent fluctuations due to the international situation, and declined rapidly. The value of exports in 1797 was about 300 million *reales,* slightly over half of which were registered as of domestic origin. In several subsequent years the value dropped to 10% of that figure, while the intervening peaks never reached the earlier highs. In 1815–21, the value of exports was typically 75 million *reales*, two-thirds of domestic origin. The demise of the colonial trade

---

21. Hamilton, *American Treasure,* p. 403; *War and Prices,* p. 34. Because of the way Hamilton constructed his indices, there is nothing in his work but these silver prices to bridge the transition between 1650 and 1651.

22. Smith, *The Spanish Guild Merchant,* p. 93.

23. Antonio García-Baquero Gonzalez, *Comercio colonial y guerras revolucionarias* (1972), p. 128.

of the eighteenth century was completed by 1828, when Spain's total foreign trade was less than a quarter of that of 1792, and exports from Cádiz totaled less than 9 million *reales*.[24]

2. The Ports and the Interior

This bare outline of commercial trends in Sevilla and Cádiz summarizes a commercial life that in the later eighteenth century represented half of all of Spain's exports and imports. Yet the ties to Madrid and the interior were surprisingly sparse, consisting of a few commercial links and a structure of credit, taxes, and political influence. This was not always the case, and it is instructive to look briefly at the history of the connections between maritime trade and the interior.

The middle decades of the sixteenth century saw a close association between the expansion of the Indies trade and the growth of the textile industries in Málaga, Granada, Toledo, Segovia, and other Castilian towns. The wine and wheat production of Andalucía was similarly affected. Consequently, the Andalusian urban system evolved like that of the Castilian towns. Córdoba, largest town of inland western Andalucía, grew from 5,851 *vecinos* in 1530 to about 13,000 by 1594. Thereafter depression set in, as demand for cloth declined, taxes rose, and epidemics hit the region. Urban growth ceased and the city began to decline.[25] This pattern was repeated in relatively small communities such as Pedroches to the north of Córdoba, where sixteenth-century expansion was also followed by rapid decline.[26]

As the sixteenth century wore on, domestic industry was unable to satisfy the Indies trade, and a growing proportion of the rising volume of exports came from foreign sources. This marks a critical phase in the separation of the Spanish interior from the economy of the Sevilla-Cádiz zone. Long before the tonnage of the Indies trade reached its peak in 1610, domestic industrial exports were in full decline, and the capture of imperial trade by non-Spanish merchants was generally recognized. It was paralleled by Italian takeover of the wool trade, as wool exports were diverted from northern outlets and taken over by Italian merchants in the southern and eastern ports of the peninsula.[27] In the early seventeenth century, Spanish America, Andalucía, and central Spain experienced depressions, each for different immediate causes.[28] The Andalusian ports remained an avenue for legal trade between

24. Ibid., pp. 122, 242, and the graphs following p. 254.
25. José I. Fortea Pérez, "La evolución demográfica de Córdoba en los siglos XVI y XVII."
26. Bartolomé Valle Buenestado, "Notas sobre la evolución demográfica de la comarca de Pedroches, 1530–1857," p. 289.
27. Carla Rahn Phillips, "Spanish Wool Exports in the Sixteenth and Seventeenth Centuries."
28. Without cheap labor, the high-cost American silver mines reduced production, and the colonial economy shifted to large, relatively self-sufficient estates; see J. H. Parry, *The Spanish Seaborne Empire* (1966), pp. 103–104, 116.

Europe and Spanish America, but played an increasingly passive role. The merchant community of Sevilla became a group of commission agents dependent on government maintenance of an obsolete commercial structure.[29]

The marginalization of Spanish commercial activity at Sevilla is illustrated by the trend of the tax that the *Consulado* collected there. The real value of its revenue rose 15–20% between 1551 and 1590, then began to decline rapidly well before the tonnage of the Indies trade. This reflects the declining participation of Castilian products in imperial trade and correlates with the decline of the smaller textile centers of the interior. The loss of contact with the interior is also apparent if we contrast the distribution of bullion from Sevilla to the interior in 1575 with the distribution of letters of credit held by a major Sevilla trading firm in 1603.[30] Of 253 peninsular credit instruments, 77% involved western Andalucía and 18% the Mediterranean coast. Only 9.8% mentioned interior locations, and virtually all of those were from southern Extremadura. This dismantling of commerce into the interior reflects the situation in Toledo, where merchants were unable to maintain their coastal trading connections after 1600.[31]

The dissolution of the commercial links between the Andalusian ports and Old and New Castile is illustrated by the *portazgo* of Zafra, owned by the Duke of Medinaceli and situated on the main route from Sevilla through Extremadura toward Madrid and Valladolid. To the extent that traffic was not being diverted to the Sevilla-Madrid route along the Guadalquivir valley, this road toll illustrates the decline of traffic from Sevilla to the interior. The scattered figures for the sixteenth century suggest a rising volume of traffic that peaked in 1604–05. Comparison with the Chaunus' figures on the tonnage at Sevilla indicates that the inland traffic through Extremadura was well developed before the expansion of the Indies trade (see Table 10.6).

Traffic at Zafra expanded 30% in the last half of the sixteenth century, while the Indies trade trebled and the real value of the *ad valorem* tax on merchandise at Sevilla increased 15–20% (1551–90). The Zafra toll revenues fell by a third between 1604–05 and 1630, then collapsed drastically with the revolt in nearby Portugal. The trend at Zafra follows closely the timing of trends in the Indies trade—but its decline, even before the Portuguese revolt, was far more rapid (58% vs. 35% to 1640). Thus while Spanish participation in the Indies trade declined, the role of the interior in the maritime economy declined even faster. The *portazgo* of Zafra continued to fall drastically in the

29. Stein and Stein, *The Colonial Heritage*, p. 47.

30. José Gentil da Silva, *En Espagne*, pp. 67–82 and tables 9–13.

31. Antonio-Miguel Bernal and Antonio García-Baquero González, *Tres siglos del comercio sevillano, 1598–1868* (1976), p. 173; Gentil da Silva, *En Espagne*, pp. 122–150; Michael Weisser, "Les marchands de Tolède dans l'économie castillane, 1565–1635."

Table 10.6. *Index Numbers of Road Toll Revenue at Zafra and Commercial Activity at Sevilla, 1536-1700*(a) *(1621-30 = 100)*

Period	Road Toll at Zafra	Tonnage to Indies	Sevilla Consulado Revenue (adjusted)
1536	65.7	—	—
1547	99.4	—	—
1551-60	99.4(b)	31.8	274.2
1561-70	—	43.7	286.8
1571-80	—	57.8	276.5
1581-90	119.6(c)	78.0	324.7
1591-1600	—	83.4	224.1
1601-10	132.7(d)	108.5	192.3
1611-20	—-	106.6	128.1
1621-30	100.0	100.0	100.0
1631-40	55.3	70.5	63.6
1641-50	25.6	53.9	37.6
1651-60	9.5		
1661-70	13.5		
1671-80	11.9		
1681-90	7.1		
1691-1700	6.5		

Sources: Chaunu, *Seville et l'Atlantique*, vol. 7, pp. 46-47; Smith, *The Spanish Guild Merchants*, pp. 140-141; Archivo del Duque de Medinaceli, legs. 60-82, 83.

a. The toll was not collected *ad valorem*, but according to a list of stipulated fees depending on the merchandise involved. Recurrent copies of the fee schedule in the documents indicate that the schedule was not changed during the period in question.

b. 1554 only.

c. 1587 only.

d. 1604-05 only.

1650's, as the war with Portugal continued; it recovered slightly in the '60's and '70's, then became negligible.

Thus traffic from Andalucía into western Spain was active in the sixteenth century and responded to the trade at Sevilla, but its seventeenth-century decline was rapid and more abrupt than the decline of traffic at Sevilla. Sevilla's contact with the commercial structure of sixteenth-century Castile was broken and its trade to the interior either declined or shifted to routes which went directly to Madrid. The pattern is repeated within western Andalucía by the collapse of Córdoba, which declined from 13,000 *vecinos* in 1594 to 7,000 in 1626–33, a trend again echoed in smaller communities such as Pedroches.[32] The new separation is apparent in the seventeenth century, as

32. Fortea Pérez, "La evolución," pp. 382–383; Valle Buenestado, "Notas."

interior regional economies declined earlier and faster than did the Sevilla trade. Its persistence is suggested by developments in the last half of the century. As Córdoba and its region recovered after 1650, they achieved a precarious stability that lasted well into the eighteenth century, but such interior trends evidence little correlation with renewed port activity at Sevilla and Cádiz.[33]

By the later seventeenth century, the underlying limitations of pre-industrial life were sharply exposed in Andalucía. The basic reliance on self-sufficiency that characterized noncoastal Spain through the eighteenth century was more prominent than ever.[34] This left only a limited market economy in which rudimentary transportation hauled valuable oil to Madrid and the north, supplied Sevilla, serviced a few mines, and provided a trickle of wine and oil for the Indies trade.[35] Agricultural output expanded only as the growing population plowed up more land, while marketable surpluses were produced largely by tithes and rents. In fact, western Andalucía saw an increase in rural output after 1715, but the peak was reached well before the end of the century and reflected the regional balance between land and population.[36]

Indicators of commercial activity in eighteenth-century Andalucía, such as brokerage fees on cargo leaving Sevilla by land and gate tolls at Córdoba, show that even at its peak, port activity had little connection with the interior (see Table 10.7). While Indies tonnage and port duty revenue at Cádiz rose steadily until 1790, the two inland duties show no such trend. That of Sevilla, when adjusted for price changes, remained stable until the inflation of the 1790's depressed its price-adjusted value, while the short Córdoba series declined noticeably from 1750 to 1779. Even without adjustment for the effects of price change, the trends verify the growing separation between regional and maritime commerce already noted in the seventeenth century.

This is further reflected in the role of Spanish products in exports to the Indies. Andalucía supplied wine and olive oil, employing commercial arrangements and landowner participation similar to those of the Madrid supply trade. But the volume of goods was not great and a generous estimate puts the Spanish share of legal exports in 1750 at 16% by value and 50% by volume. The evidence regarding manufactures originating in Spain documents the absence of interior Castile from the export trade. Of 10,000 tons of textiles shipped to the Indies in 1749–51, only 12 tons (30 mule loads an-

---

33. Fortea Pérez, pp. 391–393; Gonzalo Anes Álvarez, "Tendencias de la producción agrícola en tierras de la Corona de Castilla, siglos XVI a XIX" (1978), p. 108.

34. Anes, "Tendencias," p. 101.

35. Pierre Ponsot, "En Andalousie occidentale: Systèmes de transporte et développement économique, XVIe-XIXe siècle" (1976); García Fuentes, "Sevilla y Cádiz," pp. 404–405.

36. Anes, "Tendencias," pp. 101, 110.

Table 10.7. *Indices of Commercial Indicators in Lower Andalucia,*
1750-1806
(1771-80 = 100)

Period	Tonnage to Indies	*Aduanilla* in Cádiz (adjusted)	*Correduria* in Sevilla (adjusted)	Gate Tolls in Córdoba
1751-60	78.6	67.8	—	113.4
1761-70	98.1	88.7	107.0	124.0
1771-80	100.0	100.0	100.0	100.0
1781-90	—	105.2	105.9	—
1790-1800	—	48.3	78.7	—

Sources: Same as Table 10.6 and, for Córdoba, Table E.1.

nually) came from the largest textile complex of the interior, the royal factories at Guadalajara and San Fernando.[37] This correlates with the location of people who took out licenses to place cargo in the Indies trade. Between 1743 and 1778, 43% were from Cádiz and Andalucía, 35% from provinces on the northern coast, and 5% from Mediterranean ports. Only 11% were located in the vast interior of Old and New Castile, León, and Extremadura, and two-thirds of that 11% were in the wool-producing provinces of Soria, Logroño, and Burgos.

The very structure of the trade worked against participation by the weak industrial sector. As plantation crops (sugar, cacao, tobacco) became more important among imports, the demand for American-bound exports shifted to manufactures, the trade goods hardest for Spain to produce. In the second quarter of the eighteenth century, manufactures constituted 54% of the value of exports, while in the third quarter they reached 72%.[38] Spain's lack of participation in the trade is suggested by the origins of letters of credit and bills of exchange held by the largest commercial house of Sevilla as of 1803. Of several hundred bills, only 25 or 30 involved any part of Spain, while the vast majority came from England, France, the Low Countries, and Germany. Only the collapse of colonial trade after 1800 reoriented these commercial connections to Spain. In 1813–18, many European contacts remained, but the same trading house had numerous new connections with Madrid, Andalucía, and the Basque provinces, foreshadowing the structure of Spain's later commercial economy. By the 1850's, commercial contacts between Sevilla and Europe were much reduced, while those with the north coast of Spain persisted. Madrid became relatively more important to Sevillan merchants, and interior Andalucía became the real basis of the city's trade.[39]

37. García-Baquero, *Cádiz*, vol. 1, pp. 324–327, 330.
38. Ibid., p. 330.
39. Bernal and García-Baquero, *Tres siglos de comercio sevillano*, pp. 190, 203, 217.

C. The Mediterranean Maritime Fringe

The port complexes of western Andalucía and Catalonia mark the two extremes of Spain's long Mediterranean coast, a coast dotted with smaller seaports like Valencia, Alicante, Cartagena, and Málaga. After somewhat disparate experiences in the sixteenth century, this entire coastal fringe began a modest commercial recovery well before 1700, contradicting the prevailing impression of depression and stagnation in late Hapsburg Spain. The evidence is far from complete, but Barcelona and Cádiz were only the most obvious parts of a commercial circuit that involved other Mediterranean ports as well.

1. The Sixteenth Century

The timing of commercial trends varied during the sixteenth century depending on local factors, but most ports were involved in the upswing of commercial activity that marked the last quarter of the century in Barcelona and Sevilla. Prices in Valencia show remarkably small cyclical swings compared with Castile and generally parallel those of Barcelona, indicating that both cities relied on Mediterranean connections for important supplies. Valencian port activity indicates notable prosperity in the fifteenth and early sixteenth centuries. Ship entries and port revenues (*peatges*) were high in 1503–10, drifted downward through the 1530's to a low in the 1550's, then show a strong recovery through the last quarter of the century. The strength of this trend is uncertain, as Table 10.8 illustrates. Judging from ship entries, the actual trend was between the two sets of revenue indices. While the volume of shipping dropped with port revenues at mid-sixteenth century, in the last quarter it was just above that for the first decade.

Valencia's late medieval prosperity reflected the disturbances in fifteenth-century Catalonia, while the midcentury decline probably indicates diversion of commercial capital to Sevilla. The later recovery coincides with the *Morisco* rebellion of 1568, the breakup of Atlantic commerce, and the diversion of the wool trade and political communications to Mediterranean outlets. The little-studied port of Alicante, an outport of Valencia a third its size, followed the same outline.[40]

The recovery of port activity in the later sixteenth century reflects the internal development of the province of Valencia. The population rose 50% between 1570 and 1609, although much of the increase took place among the *Moriscos*. Settled in poorer and more isolated areas, they contributed little to

40. Álvaro Castillo Pintado, "La coyuntura de la economía valenciana en los siglos XVI y XVII" (1969), pp. 255, 257–266; Emilia Salvador, *La economia valenciana en el siglo XVI* (1972), pp. 139–173, 335–342. Castillo Pintado presents higher port duty (*peatge*) figures, but Salvador's study was made later, uses a different series of documents, and has been accepted as preferable.

Table 10.8. *Indices of Port Activity in Sixteenth-Century Valencia (1581-90 = 100)*

Period	Spanish Prices	Port Duty(a) (nominal)(b)	Port Duty(a) (adjusted)(c)
1501-10	39	65.7	168
1531-40	49	46.5	95
1581-90	100	100	100

Source: Castillo Pintado, "La coyuntura de la economía valenciana."
a. The *Peatge* of Valencia.
b. No adjustment for possible effects of price changes when goods were taxed *ad valorem*.
c. Assumes *ad valorem* tax, adjusted with Valencian prices in Hamilton, *American Treasure*, p. 273.

the market economy. The Christian population, which rose rapidly in 1548–71, grew more slowly in the later decades, but the overall pressure was strong enough to prompt migration from Valencia to Castile despite the population problems there.[41] A growing population rented more land for farming, creating a boom in the value of rents and tithes. This is illustrated by examples of the royal share of the tithe, the nominal value of which increased 525% between the 1560's and 1601–10. Even when adjusted for price changes, the increase was about 215%, implying a large jump in the amount of wealth captured by landed and urban elites.[42] This is the type of rural trend that allowed rural distress and port activity to develop simultaneously.

The pattern in sixteenth-century Málaga differed considerably. Málaga had been a center of the Moorish silk industry and served both as port of entry for goods destined for Granada and outlet for raisins and sweet wines. She was the official supply port for the African *presidios* and early became a participant in the Indies trade. The nominal value of the silk industry grew rapidly during the first half of the century, but it is difficult to measure the actual rate of growth without reliable silk prices. In 1501–50 the decennial averages of the general price index in Andalucía rose 103%, while the nominal value of the silk tax rose 175%. In the next two decades, prices rose 32% while silk tax revenues increased 92% (see Table 10.9). Thus we can infer that the silk industry in Málaga grew steadily before 1550, and then at a more rapid rate until the *Morisco* revolt at the end of the 1560's. In this, Málaga was following the pattern of towns like Florence,[43] and responding to the

41. Castillo Pintado, "La coyuntura," pp. 240–241, 244, 247.
42. Ibid., p. 272. The control used is the price of wheat in Valencia. While not the only commodity tithed, wheat was the most important one.
43. Carlo M. Cipolla, "The Decline of Italy" (1952–53 and 1968).

Table 10.9. *Silk Tax Revenues in Málaga,*
Sixteenth Century

Period	Average Annual Value(a)	Index (1540-46 = 100)
1505-10	216,915	40.4
1511-16	261,033	48.6
1531	373,147	69.4
1540	466,912	86.9
1541-46	537,312	100.0
1547-53	595,588	110.8
1554-60	761,029	141.6
1561-68	1,139,159	212.0

Source: Francisco Bejarano, *La industria de la seda en
Málaga durante el siglo XVI* (1951), pp. 103-108.
a. Figures given in *reales.*

development of Sevilla as the empire developed. Thus she avoided the midcentury slump that affected Valencia and Barcelona.

Málaga, Granada, and Jaén comprised an important segment of the urban
system of Mediterranean Andalucía. With a Moslem economic heritage that
included luxury products like silk and sugar, this region saw development of
interurban commerce in the sixteenth century, and then the same separation
of coastal and interior economies experienced by western Andalucía in the
seventeenth. We do not have serial data for Granada in the sixteenth century,
but its largest satellite, Jaén, experienced the same expansion as other Andalusian towns, growing from 4,628 *vecinos* in 1530 to 5,595 by 1594—a 20%
expansion.[44] This parallels the growth of the silk industry in Málaga and
implies growth in the Granada region until about 1570, followed by political
and demographic instability after the *Morisco* rebellion of 1568. Despite
difficulties, Málaga remained an important transit port in the Mediterranean
trade to Sevilla and Lisbon and, along with Alicante and Cartagena, was a
redistribution center for colonial products.[45]

2. The Seventeenth Century
The seventeenth century littoral is documented by data on port activity in
Valencia, Málaga, and Cartagena, and illustrated with qualitative information from Alicante. These are summarized and compared by indexing the
peatge of Valencia, the *mollages* and *renta mayor* of Cartagena, and the
revenue of the *lonja y correduría* in Málaga. Although the concordance is not

44. Luis Coronas Tejada, "Estudio demográfico de la ciudad de Jaén en el siglo XVII."
45. José Luis Barea Ferrer, "Vicisitudes en torno a la construcción del nuevo puerto de
Málaga en el siglo XVI."

Table 10.10. *Commercial Activity in Valencia, Cartagena,
and Málaga, 1601-50
(1621-30 = 100)*

Period	Index numbers of nominal values			
	Valencia *Peatge*	Cartagena *Mollages*	Cartagena *Renta Mayor*	Málaga *Lonja y Correduría*
1601-10	133.5	—	99.2	—
1611-20	105.1	—	138.1	87
1621-30	100.0	100.0	100.0	100.0
1631-40	83.8	90.4	94.7	94
1641-50	99.0	85.2	56.9	121
	Index numbers adjusted(a) for price levels			
1601-10	136.0	—	107.4	—
1611-20	109.4	—	164.2	103.5
1621-30	100.0	100.0	100.0	100.0
1631-40	75.1	87.6	91.8	91.2
1641-50	99.0	67.9	45.3	96.5

Sources: See Table E.1 and, for Valencia, Castillo Pintado, "La coyuntura de la economía valenciana."
a. Valencian figures have been adjusted with Hamilton's averages for that region, Cartagena and Málaga figures with Hamilton's Andalusian averages. The close connection between Málaga and Sevilla makes this acceptable, although the procedure is dubious for Cartagena.

perfect, by the later seventeenth century all three ports had stabilized after the midcentury decline, and two of the three show significant increases in port activity (see Tables 10.10 and 10.11).

Castillo Pintado summarizes economic trends in seventeenth-century Valencia by depicting a peak in 1605 just before the expulsion of the *Moriscos*, a 35-year decline, recovery of commercial activity lasting into the 1670's, and a plateau in the last decades.[46] Unfortunately, he did not adjust the *peatges*, which were largely *ad valorem* taxes, for price changes. The prolonged deflation of seventeenth-century Europe is apparent in Valencia, and contrasts with Castile.[47] When the indicator is adjusted for prices, the early seventeenth-century decline comes closer to 50% than the 35% that Castillo Pintado found, a trend corroborated by evidence of serious decline in agriculture. The rural situation was worst in 1610–20 and 1645–50, after which the rural economy stabilized.[48] Conversely, the last half of the century appears more

46. Castillo Pintado, "La coyuntura."
47. Vilar, *Catalunya*, vol. 2, pp. 379, 381; Hamilton, *War and Prices*, pp. 119–120; James Casey, *The Kingdom of Valencia in the Seventeenth Century*, p. 247 and Conclusion.
48. Anes, "Tendencias," p. 108.

Table 10.11. *Commercial Activity in Valencia, Cartagena,*
and Málaga, 1651-1700
(1671-80 = 100)

Period	Valencia *Peatges*	Cartagena *Mollages*	Cartagena *Renta Mayor*	Málaga *Lonja y Correduría*
	Index numbers of nominal values			
1651-60	75.0	83.6	131.3	136.9
1661-70	—	87.2	86.5	147.0
1671-80	100.0	100.0	100.0	100.0
1681-90	91.3	65.0	89.9	61.7
1691-1700	—	64.5	91.8	—
	Index numbers adjusted(a) for price levels			
1651-60	63.7	106.2	166.8	173.0
1661-70	—	90.4	89.8	152.5
1671-80	100.0	100.0	100.0	100.0
1681-90	97.0	103.3	143.0	97.5
1691-1700	—	113.8	161.9	—

Sources: See Table 10.10.
a. See note a. to Table 10.10.

optimistic than Castillo Pintado's nominal figures imply—the recovery in the third quarter is stronger and the level of the last quarter more sustained. The sequence strongly resembles that for Barcelona.

Port activity paralleled provincial population, which declined 30% due to the expulsion of the *Moriscos*, and 35% by 1650. The impact on agricultural production was softened because much of the vacated land was marginal or was quickly resettled by Christian peasants. By the 1630's, production as documented by tithes had reached the nominal value of the sixteenth-century peak, although this was offset by wheat prices that were 25% higher.[49] The expulsion of the *Moriscos* caused serious economic adjustments, while the collapse of Toledo hurt the Valencian silk industry.

Silk production declined seriously during the seventeenth century despite a shift to lower-quality products as Castilian purchasing power fell. Dependent on the Toledo-based trading network of the interior, the collapse of this industry destroyed important linkages between periphery and interior. There are signs of a revival of silk production at the end of the seventeenth century, but the only connection with the interior was the Madrid market; and in contrast with the sixteenth century, the revival depended much more on trade connections outside of Spain. This is but one of a number of indications of

49. Castillo Pindato, "La coyuntura," pp. 242–243, 249, 252.

declining association with the interior. James Casey suggests a rigidification of rural society and economy in which, despite Valencia's position as a seaport, the region was caught in a developmental stalemate of rural misery, inequality, and Mafia-style local power structures.[50]

In general, Castillo Pintado's analysis of the early seventeenth century in Valencia is overly optimistic. The partial recovery of economic life by the 1640's is clear, however, and the relative strength of the Valencian economy is suggested by the appearance of Castilian silver coinage after 1640, a reflection of the diversion of Barcelona traffic to Valencia during the Thirty Years' War.[51] The recovery of port activity appears stronger in the period 1660–80, after which it established a plateau concurrent with those in Barcelona and Málaga.

In Cartagena, the level of port activity was high well into the seventeenth century, reaching its peak in the second decade and paralleling the cycle of the Indies trade and the Mediterranean conjuncture.[52] The price-adjusted index of port activity, however, shows an extremely sharp drop after 1630, with port revenues falling a third by 1650, and the *renta mayor* by two-thirds. The price-adjusted indicators reached their nadir in the 1660's, after which the index for the *mollages* jumped 25% and that for the *renta mayor* 85% between 1671 and 1700. This fits with evidence that agricultural output in the Murcia area declined between 1604 and 1670, followed by rising production past the end of the century.[53] Thus the decline in Cartagena came later and was sharper than in Valencia, while the adjusted indices show unambiguous growth in commercial activity beginning at roughly the same time as in Barcelona and Valencia.

Other Cartagena series reflect the changing relationship of the port to the interior. The *renta mayor* and *mollages* (see Tables 10.10 and 10.11) reflect port activity and the economy of the city itself, while the *correduria* and *saca del pescado* (see Table 10.12) taxed goods leaving the city for the interior. The *renta* and *mollages* of Cartagena declined in the 1630's, although revenues on goods moving into the interior did not. The *correduria* did not collapse until the 1640's, while the volume of fish shipped inland remained large through the 1650's.

The *correduria* indicates a low volume of goods moving inland except in the 1670's—a time when American bullion began to lubricate many aspects of long-distance commerce in Spain.[54] The movement of fish inland remained

50. Casey, pp. 84–91.

51. Castillo, "La coyuntura," p. 256.

52. Fernand Braudel, in *The Mediterranean*, vol. 2, pp. 892–903, indicates that the general level of economic activity in the Mediterranean mercantile economy remained high through the first third of the seventeenth century.

53. Anes, "Tendencias," p. 108.

54. Henry Kamen, *Spain in the Later Seventeenth Century*, p. 135.

Table 10.12. *Indices of Inland-Oriented Commercial Activity*
in Cartagena, 1611-50
(1621-30 = 100)

Period	Correduría Carros (nominal)	Correduría Carros (adjusted) (a)	Saca de Pescado (nominal)	Saca de Pescado (adjusted) (a)
1601-10	—	—	—	—
1611-20	101.4	120.6	119.0	185.6
1621-30	100.0	100.0	100.0	100.0
1631-40	111.7	108.3	184.0	153.5
1641-50	54.5	43.4	238.0	166.7

a. Adjustment is based on Hamilton's New Castilian indices.

substantial until 1690, except during the crisis years in the late 1670's (see Table 10.13). Then, while the adjusted *renta* rose 62% in the last quarter of the century, the tax on fish moving inland dropped drastically and the volume of merchandise heading inland fell back to the midcentury low.

Expansion of port traffic was underway from the 1670's. Although the taxes on goods re-exported from Cartagena to the interior indicate a decline in that traffic, port traffic in Cartagena was increasing. Connections with the interior that had been important early in the seventeenth century had dissolved, and port activity was now more an outgrowth of coastal trade or the economic life in the provincial hinterland. The pattern is very like that observed for Andalucía and Valencia.

Additional light is thrown on these trends by descriptive evidence from Alicante, midway between Valencia and Cartagena. The city shows a heavy preponderance of imports which were financed with American silver and a large part of which went on to Madrid. Imports were preponderantly French (39%), English (24%), or of Low Countries origin (22%), illustrating both the nature of the Cádiz-to-Marseilles coastal trade and the narrow nature of coastal contacts with the interior. This trade is further illustrated by the activities of an established merchant in Alicante, Felipe de Moscoso. Beginning in 1661 he built up an import-export business which dealt regularly in goods from suppliers located in ports from Venice to Lisbon and occasionally in London, Amsterdam, and Hamburg; he routinely exported soap, agricultural commodities, wine, and wool while importing European manufactures and iron and colonial sugar and tobacco.[55]

The best indicator of commercial trends in Málaga is a brokerage fee on raisins and wine exported through the port. The nominal yield of this *co-*

55. Ibid., pp. 119-122, 140-144.

Table 10.13. *Indices of Inland-Oriented Commercial Activity in Cartagena 1651-1717*
(1671-80 = 100)

Period	Correduría Carros (nominal)	Correduría Carros (adjusted) (a)	Saca de Pescado (nominal)	Saca de Pescado (adjusted) (a)
1651-60	38.5	48.9	123.3	195.1
1661-70	48.5	50.3	172.5	209.7
1671-80	100.0	100.0	100.0	100.0
1681-90	30.2	48.1	117.4	198.7
1691-1700	—	—	35.2	47.8
1701-10	33.9	—	29.7	—
1711-17	33.8	—	44.7	—

a. Adjustment is based on Hamilton's New Castilian indices.

rreduría de pasas y vino (see Tables 10.10 and 10.11) reveals sustained port activity through the earlier seventeenth century. Even when adjusted for price levels, traffic appears to have fallen only 8% from 1611 to 1650. The nominal value of the revenue continued to rise until 1670 and then fell by 50% in two decades, but when adjusted for price changes the fluctuations are much smaller. The adjusted index of traffic is stable in the middle decades of the seventeenth century, drops by a third in the 1670's, then stabilizes at the lower level in the 1680's. This parallels García-Baquero's description of the volume of shipping in the Cádiz monopoly, but runs counter to the strong increase in the adjusted indices for Cádiz, Sevilla, Cartagena, and Valencia. It implies that the trading circuit as a whole was distinctly expansive in the last third of the seventeenth century, although its commerce was re-distributed away from Málaga.

The chronology of the trend suggests a delayed seventeenth-century crisis in Málaga and its hinterland, and it is likely that the decline of the regional silk industry was a contributing factor.[56] Wheat output fell considerably in the interior districts of the province by the later seventeenth century, but increased along the littoral. The latter trend coincides with the decline of wine and raisin exports, implying greater emphasis on self-sufficiency by the last quarter of the century.[57]

As the Málaga area lost its silk industry and drifted toward agricultural export and self-sufficiency, the urban network based on Granada lapsed into economic isolation and a precarious, self-contained stability. Granada's tax on sugar, an export commodity analogous to wine and raisins in Málaga,

56. Francisco Bejarano, *La industria de la seda en Málaga durante el siglo XVI* (1951), ch. 3.
57. Anes, "Tendencias," p. 108.

Table 10.14. *The* Corredería de Azúcar *in Granada,*
1635-1700
(1671-80 = 100)

Period	Index of Nominal Value	Index of Adjusted(a) Value
1635	519.7	766.7
1645-46	493.8	616.5
1651-60	157.6	178.9
1661-70	73.4	70.6
1671-80	100.0	100.0
1681-90	32.8	58.0
1691-1700	37.0	65.2

Sources: See Table E.1.
   a. Adjustment is based on Hamilton's prices for sugar in New Castile.

declined sharply, in contrast to the surprising strength of other exports from Málaga. From 1635 to the 1670's, this revenue fell 80% in nominal terms and 87% when adjusted for the price of sugar (see Table 10.14). The collapse of Spain's domestic sugar industry is clearly documented, and reflects the presence of colonial sugar in peninsular markets and reduced domestic buying power. The crises of 1677–85 brought another drop in production, and in the last decades of the seventeenth century the yield from the brokerage fee on sugar was less than a tenth of the figures for the 1630's and '40's. Thus an important link between Granada and the rest of Spain disappeared.

Despite the continued decline of sugar, Granada's population apparently followed the pattern seen in Córdoba. Revenues from the brokerage on wheat are available from the 1650's through the 1680's, and their stability suggests that any urban population decline occurred before 1650.[58] This is also the demographic trend in Jaén, Granada's most important urban satellite, where population fell from 5,596 *vecinos* in 1594 to about 4,000 around 1650 and then leveled off.[59] The increasing self-sufficiency of the inland regions is also implied by the decline of dried fish imports for distribution to the interior. In contrast to the similar duty in Cartagena, the volume taxed in Málaga declined 50% from 1631 to 1670 (see Table 10.15). This again prompts the inference that even though the population of Granada stabilized after mid-century, the regional economy was becoming much more isolated and self-contained.

58. Hamilton, *War and Prices,* p. 183.
59. Coronas Tejada, "Estudio de Jaén," p. 215.

Table 10.15. *Revenue from the* Arbitrio de Bacalao
in Málaga, 1631-1703
(1671-80 = 100)

Period	Index of Nominal Value	Index of Adjusted(a) Value
1631-40	194.8	223.1
1641-50	151.8	164.1
1651-60	114.5	170.3
1661-70	131.4	146.3
1671-80	100.0	100.0
1681-90	54.2	83.5
1691-1700	48.2	78.1
1701-1703	32.5	—

Sources: See Table E.1.
    a. Adjustment is based on Hamilton's price for dried fish in New Castile.

3. The Eighteenth Century

The War of the Spanish Succession and the arrival of the Bourbons on the throne mark a break in the long-term indicators of port traffic for all three of the seaports under discussion. The longest unbroken series indicating port activity is the combined *renta mayor y mollages* of Cartagena, supplemented by a *renta de la lonja* in the last third of the century. The nominal and adjusted index numbers of these taxes are shown in Table 10.16. The decades after the succession war suggest a slow upward drift of port activity, extending the recovery of 1675–1700 until the 1740's. Thereafter, port activity expanded rapidly as the index doubled in the 1740's and redoubled in the 1750's. Even adjusted for inflation, the *renta* series shows traffic trebling from 1750 to 1790 and doubling from the end of the Seven Years' War to 1790. The shorter *lonja* series shows similar growth from the mid-1760's and extends the expansion through the 1790's. The trends are remarkably similar to those for both Cádiz and Barcelona.

The combined tax on cartage and fish leaving the city (the *correduría*) also produced increasing revenue during the eighteenth century, but with a different chronology (see Table 10.17). After very low yields in 1720–36, it expanded substantially between 1736 and 1764, but then declined until 1785. Strong expansion is apparent only at the very end of the 1780's when, adjusted for prices, the average of the decade was 10% higher than in the 1750's.

Apparently the increased commercial activity in Cartagena was related to the growth of the city itself and its own hinterland, and revival of the naval base. Agricultural output in the Murcia region ceased to expand after the

Table 10.16. *Indices of Port Activity in Cartagena, 1721-1800*
(1761-70 = 100)

Period	Renta Mayor (nominal)	Renta Mayor (adjusted) (a)	Lonja (nominal)	Lonja (adjusted) (a)
1721-30	11.9			
1731-40	14.4			
1741-50	33.8			
1751-60	61.2	63.1		
1761-70	100.0	100.0	100.0	100
1771-80	—	—	186.0	172
1781-90	258.3	205.5	238.5	186
1791-1800	—	—	471.8	286

Sources: See Table E.1.

a. Adjustment is based on Hamilton's Andalusian price indices, adjusted to make 1761-70 = 100. This was necessary because of the gaps in the *renta mayor* series, and brings the indices into line with those for Barcelona. In the first half of the century, fairly stable prices make the nominal indices a reliable indicator. The inflation of later decades requires adjustment for prices, and the strong maritime links along the coast again suggest the Andalusian series as the best control.

middle of the century. The growth of commerce into the more distant interior is less marked, but can also be explained by decline of the port-of-entry function because of improved roads in northern Spain and the rise of nearby Alicante.[60] In any case, well before 1700 Cartagena had begun a century-long commercial expansion that reflected the development of maritime Spain and Europe and was not associated with the Spanish interior.

No indicators of port activity are available for eighteenth-century Valencia, but there is evidence of a similar trend. Following the recovery of port activity in the late seventeenth century, the provincial population rose from 255,000 inhabitants in 1718 to 960,000 in 1794. Even though the margin of error inherent in the early figure is considerable, the growth is spectacular. The city of Valencia had 75,000 to 100,000 inhabitants by the end of the century and was the center of an urban network of several towns and ports with 10,000 to 20,000 people. The city produced 2 million *varas* of silk annually, and the province exported 420,000 *arrobas* (5,200 tons) of figs a year and 330,000 *arrobas* (4,100 tons) of *barilla* for the Venetian glass industry. Its trade connections reached Venice, Sicily, Corsica, France, Africa, Cádiz, Portugal, and England.[61] With the exception of the silk industry, the eighteenth-century trade pattern was remarkably like that of Málaga.

60. Julia López Gómez, "El puerto de Alicantie" (1951); Juan Masia Vilanova, "Dos épocas en las comunicaciones alicantinas" (1954). On the role of Alicante as an entry port for Madrid, see Enrique Giménez López, "Aproximación al estudio de la estructura social de Alicante en el siglo XVII" (1977), pp. 15-18.

61. Casimir Melià Tena, *L'economia del regne de València* (1978), pp. 37-50, 87, 101-137.

Table 10.17. *Indices of the* Correduría
de Carros y Saca de Pescado *in*
Cartagena, 1721-90
(1771-80 = 100)

Period	Correduría (nominal)	Correduría (adjusted) (a)
1721-30	27.1	—
1731-40	45.8	—
1741-50	92.1	—
1751-60	168.0	173.6
1761-70	100.0	100.0
1771-80	—	—
1781-90	247.0	193.4

a. Adjusted as on Table 10.17.

It is unclear how modern these developments really were. Casey suggests a rigidification of rural society and economy by the end of the seventeenth century in which Valencia's countryside was caught in a developmental dead end of rural misery, inequality, and Mafia-style local power structures.[62] If so, behind the rapid population growth of the eighteenth century lurked a cycle of growth and stagnation in agricultural production that followed the trends in Andalucía and Murcia and implied an increasingly fragile regional economy.[63]

The eighteenth century brought to Málaga the same growth of commercial activity seen elsewhere along the Mediterranean coast, although with variations unique to the area. The trend can be followed through indicators for 1704–35 and 1742–1818 as shown in Tables 10.18 and 10.19. The *correduría* on raisins and wine doubled in the first third of the century, ending the decline and stagnation of the previous century. Between 1742 and 1790 the nominal value of the tax trebled, with only a brief recession in the 1770's. The pattern is similar to that for commerce in Catalonia.

Málaga was participating in the expansion of Europe's maritime economy, and foreign merchants and capital were entering the region in the first third of the century.[64] The city's commerce was stimulated by the reform of Indies trade, and by 1791 Málaga was the third most important peninsular port in the imperial trade, exporting wine, almonds, raisins, and other agricultural commodities.[65] The link between commercial agriculture and exports is clear,

62. Casey, ch. 9.
63. Anes, "Tendencias," p. 111.
64. Germán Rueda Hernanz, "Aportaciones a la historia de la economía malagueña en el periodo de crisis del Antiguo Régimen, 1791–1833."
65. Javier Ortiz de la Tabla Ducasse, "Contrastes regionales en el comercio colonial: Exportación de Cádiz y Málaga a Nueva España, 1785–95," pp. 137–139.

Table 10.18. *Index Numbers of Revenue from Commercial Duties in Málaga, 1704-35 (1721-30 = 100)*

Period	Lonja de Tierra	Correduría de Pasas y Vino	Arbitrio de Bacalao
1704-10	40.9	53.8	48.8
1711-20	102.0	85.1	61.8
1721-30	100.0	100.0	100.0
1731-35	—	117.5	100.0

Sources: See Table E.1.

since three-fourths of regional exports were agricultural.[66] Wheat production stagnated at a high level in the interior districts and declined along the coast,[67] but the latter no doubt reflects the spread of commercial agriculture. By the reign of Charles IV, exports included 400,000 *arrobas* (ca. 1.6 million gallons) of wine and 600,000 *arrobas* (1.5 million pounds) of raisins a year. The leading consumer was England, followed by Germany, Holland, and France.[68]

Taxes reflecting commerce oriented to the interior, however, behaved erratically throughout the century. The *lonja* fee on inland commerce recovered after the War of Succession, but remained static from 1711 to 1730. The new version of this tax fluctuated erratically from 1742 until the 1780's, when imperial trade was reformed and a *Consulado* organized in the city.[69] The 1780's saw a substantial increase in the value of general commerce, although by the end of the century growth had ceased and the real value of the export tax had declined. Indeed, as in Cádiz and Barcelona, the mid-1790's mark the beginning of extremely unstable trade conditions and a regional decline lasting well into the nineteenth century.[70] The erratic nature of interior-oriented trade (*lonja de tierra*) is paralleled by the tax on fish. The importation of cod *(bacalao)* for shipment inland doubled after the succession war, and after 1760 the nominal values indicate a rapid rise in imports, broken by a recession in the 1780's. When these figures are adjusted for the price of *bacalao* in New Castile (assuming an *ad valorem* tax), the peak in the series comes in the 1770's, when prices were relatively low.[71]

66. Rueda Hernanz, "Aportaciones," p. 209.

67. Anes, "Tendencias," p. 110.

68. Juan Jaime Lopez González, "El comercio y el movimiento portuario de Málaga durante el reinado de Carlos IV."

69. Francisco Bejarano, *Historia del Consulado y de la Junta de Comercio de Málaga, 1783–1859* (1949).

70. Rueda Hernanz, "Aportaciones," p. 210.

71. Lopez González, in "El comercio, p. 316, shows a trebling of the volume of *bacalao* from 1784 to 1791, but this period is too short to establish a trend.

Table 10.19. Index Numbers of Revenue from Commercial Duties in Málaga, 1742-1818
(1761-70 = 100)

Period	Lonja Tierra (nom.)	Lonja Tierra (adj.) (a)	Pasas y Vino (nom.)	Pasas y Vino (adj.) (a)	Bacalao (nom.)	Bacalao (adj.) (a)
1742-50	163.7	—	58.1	—	—	—
1751-60	288.9	297.8	74.7	77.0	—	—
1761-70	100.0	100.0	100.0	100.0	100.0	100.0
1771-80	—	—	92.8	85.9	250.6	257.5
1781-90	532.8	416.6	167.1	130.6	161.1	114.9
1791-1800	711.5	431.5	175.6	106.5	253.9	179.2
1801-10	—	—	135.9	—	253.9	
1811-20	—	—	71.7	—	379.0	—

Sources: See Table E.1.
a. Adjustment is based on Hamilton's general indices for Andalucía and fish prices for New Castile, as available.

This instability in part reflects a boom of coastal trade stimulated by the Indies reforms which contrasts with conditions in the regional urban network served by Málaga. Wheat and sugar brokerage revenues for late eighteenth-century Granada suggest an expansion of output in the middle decades, but their later behavior indicates that the urban economy was closely linked to regional agriculture. There are indications of a downturn in agricultural production in many parts of Andalucía at the end of the century,[72] and after the 1770's Granada sugar followed suit. The Granada wheat brokerage revenue, adjusted for Andalusian wheat prices, follows an identical pattern (see Table 10.20). Thus Granada does not fit any model of Spanish economic growth involving general or regional expansion in the last third of the eighteenth century, and its urban economy was unaffected by the commercial boom in Málaga.

II. The Northern Littoral

The Basque provinces and the port of Bilbao constituted the third Spanish center with persistent long-distance commercial connections. In the fifteenth and sixteenth centuries, Vizcaya was an active economic center with a rapidly growing population. It reputedly produced 300,000 *quintales* (15,000 tons) of iron a year around 1550. A third of that was exported, a third was used by the Basque shipbuilding industry, and the remainder was turned into finished goods, especially the helmets, swords, pikes, and armor essential to sixteenth-century infantry. Quantities of iron ore were exported to France, and Basque sailors ranged from the fishing and whaling areas off the British

72. Anes, "Tendencias," pp. 110–111.

Table 10.20. *Index Numbers of Revenue from Wheat and Sugar Broker-age in Granada, 1751-1820*
(1771-80 = 100)

Period	Sugar (nominal)	Sugar (adjusted) (a)	Wheat (nominal)	Wheat (adjusted) (a)
1761-70	67.7	65.8	89.7	90.9
1771-80	100.0	100.0	100.0	100.0
1781-90	79.4	77.9	79.5	67.7
1791-1800	36.6	20.3	126.3	87.5
1801-10	—	—	—	—
1811-20	47.4	—	159.8	—

Source: See Table E.1.
a. Adjustment is based on Hamilton's prices of sugar in New Castile and wheat in Andalucía.

Isles to Africa and Newfoundland.[73] The Basques also maintained an active trade in wheat, wine, local manufactures, salt, fish, and other goods along the French and Spanish coasts. When trans-Atlantic trade began at Sevilla, the Basque provinces supplied large numbers of sailors, merchants, and ships.

The backbone of Basque commerce, however, was the export of Castilian wool to European markets (see Table 10.21). The volume of wool exports peaked around 1560, and the 1560's saw the start of a prolonged decline of northern wool exports, reflecting the shrinking size of the Mesta flocks.[74] The 1570's brought disruption of the Castilian trade fairs and a struggle between Burgos and Bilbao for control of export trade.[75] Burgos merchants dispatched the wool through several north-coast ports until those of Bilbao gained control of the process.[76] Bilbao's victory was ephemeral, however, since in 1580–1600 the northern wool trade declined 80% because of the northern wars. Wool exports were diverted to eastern and Andalusian ports and fell into the hands of Italian merchants, while the fishing, whaling, and shipbuilding industries were unable to adapt to new conditions because of the incessant demands of the Crown.[77]

In the background, the regional economy experienced population growth,

73. Fernández Albaladejo, *El crisis en Guipúzcoa*, pp. 53–58; Emiliano Fernández de Pinedo, *Crecimiento económico y transformaciones sociales del país vasco, 1100–1850* (1974), pp. 29–30.

74. Manuel Basas Fernández, *El Consulado de Burgos en el siglo XVI* (1963), pp. 257–264; Vicente Palacio Atard, *El comercio de Castilla y el puerto de Santander en el siglo XVIII*, pp. 27–33, 119–142.

75. Luis María Bilbao, "Crisis y reconstrucción de la economía vascongada en el siglo XVII" (1977), p. 162.

76. Basas Fernández, *El Consulado de Burgos*, pp. 207–223; Vicens Vives, *Manual*, p. 338.

77. Fernández de Pinedo, *Crecimiento*, p. 31; Fernández Albaladejo, *El crisis en Guipúzcoa*, pp. 60–71; Phillips, "Spanish Wool Exports."

Table 10.21. *Wool Exports from Northern Spain, Sixteenth and Seventeenth Centuries.*

Period	Average Annual Export (in *arrobas*)	
1558-60	180,000	(3)(a)
1561-70	165,989	(10)
1571-80	127,017	(10)
1581-90	34,695	(9)
1591-96	28,099	(5)
1601-25	72,449	(16)
1652-77	85,823	(14)

Source: Based on Carla Rahn Phillips, "Spanish Wool Exports in the Sixteenth and Seventeenth Centuries." Dr. Phillips states that these are provisional estimates.

a. Figures in parentheses indicate number of years documented. The last average masks a strong upward trend after 1660, after which exports ran around 100,000 *arrobas* per year.

as elsewhere in the sixteenth century. This prompted an expansion of cereal production that can be documented as far west as Santander and Asturias, although the coast continued to maintain a balance between cereals, vines, and livestock.[78] Late in the century, however, coastal and interior trends diverged. Population and agricultural production continued to rise along the littoral until after 1600, but in interior Álava the peak was reached as early as the 1560's. The plague of 1564–65 brought stagnation to that region, and by 1583 demographic decline was unmistakable.[79]

In the seventeenth century, the Basque countryside lapsed into self-sufficiency even though certain types of long-distance trade prospered. The weapons industry, unable to convert to production of firearms, declined badly. The iron industry maintained much of its sixteenth-century volume of bar and plate, but exports increasingly featured unworked iron controlled by foreign entrepreneurs.[80]

But despite the wool crisis and decline of Basque rural industry, one type of commerce remained active (see Table 10.22). This was the transit trade between the northern ports and the elite market that was gravitating toward

78. Fernández de Pinedo, pp. 15–18, 23–24; Fernández Albaladejo, pp. 88–91.

79. Fernandez de Pinedo, pp. 15–18; Luis María Bilbao, "Transformaciones económicas en el país vasco durante los siglos XVI y XVII" (1979), pp. 114–127.

80. Fernández de Pinedo, pp. 32–37; Fernández Albaladejo, pp. 71–90; Francisco Sánchez Ramos, *La economia siderúrgica española* (1945), pp. 105–108.

Table 10.22. *Revenue from* Portazgo
de Pancorbo
(1621-30 = 100)

Period	Index
1583-91	115.2
1610-20	106.2
1621-30	100.0
1631-35	90.5

Source: See Table E.1.

Madrid. At Pancorbo, located on the trade routes reaching Castile through the mountain passes near Orduña and Vitoria, toll revenue dropped only 20% between the 1580's and the 1630's. This is slightly at odds with the timing of commercial contraction in Bilbao, where *consulado* revenues reached their low point in the first quarter of the century and then began to recover (see Table 10.23). More detailed figures from the *Consulado* show that the drop was worst in the crisis of 1626–30.[81] The contrast between Pancorbo and Bilbao indicates that the commercial crisis affected the Basque economy more severely than it did the demand for imports in the interior.

The years 1626–51 saw a 28% rise in *Consulado* revenues, but a 20% increase in Castilian prices rendered the gain negligible. Nominal revenues more than doubled from the second to the third quarter of the century, making it hard to deny an increase in the real value of trade, whatever the changes in price levels. Revenues rose another 28% between the third and fourth quarters, and the 17% decline in prices in Old Castile indicates that the real value of trade may have grown by a third. The pattern suggests that traffic was sustained by the growing demand for imports in Madrid and the concentration of Castilian trade at Bilbao.

By mid-seventeenth century the structure of Basque commerce had been radically altered. The iron industry was reduced to ore and rough metal; wool exports had declined and concentrated at Bilbao, at the expense of Burgos and other northern ports; and the arms industry, shipbuilding, and fishing had decayed, as foreign merchants took control of the trading circuit of the Bay of Biscay. Rising *Consulado* revenue reflected the revival of wool exports and its concentration in Bilbao.[82] But Bilbao now did little but organize wool export

81. Fernández de Pinedo, p. 66.
82. Luis María Bilbao, in "Transformaciones," p. 141, indicates that 70% of all wool exported from Spain passed through the port of Bilbao. This is paralleled by the improvement in the situation of the Mesta, whose finances were linked with wool exports; see Jean Paul LeFlem, "Las cuentas de la Mesta, 1510–1700" (1972).

Table 10.23. *Consulado Revenue in*
Bilbao, 1590-1701
(1601-25 = 100)

Period	Index
1590-96	109.4
1601-25	100.0
1626-51	128.3
1652-77	327.4
1678-1701	458.2

Source: Based on Smith, *The Spanish Guild Merchant*, pp. 89-90.

and pass European imports on to the wealthy elite in Madrid, and these interdependent trades explain the port's apparent commercial prosperity. As we will see, by 1650 alternative urban markets in Castile were severely limited.

As Basque commerce narrowed its focus, the agricultural hinterland of the littoral withdrew into self-sufficiency, but in a manner different from that of areas on the south and east coasts. Coastal population trends show difficulties in the important towns and manufacturing areas that were most severe in the 1620's. Despite this, the coastal areas never experienced a true demographic crisis in the seventeenth century. Expansion of farming land continued, often sacrificing vines and orchards to provide food grains. But the seventeenth century also saw the widespread adoption of maize, more intensive farming, fodder crops to maintain livestock, and rising per-acre yields. This intensified subsistence agriculture, allied with short-range coastal trade, allowed the northern littoral to avoid demographic crisis and combine a high level of population with heightened economic isolation. In 1704, therefore, the population of the coastal districts was at least as large as it was a century before.[83] Once away from the coast, however, we find the same boundary between periphery and interior that has been noted in Andalucía and Málaga. While coastal Vizcaya was adjusting to seventeenth-century conditions with some success, interior Álava, an extension of the Castilian plain, was moving into a depression before the 1580's and remained depressed and stagnant until the early eighteenth century.[84]

83. Anes, "Tendencias," pp. 102–105; Fernández Albaladejo, pp. 86–88, 186; Fernández de Pinedo, pp. 108, 178, 478; Bilbao, "Transformaciones." pp. 136–138, and "Crisis y reconstrucción," pp. 167–169. On the long-term reliance of local economies upon maritime contact, see Fernández Albaladejo, p. 41.

84. Anes, "Tendencias," p. 107; Bilbao, "Crisis y reconstrucción," pp. 169–170, and "Transformaciones," p. 138.

During the eighteenth century, the Basque economy expanded in many ways, and its commercial life was recaptured by Basque traders, but the underlying economic structure of the seventeenth century remained intact. The wool trade grew steadily, although after the 1750's it was divided between Bilbao and the developing port of Santander. By 1750 the volume of wool export matched the sixteenth-century peak and in 1795 was near that level, at 280,000 *arrobas* (7 million pounds), despite international instability.[85] Thereafter, exports declined seriously and did not recover during the first half of the nineteenth century.

The pattern was similar in the iron industry, where exports of iron and hardware rose from 20,000 tons in 1733 to 53,000 tons in 1769. Iron ore exports, which had fallen to 10,000 metric tons in the 1640's, ran about 17,000 metric tons between 1763 and 1790. Subsequently they plummeted for a quarter-century before starting another recovery in the 1820's.[86] Basque agriculture underwent further intensive development in the eighteenth century, achieving large increases in production in the middle decades. After about 1775 on the coast and 1785 inland, however, production began to decline. As before, it is important to distinguish between the littoral and the interior. On the littoral the midcentury increases in output were on the order of 170–300%, while in the interior they ranged only about 25–100%. During the decline from about 1780 to 1825, the littoral saw a modest regression of 12–15%, while output in Álava fell 40–50%.[87]

The eighteenth century saw similar changes all along the northern littoral. Santander became an important alternative to Bilbao as an outlet for Castilian wool when roads to the interior improved. This led to new tanning and milling industries in the hinterland.[88] Many of the agricultural developments seen in the Basque provinces spread along the coast and could be observed in Santander and Asturias. The trade in wheat, fish, and other staples that survived the collapse of long-distance Basque commerce in the preceding century expanded steadily.[89] This trade circuit extended from western France to Portugal, allowing regional specialization and providing maritime sources of supply when local self-sufficiency failed. Only under extreme conditions did these areas draw on Castile for foodstuffs.[90]

The later eighteenth century saw the development of fishing in Galicia, but it was based on Catalán capital and manpower. As in Vizcaya, Andalucía, and

85. Phillips, "Spanish Wool Exports," statistical appendix; Antonio Matilla Tascón, *Balanza de comercio exterior de España en el año 1795.*

86. Fernández de Pinedo, pp. 324, 325, 331.

87. Anes, "Tendencias," pp. 105–106, based on Fernández de Pinedo, ch. 8.

88. Palacio Atard, *El comercio de Castilla,* pp. 136–192.

89. Albert Girard, *Le commerce français,* pp. 387–389.

90. José Lucas Labrada, *Descripción económica del Reino de Galicia,* pp. 31–36; Antonio Mejide Pardo, *Economía marítima de la Galicia cantábrica en el siglo XVIII.*

Málaga, there was a sharp boundary between littoral and interior in Galicia, and the interior had a much simpler, less intensive economy. By the last quarter of the century, large parts of the Galician interior were oriented to producing cattle for the Madrid stockyards. A contemporary noted that this trade was one of the few activities that created buying power for the region, allowing it to participate in the regional markets of Old Castile and support a modicum of commerce at El Ferrol.[91] There were attempts at modernizing the linen industry in Galicia, but marketing problems constantly plagued the effort.[92]

The general impression is that, excepting the ports of Bilbao and Santander, the northern coast had very little contact with the interior. The seventeenth-century reconstruction of the Basque economy had greatly reduced its interaction with Castile and the north Atlantic, and local Basque economies depended on a combination of self-sufficiency and coastal trade. The major ports relied on wool exports and the import of European products for the elite market of the interior—activities that reinforced the economic structure of the interior and had few links with their own hinterlands. This reality is reflected in the surprisingly small size of these commercially important cities.[93]

III. Conclusion

Spain's coastal periphery consisted of a number of economically autonomous regions. In the sixteenth century, they had varied trajectories; Barcelona and the Valencian coast were stagnant until the last quarter, while Málaga and Vizcaya experienced considerable growth until about 1570, and Sevilla enjoyed a prolonged boom until after 1610. Barcelona and Vizcaya were in commercial difficulties by the last decade of the sixteenth century, and Valencia felt them after 1605. Sevilla and Cartagena experienced commercial crisis only in the second quarter of the seventeenth century, while Málaga fared relatively well until the third quarter.

These disparate declines had certain common features. With the possible exception of Barcelona, all of the coastal areas experienced a withdrawal of agriculture into increased self-sufficiency, a process accompanied by a decline of interurban trade. This trend is even more pronounced within the urban network of the peninsula as a whole. The interdependence of industry,

91. Pedro Antonio Sánchez, *La economía gallega en los escritos de Pedro Antonio Sánchez* (1973, written ca. 1796), pp. 20–22, 127–142.
92. Luis Miguel Enciso Recio, *Los establecimientos industriales españoles en el siglo XVIII: La mantelería de La Coruña* (1963).
93. Mercedes Mauleón Isla, *La población de Bilbao en el siglo XVIII* (1961), pp. 78–79, indicates that Bilbao almost doubled in size in the eighteenth century, but in 1800 still counted only 11,000 people.

raw materials, and markets that had linked Bilbao, Valencia, Málaga, and Sevilla with the Castilian interior broke down, and traffic with the interior fell more rapidly than port activity.

Between 1650 and 1680, all of these ports except Málaga passed through a low point in port activity and began to expand, or at the least had achieved a plateau that was sustained through the War of Succession. After the war, the eighteenth century saw striking growth of commercial activity on the coasts. This phenomenon, in which port activity everywhere in Spain exhibits a similar chronology, reflected two important developments. One was an apparent but little-understood upsurge in the volume of private bullion at Cádiz. While not apparent in official tonnage figures, this lubrication of the coastal trade circuits signaled a rise in port activity well before 1700 everywhere but Málaga. To this we must add the boom in Atlantic commerce after the Restoration in England—which, along with French penetration of Barcelona and Cádiz, drew Spanish ports into the European market. This is manifest by the eighteenth century in the importance of agricultural exports—wool in the north, wine, raisins, olive oil, *barilla*—to Europe, coupled with a flow of Catalán manufactures to Cádiz and America.

The striking thing in this development is that, unlike that of the sixteenth century, there are few indications that this revival had connections with any aspect of the Castilian interior other than the consuming market of Madrid and the wool industry. The reasons for this lie in the fate of the commercial and urban networks of the interior, as Madrid became a permanent feature of the Castilian landscape.

11. The Castilian Urban Network: Madrid and the Decline of Toledo

I. The Urban Network

The Castilian counterpart to the seaports and their commercial life was a network of towns and cities that linked the regional economies of the interior with each other and with the maritime periphery. The interior of sixteenth-century Spain contained a well-developed urban hierarchy: the principal city was Toledo, with a respectable 65,000 people, while the second-level center was Valladolid, with a population of 40,000. The network contained several third- and fourth-order centers of 10,000 to 25,000, and a developed system of local and regional markets and fairs.[1] This network organized the export of significant amounts of wool, textiles, and craft products and the import and distribution of colonial and European luxuries and manufactures. Even before 1600, the pressures of population and declining markets were encouraging the concentration of commercial and manufacturing functions in the larger centers, but before the rise of Madrid, Toledo and Valladolid were able to maintain their integrating roles in the urban network. They survived for a time partly by capturing the supplies and functions of smaller towns, but they themselves fell victim to the same process when confronted by Madrid. As the Spanish state and its capital city evolved, Madrid attracted the investments of the wealthy, who bought offices, annuities, and urban real estate and took up residence near the Court.

Consequently, the rise of Madrid produced several fields of influence that established the capital as the center of the commodity trades of Old and New Castile. This process was accompanied by the decline of other interior urban

1. Valladolid was the largest central place of Old Castile, but Toledo included a range of industrial, political, and ecclesiastical functions that placed it above Valladolid in the urban hierarchy. See Josiah Cox Russell, *Medieval Cities and Their Regions* (1972); and Michael Weisser, "The Decline of Castile Revisited: The Case of Toledo," pp. 616, 620–621.

markets after 1600, and is part of the explanation for why maritime Spain lost contact with its traditional Castilian suppliers and customers. This clearly reflects economic conditions before 1600 that favored larger towns able to command surpluses at the expense of smaller ones. The central event of the process, however, was the dramatic collapse of Toledo after 1610 and, by 1650, the effective de-urbanization of the entire interior. In this chapter we will examine the collapse of Toledo as the center of urban commercial life in the interior and, in Chapter 12, the subordination of the rest of the urban network to Madrid.

In the terms set forth in Chapter 1, a new set of urban functions (social and political centralization) was acquired by a previously minor city. Those functions required a very large investment in the facility (a capital city) needed to perform them. Given a capital-poor economy in which local economic life tended toward self-sufficiency in the face of erratic weather and food supply, this stimulated the development of a disproportionately large primate city and limited most other central places to low-order functions with geographically small fields of influence.

Thus, to the extent that the sixteenth-century urban network headed by Toledo depended on the wealth of the rentier class, its economic base was preempted. To the extent that the new situation drew commercial functions and craftsmen away from Toledo and other towns, the situation was aggravated. The discussions of population and workforce in Chapters 3 and 5 have shown us that these movements did take place. The shift of societal priorities from commercial and industrial functions to political and social ones, the choice of a new focal point for the state, and the larger fields of influence inherent in political function, led to the replacement of the old urban hierarchy with a macrocephalic one that became a permanent feature of Spanish life.

II. A Measure of Change: Population and Migration

The proximity of the "Imperial City" (Toledo) and the new *Corte* (Madrid), and the reversal of their relationship in less than 25 years (1606–30), point to a confrontation in which a booming Madrid preempted the bases of urban life in the region. The sharpness of this confrontation is suggested by the selected population estimates in Table 11.1.

The immediate economic and geographic hinterland of the two cities included the modern provinces of Madrid, Toledo, Segovia, Guadalajara, Cuenca, and Ávila (see Map 1.1). By 1600 Madrid already reached beyond that limit for some commodities (see Chapter 9), but evidence from other cities of the period indicates that 80–90% of urban immigrants came from

Table 11.1. *Population of Madrid and Toledo, Sixteenth and Seventeenth Centuries*

Year	Population of Madrid	Population of Toledo
1530		25-30,000
1546	25,000	
1563	30,000	
1571		60,000
1597	65,000	70,000
1630	175,000	20,000
1669		10,000
1685	120,000	

Sources: On Madrid, Chapter 2; on Toledo, Appendix F. The development of Toledo's population is as hard to document as Madrid's, since the estimates are based on *vecino* figures. The trend is confirmed by Weisser in *The Peasants of the Montes*, ch. 4, and "Decline of Castile," pp. 621-629.

within 75 kilometers, roughly the six provinces of the immediate hinterland.[2] Madrid and Toledo together accounted for the same 6% of the regional population in 1541 and 1591, suggesting a balance between urban and rural development. Within the region, sixteenth-century population growth was concentrated near the major cities, and the province of Toledo (city excluded) expanded 83% between 1541 and 1591, while Madrid province (city excluded) grew by 200%. The regional economy clearly responded to the presence of a new market.

The development of Toledo's population followed regional trends closely. The fastest growth took place before the crises of the 1570's, after which further expansion came slowly. This reflects the fact that, although many rural communities reached the effective limits of cultivation, the population of the region increased by another 25% between 1576 and 1590. This encouraged handicraft industry, economic specialization, and market activity oriented to the exchange network based in Toledo. By the 1590's the potential of this process had been exhausted and in the last decade of the century the

2. AVM, *Secretaria,* sigs. 2–102–8, 2–140–6; Manuel Espadas Burgos and María Ascensión Burgos, *Abastecimiento de Madrid en el siglo XVI,* p. 9, quoting AVM, *Secretaria,* sig. 2–158–149; Ringrose, *Transportation,* ch. 2; Roger Mols, *Introduction à la démographie historique,* vol. 2, pp. 378–380. In the case of Madrid, the proportion coming from coastal provinces may well have been greater. See Chapter 3 above, and also Charles L.Carlson, "The Vulgar Sort."

decline of individual income in the region was pronounced. Baptismal statistics from several villages indicate cessation of population growth, followed by gradual decline in the next decade.[3] Subsequently the decline became precipitous, reaching 20% in the decade after 1610. Population decline was matched by falling cereal production and by a 40% drop in the señorial income that Toledo received from the region. The worst of the demographic crisis was over by 1630.[4]

Toledo's population expanded briefly after the plague and subsistence crisis of 1598–99. This may reflect the temporary departure of the Court from Madrid (1602–06), but it also suggests displacement of the rural population. In the twenty years after the subsistence crisis of 1606–07 and the expulsion of the *Moriscos* (1609), the city's population declined 60%.[5] The urban decline was proportionately far more severe than that of the rural areas near the city. The timing of Madrid's growth provides an instructive counterpoint. The city grew slowly before 1563, then doubled in the next thirty years. From 1600 to 1630, the city's growth not only ran counter to the trend in its hinterland, but the population nearly trebled.

Pre-industrial European cities depended not only on the ability to extract supplies from their hinterlands, but on a flow of immigrants to maintain the population.[6] If we assume that Toledo and Madrid were at the middle of the scale of observed baptism/death ratios and had death rates of 45 per 1,000,

3. Michael R. Weisser, "Toledo in the *Siglo de Oro*" (paper presented to the Society for Spanish and Portuguese Historical Studies, 1972).

4. Weisser, "The Demography of the Heartland of Castile, 1500–1700," pp. 10–14, and *The Peasants of the Montes*, pp. 98–119.

5. An important aspect of this development that has not been discussed is the expulsion of the *Moriscos* between 1609 and 1611. Current findings suggest that from 3,600 to 4,100 persons, or about 5% of Toledo's population, were expelled. If this included skilled textile workers, the connection with the decline would be important. If, however, the *Moriscos* were primarily truck gardeners, peddlers, and rural laborers—as in Valladolid, and as Weisser suggests for Toledo—it is less important in this context. See Weisser, "The Decline of Castile Revisited," p. 624; Henri Lapeyre, *Géographie de l'Espagne morisque* (1959), pp. 158, 200, 212; Julio Caro Baroja, *Los moriscos del Reino de Granada* (1957); Ramón Carande, "Los moriscos de Henri Lapeyre, los de Julio Caro, y algún morisco mas" (1961).

6. Few cities of any size maintained their populations by natural increase, and various examples suggest rates of immigration ranging from 2 to 15 per 1,000 inhabitants, depending on conditions. E. A. Wrigley, in *Population and History*, pp. 114–115, 125–126, gives chilling figures on mortality in seventeenth-century London and on death rates in foundling homes in urban societies. Roger Mols—in *Introduction à la démographie*, vol. 2, pp. 329–338, and vol. 3, pp. 203–222—shows that in the larger centers, 45–59% of all deaths were in the birth-10-year-old age group, and the ratio of births to deaths did not exceed 96 per 100 for any long period and was as low as 66 per 100. If the death rate was 45 per 1,000, it would imply the rates of immigration suggested above. The role of immigration and the typicality of demographic deficit in such cities has long been recognized; see Adna Ferrin Weber, *The Growth of Cities in the Nineteenth Century* (1899; reprinted 1967), pp. 230–237. Some of these assumptions have been questioned recently, but, with allowance for a distinction between stable and immigrant urban population, they remain valid. See Sharlin, "Natural Decrease in Early Modern Cities."

they needed 9 immigrants per 1,000 inhabitants to maintain a given population.[7] As we saw in Chapter 3, Madrid always depended heavily on immigration. In the late eighteenth century, the capital had a relatively favorable baptism/death ratio, but in the early seventeenth century it probably did not.[8] In Toledo, the evolution of population changed as the sixteenth-century economy became unstable. The volume of births declined between 1560 and 1580; but then, reflecting the fact that the new *Morisco* districts had much higher birth rates, births increased until 1595. Given the slow growth of the city late in the century, this implies a decline of dependence on immigrants. Even so, once immigration was diverted to Madrid, population decline was inevitable.[9]

Between 1571 and 1597, Toledo expanded by no more than 700 inhabitants per year and required up to 600 more to maintain its base population. Meanwhile, Madrid was growing at the rate of 1,000 inhabitants per year and, with an internal deficit of about 430, accounted for an average of 1,430 immigrants. Together the two cities probably absorbed 2,800 immigrants yearly. Between 1597 and 1630, Madrid grew at the rate of 3,667 inhabitants per year. With an estimated natural deficit of 1,000, the total reaches 4,667 immigrants per year.[10] Possibly 600 came from Toledo, which lost an average of 1,100 inhabitants per year in the same period. Madrid had replaced Toledo as the center of attraction for internal migration.

This was a demographic phenomenon as significant as the current of emigration to America. The size and direction of the flow illustrates the attractiveness of Madrid relative to Toledo and the rural world. In particular, it reflects the rising real wages and building boom in Madrid from 1608 to 1625. The deterioration of the regional economy contributed to the contrast, as did the redirection of supplies to Madrid. The doubling of the migration to the cities between 1600 and 1630 as regional population declined, its reorientation to Madrid, and Toledo's change from recipient to source of migrants all point to a major change in the regional economy.

Population trends suggest continued economic growth in the region before

7. This is likely to overestimate the death rate in Madrid, which probably had a higher proportion of young adults. On the other hand, Madrid probably had a higher level of migration back to home communities.

8. By all accounts, Madrid was the dirtiest, filthiest, and smelliest capital in all of Europe; See José Deleito y Piñuelo, *Solo Madrid es Corte,* pp. 127–138.

9. Compared with Madrid, Toledo was older and more established, and never experienced the massive growth of Madrid after 1600. On the other hand, it was a crowded industrial center that may have resembled Amiens or Valladolid, neither of which was notably healthy. See Weisser, "The Decline of Castile Revisited," pp. 621–626; Pierre Deyon, *Amiens, capitale provinciale,* pp. 35–44; Bennassar, *Valladolid,* pp. 157–160, 183–189.

10. The role of the Court in stimulating immigration is suggested by the tremendous following which accompanied the movements of the royal establishment; see José Pellicer de Ossau y Tovar, *Avisos históricos* (1965), p. 168, entry for Jan. 3, 1642.

1600, but with the rate of growth slowing in the 1580's, disappearing in the 1590's, and turning negative in the seventeenth century. Throughout the sixteenth century, Madrid and Toledo included a steady 6% of regional population. They continued to grow into the first years of the new century as the rural economy began to decline, implying that urban migration had become the result of conditions in the countryside. After 1608, Toledo collapsed and Madrid's growth accelerated, as rural crisis was paralleled by circumstances that made the capital attractive to the people of economically troubled Toledo and New Castile.

III. Madrid Captures the Regional Supply Market

It is not easy to assign relative weights to the factors affecting Madrid, Toledo, and Castile, but analysis of long-term trends within the two cities clarifies the economic interaction of the three.[11] The displacement of Toledo as center of the Castilian urban hierarchy can be documented, and aspects of Madrid's dominance over Castile's long-distance commerce can be set alongside its domination of commodity trades in the landlocked interior. The tensions in the Castilian economy are suggested by the contrast between the declining rural population and the growth of Madrid's demand for agricultural staples. They are also reflected in the rate of growth of consumption in Madrid (see Table 11.2) and by the fact that additional demand far exceeded the supplies released by Toledo's decline.

To supply both Toledo and an expanding Madrid, the hinterland had to meet the needs of an urban population of around 100,000 in 1570 and 130,000 by 1597. Despite the decline of Toledo, by 1630 the total was approaching 200,000. Without the decline of Toledo, the region would have had to support an urban complex of over 250,000 people—roughly the population of London or Paris at the time. This would have required a market-oriented agriculture beyond the capacity of existing transport, agricultural resources, capital, technology, and labor supply. What follows, therefore, is an attempt to document the impact of the supply controls outlined in Chapter 7 and 8 upon the urban network of Castile, as Madrid expanded its economic hinterland.

11. To make the series used as indicators comparable, they are presented as indices with the base 1621–30 = 100, the decade for which the series are most complete. Price indices are presented as five-year moving averages. Other indices are presented as averages of available figures in five-year periods, since the gaps in the data make moving averages deceptive. Price series are based on Earl Hamilton, *American Treasure,* pp. 144, 149, 213; Hamilton used data from Toledo with interpolations from Alcalá de Henares. See also Jacqueline Fourastié, *Les formules des indices de prix* (1966), p. 108.

Table 11.2. *Consumption of Staple Commodities in Madrid, 1590s and 1630s*(a)

Commodity	Consumption in 1590s	Consumption in 1630s	Increase
Olive oil	126,480 gal.	239,088 gal.	189%
Wine	2,968,000 gal.	4,820,000 gal.	211
Meat	2,543,000 lb.	8,210,000 lb.	223
Wheat	270,000 bu.	775,500 bu.	287

Source: Chapter 6.
 a. Actual base periods are: olive oil, 1584, '87, '88, and 1639-43; wine, 1584, '85, '87, '88, and 1624-30; meat, 1601 and 1632; wheat, 1599 and 1630-31. Olive oil and wine are converted at the rate of 16 quarts per *arroba*; meat figures are taken directly from Chapter 6; and wheat is converted at the rate of 1.5 bushels per *fanega*.

A. Wheat

There is clear evidence of the competition between the two cities for wheat, the most important staple. The upper panel of Figure 11.1 shows the indices of the yield to Toledo from its *calahorra* (wheat brokerage) duties and of the annual consumption figures available for Madrid.[12] The indices of general prices and the price of wheat in New Castile appear in the lower panel as five-year moving averages. Toledo's consumption rose rapidly until about 1560, declined to 1570, rose considerably in the next decade, stabilized in the 1580's, and climbed to a much higher level for most of 1590–1605.[13] Madrid, meanwhile, doubled both size and wheat consumption between 1570 and 1600. This growth, and a 20% increase in the requirements of Toledo in the same period, imply a 50–55% increase in the demand of the two cities.[14] In 1598–1608, Toledo's consumption rose but slightly while that of Madrid jumped by 63%, producing another 15% increase in combined requirements and a noticeable acceleration of the rate of growth of urban demand.

Predictably, there was a sharp increase in the price of wheat in Toledo. The average annual wheat price in 1576–80 represented a 12% increase in a decade, and the average of 1586–90 was only a 9.6% increase in ten years. But the index for 1596–1600 was 37% higher than that for 1586–90, and the average annual wheat price in 1606–10 was fully 40.5% above 1596–1600. In the decade preceding 1608, Madrid and Toledo came to represent a demand

12. The wheat index is based on the two years 1628 and 1630.
13. The dip in 1596–1600 reflects the crisis of 1598–99.
14. This estimate is based on Madrid's demand for 180–200,000 *fanegas* of wheat in 1598; a 20% increase in the population of Toledo, 1575–1600; and comparable populations in the two cities in 1598.

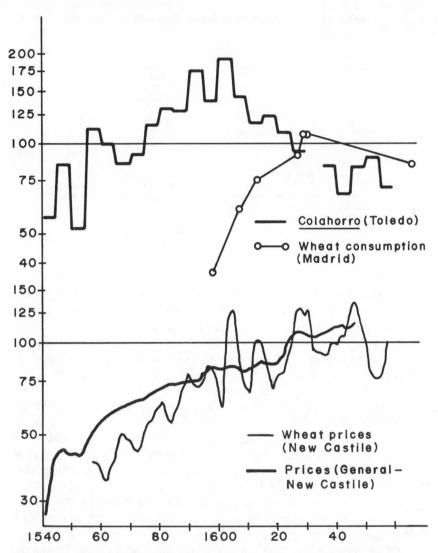

Figure 11.1 *Indices of Wheat Consumption and Prices in Madrid and Toledo*

approaching 500,000 *fanegas* (750,000 bushels) of wheat, a 25% increase in ten years. The inelasticity of the supply is amply documented by the escalating price of wheat, which rose much faster than prices in general.

The role of urbanization in intensifying price instability is demonstrated by the situation in Old Castile.[15] When harvests were good, wheat prices in Old and New Castile were similar, but in years of shortage the price of wheat in the great cities of New Castile was often double the price in Old Castile.[16] At the same time, the situation in rural New Castile was deteriorating, as population remained high while production began to decline.[17] During the decade 1601–10, urban demand and rural hardship culminated in the most spectacular fluctuation of New Castilian wheat prices of the century from 1550 to 1650. The five-year index, which masks yearly extremes, soared from 52 in 1601 to 163 in 1608, before falling back to 54.

In the twenty years before 1610, therefore, urban demand became an increasingly important factor in the behavior of wheat prices. After 1610, the collapse of both rural and urban Toledo was rapid, as the revenue of the *calahorra* shows, and brought in its train the deterioration of the rural markets dependent upon Toledo. From that date, wheat prices in the interior stabilized for nearly 15 years, reflecting the end of intercity competition for supplies. By 1630, however, Madrid alone was straining the regional supply base and was reaching far beyond New Castile for its supplies. Only after 1635, when Madrid's demand began to slacken, is it necessary to look to monetary inflation and declining production as the principal causes of higher wheat prices.

B. Wine

As we saw in Chapter 6, individual demand for wine was elastic and varied greatly with the real income of the poor. High bread prices sometimes reduced the demand for wine even when wine prices themselves did not increase.[18] Thus the market for wine behaved very differently when caught in the three-way relationship between Madrid, Toledo, and the countryside. As Figure 11.2 illustrates, between the early 1590's and 1610 wine consumption in Madrid rose only 25%, compared with a 60% growth in both wheat consumption and population.[19] If the population of Toledo reacted to high wheat prices in the same way, the demand for wine in the two cities was static between 1595 and 1610 and may even have declined.

15. José Larraz López, *La época del Mercantilismo en Castilla, 1500–1700,* p. 60.

16. Hamilton, *American Treasure,* pp. 391–392. One hundred miles of transport sometimes doubled the price of wheat: AHN, *Consejos,* leg. 6775, exp. 3. In the later eighteenth century, a *fanega* of wheat costing 25 *reales* in Palencia incurred 20 *reales* in transport costs, plus commissions and handling charges, during the trip to Madrid.

17. Parish registers in rural Toledo show that population was fairly stable as late as 1605 or even 1610. Weisser, in "Crime and Subsistence," pp. 299–311, 328–336, gives figures for 12 towns in the Montes de Toledo; in 9 cases the situation did not change until 1610.

18. Ringrose, "Madrid y Castilla," pp. 78–82, 85–86, and Chapter 6 above.

19. *Sisas* were excise taxes on the sale of various commodities. In this case it was a fixed levy of two *maravedises* per *azumbre* of wine. See our earlier discussions of consumption and

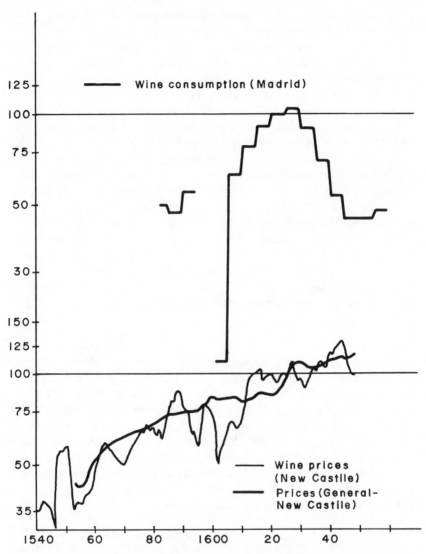

Figure 11.2 *Indices of Wine Consumption and Prices in Madrid and New Castile*

This stagnation of urban demand is reflected in wine prices, which fell 9.6% between 1586–90 and 1596–1600, and another 16.4% by 1605–1610. As with wheat, the situation in the wine market changed sharply after 1610. By the 1620's, urban consumption was 25–30% greater than in 1600. This happened despite wine prices which had risen 60% in thirty years.

The implications of this go beyond the matter of competition between the two urban economies. While wheat was generally extracted from self-sufficient local economies by nonmarket means, wine producion involved specialization and orientation to the market. Many communities were heavily dependent on viticulture and therefore relied on the market for many necessities. The *Relaciones topográficas* of the 1570's indicate surprisingly large wine sales by many New Castilian towns.[20] Yet between 1590 and 1610, wine prices fell as wheat prices soared; and while the volume of wine sold in Madrid rose 77% between 1601 and 1632, the real price per unit was virtually unchanged. As a consequence, the wine industry's share of the Madrid commodities market fell from 43% to 29%, while that of wheat rose from 37% to 46% (see Chapter 6). Thus the wine-producing towns of the hinterland faced declining incomes and rising prices precipitated by the development of Madrid.

The crisis in the wine districts contributed to the crisis in Toledo. One of the functions performed by the merchants of Toledo was the distribution of imported and regional goods throughout the regional economy. Thus the distress of the New Castilian wine towns undermined the commercial sector of Toledo's economy. By 1610–20 the wine districts were in full decline, reinforcing that of Toledo itself.[21] The expansion of the area from which Madrid drew its wine (see Chapter 9), even when urban consumption fell, verifies the disintegration of the regional market organized by Toledo.

C. Mutton

If wheat was linked to self-sufficiency, and wine was part of a regional market economy, mutton was associated with both regional supply and the long-distance wool trade. Consequently, the level of mutton consumption reflected factors external to the tension between the two cities. As a result, the market for meat was not one of the mechanisms through which Madrid affected Toledo. The Castilian grazing industry responded to two markets, the supply and demand for meat in the city and the export market for wool.[22]

Wool exports declined in the later sixteenth century, as war disrupted

---

Bartolomé Bennassar, "L'alimentation d'une capitale espagnol au XVIe siècle: Valladolid" (1970), p. 57.

20. Gentil da Silva, *En Espagne*, pp. 27, 29–30, and tables 17–23 on pp. 38–44.

21. Weisser, "Crime and Subsistence," pp. 299–311, and "Les marchands de Tolède."

22. We have little direct information on where Madrid's meat came from before 1700, and know little about the size of the Mesta flocks after 1570, or about the price of wool. See Noël Salomon, *La campagne de Nouvelle Castille*, pp. 319–321; Julius Klein, *The Mesta, A Study in Spanish Economic History, 1273–1836* (1920), p. 27; Jean Paul LeFlem, "Las cuentas de la Mesta, 1510–1700"; Hamilton, *American Treasure*, pp. 228–229. Tentative wool export figures have been offered by Carla Phillips in "Spanish Wool Exports," statistical appendix.

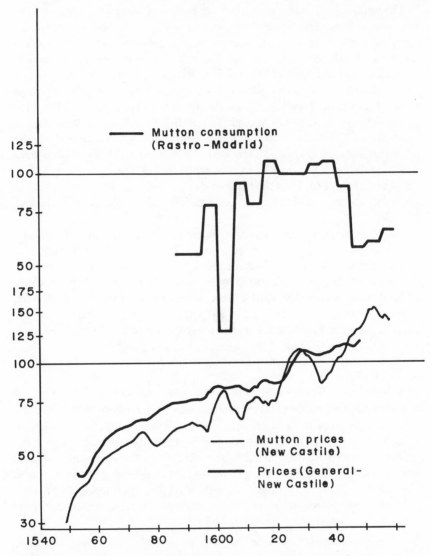

Figure 11.3 *Indices of Mutton Consumption and Prices in Madrid and New Castile*

Atlantic trade and Europe developed other sources of wool.[23] By the end of the century, there was intense competition in Europe's markets for woolens, and this contributed to deterioration of the smaller cloth towns in Castile.[24] Woolens production around Toledo, however, remained stable until 1607 and seems to have been the principal Castilian exception to incipient decline. Trade disruption and slack domestic demand for wool help explain the stability of mutton prices in the face of a substantial jump in urban demand. Between 1586 and 1610, mutton consumption in Madrid rose 75%,[25] a rate of increase only slightly below that for wheat consumption. Aside from 1602–03, however, mutton prices remained stable, and the five-year average of 1606–10 was only 6.5% above that of 1586–90. (See Fig. 11.3.)

Clearly, the supply of mutton was much more elastic than that of wheat. The link between wool and mutton is illustrated by the figures for 1601–03, when a revival of textile production in Toledo paralleled a jump in mutton prices, despite the decline of consumption in Madrid due to the absence of the Court. This suggests that sheep were being held off the meat market in order to build up the wool crop.

In a supply crisis, poor urban populations revert to bread as the cheapest staple, and demand for relatively expensive meat drops. Unless the meat supply also contracts sharply, this tends to depress meat prices. At the same time, diversion of buying power to foodstuffs reduces demand for textiles, and hence for wool. By the end of the 1620's, collapse of the domestic woolens industry, crisis in the international wool trade, and continuously bad weather in 1626–31 produced a decline in the Castilian flocks. By 1635, this contributed to a rapid rise in mutton prices that coincided with falling consumption in Madrid.[26] As with wheat and wine, if for different reasons, the early seventeenth-century disintegration of the Castilian economy contributed to a

23. Larraz López, *La época del Mercantilismo*, pp. 47, 48. Carla Phillips shows a 25% decline between the 1560's and the 1590's; see also Chapter 10 above.

24. Current research is clarifying the role of Neapolitan wool in the Italian market, suggesting that Hapsburg policy in Naples protected graziers, but also forced up the price of grazing land as demand for grain increased. See John Marino, "The Works and Days of the Dogana de Foggia in the Sixteenth and Seventeenth Centuries" (1977). On the woolens trade, see Domenico Sella, "Les mouvements longs de l'industrie lainère a Venise au XVIe et XVII siècle." (1959), pp. 29–45; Pierre Deyon, "Variations de la production textile aux XVIe et XVIIe siècles: Sources et premiers resultats" (1963); Álvaro Castillo Pintado, "Population et 'richesse' en Castille durante la seconde moitié du XVIIe siècle" (1963), p. 730.

25. This is inferred from the *sisa del rastro,* which actually was collected at varying rates for different animals; see Chapter 6.

26. Estimates indicate that the Mesta flocks declined steadily from 1600 until after 1630. Mesta accounts show a precipitous decline in profits from 1635 to 1652; see LeFlem, "Las cuentas de la Mesta," pp. 70, 77–80. Carla Phillips' estimates of wool exports show a similar pattern.

brief "golden age" in Madrid that lasted until the collapse of production and the effects of inflation reached the capital itself.

Competition between Madrid and Toledo for supplies was most direct in the case of wheat. The market for mutton depended on the price of wheat and on the demand for wool, and did not contribute directly to the urban crisis. Both the price and the demand for wine were depressed in the twenty years after 1590, weakening the market nexus between the wine districts and Toledo. Here we face a central problem that Madrid posed for Toledo. Nevertheless, the wheat market was the focal point of the situation, and in the twenty years from 1588 to 1608 the price of wheat (five-year averages) rose 92.5%, while the general price index rose only 13.9%. Purchasing power in the towns served by Toledo's regional market was badly hurt, undermining Toledo's entrepôt function in the interior.[27] Shortages of foodstuffs aggravated by Madrid depressed real wages to the subsistence level, linking labor costs in the textile industry to the volatile price of bread. Thus the growth of the capital undermined both the regional economy and Toledo's ability to compete in the international market. It can be argued that this was due to monetary inflation, and the situation clearly reflects rural supply problems, but this analysis shows that some of the pressure came from shortages generated by the rise of Madrid.

IV. The Reorientation of Commerce and the Collapse of Industry in Toledo

As the supply trades were reorganized, Madrid became the focal point of long-distance communication and Toledo declined as a mercantile center. Sixteenth-century Toledo was heavily involved in Spain's economic response to the American empire, a fact demonstrated by the flows of American bullion into the regional economy in return for exports of woolens, leather goods, and weapons.[28] This was reinforced by the city's role as an entrepôt for merchandise brought from outside of the interior and distributed to regional markets.[29] These economic functions were enhanced by Toledo's role as the site of the wealthy Archbishopric of Toledo.

Evidence that Madrid rapidly diverted commerce as well as supplies from Toledo is provided by the revenue series from the *barca de Arganda*. This ferry was near Madrid on the main road from the Mediterranean, but north of the route to Toledo (see Map 12.1). Its toll schedule, location, and apparent

27. Weisser, "The Decline of Castile Revisited," pp. 634–635.
28. Gentil da Silva, in *En Espagne,* ch. 2, analyzes bullion flows into the interior in 1570.
29. Weisser, "Les marchands de Tolède"; and Salomon, *La campagne de Nouvelle Castille,* section on *mercados* and *ferias.*

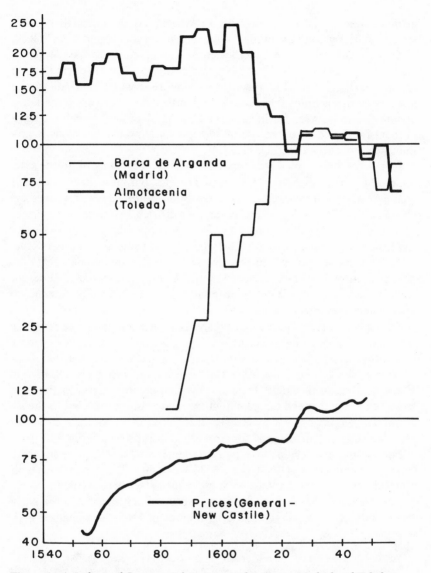

Figure 11.4 *Indices of Commercial Activity and Prices in Madrid and Toledo*

insulation from regional subsistence crises suggest that much of the traffic on the ferry consisted of Madrid's long-distance trade, travel, and communications. The spectacular growth in ferry revenues, interrupted only by the temporary move of the government to Valladolid in 1602–06, reflects the attraction of social and political life to Madrid. As the regional economy stagnated, this growth inevitably included commerce diverted from Toledo.

Toledo's *almotacenia* revenue, levied on manufactures and trade goods, changed little in the 1540's and '50's, rose in the 1560's, but suffered a mild setback in the 1570's. This coincided with the recession of the Indies trade and a crisis in government finance, leaving little doubt about the importance of connections between Sevilla and the Castilian interior. The episode helps account for the pause in the rise of Toledo's consumption of regionally produced commodities. (See Fig. 11.4.)

It is generally assumed that this crisis was the beginning of Toledo's decline, as it was for Medina del Campo and Burgos, but subsequent renewal of commercial growth contradicts that assumption.[30] *Almotacenia* revenues leveled off after 1590, as depression hit the wine districts that were an important part of Toledo's distribution network. Market activity became more clearly sensitive to regional conditions, falling during each subsistence crisis. Revenues from the ferry often did the reverse, indicating that while Toledo depended on its region, Madrid depended on more distant resources. As a result, each successive crisis allowed the capital, with more consistent demand, to attract more commercial activity.

The shifting balance between local and long-distance commerce is seen in the contrasting behavior of Toledo's *almotacenia* and *peso mayor* revenues. The latter was a brokerage and measuring fee on fruits, vegetables, fish, pork products, olive oil, fuel, and other commodities, and was more sensitive to changes in urban income.[31] Demand for such commodities was thus less elastic than the demand for manufactures and luxuries reflected in the *almotacenia,* although low income levels rendered demand for these consumables more elastic than demand for essential foodstuffs.[32] (See Fig. 11.5.)

Peso revenues in Toledo rose rapidly in the middle decades of the sixteenth century, followed by a plateau in the 1570's and '80's. This corresponds with regional economic expansion and subsequent pressure on agricultural resources by the 1580's.[33] Both of these Toledo series recovered in the early 1590's and, after the plague and crop failures of 1598–99, remained high

30. Weisser, *The Peasants of the Montes,* ch. 4.

31. See the description of the *peso* operations in Madrid in Chapter 7 above.

32. This is illustrated by a comparison of the *peso mayor* and *almotacenia* of Toledo (Figures 10.4 and 10.5). In the crisis of the 1570's, the *almotacenia* dropped 25 index points and took 20 years to recover, while the *peso mayor* fell only 10 points and exceeded its previous high within a decade. This reflects the influx of *Morisco* immigrants after 1570, immigrants whose buying power was at the lower end of the scale: Weisser, "Decline Revisited," pp. 624–625. The crisis of 1598–99 provoked a 17% drop in the *almotacenia,* but only 2% for the *peso mayor,* and the crisis of 1606–07 provoked a similar response. The brief revival of Toledo provoked by the absence of the Court from Madrid in 1602–06 sent Toledo's *almotacenia* up 23%, while the *peso* rose only 15%.

33. Vicens Vives, *Manual,* p. 421.

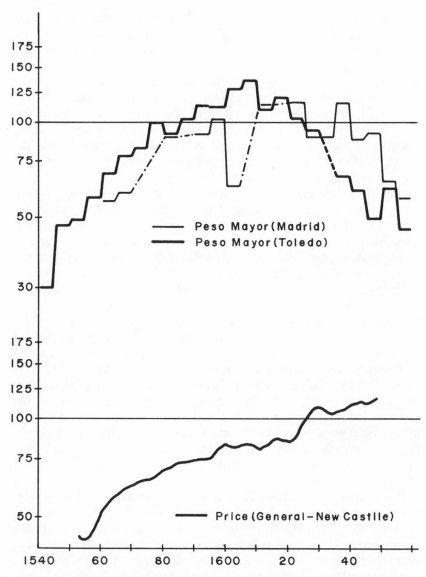

Figure 11.5 *Indices of Central Market Activity and Prices in Madrid and Toledo*

until 1608. The peak for both coincides with the Court's absence from Madrid. Given that Toledo was the center of the regional market system, the high level of economic activity indicates that regional exchange mechanisms were functioning in Castile until after the beginning of the new century.

Disintegration of the system organized by Toledo came later than has been assumed, and coincides with the collapse of that city.

The significance of the relative elasticities in the Toledo series emerges when we compare trends in the two cities. The revenue of the *almotacenía* in Toledo began to drift downward in the mid-1590's, while the *peso* and the wheat brokerage fees continued upward until 1608. This suggests that the volume of long-distance trade was declining, even though Toledo's population was still growing. The city was becoming poorer and shifting purchasing power to the basic, regionally produced commodities that flowed through the *peso*. This coincides with evidence that the poorer *Morisco* part of the population was growing faster than the rest of the city.[34]

In Madrid, the trend of the Arganda toll indicates continued growth of the new political and social functions of the capital, but the extreme polarization of wealth that we have described elsewhere was developing steadily. Revenues from the *peso mayor* stopped rising in the second decade, despite a rapidly growing population. This implies that most immigrants were from the poorest strata of rural society and were pushed off the land by disintegration of the rural economy. They were attracted to the city by high wages, stable food prices, and the construction boom of 1608–25.

When Toledo's collapse came, it was spectacular. By the 1620's, income from the *almotacenía* was 55% below the level of 1601–10, and only leveled off during the 1630's and '40's. The decline of the *peso mayor* was initially slower, since it reflected population rather than commercial trends, but in the longer run it was equally emphatic. From an index of 132 in 1601–10, it dropped to 100 in the '20's and to 56 in the 1640's—a 58% decline. The sequence indicates that first Toledo's long-range commerce (reflected in the *almotacenía*) was drawn away or undermined by Madrid. Consequently, the population became smaller and poorer (reflected in the more gradual decline of the *peso mayor*), and by 1631 the population of Toledo had fallen to 20,000.[35]

It is simplistic to assert that Madrid "caused" the decline of Toledo, but it is important to show how Madrid fit into the pattern of change that was involved. Monetary inflation and the state of the international market were clearly central to the process.[36] The *almotacenía* of Toledo was sensitive to such factors, as witnessed by its sharp reaction to the difficulties of the Crown and the stagnation of traffic at Sevilla in the 1560's and '70's. By the 1590's, however, Toledo's commerce was becoming more sensitive to regional condi-

34. Weisser, "Decline Revisited," p. 625.
35. Ibid., pp. 625–626.
36. Larraz López, *La época del Mercantilismo*, pp. 38–39.

tions than to the Sevilla trade. Indeed, the decline in Toledo's commercial activity led the decline of commerce in Sevilla.[37] While in the mid-sixteenth century Toledo was well connected with external trade, by the end of the century local conditions were much more important. These were the conditions shaped by Madrid's growing control of the supplies, trade, and mercantile services that had maintained Toledo.[38]

Thus Toledo's collapse was precipitated by a combination of factors that preempted or destroyed the city's functions and fields of influence. The process involved the disruption of foreign trade, heavy taxation, inflation, and regional overpopulation. Within that context, however, the growth of Madrid triggered a rapid and erratic increase in wheat prices, and thereby encouraged a recession in commercialized agriculture, especially viticulture. Consequently, Toledo's economy became increasingly sensitive to regional subsistence conditions. The growing strength of Madrid is apparent in the contrasting behavior of the two *peso* series. Before 1600 they reacted simultaneously to regional supply conditions, but thereafter they show opposite reactions to crises, suggesting that Toledo could attract commodities only when the population of Madrid was forced to divert its outlays to more essential goods.

Toledo's position as an urban center depended ultimately on the ability to provide quality manufactures for long-distance trade. Without such goods, the link between regional economy, regional entrepôt, and maritime commerce could not be maintained. This was the reality for the entire urban network of sixteenth-century Castile, and thus the collapse of Toledo's textile industry was an important aspect of the reorientation of Castilian urban life. Given the problems of the European textile industry in the early seventeenth century, therefore, it is an oversimplification to attribute Toledo's decline to Madrid alone.[39]

Toledo's high-quality woolens sold all over Europe, Spain, and Spanish America. By the end of the sixteenth century, however, international competition and differing rates of inflation had made it difficult for Spanish woolens to remain competitive. This has been attributed to the uneven impact of American bullion, but the inability of Castilian agriculture to meet urban demand, and the consequent rise of food prices, added labor costs to the

37. Huguette and Pierre Chaunu, *Seville et l'Atlantique* (1956), vol. 6, pp. 328–330.

38. On migration to Madrid, see Domínguez Ortiz, *Siglo XVII*, pp. 131–135. On Toledo's decline as an entrepôt, see Weisser, "Les marchands" and "Decline Revisited," pp. 630–640.

39. Toledo produced woolens, linens, and silk, and long collected small taxes on sales of woolens and linens in the city. Between them they provide a profile of the evolution of the city's industrial sector. The silk trade was considerably more valuable, but a comparable levy on silk was not imposed until after the city's decline was well under way.

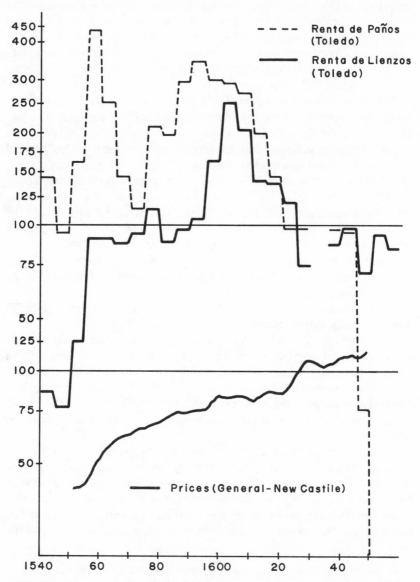

Figure 11.6 *Indices of Industrial Activity and Prices in Toledo and New Castile*

difficulties. After reaching very high levels at mid-sixteenth century,[40] woolen production fell sharply in the 1560's, corresponding with a drop in the *almotacenia* and the disruption of governmental and mercantile credit. Revenues then climbed steadily to 1591–95, after which they began a slow decline that accelerated in 1610. (See Fig. 11.6.)

In contrast, Toledo's linen trade was hardly affected by the fiscal and commercial difficulties of the 1570's, thus linking it to regional as opposed to international markets. Prior to 1595, when the index for woolens reached its second peak, the growth in linens was modest. Then, as woolens declined, linen output increased rapidly and remained high through 1601–07. As much as a century and a half later, linen was the most widely used fabric in Madrid, and it was a mainstay of the Castilian handicraft industry. Clearly, market conditions were favoring local rather than distant sales.

After 1610, linen tax revenues declined with other Toledo indicators, but much more slowly than those for woolens. Following the subsistence crisis of the late 1620's, linens retained a domestic market and escaped the total collapse of the woolens industry. The industrial base that was crucial to Toledo's ability to maintain its position as mediator between the interior and the periphery was clearly eroding, however. Confronted with rising local prices and wages, Toledo woolens export and production declined, while linen output that could be exchanged for regional agricultural commodities represented a futile attempt to offset the growing difficulties of urban supply.

V. General Considerations

Thus Toledo's economy was still expanding as late as the 1590's. The first sectors to decline were the export industries and long-distance trade, as international competition displaced Spanish textiles. This inability to compete reflects the tension between Madrid, Toledo, and New Castile, as the new capital city used the political and economic power of an imperial state to control resources within the Castiles. Tension was apparent in escalating supply crises, rapidly rising wheat prices, depression in the wine industry, and migration of the upper levels of Toledo's society to Madrid.[41] Thus, while economic conditions created hardship in other European textile centers after 1610, in Spain they precipitated the collapse of Toledo.

The growth of the regional population in the sixteenth century brought an intensification of subsistence agriculture within the local economies of the area,[42] but faster growth near the two cities reflects market-oriented special-

40. Figure 11.6 may overstate this peak, because the series is incomplete for the middle decades.
41. Weisser, "Les marchands" and "Decline Revisited," pp. 624–625.
42. Weisser, *The Peasants of the Montes,* ch. 4.

ization, and documents intimate urban-rural connections. They imply an agriculture directed at regional and urban markets, rural dependence on the market for essential supplies, and cottage industry tied to the exchange network that supported Toledo.[43] This orientation of rural society to the urban market represents both a degree of economic growth and an effort to compensate for declining agricultural productivity. The stability of the rural economy thus depended on a functioning regional market system, since the more specialized agriculture becomes, the more its population depends on exchanges for vital supplies. In Castile, the cost of bringing supplies from long distances encouraged the Crown to disrupt that market system in order to supply its growing capital city.

Officials in Toledo had no doubt that Madrid was the cause of their difficulties.[44] As Toledo had expanded, it became dependent upon wine supplied by brokers whose predecessors once produced the city's wine within the jurisdiction of the city council. Toledo had outgrown those sources, and the local vintners had become middlemen who purchased wine in more distant towns. This was part of the commerce that supported the city, but Toledo had no jurisdiction over the towns involved. By 1600, these towns were being drawn into Madrid's supply system, as the Crown increased Madrid's radius of control. Thus, while once Madrid had had to protect itself from Toledo's preemption of supplies,[45] by 1598 Toledo was vehemently protesting Madrid's tactics. Earlier the government had diverted to Madrid all wine within 12 leagues (36 miles), but in 1598 it broke all precedent and extended the radius to 15 leagues (45 miles).[46] Since the two cities are only 50 miles apart, the embargo reached into the neighborhood of Toledo, and wine destined for Toledo was being diverted to Madrid.

In better harvest years, supply remained adequate, but crises like that of 1598 increasingly put Toledo at a disadvantage. In that year the diversion of wine produced a price of 42 *maravedises* per *azumbre* in Toledo, while it was 28 in Madrid. The price differential is corroborated by the vintners of Yepes, who complained that they were forced to sell to Madrid at 3.5 *reales* per

43. For a theoretical discussion of this locational problem, beginning with Johann Heinrich von Thünen, *Der isolierte Staate* (1828), see Edgar S. Dunn, Jr., *The Location of Agricultural Production* (1954), esp. pp. 56–70 and 99–104; Janet D. Henshall, "Models of Agricultural Activity" (1969), pp. 443–445; and Carol A. Smith, ed., *Regional Analysis* (1976), vol. 1, ch. 1. For Castilian evidence, see Gentil da Silva, *En Espagne*, pp. 27–28.

44. Urban regulation of the countryside was a routine aspect of economic life, and the uniqueness of Madrid is in the scale of its application. See Eli Hecksher, *Mercantilism* (1935), vol. 1, pp. 39–40, 123–129, and vol. 2, pp. 132–135; Adna Ferrin Weber, *The Growth of Cities*, pp. 176–178; Max Weber, *The City*, pp. 187–188. The mechanics and chronology of market intervention in Castile were detailed in Chapters 7–9 above.

45. AVM, *Secretaria*, sig. 2–91–27.

46. See Chapter 7 above for details on regulation of commodity flows in New Castile.

arroba, even though brokers from Toledo were offering 5.5.[47] Similarly, in 1625 wine was available in Madrid for 38 *maravedises*, while the price was 46 in Toledo and 48 in Illescas.[48] Given that Toledo was nearer to the supplying towns, higher prices there clearly reflect the diversion of supplies to Madrid.

Toledo was also affected by the southward expansion of the system of *pan de registro*. By 1609 the capital was exacting quotas from as far as 18 leagues, a zone that enveloped Toledo and excluded only towns under its señorial authority. This produced numerous disputes, illustrated by orders that Toledo cease interfering with the shipment of bread to Madrid (1609) and stop removing bakers from towns now under Madrid's jurisdiction (1614).[49] By 1610, discriminatory bread prices (see Chapter 7) were in force, and beyond 12 leagues from Madrid the price was set at 18% below the price in the city.[50] Regulation, and the consequent erosion of Toledo's economy, help explain migration from Toledo to Madrid, the attractiveness of the latter, and the rapid change in their relative size. After 1607, emigration from Toledo became a flood, and is confirmed by edicts dated 1607, 1615, 1621, 1632, and 1641 ordering Toledans in Madrid to return to Toledo.[51]

The economic distress of New Castile in the 1580's and 1590's and the collapse in the early seventeenth century have been attributed to inflation, high taxes, subsistence crises, disease, diversion of capital from productive activities, and loss of manpower to army and empire. Any of several combinations of these variables provides an explanation, but it is not always clear just how they operated. A favored interpretation holds that the price revolution forced Spanish manufactures out of world and Spanish markets.[52] Yet 1601–20 was not an especially inflationary time in Spain, since the composite price index actually fell 7.5% between 1601 and 1610, and rose only 1.44% from 1611 to 1620.[53]

Unquestionably, an important part of the commercial life of the sixteenth-century interior depended on external markets. Nevertheless, isolation and primitive transport rendered the economy of New Castile largely autonomous. Alongside the activities of Toledo based on distant markets was the exchange of lesser-quality rural manufactures and agricultural products—a

47. On 1598 and the Toledo wine supply, see AHN, *Alcaldes,* libros for 1598, fols. 160, 169–170.

48. Ibid., libro for 1625, fols. 49, 73.

49. Ibid., libros for 1609, fol. 402, and 1614, fol. 22.

50. This was done deliberately to divert bread from Toledo to Madrid: ibid., libro for 1610, fols. 570–572.

51. Domínguez Ortiz, *Siglo XVII,* pp. 131–135.

52. Larraz López, *La época del Mercantilismo,* pp. 38–39.

53. Ural Pérez, in "El precio de los granos," p. 128, demonstrates declining pressure on grain supplies in New Castile that correlates with the collapse of Toledo.

market insulated from the rest of the world. Through the sixteenth century, Toledo functioned successfully as an interior entrepôt, keeping external and regional markets linked together. In that regional context, growing domestic demand and inelastic supply were more damaging to exchange patterns than the money supply, and aggravated the impact of international price differentials on competition abroad.

Another explanation is that increasing government demands undermined the fragile peasant economy. This explanation gives attention to rising taxes and price regulation, but the immediate realities suggest that regional as well as international aspects of the interior economy were undermined by conditions occasioned by the rise of Madrid. Unquestionably, increased taxation at the end of the sixteenth century came at the worst possible time for Castile's peasant economies, caught as they were between high population and declining yields. But the insertion of Madrid into this situation was not an autonomous event—it was another aspect of the growing societal cost of the state. The operative aspects involved supplies and regulation, rather than revenue—but conceptually, it was part of the price of empire.

The evolution of the regional economy was distorted by contradictory government policies and shifting urban consumption. This was a consequence of the relative elasticities of demand for commodities under inelastic supply conditions and of the emerging structure of income in the new capital city. This structure, with extremes of income distribution, precluded the urban-rural interactions characteristic of sixteenth-century Toledo. The crucial turning points were the selection of Madrid as the capital in 1560 and the expansion of the capital into a major urban center after 1595. The effect was to increase urban demand sharply, at a time when the rural economy was heavily populated.

In the sixteenth century, development of the urban hinterland concentrated around the two cities and featured specialization. The most striking of these was the shift to viticulture between 1560 and 1590, as wine prices rose appreciably faster than cereal prices. This left many districts dependent on city-based exchanges for vital supplies. The intensification of demand for wheat after 1590 prompted a rapid rise in its price which, as five-year averages, rose 90% in twenty years, while wine prices fell 20%. It is small wonder that many communities experienced falling incomes and soaring bread prices, rising mortality, declining fertility, and emigration.

First Toledo's export sector, pressed by competition and high costs, lost its foreign markets, then the city's mercantile function ceased to be profitable, and ultimately much of its commercial community moved to Madrid. Between 1595 and 1630, the growth of Madrid aggravated recurrent regional subsistence crises, depriving Toledo and the region of respite from negative economic pressures and forestalling stabilization. Only in the 1630's and

'40's, when defeat and revolt diverted resources from Madrid, did the capital cease to grow. Toledo was then able to stabilize at 20,000 inhabitants, with vestiges of its entrepôt function, remnants of its textile industry, and its role as site of Spain's metropolitan see.

In the process, interior agriculture was left with a single urban market—a market destined to expand and contract in response to conditions unrelated to the economic realities of the interior. The political crisis of the Spanish empire after 1635 diverted resources to warfare, and the capital itself declined. The reduction in Madrid's requirements came too late to aid Toledo or to prevent demographic calamity in Castile much worse than the stagnation experienced in the rest of Western Europe during the seventeenth century.

With the collapse of Toledo, Madrid was the only city of significance in the entire zone affected by the capital's supply network. An urban hierarchy based on specialized agriculture, craft industries, and a range of local, regional, and international exchanges had been dismantled. It was replaced with an urban hierarchy in which the provision of political and social services precipitated the redistribution of resources, demand, and urban functions so as to create a network of minor regional centers dominated by a disproportionately large primate city. The accompanying widespread reversion of rural society into subsistence production was an inevitable consequence of this change. This reorientation of the rest of the Castilian urban system to Madrid is the subject of Chapter 12.

12. The Urban Network: Madrid and the Castilian Towns

Cities exist partly because they provide political, social, and exchange functions for their immediate hinterlands. They also provide connecting links between these hinterlands and more distant sources of goods and services. These two types of function reinforce each other and are easy to identify in a great port city like Sevilla or in a primate city like Toledo because the long-distance, higher-order exchanges and services of a large city are very visible. In a landlocked interior region, however, long-distance contacts are relatively expensive, harder to maintain, and fragile, and thus play a much smaller role in the combination of local and long-distance activity in the regional economy. Thus, when we examine the development of urban economies in an interior region, it is harder to identify the changes associated with interurban connections.

This is particularly true for early modern Castile, because we know remarkably little about the interurban aspects of its regional economic life. It is clear that by the mid-sixteenth century the Castilian interior had a fairly complex urban network. We have descriptive evidence of economic life, some perception of the regional exchange economy in the 1570's, and a few studies of towns like Valladolid, León, Segovia, Ciudad Real, and Talavera—but we lack a concrete understanding of how they fit together. The best evidence that we are dealing with a coherent, integrated system is that the cities of Old and New Castile formed an urban hierarchy very similar to that predicted by location theory for a functioning system of market-oriented towns.[1]

At the head of the system was Toledo, which maintained intense relations throughout New Castile, providing both commercial and politico-social ser-

---

1. For a summary of the relevant propositions, see Smith, *Regional Analysis,* vol. 1, pp. 23–30.

vices. Toledo coordinated the long-distance and financial exchanges that linked the two Castiles with Valencia, Cartagena, Sevilla, and the Burgos-Bilbao-Flanders axis. Valladolid, with two-thirds the population, ranked second to Toledo in the urban hierarchy of the sixteenth century. Valladolid was the center of interurban activity in Old Castile. Its regular commercial contacts reached as far as Burgos, Segovia, Salamanca, Medina del Campo, and Medina del Rio Seco (Map 12.1). Only a few commercial contacts generated by the Court reached beyond that range, however, indicating a dependence on higher-order commercial functions emanating from Toledo, Burgos, or Bilbao. Valladolid's long-distance functions were as much administrative and political as commercial, depending on the Crown and the *Chancilleria,* which remained when the Crown moved away. Valladolid never contained the capitalist merchants found in Burgos, Toledo, or Sevilla; the structure of its workforce shows a surprisingly large class of legal and professional people.[2]

Below Toledo and Valladolid were a number of important towns noted for their textile industries and/or relative size (10,000–25,000 in the late sixteenth century): Segovia, Ávila, Guadalajara, Cuenca, Salamanca. At the next level were several towns that performed special trade functions: Medina del Campo, Burgos, Astorga, Talavera; and regional agricultural centers with small nuclei of urban service elements: León, Ciudad Real, Albacete, Soria, Trujillo.

Obviously, such a list is incomplete and impressionistic; but the fact that it can easily be made is suggestive of the developed nature of Castile's sixteenth-century urban system and long-distance commerce.[3] The Castilian urban network integrated the wool exports, the great trade fairs, and the cloth, pottery, leather, and silk industries of Segovia, Palencia, Cuenca, Talavera, Toledo, and other communities. This exchange network was central to the credit of the Spanish Crown before the heyday of American silver; it reached as far as Flanders and Italy and attracted international trading firms.

Madrid played a major role in reorienting that urban system; but the system itself was also weakened by the transfer of the Court from Valladolid, the late sixteenth-century reorientation of bullion flows, and diversion of the wool trade from the north coast. In the following pages we will sketch the decline of some of these interior towns as the sixteenth-century urban hierarchy broke down, and review the stabilization of an urban system in the seventeenth century that contained few centers capable of providing higher-order services. Then we will try to sort out the reactions in that system to the growth of Madrid and rural population during the eighteenth century, con-

2. Bartolomé Bennassar, *Valladolid au siècle d'or,* pp. 99–102, 116–119. Only 40% of Valladolid's *vecinos* appear to have been active in the workforce, compared with 48% in Burgos and 65% in Medina del Campo.
3. Weisser, "Les marchands de Tolède."

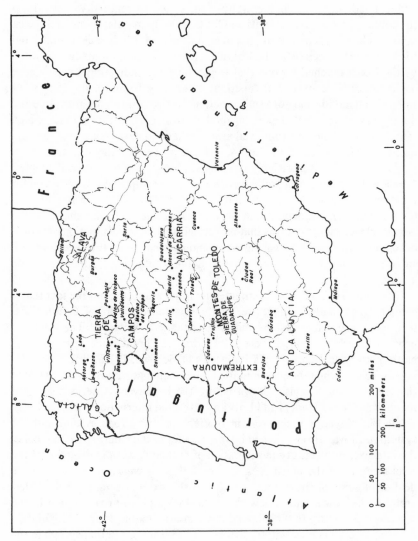

Map 12.1 *Locations Cited in Chapter 12*

cluding this chapter with some comments on the role of Madrid as the link between interior and periphery.

I. Sixteenth and Early Seventeenth Centuries: The Collapse of the Urban Network

We have already seen how Toledo, after expanding in the middle decades of the sixteenth century, experienced serious difficulties in the third quarter and then managed a qualified recovery between 1580 and 1605. Behind that recovery was a deterioration of the city's long-distance commercial function and a shift of industrial output to products more appropriate to the regional market. After the Court was re-installed in Madrid in 1606, Toledo began a precipitous decline that reduced it to the level of an economic backwater, enhanced only by the presence of the metropolitan see.

The fate of Valladolid was very similar, although the cause appears to have been connected with the loss of political and social functions rather than, as in Toledo, the loss of commercial function and supply base. As was Madrid later, the Valladolid of the 1540's and 1550's was subsidized by the presence of the Court and a large resident nobility. This produced a midcentury boom, followed by a severe setback when the Court left in 1559. The population fell from 7,000 *vecinos* in the 1550's to 5,258 in 1570 before recovering to 8,112 *vecinos* in 1591.[4] The precarious economy was bolstered by the return of the Court in 1602; but with its departure in 1606, longer-range commercial links evaporated.[5] Having reached a population of about 40,000 people in 1595, Valladolid declined rapidly after 1606 and, although the chronology of decline is unclear, by 1688 the number of *vecinos* had fallen from the 8,112 of 1591 to only 3,000.[6] Having lost its major political function, the city ceased to serve as a coordinator for long-distance exchanges within Old Castile and rapidly declined to the same status as Toledo—an economic backwater enhanced, in this case, by the presence of the *Chancilleria* of Valladolid.

As examples of cities of the next order of importance, we can consider the two cloth-producing centers of Segovia and Cuenca. Segovia, a major textile center, grew from about 14,000 inhabitants in 1531 to 21,000 in 1591. By that time, the city had passed the peak of its yearly textile production: 16,000 pieces of cloth of 40 *varas* each. In this respect Segovia's economy paralleled the industrial portion of Toledo's, where the tax on woolen cloth suggests a decline in production beginning in the 1590's. As of 1591, there were 600

4. Bennassar, *Valladolid,* pp. 125, 132–135, 141–144, 185. The pattern is similar to that shown by Weisser, in "The Decline of Castile Revisited," pp. 625 ff., for non-Morisco Toledo.
5. Bennassar, *Valladolid,* pp. 347–348.
6. This implies a maximum population of 15,000: Domínguez Ortiz, *Siglo XVII,* vol. 1, pp. 137–138.

looms in Segovia itself; but by 1620 the number had fallen to 300, and by 1691 to only 159.[7] This is paralleled by population figures, which declined over 50% in the century after 1591.[8] It is noteworthy that towns like Segovia lost a smaller proportion of their population than the larger centers. What was lost was not a fixed proportion of each city's economic base, but functions that reached beyond the regional economy. Thus a town like Segovia, with a less complex set of urban functions, had less to lose than Valladolid or Toledo, and under the developing conditions soon found itself much more of an equal to them.

This pattern was repeated in Cuenca, midway between Valencia and Madrid in a relatively well-defined regional economy of its own. A substantial regional woolens industry was organized from the city, although the volume of cloth marketed was only about half as much as Segovia's. While most of Cuenca's woolens were sold in the interregional exchanges between Toledo and the Valencian frontier, some of its cloth was regularly traded as far away as Sevilla, Valencia, and Medina del Campo, illustrating the complexity of exchanges in the sixteenth-century Spanish interior.[9]

A profile of Cuenca's commercial history is provided by the revenue figures from the city's *correduría mayor y menor y sisa vieja* from 1577 to 1670 (Table 12.1).[10] The highest revenue figures appear in the 1570's and '80's, after which a decline in both nominal and adjusted indices began. As in Toledo and Segovia, industrial activity linked to long-range commerce reached its peak before 1600, and market activity subsequently declined with the reorientation of Castilian urban resources and the breakup of interregional exchanges. By 1600, revenue had fallen 20–30%, although the trend was arrested briefly in the first decade of the new century, when pressure in the regional commodities markets was eased during the Court's absence from

7. Angel García Sanz, *Desarrollo y crisis del Antiguo Régimen en Castilla la Vieja,* pp. 45–48, 215–217.

8. Domínguez Ortiz, *Siglo XVII,* pp. 150–151. While he questions the seventeenth-century censuses, which suggest only 4,000 people, Domínguez Ortiz cannot accept more than 10,000 as of the 1690's.

9. Paulino Iradiel Murugarrén, *Evolución de la industria textil castellana en los siglos XIII-XVI* (1974).

10. As in the coastal cities, interior towns collected road and gate tolls, market inspection fees, and taxes on raw materials or manufactured items used, produced, or traded in the town. Supporting information makes possible several assumptions about these duties: The rate of taxation, whether defined in nominal monetary terms or *ad valorem,* rarely changed. When it did, it was as a result of municipal reform evident in the accounts. Taxes were farmed for one to six years, and in most cases seasonal variations are masked. Yearly variations were minimized by long contracts and by their basis on projections of future yield. We know little about arrangements that permitted tax evasion, nor can we estimate the revenue captured by the tax farmer but not represented in municipal accounts. Pending local studies, we are left with the assumption that in relatively small, close-knit towns, corruption was recognized and stabilized by custom and usage. See Vilar, *Catalunya,* vol. 2, p. 384.

Table 12.1. *Indices of Commercial Revenues in Cuenca, 1577-1670 (1621-30 = 100)*

Period	Corredurías (nominal)	Corredurías (adjusted) (a)
1577	154.0	216.8
1588-90	167.6	214.1
1591-1600	149.5	175.7
1601-10	133.9	152.4
1611-20	107.3	118.0
1621-30	100.0	100.0
1631-40	52.8	45.6
1641-50	77.0	61.8
1651-60	85.0	—
1661-70	84.0	—

Source: See Appendix E, Cuenca.
a. Adjustment was made with Hamilton's New Castile price indices.

New Castile. Revenues fell over 60% from 1600 to 1635, then stabilized despite the difficulties of the 1640's, echoing the pattern we have already seen in Toledo.

Somewhat lower in the urban hierarchy were a number of towns that served as centers of regional agriculture but also provided a specialized function such as transport center or fair site. As an example of each, we can look briefly at the towns of Astorga and Talavera. While never exceeding a few thousand people, each held a place in the urban system beyond that of simple market town.

Astorga, 40 kilometers southwest of León and 20 kilometers northwest of the market town of La Bañeza, was at the crossroads of the Camino de Santiago and the royal highway from Madrid to Galicia (Map 12.1). It was the principal town of the *maragato* district, home of an important group of long-distance muleteers.[11] After growing from 557 *vecinos* in 1571 to 656 by 1591, Astorga plummeted to 200 *vecinos* by 1659, as interregional trade declined and plague devastated the area. Astorga's transporters had prospered as a link between the cities of Old Castile and the ports of Asturias and Galicia. As urban life concentrated on Madrid, different routes to the coasts

11. Valentín Cabero Diéguez, *Evolución y estructura urbana de Astorga*, pp. 35–38. Judging from work on Galicia, the volume of this commerce was small, and the long-distance trade to the ports derived little from the economy of Galicia. See Jaime García-Lombardero, *La agricultura y el estancamiento económico de Galicia en la España del Antiguo Régimen*, ch. 3.

were favored and the Old Castile markets disappeared; when Madrid itself declined after 1635, this situation was aggravated.

This sequence was repeated in the modest fair town and industrial center of Talavera de la Reina, although there the decline was slowed by the town's functional importance in the new Madrid-oriented urban hierarchy.[12] Located on the main route from Madrid and Toledo to Extremadura, with connections to Portugal, Sevilla, and Old Castile, Talavera grew rapidly in the early sixteenth century. It received a setback in the 1560's that coincides with problems in Toledo, Valladolid, Álava, and elsewhere, but recovered in the late 1570's and '80's. The regional economy was based on a combination of subsistence agriculture, livestock, textiles, and the added element of a pottery industry. The region was suffering from soil exhaustion by the 1590's, about the time that its livestock fair reached its peak. In the last decades of the century, population fluctuated around 8,000 (2,000 *vecinos*).

But despite the plagues and subsistence crises of 1598–99, 1607, and 1626–30, the town held most of its population, declining only 25% by 1632. It is this relative stability that documents Talavera's adjustment to the rise of Madrid. The town became a way station for long-distance connections with Andalucía and Portugal and a key part of the capital's meat-supply system. Once Madrid began to decline, however, Talavera lost its vitality, and by 1646 its population was just over half that of the late sixteenth century. Even so, Talavera fared proportionately better than Toledo, Valladolid, or Astorga, and continued to perform significant supply functions for the capital.

Finally, as examples of towns that were the centers of relatively self-contained agricultural regions, with tenuous and unspecialized connections to the larger urban network, we can look at León in the north and Albacete and Ciudad Real in southeastern New Castile. In these cases regional conditions were clearly the dominant factor in urban development, and external changes had less impact.

León is some distance from both Valladolid and Madrid. Center of an isolated agricultural zone, its development paralleled José Gentil da Silva's model for New Castile. In the last half of the sixteenth century, while the total number of *vecinos* did not change much, the composition of the economically active population did. There was a notable increase in the number of day laborers and textile, leather, and construction workers, and a smaller increase in the number of miscellaneous artisans. The service sector grew, adding government employees, professionals, and a number of people engaged in commercial activity. In New Castile, as rural demographic pressure increased, local craft industries developed to compensate for diminishing re-

12. The development of Talavera is summarized from María C. González Muñoz, *La población de Talavera de la Reina, siglos XVI-XX* (1975), pp. 95, 131–133, 180–190, 245.

turns in agriculture. León shows the same pattern for the northern *meseta*, with modest textile and leather industries that bolstered the city's economic base as supplies became more expensive. By 1600, with about 4,000 people, León looked somewhat less like a large farm town and a bit more like a modest regional capital.[13]

Increased exchange activity is documented both by growth of the artisan, commercial, and service sectors and by revenue from the city's *peso de mercancías*. Revenues rose slowly in the 1560's and '70's, a period of distress almost everywhere, and then climbed rapidly in 1581–1610 (see Table 12.2). Between 1610 and 1640, the adjusted revenue index fluctuated between 85 and 100. Apparently the regional economy on which León was based remained fairly stable. Never strongly linked to the urban network, León was less exposed to the breakdown of interurban exchanges; and the city's population, which fluctuated around 900 *vecinos* from 1555 to 1594, fell by only 30% in the first half of the seventeenth century.[14] The pattern shows little correlation with trends in Madrid.

At the opposite corner of the Iberian interior, Albacete was a town in eastern La Mancha situated on the road from Madrid and Toledo to the Mediterranean. It was the center of a modest regional economy emphasizing wheat, livestock, and some wine. Adjusted for prices, the city's *almotacenia* increased 20% from 1561 to the 1580's, while the *correduría* (brokerage fee on large transactions) shows no significant trend (see Table 12.3). In the last two decades of the century, both indicators declined sharply—50–60% after adjustment for prices. Market activity then recovered sharply in 1600–10, before resuming a decline. Cereal output repeated the decline that Weisser has documented for the nearby Montes de Toledo; the wool trade was disrupted; and wine prices started to fall in the 1590's. We have seen that the temporary movement of the Court to Valladolid coincided with commercial recovery in Toledo, and this brief reprieve for the urban network may be reflected here as well.

The pattern in Albacete is paralleled in the baptismal records of nearby Ciudad Real, where population and baptisms rose erratically until 1575, fluctuated around a stable base for two decades, and then fell sharply between 1602 and 1620. The city then stabilized, and until the crisis of 1680 experienced strong cyclical fluctuations around a gradual upward trend.[15]

These urban stories fit the generally accepted version of economic change in New Castile. The expansion of the mid-sixteenth century is weaker than

13. Valentina Fernández Vargas, *La población de León en el siglo XVI* (1968), pp. 139–147; Gentil da Silva, *En Espagne,* pp. 28–30, 82.
14. Fernández Vargas, *La población de León,* pp. 162–163, Domínguez Ortiz, *Siglo XVII,* p. 150.
15. Carla Rahn Phillips, *Ciudad Real, 1500–1750,* pp. 22–23, 30.

Table 12.2. *Indices of Commercial Activity in León,*
1561-1656 (1621-30 = 100)

Period	Peso de Mercancías (nominal)	Peso de Mercancías (adjusted)
1561-70	30.5	50.0
1571-80	34.4	52.7
1581-90	50.3	72.6
1591-1600	62.0	77.7
1601-10	82.9	91.1
1611-20	73.3	87.4
1621-30	100.0	100.0
1631-40	88.1	85.1
1641-50	155.1(a)	135.5
1651-56	237.7(a)	—

Source: See Appendix E, León.
a. Given a falling population, it is likely that these figures
represent higher tariffs, not increased market activity.

some surveys imply, but the distress of the last two decades is evident. The
contrast between these smaller towns and Toledo suggests that they were
more vulnerable to localized conditions than the larger city. Thus, while the
lower echelons of the urban hierarchy were being affected by the problems of
rural Spain, the entire urban network was being distorted by the impact of the
Court. The last three towns we have examined were more sensitive to local
conditions, however, than to conditions that disrupted higher-order interurban activity.

Taking the urban system as a whole, the rise of Madrid prompted a redistribution of urban resources and high-order functions. This undermined
long-distance retailing and deprived the larger sixteenth-century cities of
functions that had made them important. As this situation developed, the
urban network faced increasingly sharp supply shortages and rising food
prices. The larger and stronger centers—Valladolid, Segovia, Toledo—maintained their positions for a while by diverting the surpluses that earlier had
supplied the smaller centers. Many lesser cities declined fairly early in the
last half of the century; Cuenca, Albacete, and Ciudad Real reflect this
pattern. Up to 1610, the process was more apparent in New Castile, reflecting
its closer proximity to the Court. The departure of the Court from Valladolid
in 1559 crippled that city; its presence in Madrid put pressure on Toledo; and
its temporary return to Valladolid clearly relieved that pressure in the commodities markets surrounding Toledo, Albacete, and Cuenca.

Thus the commercial network that grew up with sixteenth-century expansion, linking regional and external exchanges, changed but continued to func-

Table 12.3. *Indices of Commercial Activity in Albacete, 1543-1611*
(1611 = 100)

Period	Almotacenía (nominal)	Almotacenía (adjusted)	Correduría (nominal)	Correduría (adjusted)
1541-50	59.0	—	53.6	—
1551-60	73.2	162.3	122.5	271.5
1561-70	91.1	154.1	154.6	261.5
1571-80	131.8	199.2	176.1	266.2
1581-90	109.4	150.0	95.4	130.8
1591-1600	85.4	108.8	83.1	105.7
1601-10	115.0	138.7	148.9	179.5
1611	100.0	100.0	100.0	100.0

Source: See Appendix E, Albacete.

tion after rural expansion had reached its limits. Then, between 1598 and 1608, plague, subsistence crises, expulsion of the *Moriscos*, and the sudden expansion of demand in Madrid revealed the fragility of the urban network and knocked it apart.

The development of Madrid as it competed with Toledo for supplies thus provides a suggestive counterpoint to the evolution of the rest of the urban network. Arbitrarily selected as the site of the government in 1560, Madrid began to grow steadily, and by the turn of the century matched Toledo in population. After a setback in 1602–06 while the Court was in Valladolid, Madrid nearly trebled in size by 1630, after which it declined 40% by 1680. This is clearly reflected in the development of commercial activity and consumption in the city.[16]

The heavy pressure of Madrid on the regional commodities markets is evidenced in meat, oil, wine, and wheat consumption and prices. As the city grew, prices rose, and demand was increasingly focused upon stocks of basic foodstuffs that were essential to the urban network. From the 1590's to the 1630's, Madrid's use of olive oil almost doubled, wine and meat consumption more than doubled, and wheat consumption trebled. These supplies were produced by a combination of rent- and tithe-paying subsistence producers, rentier accumulation, and specialization in activities like viticulture in the context of declining per-capita agricultural output.[17] The pressure of the capital on these stocks undermined the rest of the regional urban network.

At the same time, urban populations were hard put to buy the less essential

16. See data on Madrid in Chapters 2, 6, and 11.

17. Gonzalo Anes, in "Tendencias," p. 100, makes this observation and notes that most Castilian urban growth took place in the first half of the sixteenth century, and expansion was much more tentative thereafter. The sense of reaching a ceiling on urban expansion is clear.

handicraft manufactures that represented the traditional resort of rural populations forced to compensate for declining living standards. This is reflected in the decline of *peso* revenues in most towns prior to 1600 and in the failure of Madrid's demand for such goods to increase as fast as its population. Thus while Madrid's pressure on the commodities market reduced the ability of other towns to obtain rural manufactures, Madrid itself did not become the alternative market that its growth might imply. The plausibility of this hypothesis is reinforced by the immediate rise of commercial indicators in New Castile while the Court was at Valladolid in 1602–06.

Thus the revival of Madrid's demands after 1606 broke the back of the regional urban network of Castile, and cities that had managed to sustain their commercial life into the seventeenth century collapsed in the next twenty years. Madrid's power to command resources was based on a political and economic empire that supported the capital's wealthy elites despite the rising cost of local foodstuffs. The extra-regional connections that this implies are illustrated by the startling rise of revenues from the *barca de Arganda*. Those revenues quintupled from the 1580's to the 1630's and were little affected by subsistence crises. While one road toll does not document a commercial network, the political and international basis of the capital's economy is patent, and insertion of the attendant political and social functions into an unstable regional economy inevitably caused a restructuring of the urban network. As a consequence, the region lost many middle-level urban functions, especially market coordination, and withdrew into local and regional subsistence. The worst of this shock had been absorbed by 1650, but by then the urban system outside of Madrid had acquired a homogeneity and rudimentary quality that was striking.

II. The Later Seventeenth Century in Castile

The later seventeenth century was characterized by a new balance between subsistence and exchange because of changes in the urban hierarchy of Old and New Castile. The economic life of the Spanish interior after 1650 was very different from the commercial development in Barcelona and around the coastal periphery. Stability here was achieved amid the ruins of the urban network of the previous century and in the context of heightened rural self-sufficiency. This reflects Madrid's preemption of urban resources and functions, a process that concentrated urban markets, economic incentives, and urban functions so that they were more distant from and less accessible to much of the interior. This blend of stability and isolation appears everywhere in Castile from Burgos to León, from Talavera to Cuenca. Outside of Madrid, there is little to distinguish levels in an urban hierarchy, and the monotonic character of the urban network is apparent in the following survey of towns which indicate market trends.

The road and gate tolls of Burgos (Table 12.4) offer us a glimpse at the contrast and separation between the local economy and long-distance pass-through trade between Madrid and Bilbao which suggests that regional economic activity may have been less sensitive to the international situation than the transit trade through Pancorbo. The nominal value of the five-year average of duties at the Burgos city gates dropped 15% between the late 1670's and the '80's; but adjusted for price levels, real value rose 49% and then remained stable until the end of the series. This indicates stability in market activity oriented to the city itself, suggesting that Burgos' seventeenth-century crisis had long since passed. This impression is reinforced by the road toll at Barbadillo del Mercado, on the route from Soria to Burgos. Here the five-year average dropped 20% after 1675–80, but recovered in the last decade of the century. The commodities most likely to pass this toll were wool and lumber from Soria bound for Bilbao. Thus there are signs of recovery that reflect increased export of regional raw materials.

Pancorbo revenues, however, declined until the last few years of the century, indicating that long-distance trade into the interior was less dynamic than regional exports. The strongest signs of regional change in the period thus resemble the response of various coastal regions to external demand. Wool exports in particular were recovering, but this represented a kind of enclave industry in an isolated interior, and the regional economy was otherwise disengaged from interior-periphery market associations.

This situation was reproduced in the province of León. At Astorga, where the regional economy was connected with the larger world by the *arrieros maragatos,* specialists in transport between the northwestern ports and Cas-

Table 12.4. *Indices of Road and Gate Tolls, Burgos, 1675-99*
(1675-80 = 100)

Period	Portazgo de Pancorbo	Portazgo de Barba del Mercadillo	Barras y Medidas (nominal)	Barras y Medidas (adjusted)
1675-80	100.0	100.0	100.0	100.0
1681-85	84.1	80.1	86.9	149.3
1686-90	66.4	84.4	79.2	144.5
1691-95	59.6	110.0	95.9	150.6
1696-99	90.0	117.6	102.0	152.7

Source: See Appendix E, Burgos.

tile, the population of the town fell from some 650 *vecinos* in 1591 to only 200 in 1659, and was still at that level in 1713. The town did not recover until the transporters of the region succeeded in reorienting their services from the markets of Old Castile to those of Madrid in the eighteenth century. This is also apparent in nearby Benavente, which by the end of the seventeenth century experienced a modest growth based on regional market activity and local woolens. The town had few external contacts other than its location on the road to the fair center at La Bañeza.[18]

Northwest of Valladolid and midway between Burgos and the towns of Astorga and Benavente lies the regional center of Palencia, long noted for woolens production. By the 1660's, when our series begins, the seventeenth-century decline had passed and market indicators had stabilized (see Table 12.5). Nominal income from the *corredurías del pueblo* (merchandise brokerage) rose sharply after 1680. When adjusted for prices, the increase is even more remarkable, although much of it is probably a recovery from the difficulties of the 1670's. Taxes on wood and fuller's earth give conflicting trends—the former rising significantly in both nominal and adjusted terms, while the latter declined with equal lack of ambiguity. The modest size of the town suggests that increased market activity reflects a reintegration of regional markets in which woolens production was now ruralized, but coordinated from the city.

This echoes the pattern in Segovia, where the quality textile industry languished, but rough cloth continued to appear in local markets. Agricultural production there stabilized by mid-seventeenth century, but shifted to crops such as rye and barley that required less labor and were better suited to regional markets than the wheat and wine earlier demanded by larger cities.[19]

The stabilization of regional subsistence exchanges apart from long-distance trade is also apparent in New Castile. There are close parallels between market trends in Toledo, now stripped of its higher-order urban functions, and Benavente, Astorga, Palencia, or Burgos as regional centers (see Table 12.6). A close examination of rural production in the area would probably yield results similar to those found in seventeenth-century Segovia, since the changes in landholding show the same concentration of ownership.[20] Within the city of Toledo, general market activity (the *peso*) declined into the 1670's, and by the end of the century was at best below the level of the 1650's. The

18. See Table 12.12 and accompanying discussion.
19. This is apparent in a quick review of the sections in García Sanz, *Desarrollo y crisis,* on the seventeenth century, and in the brilliant piece by Gonzalo Anes and Jean Paul LeFlem, "Las crises del siglo XVII: Producción agrícola, precios e ingresos en tierras de Segovia" (1965).
20. Weisser, *The Peasants of the Montes.*

Table 12.5. *Indices of Commercial Activity in Palencia, 1651-1700*
(1671-1680 = 100)

Period	Peso (nominal)	Peso (adjusted)	Corredurías del Pueblo (nominal)	Corredurías del Pueblo (adjusted)
1651-60	—	—	—	—
1661-70	105.5	118.4	—	—
1671-80	100.0	100.0	100.0	100.0
1681-90	80.6	128.5	167.9	267.8
1691-1700	82.6	130.9	163.8	260.0

Period	Poyo (nominal)	Poyo (adjusted)	Greda (nominal)	Greda (adjusted)
1651-60	94.5	136.6	—	—
1661-70	106.6	170.0	134.5	151.6
1671-80	100.0	100.0	100.0	100.0
1681-90	107.8	166.4	53.1	82.0
1691-1700	123.1	183.6	58.9	87.8

Source: See Appendix E, Palencia.

Table 12.6. *Indices of Commercial Activity in Toledo, 1651-1700*
(1671-80 = 100)

Period	Peso (nominal)	Peso (adjusted)	Almotacenía (nominal)	Almotacenía (adjusted)
1651-60	127.5	175.5	154.6	213.6
1661-70	107.0	120.0	79.5	89.4
1671-80	100.0	100.0	100.0	100.0
1681-90	86.6	143.2	106.2	164.1
1691-1700	96.8	163.0	126.7	188.8

Source: See Appendix E, Toledo.

almotacenía collected on merchandise showed greater volatility and reached its low point a decade earlier, but closed the century well below the level of the 1650's.

The situation in Cuenca, with its links to Valencia, was somewhat different. The decline in market activity that became pronounced in the first half of the century continued to the end of the first Cuenca series in 1670, but was less pronounced than in Toledo (see Table 12.7). Nominal revenue remained stable and the adjusted revenue fell only 30% to the 1670's, a decade marked by depression everywhere. The relative stability in the third quarter of the

Table 12.7. *Indices of Commercial
Activity in Cuenca, 1651-1680
(1671-80 = 100)*

Period	Correduría (nominal)	Correduría (adjusted)
1651-60	100.8	141.8
1661-70	98.9	117.0
1671-80	100.0	100.0

Source: See Appendix E, Cuenca.

century, and the expansion of activity thereafter (see discussion of eighteenth-century Cuenca below), indicate a commercial life conditioned by the
revival of wool exports and by the growth of Valencia and its port activity.

The regional background is illustrated by Ciudad Real, where the same
process of consolidation of landholding that has been noted in rural Toledo
and Segovia took place. At the same time, the urban population stabilized
soon after 1630 and, despite the crises of 1677–85, the base level of the town's
population drifted upward.[21] Although Madrid's total consumption of wine
dropped drastically after the first third of the century, La Mancha (modern
Ciudad Real province) appears to have become relatively more important in
the trade; this may help explain the stabilization of the region.

These are some of the parallel trends that explain the levels of market
activity noted in Toledo, Palencia, and elsewhere. They are also apparent in
Talavera de la Reina, where the population developed as in Ciudad Real and
there was a survival and concentration of specialized craft industry among
urban notables similar to the concentration of land control elsewhere.[22] The
pattern is also seen in a minor boat toll near Alcalá de Henares where,
reflecting local and regional traffic, revenues dropped sharply in the first half
of the century and then fluctuated at around 60–70% of 1670's levels as late
as 1720 (see Table 12.8).

Although the contrast is not strong, trends in Madrid and its university
satellite, Alcalá de Henares, suggest that commercial life in the capital was
continuing the dual pattern created by the structure of the city's economy.
The strongest indicators of economic activity were those connected most
closely with the political and social functions of the capital city. During the
entire half-century beginning in 1670, only one ten-year period shows the
revenue of the *barca de Arganda* significantly below the peak of the early

21. Phillips, *Ciudad Real*, ch. 2 and pp. 34–35.
22. González Muñoz, *La población de Talavera*, pp. 189–257.

Table 12.8. *Indices of Commercial Activity in Alcalá de Henares, 1638-1720 (1671-80 = 100)*

Period	Corredurías y Pesos (nominal)	Corredurías y Pesos (adjusted)	Barca del Río Henares (nominal)
1638	274.0	—	272.0
1649-50	110.0	—	84.0
1651-60	80.0	111.4	96.9
1661-70	66.2	74.1	82.0
1671-80	100.0	100.0	100.0
1681-90	95.3	152.8	81.0
1691-1700	176.5	277.5	72.7
1701-10	325.9	—	78.2
1711-20	351.1	—	69.8

Source: See Appendix E, Alcalá de Henares.

seventeenth century, and in its worst decade (the 1650's), the boat toll fell by only 25% (see Table 12.9).

The chronology of the boat toll revenue is very like that of commercial or port activity in many coastal regions, reflecting its links with the economic base of the controlling elites in the capital. There is strong expansion of traffic in the third quarter of the seventeenth century, followed by a plateau lasting through the succession war. Unlike most interior indicators, however, the actual revenue of the boat toll never fell much, and matched the highs of the 1630's through most of the later seventeenth century, indicating a strong concentration of surviving long-distance trade upon the capital. The economic strength of Madrid's elites is reflected in the market duty at Alcalá, a university town whose major industry depended upon the wealth and patronage of the bureaucratic elites in the capital.[23] The Madrid *peso* was also stronger than those of other Castilian towns, reflecting relative urban prosperity as it filtered down to the middling-income levels. Not surprisingly, since the population of the city was stable for several decades, the consumption of basic staples changed little.

Thus we can clearly see the differing elasticities of demand at work in the capital, as the beginnings of peripheral prosperity and the presence of the state apparatus supported a commercial life connected with urban elites, even though other aspects of urban demand changed little. Only as commer-

23. Richard Kagan, in *Students and Society in Early Modern Spain* (1974), pp. 144, 237–238, and 249, shows that while university matriculations fell drastically in the seventeenth century, the lowest level at Alcalá was 864 in 1710. Furthermore, a growing proportion consisted of affluent members of the exclusive *Colegios Mayores*.

Table 12.9. *Indices of Commercial Activity in Madrid,*
1651-1700 (1671-80 = 100)

Period	Peso (nominal)	Peso (adjusted)	Barca de Arganda (nominal)
1651-60	111.9	157.3	68.8
1660-70	135.7	152.4	83.1
1671-80	100.0	100.0	100.0
1681-90	115.2	183.7	98.3
1691-1700	145.2	230.3	81.4

Source: See Appendix E, Madrid.

cial and imperial prosperity became more pronounced in the next century did the entire city begin to expand and change the relationship between urban consumption and the subsistence-oriented countryside.

III. The Eighteenth Century

Outside of Madrid, evidence for a revival in eighteenth-century Castile is ambiguous. The population increased gradually—although the margin of error in the earlier estimates is large—and the rapid growth of the coastal districts renders expansion in the interior a bit shadowy.[24] It is not surprising, therefore, that most of the interior exhibited a lack of sustained commercial trends, and the only dynamic elements were related to the capital.

Nevertheless, the eighteenth century is generally regarded as one of expansion in Spain, and we have seen that most port areas enjoyed a long rise in market activity. Even within the maritime provinces, however, there are indications of persistent dualism. Away from the coasts and ports, population trends, agricultural output, and markets based on the rural economy document an expansion in the first half of the eighteenth century that slowed markedly after the 1750's. Inland from Cartagena and Málaga and around Granada, this was apparent after 1760. It developed in Vizcaya about 1775 and in Álava around 1785, while overland commerce was stagnant or declining around Sevilla and Córdoba after 1770.

With such trends developing in the interior zones of the maritime

24. Uztáriz himself believed that the *vecindario* of 1707–23 underestimated the population by 20%, and that margin of error is separate from the problem of what a *vecino* meant demographically. See Anes, *Las crises agrarias*, pp. 129–142; and Francisco Bustelo García del Real, "El Vecindario General de España de 1712 a 1717: Censo de Campoflorido" (1973 and 1974), "Algunos reflexiones sobre la población española de principios de siglo XVIII," and "La población española en la segunda mitad del siglo XVIII." Also of interest is *La Renta Nacional de la Corona de Castilla*, ch. 3.

provinces, it is hardly surprising that similar indications are found in León and Benavente in the west, Palencia and Segovia in the north-central areas, and Cuenca, Albacete, Toledo, Ciudad Real, and Talavera de la Reina in New Castile. Eighteenth-century expansion was more complicated than a general survey might suggest.[25]

A. Old Castile and León

At León, in contrast to the expansion of commercial activity that accompanied peninsular prosperity in the sixteenth century, the tax on market activity (the *peso*) declined about 30% between 1721 and 1740, then remained static from 1740 to 1780 (see Table 12.10). Adjusted for prices, the decline amounted to almost 40% from 1721 to 1760; and after stabilizing in the 1760's, revenue fell another 10% in the 1770's. Beginning in 1751, the tax on merchandise is virtually static, varying only 5% from 1751 to 1780. Not until the 1780's is there an indication of expansion of commerce, as revenues rose about 35% after adjustment for inflation. The wine and olive oil series (the *peso de San Francisco*) declined from 1750 to 1770, started to rise sooner (in the mid-1770's), and in the 1780's averaged 47% higher than in the 1770's, doubling the 1760's average even after adjustment. By the last decade of the century, however, the signals are contradictory. The revenue of the general *peso* trebled between decades; and even adjusted for prices, the increase is about 240%. This abrupt change suggests a change in the rates of taxation. Since the revenue collected on merchandise rose only 20%, and adjusted for prices fell 5%, the behavior of the *peso* cannot reflect the actual flow of commodities.

Table 12.10. *Indices of Commercial Activity in León, 1721-1800 (1771-80 = 100)*

Period	Haber del Peso (nominal)	Haber del Peso (adjusted)	Peso de Mercancías (adjusted)	Peso de San Francisco (adjusted)
1721-30	141.5	198.8	—	—
1731-40	118.0	152.4	—	—
1741-50	97.7	125.8	—	—
1751-60	98.0	109.2	100.0	78.4
1761-70	107.3	111.6	104.9	68.3
1771-80	100.0	100.0	100.0	100.0
1781-90	138.7	141.7	134.9	147.1
1791-1800	496.7	350.5	126.1	—

Source: See Appendix E, León.

25. Anes, *El Antiguo Régimen: Los Borbones* (1975).

The growth of urban consumption and market activity in the 1780's is undeniable, and may reflect the growing dependence of the rural economy on market exchanges, as population pressed on resources. Given the comments of Antonio Sánchez on the Galician economy in the 1790's, the importance of the nearby Tierra de Campos and fairs at La Bañeza, and the role of the Astorga muleteers in the Madrid trades, market expansion may also reflect the increased flow of disposable wealth from Madrid to the provincial rentier class. Thus market activity increased in León between 1775 and 1790, but this episode was apparently cut short in the 1790's. Compared with the general economic expansion of the sixteenth century, León in the eighteenth experienced only a fleeting reflection of the commercial prosperity of Spain's coastal regions.

Evidence from the nearby towns of Benavente and Astorga supports this pattern, since with León the three towns surround the fair center at La Bañeza. The Astorgan *arrieros maragatos* operated between Galicia, León, and Valladolid in the sixteenth century, and in the eighteenth they were drawn to the long-distance transport of imports into Madrid and of Castilian agricultural products to the mountains and Galician ports. Concurrently, the population of Astorga rose from 1,200 in 1709 to 2,900 in 1753, when the city counted 700 *vecinos*. By 1808 it had dropped to only 500 *vecinos*, and as late as 1845 the town was no larger than in 1753. The principal change in the economic structure of the town as it grew was an increase in the number of long-distance transporters.[26] This documents the rise of commerce between Madrid and the maritime world and provides a counterpoint to the largely self-contained regional economy of León, situated outside the fields of influence of any large city.

Benavente is represented by taxes on general market activity and wool traded in the town. The town-based revenues are complemented by the revenues from two tolls (Table 12.11), one of them on the route between Galicia and Castile. The *peso y medidas* revenue indicates that the nominal value of market activity rose gradually through the century, with recessions in the 1720's and 1740's, and that the yield doubled between 1690 and 1790. After adjustment for changing prices, however, what appears is a strong increase to the 1740's, followed by a downward secular trend broken only by a few years in the 1780's. Thus by the 1790's, the real value of revenue was only 15% more than a century before.

The chronology is roughly the same for the wool tax; the nominal value shows a plateau between 1700 and 1750, a decline in the third quarter, and a sharp increase in the last decade. When adjusted for prices, the wool tax reached its peak in the 1730's and 1740's, then fell sharply until 1770. It then

26. Cabero Diéguez, *Evolución y estructura urbana de Astorga*, pp. 38–39, 47.

Table 12.11. *Indices of Commercial Activity in Benavente, 1691-1800*
(1771-80 = 100)

Period	Pesos y Medidas (nominal)	Pesos y Medidas (adjusted) (a)	Renta de Lanas (nominal)	Renta de Lanas (adjusted) (b)
1691-1700	50.3	64.6	103.0	105.8
1701-10	59.2	74.8	125.4	134.2
1711-20	63.1	80.4	121.2	146.4
1721-30	56.9	79.9	89.9	111.3
1731-40	81.6	105.4	126.6	162.1
1741-50	71.3	91.8	126.6	153.1
1751-60	84.6	94.2	95.9	100.7
1761-70	85.0	88.4	74.3	79.4
1771-80	100.0	100.0	100.0	100.0
1781-90	100.1	85.9	126.8	112.9
1791-1800	106.4	75.1	185.5	140.2

Source: See Appendix E, Benavente.

a. *Peso* revenues are adjusted using New Castilian indices.

b. Wool revenue is adjusted using an index constructed from prices of wool products in Hamilton, *War and Prices*, pp. 250-257.

began to recover, but by the end of the century was still lower than in the 1730's and '40's. The general pattern parallels that for León, with high levels of activity early in the century; a weakening in the third quarter; recovery in the 1780's; and mixed signals, with an apparent decline, in the last decade. This coincides with the well-documented cycle for Segovia, where rising population and production prior to 1760 were followed by growing tension between local subsistence and the requirements of the urban network, a tension which cut off regional demand for nonessential commodities.[27]

The two ferries near Benavente reflect the actual movement of goods destined for the market (Table 12.12). The boat revenue at Villafer, on a secondary route, indicates an expansion of traffic from 1690 to 1725, but then a decline of over 50% by 1784. Traffic recovered sharply at the same time that market activity rose in León, just as Madrid was increasing its demand for Old Castilian supplies. The ferry at Santa Cristina, on the Galicia-Madrid highway, shows a century-long upward trend, with a cumulative 50% increase in traffic. This was broken by recessions in the 1720's and in 1750-70, but the pattern is not unlike that for port activity in Cádiz and reflects the recovery and reorientation to Madrid of the muleteers of Astorga and the integration of Galicia into the supply commerce of Madrid.

The contrasts between the four series from Benavente suggest the separa-

27. See the discussions and references from García Sanz, *Desarrollo y crisis*, in Chapters 7 and 8 above.

Table 12.12. *Indices of Boat Toll Revenues near Benavente, 1691-1800
(1771-80 = 100)*

Period	Barca de Santa Cristina	Barca de Villafer
1691-1700	73.4	127.8
1700-10	77.5	149.1
1711-20	83.1	183.9
1721-30	71.2	222.6
1731-40	88.1	203.0
1741-50	90.2	163.0
1751-60	78.0	109.0
1761-70	75.5	144.4
1771-80	100.0	100.0
1781-90	80.9	148.3
1791-1800	113.2	228.2

Source: See Appendix E, Benavente.

tion of the two Spains, if in a complex way. The town, center of a largely self-sufficient region, experienced the same lackluster eighteenth-century trends as León and Segovia. The long-distance traffic passing by from Galicia and Asturias to Castile and Madrid, however, echoed the fluctuations of maritime trade from coast to capital city. The turn-of-the-century depression in Ástorga indicates that the crises after 1795 cut short the growth of this traffic.

The same pattern of early eighteenth-century growth, third-quarter recession, and end-of-century rise of commercial activity also appears in Palencia, which is represented by two indicators of market activity and two taxes on raw materials, supplemented by cloth production figures for 1763–86 (Tables 12.13 and 12.14). On the edge of the Tierra de Campos, Palencia was a major link in the urban network centered on Valladolid, and in its own right was a center of textile manufacturing that produced rough woolens and blankets traded throughout the interior.[28] As measured by nominal revenues from the *peso real,* market activity rose from the 1680's to the 1720's, drifted downward to the 1750's, and then rose to the 1770's—but the century-long increase was only 15%. Adjusted for changes in the price level, the trends are more pronounced. Market activity rose 70% from the 1670's to the 1720's. It then fell rapidly for 30 years and leveled off at an adjusted value only 12% above the seventeenth-century low and well below the level of the 1660's and '70's. The nominal value of the *corredurías* taxing manufactured goods was

28. Eugenio Larruga, *Memorias políticas y económicas sobre los frutos, comercio, fábricas y minas de España* (1785–1800), vol. 33, p. 170.

stable during 1680–1710, and fell in the 1740's, but overall experienced a slight upward trend from the 1690's to the 1760's. Adjusted for prices, however, the series drifts upward to the 1740's and then begins a sharp 30-year decline to 1780, when the tax series ends.

The impression is one of slow expansion in the first third of the eighteenth century and of decline or stagnation in the second third. The nominal figures suggest a recovery beginning in the 1760's, while the price-adjusted ones indicate that the decline reached into the 1770's. The volume of activity as of 1780 was little more than in 1690 (see Table 12.13).

Table 12.13. *Indices of Commercial Activity in Palencia, 1681-1780 (1771-80 = 100)*

Period	Peso Real (nominal)	Peso Real (adjusted)	Corredurías del Pueblo (nominal)	Corredurías del Pueblo (adjusted)
1681-70	87.9	114.6	94.7	123.5
1691-1700	90.1	116.3	92.4	119.2
1701-10	96.1	121.5	96.8	122.4
1711-20	94.4	120.3	77.0	98.1
1721-30	104.4	146.5	91.2	128.1
1731-40	95.8	123.8	92.3	119.2
1741-50	90.1	112.2	106.1	136.6
1751-60	86.4	96.3	104.5	116.4
1761-70	–	–	110.9	115.4
1771-80	100.0	100.0	100.0	100.0

Sources: See Appendix E, Palencia.

This is echoed in the *renta del poyo,* a tax on wood, which shows moderate expansion from the end of the seventeenth century to the 1730's, followed by rapid decline to the middle 70's, when the series ends. The most puzzling series is the *renta de la greda,* a tax on fuller's earth. Revenue remained fairly stable from 1680 to 1730, after which the yield fell rapidly (see Table 12.14). This conflicts with woolens production figures—suggesting that while the industry was commercialized in the city, production developed in the countryside, where it escaped the tax. Indeed, production figures contradict the evidence of urban market decline. While production of *bayetas* remained static, output of coverlets, a traditional specialty of Palencia, began to rise after 1767 and had trebled, from about 65,000 units to 168,000, by 1786.[29]

In general, the commercial life of Palencia stabilized in the later seventeenth century and experienced a modest expansion in the first half of the eighteenth. This was followed by a deterioration that probably reflects a rural

29. Ibid., pp. 119–131 and 186, gives totals for 13 years between 1763 and 1786.

Table 12.14. *Indices of Commercial Activity in Palencia, 1681-1800*
(1771-80 = 100)

Period	Renta del Poyo (nominal)	Renta del Poyo (adjusted)	Renta de la Greda (nominal)	Renta de la Greda (adjusted)
1681-90	153.5	191.9	242.7	303.3
1691-1700	175.4	211.8	269.3	325.3
1701-10	180.2	210.6	192.6	226.2
1711-20	178.3	212.5	192.7	229.6
1721-30	192.8	255.0	256.9	339.8
1731-40	176.3	225.4	166.4	212.9
1741-50	98.6	120.8	148.7	182.2
1751-60	160.1	176.6	116.2	128.2
1761-70	113.4	118.2	—	—
1771-80	100.0	100.0	100.0	100.0
1781-90	—	—	—	—
1791-1800	141.8	99.9	5.0	4.2

Source: See Appendix E, Palencia.

situation which ultimately encouraged textile production to compensate for declining individual income in agriculture. The fact that the city declined from 11,430 to 11,203 inhabitants between 1751 and 1787 indicates that the textile industry was rural and expanded with the rural economy.[30] The cycle is again different from that of the coasts. The modest signs of growth came early in the eighteenth century, and as of 1780 revenues were again the same as in 1690. The expansion of woolens production introduces a new note; but even in a region where highway and canal construction reduced the isolation of the interior, the evidence for expansion suggests a version of the "static growth" seen elsewhere in the eighteenth century.

The limited and self-contained industrial and commercial activity suggested by serial data from León province and Palencia is also apparent in the more carefully studied province of Segovia, where García Sanz' study is supplemented by figures on cloth production for the entire century (see Table 12.15).[31] In this case we have proof that the textile industry was coordinated from within the city, while actual production was carried out in the countryside. There was a gradual expansion of output from 1710–19 through the 1750's, with a midcentury peak in 1759. Output then fell for twenty years, and even the most generous figures indicate an output in the 1780's only 6% above the peak of 1759, itself well below half of sixteenth-century volume.

Woolens production in Segovia thus parallels commercial activity in Palen-

30. García Sanz, *Desarrollo y crisis*, pp. 45–48, 215–217.
31. Production is in pieces of cloth of about 40 *varas* length. There is ambiguity in the sources, since Larruga and García Sanz offer the same figures to 1778, but thereafter Larruga

Table 12.15. *Wool Cloth Production,*
Segovia, 1700-89
(1770-79 ━ 100)

Years	Average Annual Production	Decennial Index
1700-09	3,745	89.9
1710-19	3,206	76.9
1720-29	3,840	92.2
1730-39	4,319	103.6
1740-49	4,191	100.6
1750-59	5,005	120.1
1760-69	4,507	108.2
1770-79	4,130(a)	99.1
1770-79	4,204(b)	100.9
1780-89	4,389(a)	105.3
1780-89	5,299(b)	127.2

Sources: Based on Larruga, *Memorias*, vol.
12, pp. 1-225; and García Sanz, *Desarrollo y
crisis*, pp. 222-223.
   a. Based on Larruga's extra-urban figures.
   b. Based on García Sanz' use of larger
totals.

cia and the *renta de lana* of Benavente. All three show high levels of activity
in the middle decades of the eighteenth century, recessions in the 1760's and
'70's, and rising textile production in the 1780's. At the same time, market
activity and population suggest that Segovia and Palencia as cities were
static, and our knowledge that Segovian textile production was largely rural
and expanded with rural population and economic stress indicates the same
pattern in the other two regional economies. Some textiles were sold into
Madrid, but we know that for Segovia this was a small share of output. Most
cloth was low-grade and used in interregional exchanges to cover local subsistence deficits.[32] Thus, as in the late sixteenth century, industrial expansion
was a function of changes in the regional subsistence economies rather than a

separates urban and regional production without specifying if both are included in the earlier
series. Larruga's earlier totals line up best with his later figures for the region outside the city.
García Sanz claims to use total production figures all through, but several of his totals for the
1780's correspond with Larruga's data for production outside the city, while after 1784 his
figures match Larruga's total figures for each year. Using the extra-urban production figures
after 1779 as an extension of the earlier series, the relative increase in output in the 1780's
seems much smaller than García Sanz suggests, and never exceeds the midcentury peak.

   32. The marketing pattern and volume of production resemble that of sixteenth-century
Cuenca; see Iradiel, *Evolución de la industria textil.* For references to Segovian cloth in
Galicia, see Pedro Antonio Sánchez, *La economia gallega.* Palencia blankets or coverlets were
used all over Spain.

response to urban demand. The entire output of Segovia was but 20% of the woolens and 3% of all textiles sold in Madrid yearly, and only a fraction of Segovia's output was actually destined for that market.

Thus the classic confrontation between population growth and resource limitations recurred in the interior regions of eighteenth-century Old Castile, but no urban network based on exchange and regional specialization developed along with it as had happened in the sixteenth century. The same indicators that document rising market activity everywhere in the earlier case, and on the coasts in the eighteenth century, show much smaller changes in the eighteenth-century interior. Moreover, the interior cities do not reflect the corresponding rural population growth. All over Old Castile, regional economies expanded in the first two-thirds of the eighteenth century without the growth of the provincial urban centers that marked the sixteenth century. After midcentury, the market indicators became more volatile, as local economies supplemented self-sufficiency to obtain movable stocks of basic commodities that were becoming scarce. This helps explain the late revival of woolens production.

By contrast, indicators of commerce between the seaports and the interior reflect the prosperity of Madrid and reaffirm our proposition that the biggest change in the structure of extra-regional exchanges between the sixteenth and eighteenth centuries was the insertion of Madrid into the urban network. This is even more apparent when we look at New Castile, with its proximity to the capital.

B. New Castile

New Castile's evolution after 1700 resembles that of Old Castile, but the region is geographically more complex. In our discussion it includes the modern provinces of Toledo, Cuenca, Madrid, Guadalajara, and also Cáceres, Badajoz, Ciudad Real, and Albacete (traditional Extremadura and La Mancha—see Maps 1.1 and 12.1). This territory has less geographic coherence than Old Castile-León, since it is broken up by the highland systems of Alcarría, the Montes de Toledo, and the Sierra de Guadalupe. Extremadura and western Ciudad Real emphasized grazing, which was interspersed with dry farming and vineyards in eastern Ciudad Real and Albacete; grain and vines prevailed in the central provinces; forest industries dominated in the mountain districts. While in the sixteenth century Toledo headed the Castilian urban hierarchy, by the eighteenth Madrid had long since usurped that role, emphasizing political and imperial functions at the expense of regional market functions capable of supplementing local subsistence.[33]

33. See Chapter 9.

Table 12.16. *Indices of Commercial Activity in Toledo, 1701-70*
(1761-70 = 100)

Period	Almotacenía (nominal)	Almotacenía (adjusted)	Peso Real (nominal)	Peso Real (adjusted)
1701-10	129.1	144.8	155.2	205.9
1711-20	101.1	115.7	120.0	158.0
1721-30	101.6	129.1	115.0	165.8
1731-40	72.3	88.7	85.3	107.1
1741-50	62.4	73.5	98.7	128.6
1751-60	88.2	93.4	144.0	153.7
1761-70	100.0	100.0	100.0	100.0

Source: See Appendix E, Toledo.

This is most apparent in Toledo, where indicators of commercial activity in the eighteenth century show persistent stagnation, and reach bottom as the series ends in 1769 (see Table 12.16). The temporary expansion of *peso* revenue in 1740–60 coincides with the efforts of the *Compañía de Comercio de Toledo* to revive the silk industry in Toledo and Talavera. After investing several million *reales*, and temporarily reviving the regional economy, the company went bankrupt. It failed because of poor technology, inadequate capital, and cumbersome management; but above all, it lacked appropriate markets.[34] If we are to judge by Toledo, there never was a period of regional prosperity based on local development and, fleeting as it was, the 1750's marked the peak of Toledo's prosperity for the next century.

The subsequent fate of Toledo is measured by its population, and signifies the inability of a once-great city, still a metropolitan see, to recapture significant urban functions from Madrid (see Table 12.17). Except for a brief increase in 1750, the city continued to shrink. The population of the countryside expanded, as it did in Segovia, but without reviving the old urban network of the region, whose resources we have seen being preempted by Madrid. Thus while Madrid did not greatly affect the rural subsistence economy, it precluded urban development that might have facilitated intra-regional exchange and specialization.

The evolution of the smaller town of Talavera de la Reina is equally suggestive of the situation in eighteenth-century New Castile. Talavera, 70 kilometers west of Toledo and 120 kilometers southwest of Madrid, was the major link between New Castile and Extremadura. Unlike the old provincial capi-

34. Larruga, *Memorias,* vol. 7; also James C. LaForce, *The Development of the Spanish Textile Industry, 1750–1800* (1965).

Table 12.17. *Population of Toledo,
Seventeenth to Twentieth Centuries*

Year	Population
1607	80,000
1630	20,000
1669	15,000
1750	20,000
1787	15,391
1842	14,778
1912	22,274

Sources: See Table 11.1 and Appendix F.

tals, Talavera more than doubled its population between 1713 and 1768, although it never attained its sixteenth-century size. As in Toledo, midcentury growth reflected population drawn by the Crown's encouragement of the silk industry. After 1760 the industry lost its subsidies and markets and the population declined slightly, but the town's importance as a clearing-point for supplies and livestock destined for Madrid sustained its economy. Traffic grew with the demands of Madrid, and Talavera was granted a second yearly fair by Charles III. Here we have an example of a secondary center losing some of its functions and acquiring others that left it more clearly subordinated to the economic structure of the market in the capital city.[35]

La Mancha is again represented by Albacete and Ciudad Real. Trends in eighteenth-century Albacete are illustrated by revenue from the combined *almotacenia* and *correduria* for the last forty years of the century. The series starts in 1762 and indicates that, in nominal terms, market activity rose 50% by the mid-1780's. Adjusted for New Castilian prices, however, the increase was more like 20%, and both nominal and adjusted indices show that the trend reversed in the last decade of the century.[36]

At a crossroads between the Mediterranean ports and Madrid and between the eastern ports and Andalucía, the expansion of Albacete's commercial activity reflects long-distance trade passing through the area. Except for the last three years of the century, the *almotacenia* at Albacete paralleled the earnings of the *barca de Arganda* on the same coast-to-Madrid corridor. Thus the brief Albacete series reflects long-distance trade across the interior more than the condition of the regional economy.

35. Gonzalez Muñoz, *La población de Talavera*, pp. 215, 340–367. Chapter 7 above shows livestock brokers in Talavera attempting to break into the meat supply contracts of Madrid in 1790–1808.
36. See Appendix E.

Table 12.18. *Indices of Commercial Activity in Cuenca, 1691-1800 (1771-80 = 100)*

Period	Corredurías (nominal)	Corredurías (adjusted)
1691-1700	39.9	51.5
1701-10	—	—
1711-20	49.6	63.1
1721-30	53.1	74.5
1731-40	71.1	91.8
1741-50	74.0	95.3
1751-60	75.7	84.3
1761-70	104.5	108.7
1771-80	100.0	100.0
1781-90	161.5	138.5
1791-1800	159.7	112.7

Source: See Appendix E, Cuenca.

The latter, however, is illustrated by the evolution of Ciudad Real, some distance from long-distance routes. There the demographic evidence reflects general expansion in the early eighteenth century and subsequent stagnation. By 1750, Ciudad Real had grown to 2,000 households, approaching sixteenth-century levels. It then remained at that level throughout the eighteenth century, indicating the same deadlock in regional conditions seen around Toledo and Segovia.[37]

The city of Cuenca is something of an anomaly as an interior town, in that its market revenues show sustained growth during the entire eighteenth century. From 1691, the city's revenue from its *correduría mayor* rose steadily until 1800, and the unadjusted average of the 1790's is four times that of 1691–1700. Adjusted for price levels, however, commercial activity rose 80% from 1690 to 1720, remained static during 1730–60, and then grew about 50% from 1760 to 1790, when it was two and a half times higher than in the 1690's. During the 1790's, the adjusted index shows a substantial decline in commercial activity (Table 12.18).

The reasons for the expansion are not clear, but the province sent wool to the Mediterranean ports and was a major supplier of wood and charcoal for Madrid, and of wood, charcoal, and meat for Valencia. The eighteenth century saw attempts to revive the woolens industry of Cuenca, indicating the persistence of a rough textiles industry for the interior market. The city was also on the overland route from Valencia to Madrid; and with the tariff

37. Phillips, *Ciudad Real*, pp. 34–35.

reforms of the Bourbons and the development of a silk industry around Requena, traffic that once used the southern route via Murcia may have shifted north and used Cuenca as a stopping point. It is striking, if inconclusive, that the rise of Cuenca's market revenue parallels closely the chronology of port activity in the Mediterranean, and it may be that the city's apparent isolation is deceptive. The parallel with the revenue from the *barca de Arganda*, through which the Valencia-Cuenca-Madrid traffic flowed, is certainly clear.

By now it should be apparent that—compared with the commercial life of towns of 2,000 people (Talavera), 8,000 (Ciudad Real), 11,000 (Palencia), or 15–20,000 (Toledo, Segovia, Valladolid)—the impact of Madrid as it grew from 125,000 to 200,000 during the eighteenth century was inevitably a major factor in shaping the long-range commercial activity of Castile, and was bound to influence the interregional functions of those towns. The zones of influence shown in Chapter 9 seem tenuous, and the volumes of goods documented in Chapter 6 may sometimes appear small, but they were vitally important for the ability of local elites to operate outside of local subsistence economies. To the extent that it could not break down subsistence patterns, commercial life was clearly vulnerable to population growth. A growing rural population stimulated local industry, but it also retained foodstuffs in local economies. This raised urban supply costs and food prices, restricting the ability of the Madrid market to buy what the countryside manufactured. The evidence for this is apparent when we examine the behavior of commercial indicators and consumption in Madrid.

IV. Madrid: Link Between Interior and Periphery

After 1610, the only city that linked periphery and interior was Madrid, the imperial capital. By 1650, Madrid was ten times larger than any Castilian competitor, and had developed a supply system blanketing the interior and an import commerce of similar magnitude. Only the concentration of trade at Cádiz exceeded the value of Madrid's commerce in the seventeenth or eighteenth centuries. With the collapse of empire in the nineteenth century, Madrid became relatively more important still in the peninsular structure of wealth and power. Its erratic growth, coupled with the city's tremendously greater size compared to any other interior town, identifies Madrid as a major dynamic element in the economy of the Spanish interior.

In the interior, economic decline appeared as early as the 1560's in Álava and the 1580's in Cuenca, Albacete, and Ciudad Real. Everywhere we see the cycle of rural economic life which has been documented for Segovia by García Sanz—early and mid-sixteenth-century expansion, overpopulation in the last decades, decline to a lower base population in the early seventeenth century, and the recovery of stability leading to a new, if more gradual expansion which culminated in the third quarter of the eighteenth century. After 1605–10, the collapse of market activity in the interior is awesome. It was over by 1650; but most interior market indicators stagnated or drifted downward until the eighteenth century, while the first two-thirds of that century saw rural expansion without significant urban growth outside the capital. Most rural districts experienced population and production problems by the end of the century, and even those indicators of interior market activity that suggest expansion turned downward in the 1790's.

Trends in the maritime areas varied greatly during the sixteenth century, as the trading network was reoriented toward Sevilla, and the northern European connections were disrupted. Thus commerce at Bilbao was falling well before the volume of trade in Sevilla peaked in 1610. Our data are incomplete or inconclusive for Barcelona and Málaga during the first part of the seventeenth century; but it does not appear that the decline of the Indies trade in the 1630's and '40's had much impact either in Málaga or in Cartagena. Even trade at Sevilla shows only modest decline until about 1630, after which it fell rapidly. Braudel's conclusion that high levels of maritime commerce persisted in the Mediterranean well into the seventeenth century appears valid. By the end of the third quarter of the century, the data for every port cited except Cartagena suggest stabilization or unmistakable, if erratic, growth in port activity. This trend was interrupted by the War of Spanish Succession; but by 1720, all five ports from which we have clear indicators had embarked upon long-term commercial expansion that not only lasted until 1790, but can be seen as a continuation of trends established well before 1700.

These same coastal areas show clear indications of declining commercial connections with the interior, as in Cartagena, Málaga, and Zafra. Moreover, the new economic growth of the eighteenth century did not prompt a renewal of those contacts between coast and interior. The links that did develop after 1650 were between port cities and Madrid—the Benavente toll, the Arganda toll, and customs revenues in the passes on the roads south from Bilbao.[38]

Madrid was an important factor in this dual pattern of interior self-sufficiency and maritime orientation to distant markets. From 1590 to 1630, Madrid's development bore little relationship to conditions in the region where the city was located, and the capital expanded for 20 years after the urban network and market systems of the Spanish interior began to disintegrate. This precipitated the decline of Toledo, and the three-way interaction between the two cities and the countryside helps explain the severity of Spain's seventeenth-century crisis. Only after 1635 did the disintegration of

---

38. Between 1720 and 1780, after adjustments for rate changes, these revenues rose by 60%. See Emiliano Fernández de Pinedo, *Crecimiento económico y transformaciones sociales del país vasco, 1100–1850*, p. 388.

Spain's European empire force a significant contraction of markets in the capital, a decade after the Indies trade started to decline seriously. By the last third of the century, revenue from the *peso* suggests recovery of some urban markets, while the persistent strength of the boat toll revenue suggests the strong association between Madrid and the maritime world. This marks the beginning of a half-century in which the size of the city and its consumption of regionally supplied staples changed little, while long-distance commerce serving the urban elites gradually expanded. After the succession war, Madrid began to expand at an accelerating rate that reflects the trends of the maritime sector rather than the tendency of the rural interior to stagnate after midcentury.

These trends document the developing relationship between periphery, capital, and interior. Until 1630, Madrid expanded its market and central-place functions rapidly—an expansion that persisted beyond the collapse of the market network of the interior and the decline of the official Indies trade. The closest correlation may well be with the total volume of bullion receipts, royal, legal, and illicit. Total shipments remained fairly high until 1630, after which official receipts plummeted, until by 1660 they were one-seventh the average of 1625–30.[39] The real flow of bullion in the middle decades remains something of a mystery, but there was a strong recovery of private receipts after 1630.[40] This correlates with the upturn of long-distance trade to Madrid and the recovery of commerce in various Spanish ports.

Through much of the seventeenth century, the Hapsburg state persisted in maintaining policies in Europe which flew in the face of economic reality in both Castile and the Indies. The degree to which the Lerma and Olivares regimes were divorced from reality during the reigns of Kings Philip III and Philip IV is evident in the frustration of politically aware contemporaries over their inability to influence a misguided government.[41] The persistence of Hapsburg policies in the 1620's and '30's was both cause and result of this blindness of leadership, and the fortunes of the regime's capital city projected the results of those policies into the Castilian heartland and suggest why Madrid played a role as a dynamic factor in the economy of early seventeenth-century Castile. Thus we are led again to a close relationship between the precipitous and persistent decline of the interior and the rise of Madrid as the urban base from which Hapsburg policy emanated.

By the late seventeenth century, the new relationship was well established.

39. J. H. Elliott, *Imperial Spain* (1965), p. 175, following Hamilton.
40. Henry Kamen, *Spain in the Later Seventeenth Century*, pp. 134–135.
41. On this frustrated political opposition, see Jean Vilar, *Literatura y economia: La figura satirica del arbitrista en el siglo de oro*, pp. 240–247, 267–276, 288–293; Gonzalo Anes, ed., *Memoriales y discursos de Francisco Martínez de la Mata* (1971), pp. 16–33; and José Antonio Maravall, *La oposición politica bajo los Austrias* (1972), pp. 211–229.

The economic situation of the periphery had stabilized, and expanding port activity is evident. Volume remained relatively small, and the emphasis on agricultural exports to European markets was greater than in the sixteenth century, but the trend is general. Elements of the economy of the capital city followed suit, despite the persistent economic stagnation of most of Old and New Castile. Renewed vitality in the port cities reflects the influx of French and British capital, the revival of unofficial American trade and remittances sought by foreign interests, and an incipient drift toward export-oriented agriculture. More than in the sixteenth century, the state and capital city of eighteenth-century Spain depended on this link, a consequence of the distance that the Bourbon state put between itself and the high aristocracy.

The connection is convincingly illustrated by the parallel growth of legal trade at Cádiz and Sevilla and commercial activity at Madrid—a pattern echoed by all the eighteenth-century ports—and by the simultaneous crisis of American empire, Indies trade, and peninsular authority after 1795. Thus we are presented with a situation in which Madrid projected new trends into the interior and became a kind of economic leading sector. But the rural interior could not easily be led and, because of its internal structure, the capital did not present very diverse or very strong incentives to its hinterland.

The static aspect of the interior is more apparent in the first half of the nineteenth century. The unreliable censuses suggest a general population increase, and there is evidence of land enclosure for farming in the 1820's and before. This trend was institutionalized with the sale of Church lands in the 1830's.[42] At the same time, cities all over Spain suffered a decline in vitality and population, and rural population was drifting from the larger to the smaller towns.[43] This process of de-urbanization has been very little studied. It demonstrates the degree to which the empire had subsidized the peninsular commercial and urban networks, as the massive deficit in Spain's European trade suddenly had to be covered from domestic sources.

It is in this context that Madrid as an independent factor in Castile, reinforcing stagnation by its own growth, becomes crucial to understanding the evolving duality of the Iberian economy. For almost three centuries, the infertile interior of Spain supported a capital that was one of the great cities

---

42. Massimo Livi-Bacci, "Fertility and Population Growth in Spain in the Eighteenth and Nineteenth Centuries" (1968), pp. 523–535; Ringrose, *Transportation*, pp. 130–131; Raymond Carr, *Spain, 1808–1939*, pp. 197–198.

43. Barcelona fell from 115,000 in 1800 to 83,000 in 1818; Cádiz from 100,000 to 56,000 in 1840; Cartagena from 60,000 to 30,000. The smaller interior towns often had similar experiences. The economic bases of the peninsular urban system had been seriously damaged. See Antoni Jutglar, *La era industrial en España* (1963), p. 70; Vicens Vives, *Manual*, p. 565; Richard Ford, *Handbook for Spain* (1845), vol. 1, p. 315, and vol. 2, p. 618; María Dolores Marcos González, *La España del Antiguo Régimen: Castilla la Nueva y Extremadura*, pp. 35–37.

of pre-industrial Europe, perhaps the largest city without access to water transport in European history. Because of its dependence on primitive overland transport, the size of Madrid was a factor of extreme importance in the economy of Castile, if only because the city constituted a market for agricultural products with few alternative sources of supply. The structure of that market was such as to provide its hinterland with only a limited range of incentives, and the city could not provide the variety and depth of demand needed to draw the Castilian interior out of subsistence agriculture embedded in a self-contained regional economy. Madrid could mobilize surpluses that the traditional systems of rural control accumulated, but had little effect on productivity. At the same time, Madrid came to dominate the urban life of the interior from the Cantabrian Mountains to the Sierra Morena and from the Portuguese border to the frontier with Aragón.

Through its capital, the Spanish state went no small way toward converting Castile into a colonial dependency of the Madrid-Sevilla-Indies network analogous to rural Mexico or Peru in its structure. With the collapse of that network, the state fell to the control of domestic elites from within this "colonialized" interior, oriented to Madrid. Hence the close parallels in the struggle for internal power between nineteenth-century Spain and nineteenth-century Latin America.

13. Conclusion: Spain and the Heritage of Madrid

Pre-industrial city life represents an economic, social, and cultural milieu different from that of the surrounding countryside and one which seems superficially familiar to investigators from an industrial and urban world. As a result, the city is often viewed as the source of change and modernity and searched for social forces, attitudes, and patterns of behavior that prefigure a modern society and economy. While this approach often identifies the beginnings of modernity, it frequently fails to explain those beginnings or why some cities are slow to produce signs of impending modernization. This is because the pre-industrial city exists not only as part of a larger system of economic and social activity, but is dependent upon the non-urban parts of that system to a degree that is hard for modern individuals to appreciate.

Many modern cities dominate the systems within which they are imbedded; but in an era when over 80% of the people and two-thirds of the gross national product were rural, the autonomy of the city was far less real. The countryside was not devoted to the needs of the city; the city existed to provide goods and services useful to the economically productive countryside. This does not mean that the city did not have a dynamic of its own, nor that it did not affect the rural world around it. It simply means that what took place within the city cannot be understood unless we also understand the complex interconnections between urban and rural components in a basically agricultural civilization.

This study has relied heavily on the concept that urban centers perform a number of economic and social functions for society, and that those functions vary in the distance across which they can be provided effectively. Thus a region such as Castile is serviced by a network of urban centers. Although a few of these centers are quite large, and provide many services, most of them are small and provide only local, short-range services.

Cast in these terms, the heritage of Madrid was a radical reorientation of the functions that cities performed for Spanish society. This in turn reshaped the urban system of Spain's interior in a manner which sacrificed a large part of the limited developmental potential of the Castilian economy to the maintenance of a political and social system that subsequently had great difficulty adapting to modern conditions.

I. Sixteenth and Seventeenth Centuries: The Hapsburg Empire

The active urban life of sixteenth-century Castile included a range of craft industries, local and regional markets, a relatively dense population, and long-distance trade. Later in the century, as agricultural output stagnated, food shortages and American bullion pushed up Spanish prices and labor costs, allowing foreign products to capture Spain's overseas markets and penetrate her domestic ones. At the same time, rising taxes in a static rural economy weakened domestic demand and regional exchanges. A fragile regional economy beset by disease and soil exhaustion was being stretched beyond its limits.[1]

Meanwhile, the Hapsburg state was attempting to govern a vast military and political system, and in the process developing an alliance with the landed nobility. This group of wealthy families maintained a tradition of military effectiveness and a powerful social and economic position in rural Spain. They were quite pragmatic about their sources of wealth, investing in commerce, commercial fishing, and colonization and often combining Spanish military prowess with Italian investment capital.[2] As the Hapsburg state evolved and the agricultural economy stagnated in the late sixteenth century, noble investments shifted toward government annuities and offices, urban real estate, and the jurisdictional authority of the Crown.

This alliance of politics and landed class took concrete form in the development of Madrid as a permanent administrative center. Philip II named Madrid as capital in 1561, and gradually the lawyers, clerks, officials, and nobility congregated there. Madrid's development was relatively slow under Philip II, and in forty years the city expanded from about 35,000 to 65,000 inhabitants. Madrid was primarily a political center; industry, commerce,

1. Bartolomé Bennassar, *Recherches sur les grandes épidémies dans le nord de l'Espagne à la fin du XVIe siècle;* Domínguez Ortiz, *Siglo XVII,* vol. 1, pp. 53–160; Gentil da Silva, *En Espagne,* pp. 97–189; Noël Salomon, *La campagne de Nouvelle Castille à la fin du XVIe siècle,* pp. 303–304; Vicens Vives, *Manual,* pp. 373–393. Aspects of this are discussed in Chapters 8, 9, and 10.

2. Ruth Pike, *Enterprise and Adventure: The Genoese in Seville and the Opening of the New World* (1966), and *Aristocrats and Traders; Sevillian Society of the Sixteenth Century* (1972); Charles Verlinden, "Italian Influence in Iberian Colonization" (1953), pp. 199–211, and *The Beginnings of Modern Colonization* (1970), pp. 113–157.

and the economic and social life of the elite continued to center around Toledo and Sevilla.[3] As late as the 1590's, the Castilian urban system had an urban hierarchy that provided complex local, regional, and long-distance markets as well as political and social integration. But Madrid had become a second primary center alongside Toledo, and many lower-order centers were suffering because of subsistence problems and changing long-distance markets. Nevertheless, the sixteenth-century system continued to function.

The next half-century, however, saw a complete reorganization of the urban network and with it a restructuring of Castilian economic life that reduced interregional exchanges and heightened dependence on subsistance agriculture throughout the interior. With the accession of Philip III, the Court became an extravagant and lively place where favors, offices, patronage, and pensions flowed freely. The movement of noble families to the capital accelerated; and after the brief sojourn in Valladolid, "the Court" and Madrid became synonymous. The population of the capital exploded from 65,000 to 175,000 between 1606 and 1630, giving impetus to a building boom.

This rapid growth posed severe supply problems for the Crown, and the solutions had serious implications for Castile.[4] Urban needs were confronted by a densely populated and inelastic agricultural hinterland in a precarious equilibrium. Each poor harvest was harder for supply officials to overcome than the last, forcing constant expansion of the area that Madrid sought to control. The embargo of more and more supply zones absorbed the sources of supply for Toledo, the principal urban center of the interior until 1608. This redirection of supplies away from Toledo created shortages and high food prices, aggravating Toledo's marketing problems by forcing up industrial wages. The array of controls included ceiling prices on grain as it left the farms, embargoes on grain shipments to destinations other than Madrid, adjustment of bread prices to draw it to Madrid, and bread delivery schedules imposed on towns up to 40 miles away. The effectiveness of price control (the notorious *tasa*) has long been questioned, but it apparently was taken seriously through the critical first third of the seventeenth century.[5] The effect was to preclude the small producer from benefiting from high wheat prices in bad years, when he had to buy rather than sell, while good harvests meant low prices and a modest return for his surplus. Meanwhile, those able to store surpluses in good years could wait and sell in short years on favorable

3. Domínguez Ortiz, *Siglo XVII,* pp. 129–139; Weisser, "Les Marchands de Tolède."

4. Aspects of this are inferred in Weisser's "Crime and Subsistence: The Peasants of the *Tierra* of Toledo, 1550–1700." The specific problems are documented in Chapter 11 above.

5. Earl Hamilton, in both *American Treasure* and *War and Prices in Spain, 1651–1800,* p. 98, maintains they had little effect. Carmelo Viñas y Mey, in *El problema de la tierra en la España de los siglos XVI-XVII,* assumes considerable impact. If Segovia was typical, the *tasa* governed large sales well into the seventeenth century: Anes and LeFlem, "Las crises del siglo XVII," pp. 22–23.

terms. This undermined the small farmer and encouraged consolidation of landownership.[6]

Moreover, as wheat became expensive, urban buying power shifted and per-capita use of wine declined. Consequently, while five-year average wheat prices rose 90% from 1590 to 1610, wine prices fell 25%. As a result, the wine-producing districts of New Castile declined rapidly after 1590.[7]

Between 1600 and 1630, therefore, the rise of Madrid turned the normal variations in harvest yield into a spiral of recurrent food shortages and high prices, rural distress and dislocation, and migration to the capital. Each new crisis required stronger efforts to supply the city, further exacerbating the developing rural crisis. This was paralleled by the final collapse of the urban hierarchy between 1610 and 1630, leaving Madrid as the only significant market for agricultural surpluses in Old and New Castile.

As an economic center, Madrid was qualitatively different from Toledo and displaced its function as moderator of a complex exchange network. Madrid exported political services (government) in return for taxes and revenue. This attracted resources from the empire beyond the immediate hinterland. Madrid also functioned as a nexus providing the wealthy elite with social integration and access to the wealth of the state. To enjoy this amenity, such families moved tò the city, bringing with them the rents from their estates. This produced a consumption-oriented market and extreme inequalities in the distribution of income that prompted the state to subsidize urban supply for the sake of public order. This provided an income for those who controlled disposable commodities in the countryside, lubricating the flow of taxes and rents back to the capital. Much of the money never left the city, being paid by urban officials and contractors to rentiers living in the city in return for the sale of landed income received as agricultural products and brought to the city.

At the same time, Madrid's narrow market locked urban crafts into quality-oriented production that further separated the city from the hinterland, which could afford few luxuries. The city increasingly attracted long-distance trade from the seaports; and as income became more concentrated, the preferences of the elite became more cosmopolitan and the city purchased an increasingly narrow range of goods from its own hinterland. Thus the city provided a kind of cash economy for the landed elites, while encouraging a more rudimentary and self-sufficient rural economy.[8] This change in the

6. See Chapters 3 and 6. The pattern follows Ernest Labrousse's formulation, in *Fluctuaciones económicas e historia social* (1962), pp. 371–379, regarding the prerevolutionary decades in France.

7. Weisser, *The Peasants of the Montes,* ch. 4.

8. Of 800 commodity transfers documented for the later eighteenth century in Castile, half involved Madrid as destination, and only two implied that Madrid was acting as a center of distribution or production. See Ringrose, *Transportation,* maps 3–13 (additional detail in the

nature as well as the location of urban demand helped to undermine rural economies that had specialized under demographic pressure in the sixteenth century, only to lose their markets in the seventeenth.

In one short generation, Madrid had acquired a near monopoly on the provision of higher-order political and social services for the Spanish elite. In the process, the capital coopted the resources that might have allowed other cities to provide the exchange functions needed to integrate the rural economy. Thus the only large market of the interior depended heavily on state and rentier income.

Madrid's primacy was no sooner established, however, when it suffered a serious decline in the resources that the state could provide. By the 1630's, American bullion remittances accessible to the Crown were falling dramatically. France entered the Thirty Years War in 1635, expanding Spain's military budget to colossal proportions. The situation became even bleaker when Catalonia and Portugal revolted in 1640, followed by Naples in 1646. The hard-pressed government reordered budget priorities, exploited the monetary system, and raised taxes. The new taxes in the 1630's took the same form as earlier *sisas* levied for public works, but were dedicated to servicing loans raised for European campaigns. Madrid had lived from a set of institutions that channeled public and private wealth to it. But the new taxes, instead of reinforcing that flow, reversed it. The impact on the city's economy was evident by the mid-1630's, when consumption of wheat, wine, meat, and olive oil began to decline. The government also sought to tax the nobility, and captured much of their income by selling them jurisdiction over hundreds of villages. The Crown thus surrendered much of its rural authority and, having made Madrid the preeminent city of the interior, caused a major contraction of the market that the city represented, furthering the withdrawal of the countryside into self-sufficiency.[9]

By the later seventeenth century, the Spanish economy had undergone sweeping reconstruction.[10] Excepting Madrid, the former cities had become large towns, and many provinces were left lightly populated and barren. Agriculture had withdrawn to the better land and emphasized cereals with local markets and lower labor requirements.[11] Intrinsically more valuable

---

Spanish edition, *Los transportes y el estancamiento económico de España, 1750–1850* (1972), Appendix). In 1789, only 13 of over 300 commodities used in the city were exported or re-exported, and they amounted to only about 3% of imports; see Chapter 6 for analysis of this market.

9. Domínguez Ortiz, "Ventas y exenciones de lugares durante el reinado de Felipe IV"; Charles J. Jago, "Aristocracy, War, and Finance in Castile, 1621–1665: The Titled Nobility and the House of Bejar During the Reign of Philip IV" (Ph.D diss., 1969), pp. 150–151.

10. Gentil da Silva, *En Espagne*, pp. 161–179; Domínguez Ortiz, *Siglo XVII*, pp. 115–160; Vicens Vives, *Manual*, pp. 375–393.

11. Anes and LeFlem, "Las crises," pp. 16–17.

and mobile products were stressed, along with an expansion of grazing.[12] Land had become concentrated in the hands of the aristocracy and Church, and sharecropping and day labor were more prevalent. Total output had declined, and the distribution of wealth favored the elite. The basic lines of Spain's rural society for the next 250 years were emerging: sharply unequal distribution of wealth, estate management and control of local jurisdiction by the *señor* and *labrador rico,* self-sufficient agriculture, and limited markets. By 1700 Madrid and Castile were locked into a rigid relationship, while the periphery continued to show varying responses to external forces.

II. The Eighteenth Century: Bourbon Revival

If in the seventeenth century Madrid had contributed to the de-urbanization and isolation of rural society in Castile, in the eighteenth it played an equally important role in turning wealthy families into the agro-commercial oligarchy that dominated Spain in the nineteenth. As the trade that supplied Madrid evolved, the political and economic elements which dominated Spain were changing their concept of a "normal" framework for economic life. The ideas of French physiocracy and English liberalism were pervasive and influential, and from the mid-eighteenth century they were cited with increasing frequency and explicitness by the highest authorities. Thus when crisis disrupted old arrangements, their replacements were well established as partial reforms and ideas familiar to the political class of the country. The commercial and financial sectors of Madrid's society were becoming larger and more sophisticated as they captured functions previously dominated by the state. Concurrently, the rentier elements controlling agricultural products were being drawn into interaction with the evolving market, its premises, and the men who operated it. The developing community of interests included not only urban middlemen and wealthy nobles of the capital, but also provincial notables, estate stewards, and the wealthy peasants who dominated many villages, thus incorporating the central elements of the *Moderado* state of the nineteenth century.

Once again there was a correlation between the fortunes of the Spanish empire and those of its capital. Before 1715, imperial reforms were tentative;[13] but after the War of the Spanish Succession, relations with France

12. While olive oil was an important crop in the eighteenth century, there is little evidence of it in the sixteenth. See Salomon, *La campagne de Nouvelle Castille,* pp. 86–87; and Carmelo Viñas y Mey and Ramón Paz, *Relaciones de los pueblos de España ordenadas por Felipe II, Provincia de Madrid* (1949) and *Provincia de Toledo* (1951, 1963). Helen Nader finds evidence of it in local commerce in Guadalajara in the late sixteenth century (seminar, 1979) .
13. There were some attempts at stimulating commerce, and the center of the Indies trade was shifted to Cádiz. The monetary system remained relatively stable after 1680 according to Hamilton, *War and Prices,* pp. 53–54.

were regularized and the higher administration was reorganized. The late 1720's saw renovation of the Spanish navy and restriction of smuggling and privateering in the Caribbean. The empire was recovering; renewed silver production provided Spain with vital foreign exchange; and by the second quarter of the eighteenth century, population and consumption began to rise in Madrid. After hovering around 120,000 inhabitants until after the War of Succession, population rose to 150,000 inhabitants in the 1750's, 180,000 in 1787, and 195,000 in 1799.[14] The growth of the capital constituted an important dynamic factor in the economy of the peninsula. The market value of imports into Madrid in 1789 was well over 400 million *reales,* half the estimated value of imports and exports at Cádiz and considerably more than the 250 million *reales* that Pierre Vilar attributes to Barcelona.[15]

In Chapter 6 we analyzed the structure of the urban market behind the estimated total value of what the city consumed, indicating that it involved a massive imbalance in trade. The overall coherence of the economic structures that supported the city can only be appreciated if we understand clearly the role of political and rentier income in maintaining them. To compensate for the goods consumed by the capital, some combination of goods and services had to be exported. Ultimately, the services that compensated for the trade deficit were government (imperial and peninsular policy-making and administration), rural management (theoretically a function of landlords resident in Madrid), and provision of a focal point for Spanish elite socialization, culture, and definition of status. Some of the exchange of goods for services was direct. The Crown owned extensive estates from which it directly mobilized revenue in kind. It also controlled two-ninths of the tithe in much of Spain. This income in kind was managed administratively to supply the military and the capital city. Similarly, many noble families and religious institutions had estates from which supplies were brought directly to urban palaces, convents, and monasteries.

Most of the process of paying for urban supplies involved sales and monetary transfers. The services created by the capital "earned" payments in the form of taxes, rents, and endowment income. This income passed through the internal economy of the city, then flowed outward again to pay for the goods the city required. The origin of these incomes provides an important key to the city's relationship with its hinterland and the larger political system.

By the 1780's, government outlays associated with Madrid were about 200 million *reales* a year, nearly a third of the Crown's net revenues. Almost half

14. See Chapter 2 and Canga Argüelles, *Diccionario de hacienda,* vol. 1, "Madrid," for census of 1797; RAH, leg. 9–6235 (census of 1787); AVM, *Secretaria,* sig. 4–4-37 (census of 1804); Matilla Tascón, "El primer Catastro de la villa de Madrid" (census of 1757); and Biblioteca Nacional, ms. 2274 (census of 1720).

15. Vilar, *Catalunya,* vol. 4, p. 129.

of the money went to support the royal household, its palaces, hundreds of servants, and extensive stables. The remainder went to over 5,000 state employees and the 7–10,000-man garrison and royal guards.[16] The revenues brought to the city privately clearly exceeded the contributions of government: a combination of hearsay and documentation suggests that the combined income of the Alba, Berwick, Arcos, and Infantado families alone reached 20 million *reales* at the end of the eighteenth century. As we saw in Chapter 4, the titled nobility in Madrid had an admitted rental income of over 144 million *reales* in 1808, and an annual income of 880,000 *reales* was considered modest for a grandee at court. The census of 1797 registered 57 grandees and 68 other titled nobles in addition to over 300 owners of lesser entailed estates and several thousand nobles residing in the city. The bulk of those revenues went into salaries, legal fees, living costs, and interest payments dispersed in the capital. These señorial revenues, combined with even a modest estimate of analogous ecclesiastical ones, more than match the contributions of the state to the urban economy.[17] Thus public and private flows of revenue into Madrid easily cover the massive deficit in the balance of trade. To many observers, the pattern is a measure of how, while Spain was exploiting America, Madrid and its elites were exploiting Spain.[18]

These basic facts about Madrid's economy help us to understand the contrast between the impact of the Spanish capital and that of other cities upon their surrounding provinces. The city's rate of growth was substantial, but below that of London in the same period and less than half of the 180% increase in the population of Barcelona.[19] Madrid's moderate growth, combined with her economic structure and the government's willingness to subsidize traditional supply organization, did not stimulate much reorganization of rural economic life. The principal response was one of adjustment within the structure of production that had emerged in the seventeenth century with the breakdown of the urban hierarchy, and it is hard to separate the rural response to urban demand from adjustments to rising rural population. Mov-

16. This is partly offset by taxes which the government collected in Madrid, but these did not amount to 5% of total revenue: Canga Argüelles, *Diccionario,* vol. 2, pp. 402–403; Vilar, "Estructures," p. 31; Matilla Tascón, "El primer Catastro de la villa de Madrid," pp. 524–525; AVM, *Secretaría,* sig. 4-4-37; Joseph Townsend, *A Journey Through Spain in the Years 1786 and 1787* (1792), vol. 2, p. 187.

17. Townsend, *Journey,* vol. 2, pp. 135–138; AHN, *Osuna,* leg. 4339; Canga Argüelles, *Diccionario,* vol. 2, p. 68; AVM, *Secretaría,* sig. 4-4-37; Domínguez Ortiz, *Siglo XVIII,* p. 90. Also see Chapter 4 above.

18. For the perspective on this from colonial Spanish America, see Stanley and Barbara Stein, *The Colonial Heritage of Latin American.*

19. George Rudé, *The Crowd in the French Revolution* (1959), pp. 10–13; E. A. Wrigley, "A Simple Model"; Iglesias, ed., *El cens de Comte de Floridablanca,* pp. 51–52.

able surpluses may actually have shrunk, and the city had to develop a remarkably widespread network in order to satisfy its needs.[20]

Urban-rural interaction around Madrid was further constrained by the city's connection with the maritime economies of the Spanish world. Roughly 40% of Madrid's trade consisted of goods from outside the Spanish interior that fed the city.[21] The regionally produced commodities were primarily food and fuel for the low-income portion of the population, and there was almost no interaction between the two market structures which met at the city gates. The location of the city prevented the commerce of Madrid from offering entrepôt services to the interior, and it remained cheaper for rural communities to use the slack periods in the agricultural economy to trade directly with the seaports for the little merchandise they could afford. Unlike London, Madrid could not provide cheap imports to the countryside, stimulating rural production by offering improvements in the rural standard of living.[22]

Until the later eighteenth century, the rate of growth of the city's own needs was accommodated within the traditional economy. Madrid's distribution of income meant that urban prosperity brought increased emphasis on imports, and declining real income for most city-dwellers. This shifted the demand for products from the interior toward a narrow range of agricultural commodities. This is suggested both by the volume of consumption of various commodities and by the changing distribution of gross revenue within the market for Castilian staples. At the same time, the government discouraged intensification of agriculture near the city by encouraging rural grain reserves and accepting the higher costs of a wider radius of supply based on the existing rural arrangements.

These conditions did not, however, preclude the development of an urban economic elite which increasingly preferred market to administered economic decisions. This urban elite adopted many tenets of Liberal economics relative to the marketing of primary products, while remaining tied to traditional structures of production in the countryside. The logic in this is apparent when we recall the nature of the revenues that supported Madrid and its rentier elite. The result was the paradoxical situation of a growing city that encouraged stagnation in the rural economy around it.

The reduction of direct government interference in the supply trades is apparent in many ways. By the eighteenth century, there is no evidence of control of rural bread prices or of embargoes directing the movement of wheat. The ceiling (*tasa*) on the price of grain leaving the farm was not

20. See Chapter 7. The most coherent regional case study illustrating this is García Sanz, *Desarollo y crisis*.
21. See Chapters 4, 5, and 6 on income distribution and the evolution of urban demand.
22. Wrigley, "A Simple Model."

enforced and was formally abolished in 1765. When crops were adequate, most of the grain entering the city came through market operations at prevailing prices. In the background, the wheat depot continued to monitor the market and to supplement supplies so as to dampen price movements. This entailed development of a considerable administrative mechanism that arranged contracts with suppliers in La Mancha, maintained a system of purchasing agents and depots throughout Old Castile, regulated the supply of transport services in Castile, and provided a third of Madrid's wheat by 1790. Thus the government oversaw rather than directly administered a large share of the wheat supply and, even where control was more direct, deferred to market prices in the supplying regions.

The gradual withdrawal of the state, while far from total, was apparent in other supply trades as well.[23] The wine supply had evolved into a system of government licenses for several purveyors, while most of the ostensibly monopolistic concessions contained provisions for interlopers in the market. The concessions themselves provided speculative opportunities for a variety of contractors, partnerships, and established entities like the *Cinco Gremios Mayores*. By 1800 the government was skeptical of the cost of supply administration, and in 1805 sold off the entire charcoal system. Thus, although the eighteenth-century state played an active role in the supply of Madrid, the drift was toward a market-driven commerce involving private entrepreneurs—an arrangement made possible by the politically and rentier-supported urban economy.

The nature of the business world behind these eighteenth-century developments has not been examined carefully and is probably obscured by the formal categories of Old Regime society. For instance, we know little about the pressures behind the reform of the grain trade in the 1760's. It is sometimes treated as an ill-conceived application of physiocratic ideas by doctrinaire reformers;[24] but given the inelasticities of supply imposed by transport and weather, a freer system clearly benefited rentiers and middlemen able to withhold grain from the market. If the nobility of eighteenth-century Toulouse could see this and espouse free trade, it should not be startling to see landed elements in Castile reacting in the same way.[25] Indeed, there are numerous other indications that the elites in Madrid were forming economic interests and attitudes that cut across traditional class and status distinctions. This was not a narrowly urban process, but reached across the countryside via agents, commodity fairs and markets, merchants, and mar-

23. See the detailed discussion of supply arrangements in Chapter 7.
24. Vicens Vives, *Manual*, pp. 467–470.
25. Robert Forster, *The Nobility of Toulouse in the Eighteenth Century* (1971), pp. 70–72.

ket-oriented estate management to touch estate managers and the *labradores ricos* who dominated village politics.

Rentier concern for profitable investment is also apparent in the flurry of interest in joint-stock trading companies, and a wide variety of noble families participated as stockholders in the Zaragoza, Toledo, Granada, and Extremadura companies.[26] Most of the companies foundered, but at least one, the Caracas Company, was successful for 60 years.[27] Noble participation in commercial activity, obviously not an alien concept for the second estate, intersected with the activity of the *Cinco Gremios Mayores.* An agency of the commercial patriciate of Madrid, the *Cinco Gremios* dominated wholesale and retail trade in manufactures in the capital and were involved in the same joint-stock companies. Their *Compañía General de Comercio,* founded in the 1760's, managed royal factories, farmed important taxes, traded with America and the Philippines, and at times supplied both the army and the capital. By 1790 the company had accumulated over 300 million *reales* in deposits, which were used to extend credit to public and private customers.[28] These activities suggest numerous points of contact between the various wealthy elements of the interior.

By the 1780's, the Banco de San Carlos, predecessor of the Bank of Spain, was functioning, with a long list of stockholders from a variety of social groups.[29] The bank in turn launched the grandiose *Real Compañía de Filipinas,* which absorbed the Caracas Company and was to undertake overseas trade, supply credit to the Crown, and construct interior canals.[30] This is further evidence of the mutual concerns of commercial and landed elements for mobilizing the products of the interior, as well as participating in the Atlantic trade. These common concerns were proclaimed through the Economic Societies, an amalgam of landed and urban interests espousing modernization and improved interior commerce and transport.[31]

The economic modernity of Madrid's elites had important limits, however.

26. For an account of the Toledo Company, with some references to others, see Larruga, *Memorias políticas y económicas,* vol. 7, pp. 59–418, and vol. 8, pp. 1–94. See also William J. Callahan, "Crown, Nobility, and Industry in Eighteenth-Century Spain" (1966).

27. Roland Dennis Hussey, *The Caracas Company, 1728–1784* (1934).

28. In 1775, the operating capital of the five participating guilds was estimated at 209 million *reales.* Capella Martínez and Matilla Tascón comment, in *Los Cinco Gremios,* pp. 17, 124, 315–316, on the growing sophistication of their business activities. By the end of the century, the *Compañía de los Cinco Gremios* had accepted deposits (technically loans) amounting to 397,994,401 *reales.* See also Vicens Vives, *Manual,* pp. 522–524.

29. Earl Hamilton, "Plans for a National Bank in Spain, 1701–1783" (1949), "Foundation of the Bank of Spain," parts 1 and 2 (1945 and 1946), and "El Banco Nacional de San Carlos, 1782–1829" (1970).

30. María Lourdes Díaz-Trechuelo Spinola, *La Real Compañía de Filipinas* (1965).

31. Robert Jones Shafer, *The Economic Societies in the Spanish World, 1763–1821* (1958).

Commercialization of commodities accumulated as rents and tithes does not necessarily stimulate change in the rural society producing them. In Castile, it led to competition for control of traditional rents and tithes within the pattern established in the seventeenth century. The dependence of commerce on Madrid and the wool trade reflected the stagnation of the other cities in the interior and the one-sided nature of the countryside's trade with the capital. Lacking convenient urban markets and services, and without adequate transportation, the response of the rural population was shaped more by rural conditions than by demand from Madrid.

Moderate population growth produced some signs of rural prosperity in the middle decades of the eighteenth century, but the interior cities were little affected. Toledo, Albacete, León, Ávila, Benavente, and Segovia appear virtually stagnant until 1770, with at best moderate and temporary expansion thereafter. A certain amount of enclosure went on, and there are indications of some concentration of enclosures near Madrid, but signs of increased large-scale farming or intensive techniques are scarce. The volume of movable agricultural commodities rose primarily because enclosure of land for farming created new tenants who added to the flow of traditional rents and tithes. Evidence of diminishing returns suggests the extension of traditional farming onto less fertile land.[32] Consequently, the sale of larger quantities of produce at Madrid had little effect on rural buying power, and hence the stagnation of local centers. Indeed, most of the rewards from the supply trades ended up in the pockets of absentee landlords, tax collectors, tithe collectors, and supply agents often resident in the capital.

This perception of the rural economy is reinforced by the history of consumption in Madrid once the seventeenth-century reorganization of the urban hierarchy was complete. The rapid increase in olive oil consumption was possible because the seventeenth-century response to declining population and demand was a shift to such low-labor, high-value commodities, and meshed with the concentration of buying power in the city which created a relatively stable market for items of elite consumption. The parallel shift to grazing similarly explains how, by 1800, Madrid was able to consume more meat per-capita than any other large city in Europe.

The seventeenth-century loss of markets and labor dismantled the commercial wine industry of New Castile. As a consequence, wine became relatively expensive, total urban consumption rose slowly, and per capita use fell below half the early seventeenth-century level. Moreover, to provide for a much smaller annual consumption it proved necessary to extend the supply region far south into La Mancha, an area only marginally important before

---

32. See Chapter 9. The carters' associations complained of enclosure of their reserved pastures for sheep and tree-planting, but only occasionally for agriculture.

1650. The districts that had once produced wine for Toledo and Madrid did not respond to renewed demand. Nor did New Castile respond to stronger demand for cereals. Important amounts continued to come from all over New Castile, but far less than in the sixteenth century, and the scanty evidence shows declining production in many areas around Madrid and Toledo between the 1730's and the 1780's. Occasional recourse to Old Castile and Andalucía for wheat gave way to an elaborate procurement system in Old Castile in order to meet the city's regular needs.

Logically, renewed urban demand should have shifted the region back toward cereals and vines. The failure of New Castile to respond in this manner is associated with structures that separated the actual farmer from market forces outside the immediate locale and enforced a very uneven distribution of rural wealth. As population rose, plots got smaller and smaller, and peasants were caught short in subsistence crises—and pushed into wage labor—which encouraged them either to emigrate from the villages or to develop extremely marginal farming patterns.[33] Yet this organization of production was so much bound up with rural power that the risks to the elite inherent in changing the organization and providing direct incentives to the peasant outweighed the long-term collective benefits of increased total production.[34] Thus the controlling elites, while behaving in an increasingly "modern" fashion in dealing with the wealth extracted from rural society, continued to maintain traditional arrangements within that society. In Castile, commercialization of necessity focused on Madrid, creating a community of interests between rural and urban elites. This pattern helps explain the apparent ambivalence of eighteenth-century domestic reforms in Spain. "Enlightened" elites often supported "liberal" reforms, such as free internal grain trade, better roads, rural industry, credit facilities, and modernization of maritime commerce and imperial administration. At the same time, they resisted serious land reforms and maintained policies of social control that made it pointless for the peasant to improve yields, because the results would quickly be lost as rent.[35]

33. Ester Boserup, in *The Conditions of Agricultural Growth: The Economics of Agrarian Change Under Population Pressure,* chs. 4 and 5, discusses some of the "low-income" traps possible under such circumstances.

34. The situation may have resembled that discussed by Alfred Cobban for France, where feudal dues and rent collections, rather than the actual exploitation of the land, were commercialized. Relative to Spain, Fontana Lázaro cites as causes of low productivity the lack of an internal market and the inefficient management of a large share of the land by the clergy; he explicitly rejects Cobban's type of analysis. See Cobban, *The Social Interpretation of the French Revolution* (1965), pp. 25–35; Fontana Lázaro, *La quiebra de la monarquia absoluta,* pp. 39, 48, 52.

35. Vicens Vives, *Manual,* pp. 472–474. On the resistance to reduction of the nobility's jurisdictional powers in the late eighteenth century, see Manuel García Pelayo, "El estamento de la nobleza en el despotismo illustrado español" (1946), pp. 45–49, 59.

Thus the largest single center of commercial and industrial activity in eighteenth-century Spain was entirely dependent upon the political structure of the empire and the landed wealth of the peninsula. The counterfactual implications of this are intriguing, given that in less isolated areas such as England, or even Spain's own Basque provinces, landed elements did respond to new investment opportunities. One of the reasons offered for the prominence of conspicuous consumption and swollen staffs of retainers in the Spanish aristocracy was the lack of more profitable investments. In eighteenth-century Madrid, the most common high-security investment other than land was apparently "loans" (actually savings deposits) to the Five Greater Guilds, which paid only 2.5% until after 1780.[36] Had the potential market and investable capital of Madrid been concentrated in a city such as Lisbon or Sevilla, with much greater potential for commercial and industrial enterprise, the pattern of economic development in Spain would have been significantly different.

Madrid's economy can now be fitted into the larger perspectives suggested earlier. The capital depended on the Spanish interior for over half of its income and for its basic supplies. Through the state and the señorial system, taxes and rents were collected in the countryside. These flowed to the city, financed one-way flows of commodities to Madrid, and thus returned to the countryside, completing the circular flow of a largely autonomous and essentially static economy. The weakness of the impact on rural society is heightened by the fact that in practice the payment for rural products often passed directly to rentiers within the city. The actual city-country relationship in that case was a one-way shipment of rural products to the urban market. Any purchasing power thus created was retained within the consumption-oriented economy of the capital city. At the same time, the capital was dependent upon the imperial system as the source of much of the revenue that subsidized the costs inherent in the city's location, thus providing a focal point for wealth captured by the landed elite. In its turn, this dependence on distant sources of wealth financed much of the trade between Spain and Europe, discouraging the diversification of the interior by directing urban demand elsewhere.[37]

III. The Nineteenth Century: An Era of Retrenchment

Our perception of Madrid and Castile in the eighteenth century provides valuable perspective on the agro-commercial oligarchy that became the basis of the dominant *Moderado* party after 1833. This oligarchy is conventionally

36. Domínguez Ortiz, *Siglo XVIII*, p. 90; Capella Martínez and Matilla Tascón, *Los Cinco Gremios*, pp. 262–263.

37. These preferences were strongly oriented toward French customs and luxuries. See J. F. Bourgoing, *The Modern State of Spain*, vol. 2, pp. 308–309.

described as consisting of landed nobility, "bourgeois" owners of disentailed Church and municipal lands, speculators in railroads and urban real estate, the army officer corps, and wealthy commercial families. This elite and its political opposition are often depicted as part of a structure of horizontal and national classes,[38] but that perception of Spanish society is anachronistic. Only for the twentieth century can a case be made for class conflicts that have national coherence. In the nineteenth century, the basic cleavages reflected well-defined geo-economic patterns. Certain coastal areas persistently opposed the policies of the dominant oligarchy, and only in those areas did industrial working and middle classes develop. Interior and coast still confronted different economic realities that offered little room for compromise. This is not to deny that coastal areas like Galicia and Asturias maintained traditional economic and social structures, but they did not have to cope with the extremes of subsistence crisis common in the interior. Nor does it deny that as an urban center, Madrid imported many elements of modernity and developed social groups accordingly.

Nevertheless, the elite of Madrid and the interior strove to reinforce the structures of the traditional interior. They backed protective agricultural tariffs, free trade in non-agricultural imports, control of colonial markets for agricultural exports, a strong Church, limited franchise, and limited education. The "liberal" elements of the coasts sought free entry of foodstuffs, tariffs to protect industry, control of colonial markets for manufactures, extensive and secular education, and a broader franchise. The structural bases of these differences meant that issues could easily become polarized along sectional lines and create serious disruption in the form of revolution and civil war.

Inevitably Madrid was a central feature of the structures that typified the interior, although other factors were also at work. Castilian agriculture expanded considerably in the 1840's, and it is an open question whether it was due to sale of entailed lands, to gradual penetration of market forces, or simply to better documentation of the effects of increased rural population.[39] In any case, export surpluses appeared, and the problem of bread that governed the budgets of Madrid's poor was eased. In the wake of this stabilization of its bread supply, the capital city renewed its demand for other agricultural commodities. Thus meat, wine, and olive oil consumption increased, despite rising prices for the last two. The nineteenth-century capital not only contributed to the long-term expansion of olive culture in the south,

38. On regional polarization, see C. A. M. Hennessy, *The Federal Republic in Spain: Pi y Margall and the Federal Republican Movement, 1868–74* (1962).

39. Miguel Artola, *La burguesia revolucionaria, 1808–1869*, pp. 58–78, 107–112; Richard Herr, *An Historical Essay on Modern Spain*, pp. 93–94; Pedro Voltes Bou, *Historia de la economia española en los siglos XIX y XX* (1974), vol. 1, pp. 117–138.

but absorbed a growing volume of meat and, more significantly, began to recover as a domestic market for viticulture.

The disentailing of Church lands may have stimulated agricultural production in Castile,[40] but it can be argued that this reflected more basic politico-economic developments. In addition to long-term rural population growth, the 1840's saw reestablishment of an effective state controlled from Madrid by Madrid-based interests. This produced tax reforms and an increase in the budget dispensed from the capital. At the same time, economic policy created captive markets in Cuba and in the peninsular seaports. Paying for Castilian products with colonial goods or manufactures, these markets provided a pale reincarnation of eighteenth-century patterns. Once again, empire meant commerce and a prosperous capital city. This was the context for land sales, and for a few years the response allowed a grain trade to Cuba and stable bread prices in the capital. This meant that Madrid's renewed prosperity could turn into demand for other products of Castilian agriculture. This was a brief phase broken by serious shortages in 1857–58, a crisis in the remnants of the empire, renewed instability of urban supply, and another breakdown in the centralist structure of power. By the mid-nineteenth century, little had happened to solve the long-standing problem of low rural productivity—an indication of the marginal impact of land reform, restoration of an imperial subsidy for domestic commerce, and the coming of the railroads. Structural contrasts remained to complicate Spanish politics well into the twentieth century.[41]

Basic economic realities included an endowment of resources that dictated a dispersed, low-yield agriculture or livestock-raising in the interior.[42] Transportation was caught in a technological deadlock that left the transport system of 1850 little better than that of 1790, and maintained regional isolation.[43] Prices reveal recurrent crises and sharp regional contrasts as late as 1880. In 1865–68, for example, wheat prices rose up to 190% in the interior but only 60% in the coastal provinces. This illustrates a profound lack of economic integration long after the period during which the nineteenth-century oligarchy was supposedly forming.[44] Consequently, the commercial activity of the interior remained restricted to import of a small volume of manufactures, mostly for Madrid, and sale of agricultural products to controlled markets in Cuba, the coastal towns, and Madrid.

40. Raymond Carr, *Spain,* pp. 275–276.
41. Ibid., pp. 280, 290–300, 547–557; Vicens Vives, *Manual,* p. 311, Sánchez-Albornoz, *España hace un siglo,* chs. 1, 2, 3, and 5.
42. Carmelo Viñas y Mey, "Apuntes sobre historia social y económica de España," pp. 35–38.
43. Ringrose, *Transportation,* pp. 135–136.
44. Sánchez-Albornoz, *España hace un siglo,* pp. 46–56, and a paper, "Mercado nacional, dualismo y ruptura: Los precios del trigo de España durante la segunda mitad del siglo XIX."

None of this represents a significant structural change since the eighteenth century. Regional price differences in 1867 were virtually identical to those of 1790.[45] Except for the decline of wool exports, the pattern of commerce in the Castilian interior was basically that of the eighteenth century, with limited exports and manufactures and luxuries supplied to Madrid from Barcelona, Bilbao, and Europe. Agricultural commodities were more uniformly accumulated as rents rather than tithes, or through direct management, as in the cases of livestock or charcoal, before they moved into supply systems focused on Madrid. The changes of a century seem modest. By the 1860's Madrid was perhaps 50% larger than in 1800, but was still under 300,000 inhabitants. Its demographic structure was unchanged, income distribution had worsened, and urban function was more narrowly political and residential. More and more of the goods demanded by the affluent of the city were produced outside the Castilian interior. Traditional industry in central Spain and in Madrid declined, forcing the countryside into heavier reliance on basic agriculture.[46]

Such changes in the economic framework of the interior seem an inadequate explanation for the agro-commercial oligarchy of nineteenth-century Spain. Unquestionably, Spain saw rapid changes in the formal definitions of society and economy and their institutions after 1833. The sanctions behind the state were secularized, and the monarchy became constitutional. Traditional law codes were replaced by modern "liberal" ones, and the old estates with prescriptive rights were officially dismantled. The legal context of commerce was modernized, removing obstacles to the free movement of goods. Land became a commodity in the classical Liberal sense, as entail was abolished, Church and municipal lands were sold at auction, and resources were freed for optimal use, as defined by Adam Smith's invisible hand.[47]

Given the permanence of underlying economic conditions, however, we must be careful about seeing in this a "revolution" by a "conquering bourgeoisie" such as Morazé depicts for France, and we must not make too much of the mobility into the elite that appears in the mid-nineteenth century.[48] If the protagonists are "bourgeois," it is within a socio-economic context more reminiscent of eighteenth-century Madrid than nineteenth-century France or England. Since land and status were still connected, it would be remarkable if the great land sales had not produced candidates for noble title. It is worth noting that the number of entries into the nobility in the seventeenth and

45. Anes, *Economia e "Ilustracion" en la España del siglo XVIII*, pp. 43–70.

46. Carr, *Spain*, pp. 264–277; Fernández García, *El abastecimiento de Madrid*, chs. 3, 4, 5; Pascual Madoz, *Madrid: Audiencia, Provincia, Intendencia, Vicaria, Partido y Villa* (1848), pp. 434–468.

47. José Luis Comellas García-Llera, *Los Moderados en el poder, 1844–1854* (1970), ch. 1.

48. Ibid., pp. 66–69; Fontana Lázaro, *La quiebra*, chs. 1 and 2; Charles Morazé, *The Triumph of the Middle Classes* (1968), ch. 5.

eighteenth centuries was also not inconsiderable.[49] Most of the legal and commercial reforms formalized in the nineteenth century had been discussed and even begun in the eighteenth. The sale of religious endowments was started by the Old Regime, and it never brought a significant land reform. Rather, the nonclerical segments of the agro-commercial oligarchy got less ambiguous control of more land at the expense of religious institutions. This meant that more land was in "bourgeois" hands, but the beneficiaries were already part of a network of interior commerce and estate management that had common interests with older landed elements. The lawyers, professionals, and speculators who are cited as the vanguard of bourgeois capitalism by some writers were really part of an urban-rural continuum in which most economic life was closely tied to land and agriculture.

Life in the countryside saw even less change. The amount of land under wheat expanded, as did total output, but yields per acre declined, indicating that traditional methods of production were being applied to lower-quality land.[50] Whoever the landlord may have been, and whatever his relationship to the market, relationships between landlord and tenant or laborer changed little, and production was not significantly capitalized. Market-oriented rentier class and self-sufficient peasantry persisted together through the nineteenth century in a balance that depended on the Madrid market.[51]

Thus nineteenth-century Madrid remained fundamentally elitist, dominated by a small, wealthy upper class and populated by rural and urban masses no better off than 100 or 200 years before. If one looks at sources and distribution of wealth in Spain, the structure of the nineteenth century looks very like that of the eighteenth.[52] The process follows closely the model discussed by Robert Brenner for the impact of a city/market on a "serf-society." Despite an air of modernity, maximizing attitudes can freeze or restrict change in rural production, limiting city-country interaction because of the shape assumed by the overall market. The result is a city limited by the rural product that can be "captured."[53] The unique thing about Madrid was its access to a transregional power base that made possible a widespread regional system of "capture."

49. Comellas, *Los Moderados*, pp. 66–67; Domínguez Ortiz, *Siglo XVII*, pp. 209–210.

50. It can be argued that the disamortization lasted most of the nineteenth century, having begun in 1798, while discussion of the topic began long before. See Francisco Tomás y Valiente, *El marco político de la desamortización en España* (1971), passim; Vicens Vives, *Manual*, p. 585; Richard Herr, "Hacía el derrumbe del Antiguo Régimen: Crisis fiscal y desamortización bajo Carlos IV" (1970), pp. 45–50.

51. García Sanz, *Desarrollo y crisis,* pp. 376–388.

52. This is a conceptual approach easier to accept for Spain than for England—as presented by Peter Laslett in *The World We Have Lost* (1965), chs. 1, 2, and 9, in his discussion of change in English society.

53. See Robert Brenner, "The Origins of Capitalist Development," pp. 45–47.

This suggests that the origins of the agro-commercial oligarchy of the nineteenth century are to be found in the association between Madrid and its hinterland that was stimulated by the growth of the city in the eighteenth century. The changes of the nineteenth century reflect shifts in alliances and land control within the elite, and a recasting in Liberal terms of the rationales by which the rentier elite justified its preeminent position. Through land purchases, intermarriage, and the political alliances made possible by the *Moderado* state, barriers between *título, hidalgo, rentista,* and *labrador rico* were blurred, bringing greater coherence to the landed elites.[54] The *Moderado* state and its constitution of 1845 have justifiably been characterized as the codification of an elitist liberalism in the service of the evolving oligarchy.[55]

The alliance of state and oligarchy was reinforced by yet another factor, which also served to attract resources to the state and its capital. Beginning in the 1790's, Spain drifted into recurrent balance-of-payments deficits and massive government debt. This diverted large quantities of capital to state finances in support of a power structure that perpetuated the dominance of Spain by Madrid and Castile. The great land sales were inseparably linked to the problem of public debt; and the perception of land and the state as secure, if low-yield, investments reflects traditional attitudes. For all of its involvement with capitalism, railroads, gas lighting, and Church expropriation, the elite of middle and late nineteenth-century Madrid were not so much something new as the end product of over two centuries of economic, social, and institutional evolution in the interior of the country.[56]

What did change in nineteenth-century Spain was the structural relationship between capital city, country, and empire—a change that pushed to the center of the political stage those economic and social elements of the eighteenth century whose fortunes best survived the catastrophe of imperial collapse between 1800 and 1825. It is hardly surprising that the elements that had long been coalescing around the one-way commerce between the Castiles and Madrid came to dominate the Spanish state. Already in the seventeenth century, Madrid had become the dominant city of the country—a city in

54. Richard Herr, "Spain," pp. 103–115; see also Miguel Artola, *Antiguo Régimen y revolución liberal,* pp. 115–118, 299–300.

55. José Luis Aranguren, *Moral y sociedad: La moral social española en el siglo XIX,"* pp. 91–96.

56. Gabriel Tortella's study of mid-nineteenth-century Spain—*Los orígenes del capitalismo en España: Banca, industria y ferrocarriles en el siglo XIX* (1973), chs. 2, 3, 5, and 6—shows that as late as the 1850's and 1860's, Spanish capital was readily diverted to overinvestment in railroads, to the detriment of industrial production. Speculative aspects aside, the commercial possibilities inherent in breaking the transport bottleneck in the interior represented opportunities of a type more easily appreciated by the economic elite than did investment in industrial capacity.

which most commercial life consisted of final distribution rather than the transformation of goods or creation of value-adding commercial services, and a city in which most incoming wealth belonged to an agricultural elite and those who serviced that elite. In the nineteenth century, the loss of empire crippled maritime commerce and government finance, leaving the complex of Madrid rentiers, suppliers, and middlemen relatively more important in the national political and economic framework. A greater share of government revenue had to come from interior sources, while the agricultural sector replaced the Indies trade as the preeminent source of wealth.[57] The collapse of imperial and foreign trade, which fell 75% between 1792 and 1827,[58] drastically weakened the port cities, leaving Madrid in a position of relatively greater importance. Despite the midcentury land sales and some response to market pressures, little occurred to alter the basic interactions between capital and country. Madrid emerged politically and economically dominant within Spain, shaping events to meet its own needs.

57. Jordi Nadal Oller, in *El fracaso de la revolución industrial en España,* p. 27, shows that while in the 1790's 22% of government revenue came directly from customs duties, by the 1830's this had fallen to only 8% and as late as the 1850's was only 11%. These figures ignore the secondary effects of commerce in augmenting ostensibly domestic revenue sources.

58. Josep Fontana Lázaro, in "Colapso y transformación del comercio exterior español entre 1792 y 1827" and *La quiebra,* pp. 49–50 and 210–218, effectively outlines the collapse of agriculture and commerce in the periphery, but refuses to admit any degree of commercialization oriented to Madrid that would have been insulated from the empire.

Appendix A: Population of Madrid; Figures and Estimates

Table A.1. *The Population of Madrid: Figures and Estimates, 1500-1900*

Year	Vecinos	Communicants	Inhabitants	Source
1513	3,000		12-15,000	1.
1530	1,000		4,775-5,000	2.
	748-1,000			3.
1542			18,000	4.
1546	6,000		25-30,000	1.
1563	2,520(a)		12-14,000	5.
			35,000	1.
1570	4,000(a)		14,000	6.
			40,000	1.
1572			35,000	10.
1594	8,524		43,320	3.
	9,541(b)		47,705	2.
			46,209	2.
1597	7,016(a)	45,422	101,550	8.
	11,857(c)			
			57,285	9.
			65,000	10.
1617		108,332		11.
			75-80,000	2.
1619			130,000	1.
1621		112,000		1.
1622-26			69,418	2.
1626			300,000	12.
1630			2-300,000	13.
1646	58,664(d)		392,175	14.
	74,435		76,430	15.
1659			129,633	1.
1685		96,000(e)		1.
1723	24,344	95,473		16.
	30,000			
			180,000	17.
			121,720	18.
			-129,473	

Table A.1. *The Population of Madrid: Figures and Estimates, 1500-1900* (*cont.*)

Year	Vecinos	Communicants	Inhabitants	Source
			150,000	19.
1740			109,550	20.
1743			111,268	21.
1757	30,626		109,753	22.
			150,000	23.
			147,543	2.
1766	32,745			24.
1769			121,038	25.
1787			156,672	26.
1797			167,607	27.
1799			184,404	28.
1804			176,374	29.
1821			135,629	30.
1825	50,336		201,344	31.
1831	49,400		211,127	32.
1833			166,607	33.
1836	50,440		224,312	33.
1842	44,000		157,397	33.
			194,312	33.
1843	44,980		166,283	33.
	55,267		212,225	33.
1844			166,283	33.
1845	48,108		202,570	33.
			206,714	34.
1846			205,848	33.
			174,564	33.
	58,750		235,000	35.
			215,000	36.
1850			216,571	37.
			221,707	36.
1851			234,178	36.
1852			236,108	36.
1853			231,866	38.
1857			281,170	39.
1860			298,426	40.
1862			288,373	40.
1864			285,174	40.
1865			283,917	36.
1866			282,976	40.
1868			282,635	40.
1869			292,483	36.
1887			470,283	41
1895			547,399	41.
1900			539,835	41.

a. "*Casas.*"
b. Includes 7,500 taxpayers.
c. "*Familias.*"
d. "*Contribuyentes.*"
e. Persons "over 7 years."

References:
1. Domínguez Ortiz, *Siglo XVII*, pp. 129-134.
2. Martorell, *Aportaciones*, pp. 31-34, based on Tomás González, *Censo español del siglo XVI* (1828).
3. Madoz, *Diccionario*, vol. 10, pp. 584-585, based on González, *Censo español.*
4. Espadas Burgos and Burgos, "Abastecimiento," p. 104, based on Gaspar de Barreiros.
5. Agustín G. de Amezua y Mayo, "Las primeras ordenanzas municipalies de la villa y corte de Madrid" (1926), pp. 401-404, based on Jerónimo de Quintana.
6. Martorell, *Aportaciones*, pp. 31-34, based on González, *Censo español*, but confusing *vecinos* and *habitantes*.
7. Espadas Burgos and Burgos, "Abastecimiento," p. 104, based on reports by the Venetian ambassador.
8. AGS, *Expedientes de hacienda*, leg. 121, *Padrones de Madrid*; est. 56,128 *"personas fuera del precepto de comunión."*
9. Tomás González, *Censo español del siglo XVI* (1828), p. 96, based on AGS sources, accepted by Amezua, Martorell, Madoz.
10. Domínguez Ortiz, *Siglo XVII*, pp. 129-134, incl. est. of transients.
11. BN, ms. 2274, fol. 37; incl. religious, excl. transients and troops
12. Contemporary est., AHN, *Consejos*, leg. 51538.
13. Patricia Shaw Fannian, "El Madrid y los madrileños del siglo XVII"; Rodrigo Diez de Noreña y Carranza, *Respuesta política* (1678), ch. 4, p. 265.
14. AGS, *Diversos*, leg. 23; González, *Censo español*, p. 96, adds 20,000 transients; these estimates are accepted by Amezua, Madoz.
15. Martorell, *Aportaciones*, pp. 31-34, assuming that González confused *vecinos* and *habitantes*.
16. BN, ms. 2274; excl. troops, religious, *hospicio* residents.
17. Gerónymo de Uztariz, *Theórica y práctica de comercio* (1742), p. 35, commenting on BN, ms. 2274.
18. Martorell, *Aportaciones*, pp. 20-21.
19. Domínguez Ortiz, *Siglo XVIII*, pp. 73-77, incl. 20,000 transients.
20. Juan Antonio de Estrada, *Población general de España* (1748), vol. 1, pp. 81-82, incl. *"matriculados."*
21. María Carbajo Isla, "Primeros resultados," p. 73, excl. *"parvulos, religiosos, soldados, hospicios, hospitales."*
22. AGS, *DGR, Unica contribución*, leg. 1980; Matilla Tascón, "Primer Catastro," pp. 464-465.
23. Matilla Tascón, "Primer Catastro."
24. Arriquibar, *Recreación política*, letter 4, as cited from Sempere y Guarinos by Domínguez Ortiz.
25. Fernando Jiménez de Gregorio, *"Censo de Aranda,"* incl. religious, excl. troops, transients.
26. RAH, *Censo* 1787, leg. 9-6235; Madoz, *Diccionario*, vol. 10, p. 593; Martorell, *Aportaciones*, pp. 20-21.
27. *Censo* of 1797, as cited by Martorell, *Aportaciones*, pp. 20-21; Madoz, *Diccionario*, vol. 10, p. 503.
28. José de Canga Argüelles, *Diccionario de hacienda* (1834), vol. 2, pp. 67-69, incl. troops, religious, excl. transients estimated at 30,000.
29. AVM, *Secretaría*, sig. 4-4-37, incl. troops, etc., but not transients.
30. Cristóbal y Mañas, *La hacienda municipal*, p. 39.
31. Sebastian Miñano, *Diccionaro geográfico-estadístico* (1826-27), vol. 5, p. 345, police census; Romero de Solis, *La población española*, p. 170.
32. Mesonero Romanos, *Manual* (1833), pp. 44-45, incl. religious, excl. troops.
33. Madoz, *Diccionario*, vol. 10, p. 593.
34. AVM, *Secretaría*, sig. 6-61-47; Fernández García, *Abastecimiento de Madrid*, p. 148.
35. Madoz, *Diccionario*, vol. 10, p. 593, with Madoz' own estimate.
36. Fernández García, *Abastecimiento de Madrid*, p. 148, based on municipal sources.
37. AVM, *Secretaría*, sig. 6-61-49, incl. foreigners.
38. Mesonero Romanos, *Manual* (1854).
39. Fernández García, *Abastecimiento de Madrid*, p. 148; Vicens Vives, *Manual*, p. 565 (from census of 1857); AVM, *Secretaría*, sigs. 6-62-1 and 6-63-29.
40. Fernández García, *Abastecimiento de Madrid*, p. 148, taken from the *Anuario provincial de Madrid.*
41. Carmen Diaz del Moral, *La sociedad madrileña de fin de siglo* (1974), p. 46.

Appendix B: Demographic Structure of Madrid

Table B.1. *Baptisms in Madrid, Selected Years*

Year	Number of Baptisms
1594	2,831
1595	2,911
1596	3,202
1597	2,999
1598	3,183
1622	4,214
1623	4,092
1624	4,095
1625	4,108
1626	4,310
1784	4,692
1785	4,635
1786	4,861
1787	4,446
1788	4,837
1803	4,962
1804	5,024
1805	4,838
1806	4,637
1807	5,282

Sources: Ricardo Martorell Téllez Girón, *Aportaciones al estudio de la población de Madrid en el siglo XVII*, pp. 85, 87; María Carbajo Isla, "Primeros resultados cuantitativos de un estudio sobre la población de Madrid, 1742-1836."

Table B.2. *Origins of Population of Madrid in 1850-51, by Province*

Province	Migrants			Province	
	Number in Madrid	% Female	as % of City Pop.	Pop. in in 1857	Migrant %
Álava	1,244	50.3%	0.56%	96,398	1.29%
Albacete	1,062	55.9	0.48	201,118	0.58
Alicante	4,670	51.4	2.11	378,958	1.23
Almería	352	34.1	0.16	315,664	0.11
Ávila	1,044	62.6	0.47	164,039	0.64
Badajoz	1,085	45.3	0.49	404,981	0.27
Baleares	449	45.7	0.20	262,893	0.17
Barcelona	1,701	48.6	0.77	713,734	0.24
Burgos	3,537	49.3	1.60	333,356	1.06
Cáceres	709	47.2	0.32	302,134	0.23
Cádiz	2,598	59.5	1.17	390,192	0.67
Canarias	70	50.0	0.03	234,046	0.03
Castellón	459	50.8	0.21	260,919	0.18
Ciudad Real	5,349	52.2	2.41	244,328	2.19
Córdoba	1,036	44.5	0.47	351,536	0.29
Coruña	2,377	42.5	1.07	551,980	0.43
Cuenca	4,178	58.4	1.88	229,959	1.82
Gerona	333	43.8	0.15	310,970	0.11
Granada	1,875	50.6	0.85	444,629	0.42
Guadalajara	6,521	68.7	2.94	199,088	3.28
Guipúzcoa	1,745	66.7	0.79	156,493	1.12
Huelva	128	50.8	0.06	174,391	0.07
Huesca	682	54.8	0.31	257,839	0.26
Jaén	1,060	46.3	0.48	345,879	0.41
León	1,436	34.8	0.65	348,756	0.41
Lérida	339	51.3	0.15	306,994	0.11
Logroño	2,170	47.4	0.98	173,812	1.25
Lugo	5,960	27.9	2.69	424,186	1.41
Málaga	1,300	52.8	0.59	451,406	0.29
Murcia	3,439	49.7	1.55	380,060	0.90
Navarra	2,041	62.0	0.92	297,422	0.69
Orense	834	27.9	0.38	371,818	0.22
Oviedo	17,195	25.4	7.76	524,529	3.28
Palencia	1,217	50.4	0.55	187,231	0.65
Pontevedra	790	32.9	0.36	428,886	0.18
Salamanca	1,313	50.0	0.59	263,516	0.50
Santander	3,388	48.1	1.53	214,441	1.58
Segovia	3,458	61.9	1.56	146,839	2.35
Sevilla	2,119	52.9	0.96	463,486	0.46
Soria	1,636	54.8	0.50	147,468	1.11
Taragona	583	52.5	0.26	320,593	0.18
Teruel	1,000	48.7	0.45	238,628	0.42
Toledo	10,980	59.7	4.95	328,755	3.34
Valencia	3,539	52.4	1.61	606,608	0.59
Valladolid	2,943	55.2	1.33	234,043	1.21
Vizcaya	2,881	65.0	1.30	160,579	1.79
Zamora	892	53.1	0.40	249,162	0.36
Zaragoza	3,354	54.2	1.51	384,176	0.87

Table B.2. *Origins of Population of Madrid in 1850-51, by Province*   (*cont.*)

Province	Number in Madrid	Migrants % Female	as % of City Pop.	Province Pop. in in 1857	Migrant %
Unknown origin	1,895	46.7	0.89		
Foreigners	4,848	35.5	2.19		
Madrid, city and province	95,863	54.4	43.23	475,785	20.15

Source: AVM, *Secretaría*, sig. 6-61-49.

Table B.3. *Age and Sex Distribution of City Population Born Outside the Province of Madrid, 1850-51*

Cohort	Single Males	Females	Married Males No.	%	Married Females No.	%	Widowed Males	Females
0-6	1,327	1,483	0	0.0%	0	0.0%	0	0
7-15	4,859	4,674	5	0.1	12	0.3	0	2
16-24	11,646	12,339	1,060	8.3	2,416	16.2	54	146
25-39	11,393	9,487	13,547	53.0	12,937	52.6	632	2,159
40-49	1,977	1,807	7,459	72.4	5,677	54.5	862	2,934
50+	1,525	1,408	6,413	61.9	3,886	32.8	2,421	6,544
Total	32,727	31,199	28,484	43.7%	24,928	36.7%	3,060	11,785

Source: AVM, *Secretaría*, sig. 6-61-49.

Table B.4. *Age and Sex Distribution of Total Population, Madrid, 1850-51*

Cohort	Single Males	Females	Married Males No.	%	Married Females No.	%	Widowed Males	Females
0-6	12,435	12,563	0	0.0%	0	0.0%	0	0
7-15	13,608	13,142	10	0.1	34	0.3	0	4
16-24	17,233	18,564	1,618	8.6	3,953	17.4	68	201
25-39	14,732	12,801	17,917	53.4	17,609	53.1	900	2,749
40-49	2,660	2,623	9,021	70.3	7,744	54.5	1,150	3,844
50+	2,032	2,056	8,198	61.2	5,040	32.4	3,166	8,463
Total	62,700	61,750	36,764	35.1%	34,380	30.9%	5,284	15,261

Source: AVM, *Secretaría*, sig. 6-61-49.

Table B.5. *Age and Sex Distribution of City Population Born in Madrid Province, 1850-51*

Cohort	Single		Married Males		Married Females		Widowed	
	Males	Females	No.	%	No.	%	Males	Females
0-6	11,108	11,080	0	0.0%	0	0.0%	0	0
7-15	8,749	8,468	5	0.1	22	0.3	0	2
16-24	5,587	6,225	558	9.1	1,537	19.7	14	55
25-39	3,339	3,314	4,370	54.8	4,672	59.4	268	590
40-49	683	816	1,562	61.7	2,067	54.5	288	910
50+	507	648	1,785	58.0	1,154	31.0	745	1,919
Total	29,973	30,551	8,280	20.9%	9,452	21.8%	1,315	3,476

Source: AVM, *Secretaría*, sig. 6-61-49.

Table B.6. *Age and Sex Distribution of Total Population, Madrid, 1787*

Cohort	Single		Married Males		Married Females		Widowed	
	Males	Females	No.	%	No.	%	Males	Females
0-6	8,843	8,554	0	0.0%	0	0.0%	0	0
7-15	8,435	8,398	3	0.0	29	0.3	0	1
16-24	11,321	10,046	1,820	13.8	3,645	26.4	38	135
25-39	9,335	4,508	13,611	57.9	13,923	69.2	549	1,675
40-49	2,165	882	7,319	71.6	5,933	66.6	738	2,095
50+	1,961	887	7,462	64.3	4,783	40.1	2,180	6,272
Total	42,060	33,275	30,215	39.9%	28,313	39.5%	3,505	10,178

Source: RAH, leg. 9/6235.

Table B.7. *Age and Sex Distribution of Total Population, Madrid, 1804*

Cohort	Single		Married Males		Married Females		Widowed	
	Males	Females	No.	%	No.	%	Males	Females
0-6	8,744	8,016	0	0.0%	0	0.0%	0	0
7-15	7,932	7,273	0	0.0	1	0.0	0	0
16-24	14,208	13,388	2,078	12.7	3,519	20.5	48	223
25-39	9,064	6,390	11,698	54.8	12,741	60.1	576	2,068
40-49	2,803	1,470	8,745	70.1	7,432	63.6	919	2,782
50+	2,601	1,481	7,380	64.7	4,902	37.8	2,419	6,594
Total	45,352	38,018	29,901	37.7	28,595	36.5	3,962	11,667

Source: AVM, *Secretaría*, sig. 4-4-37.

Appendix C: Occupations and Incomes in Madrid

I. Occupational distribution of the economically active population

The principal sources for the occupational structure are two versions of the *Catastro* of 1757. One was published by Antonio Matilla Tascón and compiled in 1757. The other, compiled in 1770, was found in the municipal archives. The two are structured differently and were drawn from the same missing data bank for different purposes. The earlier version was drawn up as a report on the aggregate income of the city for use in general calculations of the ratio of national income to royal revenues. This was the first step in developing quotas for a new single tax. The version of 1770 was developed in connection with the effort to actually implement the tax and assign obligations in conformity with the rates designated for different types of income. Neither source was constructed with the objectives of this analysis in mind, and both reflect the fiscal concerns of the project for which they were compiled. As a result, aggregate income figures are attributed to many corporate groups, royal offices, and guilds without showing internal distribution. Much of this more detailed data was presumably available in the original supporting data, and a good deal of it came out in the comparison of the two versions. Nevertheless, it was sometimes necessary to make tentative estimates of the numbers of individuals and of individual incomes. Where this was done, it was by analogy with comparable cases where the data was less ambiguous.

The two most difficult occupational groups to estimate were the bureaucracy and the Church. For the bureaucracy, incomes were listed by bureau or administrative unit. Here it was necessary to go outside the two versions of the *Catastro*. The census of 1787 gives total royal employees at that time, while the *Guia de Forasteros* allows a count of the relatively important officials in the city. By counting the latter, and comparing the number with royal

employees recorded in 1787, a ratio was established which allowed an extrapolation from the number of officials in the *Guía* at the time of the *Catastro* to
an estimate of government employees at that time. This is the source of the
estimate of 3,000 inserted in Table 4.1. While the procedure is less than ideal,
the margin of possible error is not large enough to affect the overall structure
that emerged. The one part of the government sector that could not be
checked was the membership of the royal family and its dependents.

The religious personnel of the city presented a different and partly seman-
tic problem. Contrary to Old Regime tradition, adult religious personnel have
been classified as part of the active population. This is done on the grounds
that they were performing spiritual functions (and often economic and social
ones) valued by the society. Indeed, monasteries and convents ran bakeries,
wine shops, schools, orphanages, and hospitals. Analysis of the city census
that accompanies the 1757 version of the *Catastro*, combined with lists of
individual incomes received by segments of the religious personnel of the
1770 version, allowed a fairly complete count.

Lesser problems emerged in the enumeration of staff members of religious
bureaucracies and of the nonprofessional employees of the medical and legal
professions and the Five Greater Guilds. The 1770 version allowed separation
of the aggregate incomes of ecclesiastical bureaucrats, doctors, lawyers, and
merchants from the aggregate income of their employees, and allowed some
occupational classification as well.

The sector for which numbers of economically active persons could not be
estimated separately included educational institutions, hospitals, and
hospicios. The institutional occupants were not economically active, but
teaching and administrative personnel obviously were. Since these institutions were tied to Church and state by both personnel and endowment, it was
assumed that their active personnel was accounted for in one or the other. In
cases such as company and agency chaplains, or teaching and nursing nuns
and monks, they were included with other members of corporate entities.

Classification of the food, construction, and manufacturing sectors was
generally straightforward. The 1757 version of the *Catastro* gave considerable detail on active individuals and individual wages. The servant class
posed a more difficult problem. In one place there is a single entry for 8,000
sirvientes of all types, with an aggregate income figure. This appears to
include servants with long-term contractual employment. The tabulations
also show a group of some 3,000 *"gente de librea,"* who are distinct from the
day-laborer category. This phrase is associated in other sources with *la-
cayos*—lackeys, grooms, footmen, and other manservants. Listed with a variety of daily rates of pay, these "men for hire" are classified separately from
construction labor, commercial porters, and servants with long-term contractual arrangements. By a process of elimination, these men-for-hire have been

defined as casual servants and grouped with the *criados* and *sirvientes* as part of the service sector.

The concrete numbers in the sources and the guesses, estimates, and extrapolations mentioned above were used to construct the figures summarized in Table 4.1. The estimated total active population thus developed could be used to establish the percentages given in Table 4.2.

II. Distribution of income among the economically active population

The income attributions in Table 4.5 reflect the same estimates and approximations used in establishing occupational distribution. The main part of Table 4.5 shows those income attributions which are given in one way or another in the two versions of the *Catastro*. In some cases, as suggested in the preceding section, this involves use of income figures in analogous cases to estimate the numbers of persons and average incomes in groups such as the dependents of professional and business enterprises. The largest aggregate which could not be broken down was the 8,000 *"sirvientes de todas clases,"* with the result that the mean income of that large group is shown. The effect is no doubt to reduce the relative size of the 0–1000-*reales* income group, since it is hard to believe that most of the women servants were paid anything like the mean of the group. The relatively high average income of the servant group reflects the way in which annual incomes were calculated. Artisans, *jornaleros,* and *gente de librea* were attributed with 180 days of work per year. *Criados* were assumed to work 250 days, and meals were included as part of salary. As a result, even a relatively low daily wage produced the impression of relatively high annual incomes. To the degree that these conventional assumptions of the time were accurate, it appears that household service was far from the least attractive economic niche in the city.

In the case of propertied and titled persons, the listing in the main body of the table is based on the city-derived incomes attributed to them by the compilers of the *Catastro*. That same group is repeated at the bottom of the table, but redistributed according to the adjustments mentioned in the text for income from outside the city.

Also at the bottom of Table 4.5 is a tentative income distribution for government personnel. It is based on a survey of the *Guía de Forasteros,* available detail on agencies given in the version of 1770, and indications of pay and numbers of subalterns in various sources. It may reflect overestimates in the middle ranges, but salary figures for public and large private organizations from later periods suggest that even relatively minor employees got a "living wage" from the Crown—a fact which is confirmed by the demand for such positions.

Many professional groups appear with corporate income attributions that could not be disaggregated, and it was necessary to settle for the mean incomes in each group. Where possible, distribution of incomes among their employees was estimated by analogy with similar personnel shown individually in the records. Similarly, distribution of endowment income within many institutions and offices could not be estimated, and it was necessary to resort to averages.

A preliminary comparison of the income figures in the two available versions of the *Catastro* showed a number of discrepancies which suggested that the 1770 figure had been updated. A careful analysis of the figures for a number of guilds revealed that in fact the data base was identical, but that the calculations for 1770 were somewhat less precise. The early version, for example, listed widows of masters with shops separate from masters with shops, so that the widows could be shown with a commercial income but without a daily wage from industrial activity. The later version simply assumed that all masterships received daily wages as well as commercial profits. This type of discrepancy accounts for virtually all conflicts between the two sources on this point; and where possible, calculations were based on the more detailed data of the earlier version published by Matilla Tascón.

In general, most income attributions that had to be estimated or extrapolated are biased upward when any uncertainty is involved. One of the points of the analysis is to show the extreme inequality of income distribution in Madrid, and any upward bias works against that hypothesis. Thus such inequality is almost certainly somewhat less extreme in the findings than in reality. Table C.1 presents a more detailed version of the distribution of income among occupational groups than could be fitted comfortably into the text.

III. Average annual income in occupational groups

The following tabulation shows the composite annual income, including wages and commercial and property income, for most professional and skilled groups in the city—officials, doctors, guild-masters, etc. It is not a complete listing of economically active persons and does not include the incomes of subalterns or wage-earning employees in these groups. Government officials excepted, it illustrates the relative income levels of various occupations in more detail than was possible in the text. It also illustrates the nature of the urban market by documenting the wide range of special occupations and the small number of practitioners in each specialty. This speaks to the narrowness of elite demand in the city and the lack of industry oriented to export from the urban economy.

Table C.1. *Distribution of Economically Active Population by Occupational Subgroups, Madrid, 1757*

Occupational Group	Number	Percentage
Royal and city government	3,000 (est.)	7.06%
Church-related:		
Chapels, parishes, charities	1,496	3.52
Convents, monasteries	3,333	7.84
Propertied individuals	1,351	3.18
Professions(a)	1,758	4.14
Business and finance:		
Five Major Guilds and other wholesalers	1,342	3.17
Business agents and money-changers	285	.67
Petty retailers	320	.75
Food industries:		
Basic foodstuffs	1,691	3.98
Other foods	983	2.31
Construction:		
Skilled	2,022	4.76
Unskilled	4,710	11.08
Manufacturing:		
Quality textiles, leather, finished goods	3,273	7.70
Precious metals	820	1.03
Mechanical and metallurgical	1,449	3.41
Rough textiles, leather, unfinished goods	1,296	2.98
Miscellaneous crafts	487	1.15
Personal services:		
Barbers, entertainment	1,086	2.55
Servants, casual labor	11,904	28.00

a. Professions include law, medicine, and teaching.

To supplement Table C.2 and provide a fuller sense of urban income distribution, Table C.3 indicates the annual incomes attributed to a number of unskilled types of employment in the city.

Table C.4 elaborates further on income levels, showing the range of wages earned by employees of guild masters in the city. The extreme range of the *oficiales* or journeymen reflects (a) the inclusion of a number of highly skilled journeymen in precious-metal-working and (b) individuals in some royal establishments who obviously were functioning as foremen or overseers.

Table C.2. *Size and Average Income of Occupational and Professional Groups in Madrid, 1757*

Occupation or profession	No. of Individuals	Average Income in Group
A. PROFESSIONS, ADMINISTRATORS		
Abogados	182	6,864 rs.
Procuradores, consejos and villa	64	12,270
Tenientes del juzgado, villa	2	41,364
Escribanos del juzgado, villa and provincia	33	20,452
Escribanos-oficiales, sala juzgado prov.	18	5,867
Alguaciles, juzgado provincia	40	2,889
Escribanos reales	213	5,269
Escribanos, cámara del consejo	20	33,268
Relatores, reales consejos	20	23,835
Receptores del número	53	5,520
Visitadores eclesiásticos	18	17,482
Notarios and escribanos, trib. visita eccles.	16	6,876
Jueces, trib. nunciatura	6	6,912
Procuradores, trib. nunciatura	10	11,879
Notarios, tribunal nunciatura	13	4,244
Tribunal vicaria, vicar y fiscal	2	50,536
Notarios, vicaria	13	9,390
Médicos	85	12,789
Cirujanos-Barberos	381	4,817
Boticarios	71	9,391
Boticarios, conventos y hospitales	8	17,826
Maestros, primeras letras	27	6,669
B. BUSINESS, COMMERCE, FINANCE		
Agentes de negocios	237	10,782
Corredores de cambio and de lonja	23	6,457
Cambistas de letras	25	49,269
Cinco Gremios Mayores, comerc., lonjas cerradas	363	20,901
Joyeros sueltos	173	4,890
Tiendas ferretería sin gremio	18	13,756
Lonja de ferretería, buhoneros	95	2,624
Comerciantes de madera	10	21,071
Comerciantes, tiendas de cristales	11	22,476
Mercaderes, Calle San Cristóbal	7	4,293
Tratantes trapo, sin gremio	51	2,642
Herbolarios	28	1,555
Lonjas extramarinos, sin gremio	10	7,710
C. ARTS, CRAFTS, GUILDS (MASTERS WITH SHOPS ONLY)		
Albeitares and herradores	80	4,766
Alfareros	1	13,180
Alojeros	36	5,306
Altareros y tramoyistas	5	8,220
Arcabuceros	15	8,532
Arquitectos and maestros de obras	72	17,239
Aseradores de madera	5	4,140

Table C.2. *Size and Average Income of Occupational and Professional Groups in Madrid, 1757* (*cont.*)

Occupation or profession	No. of Individuals	Average Income in Group
Batidores de oro	15	14,644
Bodegoneros	108	3,305
Bordadores	57	6,273
Boteros	8	6,067
Botilleros	14	12,136
Cabestreros and alpargateros	10	22,268
Cabreros and ganaderos	48	3,618
Cabrero con obejas	1	26,484
Caldereros	25	9,942
Cantería, Arte de	30	8,935
Carpinteros and cofreros	128	5,274
Carreteros	9	11,564
Cedaceros	10	4,478
Cereros	22	26,710
Cerrajeros	56	7,210
Cesteros and palilleros	8	7,156
Cocheros, maestros de hacer	79	8,977
Colchas, mantas, fabricantes and maestros	7	14,631
Colchoneros, Comunidad de	34	3,044
Coleteros	11	3,591
Confiteros	90	13,120
Confiteros: hornos bizcorcho	8	3,504
Cordoneros	2	12,250
Cordoneros	59	5,650
Cosecheros de vino, Cabildo de	26	14,678
Cosecheros de vino, bodegas de	2	21,600
Cotilleros and Gollilleros	46	3,036
Cuchilleros	43	6,471
Curtidores	16	7,122
Doradores a fuego	14	5,997
Doradores a mate	78	7,313
Ebanistas	45	3,488
Empedradores, Cuadrilla de	13	900
Escultores and estatuarios	26	9,221
Espaderos	13	4,615
Esparteros	22	13,214
Estañeros	9	1,214
Estereros de palma and junco	12	9,211
Fontaneros	8	7,288
Frutas, tratantes en, Gremio de	14	16,089
Gallinas, huevos, revendidores (est.)	25	2,467
Guanteros	6	8,786
Guardamacileros	3	3,533
Guarnicioneros	73	9,177
Hachas de viento, fabricantes	8	8,075
Herreros de grueso	24	26,227
Herreros de menudo	13	10,412
Hierro, mercaderes	21	3,370

Table C.2. *Size and Average Income of Occupational and Professional Groups in Madrid, 1757* (*cont.*)

Occupation or profession	No. of Indivi- duals	Average Income in Group
Hoteleros, hosterías, posadas, figones	31	22,297
Impresores	27	20,153
Jalmeros	24	11,219
Juegos varios	35	7,317
Laneros and cardadores	27	7,833
Latoneros and campaneros	15	36,613
Libreros and bookbinders	70	9,141
Lienzos, tejedores de	20	4,333
Manguiteros and peleteros	10	14,115
Marmolistas	21	15,614
Menuderos	16	18,301
Mesoneros: mesones	40	18,444
Mesoneros: posadas	6	7,009
Molenderos de chocolate	120	28,114
Molenderos de chocolate: molinos	5	37,462
Monteros	17	3,614
Organeros and clavicorderos	7	14,954
Panaderos and tahoneros	129	18,105
Panaderos and tahonas de comunidades	6	35,666
Papel estraza y cartón, fabricantes	2	16,100
Pasamaneros	54	6,297
Pasteleros	19	9,063
Peineros	11	4,609
Peluqueros	158	2,694
Peluqueros: maestros, de papillote	31	4,162
Pieles para guantes, fabricantes	25	12,097
Plateros: comercio mayor de joyas	22	56,918
Plateros: de oro	54	13,139
Plateros: de plata	96	9,475
Plateros: cincelidores, vaciadores, obra sellos	19	4,984
Plateros: lapidarios, abrillantadores diamantes	10	10,132
Plateros: forjadores	7	9,551
Plateros: venta de dijes	4	3,423
Polvoristas	8	5,987
Polleros and hueveros	24	12,522
Puertaventaneros	19	7,814
Relojeros	36	7,137
Revocadores de casas	7	8,578
Ropavejeros, tratantes ropas usadas	123	3,461
Roperos de nuevo	43	10,787
Sastres y casulleros	420	5,714
Seda, tejedores and torceres	62	9,249
Silleros de paja y jauleros	18	5,593
Soladores	12	5,316
Sombrereros	22	13,740
Taconeros	21	1,080
Tafetanes, picadores de	13	9,788
Tallistas y ensambladores	34	9,132

Table C.2. *Size and Average Income of Occupational and Professional Groups in Madrid, 1757 (cont.)*

Occupation or profession	No. of Individuals	Average Income in Group
Tapiceros	16	17,110
Taverneros: particulares	239	5,396
Taverneros: comunidades	15	16,347
Tenderos de aceite y vinagre	242	2,991
Tintoreros	14	21,224
Tiradores de oro	3	2,073
Torneros	21	7,873
Vidrieros de loza	42	6,304
Vidrieros and hojalateros	57	6,395
Violeros and guitarreros	5	7,570
Yeso, fabricantes de	19	18,966
Zapateros de nuevo y de viejo	272	2,632
Zurradores	16	7,433

Table C.3. *Yearly Wages of Various Services and Unskilled Occupations*

Occupation	Wage
Aguadores	2,559 rs.
Mozos de aduana	1,825
Machacadores de yeso	1,440
Componedores de sillas	1,440
Ayundantes en carpintería, construcción	1,080-1,260
Peones en carpintería	900-1,080
Polvilleros de yeso	900
Mozos de arriería	900
Mayorales de ganado	900
Labradores and hortelanos	900
Tostadores de chocolate	900
Jornaleros de campo	720-900
Revendidores de vidrio	720
Esquiladores de mulas	720
Peones de albañil	720
Pastores	540-720
Zagales de ganado	540
Gente de librea (range)	360-1,440
Gente de librea (median)	800

Table C.4. *Range of Yearly Wages for
Various Categories of Guild Workers*

Grade	Salary range
Maestros (as employees)	1,080-1,800 rs.
Oficiales	540-2,700
Mancebos	720-1,080
Meseros	720-900
Apréndices	360-720

IV. Estimation of annual value of urban imports

Without a measure of the value of the goods involved in Madrid's trade, the elaborate contemporary list of urban imports and consumption compiled in 1789 is of little analytic value to us. Recognizing that at best any such calculation can yield but a rough approximation distorted by unknown product variety, variations in measurement, and outright fraud, an attempt was made to attach prices to as many imports as possible. Our preferred source was Earl Hamilton for the late 1780's, since the commodity prices he gives are based on the market in Madrid. Where possible, these were compared with other sources, including some of the commodity prices given in the work of Gonzalo Anes, which come from different documents and have proved generally reliable. Prices for foodstuffs of all sorts were found in the lists of price ceilings published in the *Correo Mercantil* during 1793. Hamilton's figures suggest that prices did not differ greatly between 1789 and 1793, so that the ceilings given provided a rough approximation. In addition, the *Correo Mercantil* published the current prices of several commodities in various ports. The prices of a number of urban imports were established by taking quotations from the most obvious port of entry or point of origin for goods en route to Madrid. Such figures are unavoidably low, since they do not include the cost of transport and handling en route to Madrid. In some cases, prices for manufactures could be estimated by reference to the *Balanza de Comercio* of 1795, although these suffer even more from various deficiencies. Many commodities that could not be priced directly were close substitutes for those that could be priced, and in those cases the prices of the substitutes were used.

Throughout these calculations, three biases were unavoidable, and therefore they were handled in a consistent way. Food prices from 1793 are assumed to have a slight upward bias relative to 1789, although they tended to include processed goods and luxuries which were relatively expensive anyway. The goods priced through port-city quotations were colonial products or metals, and the bias is clearly downward in those cases. In the case of goods which appear to have been near substitutes, the prices which were assigned are probably lower than the missing prices they replaced. The effect of these distortions is a slight overstatement of the value of subsistence commodities, most of which came from the Castilian interior, and a definite understatement of the value of colonial and other imports which were seldom part of the subsistence commodities that everyone needed. As a result, the proportionate value of the city's imports that were luxury-oriented or nonessential manufactures and raw materials is understated.

About 75% of the goods recorded have been priced, and the estimate that this represents 75% of their value is very rough and tentative. More than 25% of the named items could not be meaningfully priced, but a great many of them were recorded in small quantities. The most serious omission, for which no correction could be made, was the price of building materials. Bricks, plaster, stone, and lumber simply did not show up in any sources. Wood of some types did appear, but the tremendous variety in wood types, qualities, and units of measure made it necessary to abandon the few available quotations. Thus the totals cannot be used for precise calculations, but they do establish the magnitude of values. This magnitude fits well with other figures on the urban economy, and the internal proportions of the total are likely to be fairly accurate.

Appendix D: Data on Urban Consumption

I. Sources and estimates of wheat consumption

A. Sources for the totals in Table 6.1

1561: Given as 100 *fanegas* per day in Manuel Espadas Burgos and María Ascensión Burgos, "Abastecemiento de Madrid en el siglo XVI" (1962), p. 110.

1599: From a report of a decision by the Pósito of Madrid to take charge of the bread supply of the city and buy 180,000 *fanegas* of flour for the year. AVM, *Secretaría*, sig. 2–96–1.

1608: Based on various documents on the daily and weekly entry registry, and production of wheat and bread in Madrid. These indicate that the government handled more than 800 *fanegas* per day. AVM, *Secretaría*, sig. 1–455–2; AHN, *Consejos, Sala de Alcaldes, libros, año* 1614, fol. 350.

1614: The total is based on the decision to guarantee that the *Pósito* would be able to distribute 1,000 *fanegas* of wheat daily during the period of scarcity. AHN, *Consejos, Sala de Alcaldes, libros, año* 1614, fol. 350.

1628: Based on estimate of 1,000 *fanegas* as a daily minimum in addition to the supplies of private households, convents, the palace, etc., for a daily total of 1,200 *fanegas*. AHN, *Consejos*, leg. 51438–7; and notes made available by Prof. Antonio Domínguez Ortiz.

1630–31: This figure is based on two complementary sources:

    a. The registry of bread entering Madrid from surrounding villages for three days in September 1630, with daily totals of 1,121, 1,031, and 1,018 *fanegas*, exclusive of bread manufactured within the city. AVM, *Secretaría*, sig. 2–99–4.

    b. Detailed accounts of the efforts of the city government to supply the entire city after the bad harvests in the two Castiles in 1629 and 1630. The summary lists the very high total of 1,034,113 *fanegas* delivered to Madrid. Assuming that this is the total for two years, this suggests a minimum annual consumption of 517,051 *fanegas*, or 1,420 per day. Allowing for baking within the city, this coincides with source (a). AVM, *Secretaría*, sigs. 2–102–8, 2–140–6.

1667: This total is based on a list of the bread suppliers and bakers of the city, which suggests a maximum output of 1,025 *fanegas* per day. The same source indicates that the surrounding towns were obligated to supply 46,454 *fanegas* of bread per year. AVM, *Secretaría*, sig. 2–190–5.

1767: These figures are taken from an official report to the effect that the bare minimum necessary was 1,200 *fanegas* per day, while normal consumption, as in the spring, was 1,500, and the highest levels were around 2,000 *fanegas* in late summer. AVM, *Secretaría*, sig. 2–122–1.

1779–80: Based on monthly reports of grain entering the city, with detail on types of purchase. AHN, *Consejos*, leg. 6775–3.

1784: Based on a report which concludes that the output of the *panaderos* supplying the city was 2,000 *fanegas* per day, while maximum consumption reached 2,233 *fanegas* per day. AVM, *Secretaría*, sigs. 2–126–7, –9, –22.

1789: AVM, *Secretaría*, sig. 4–5–67.

1792: AHN, *Consejos*, leg. 6780–18.

1797: Based on weekly reports of wheat dispensed from the *Pósito* at a time when it was apparently the sole source of supplies. These averaged about 2,570 *fanegas* of wheat, equivalent to 2,800 of bread. These registers exist for many years, but only in a few cases is it possible to know what share of total consumption they represent. For 1797, the totals are high enough to preclude other sources of any note. AVM, *Secretaría*, sigs. 1–131, 1–126, 2–135, esp. document 17.

1812: From a report on the bread supplied to the city, dated July 8, 1812. At that time daily supplies were about 1,367 *fanegas*, which was considered barely adequate, but contrasted sharply with the 618 per day of the previous June. AVM, *Secretaría*, sig. 2–137–3.

1815: Derived from a report of the bread-baking facilities of the city and estimated daily capacity of 1,697 *fanegas*. AVM, *Corregimiento*, sig. 1–87–21.

1818 and 1820: Manuel Espadas Burgos, "Abasto y hábitos alimenticios en el Madrid de Fernando VII," p. 257, citing AVM, *Secretaría*, sigs. 2–138–20 and 2–138–42.

1824 and after: Pascual Madoz, *Diccionario geográfico*, vol. 10, pp. 1015–1072, various tables.

B. Comparisons between normal and minimal consumption

The estimate of long-term normal wheat consumption illustrated on Figure 6.1 depends on contemporary statements about the difference between normal and minimum or crisis-level requirements. Since the latter type of figure is all we have for earlier periods, it was necessary to establish the difference between the two, and the assumption that a year with minimum or crisis-level consumption represented 70% to 80% of a normal consumption level is based on three calculations:

1. In 1767, it was reported that the minimum was 1,200 *fanegas* against a normal level of 1,500. Thus the minimum here is 80% of normal.

2. In 1824–29, the average consumption was 682,164 *fanegas*, while the lowest year, 1824, was 522,343, or 77% of the average.

3. In 1839–47, the average of the available totals was 705,621 *fanegas*, while the lowest for the bad year of 1847 was 491,453 *fanegas*, about 70% of the average.

II. Serial data on consumption of commodities

A. General comment on the use of municipal tax data

Many sections of this book depend upon analysis of economic trends as indicated by taxes collected on various commodities, market transactions, and similar types of activity, but it is often difficult to use municipal tax data as they appear in the sources. Municipalities farmed out their taxes with contracts lasting one to six years; this implies an unknown margin of profit for the contractor, and a corresponding difference between figures shown in municipal accounts and the revenue actually collected. Accounts were figured yearly, and thus tax data seldom reflects seasonal changes. When the rental contracts were relatively long, they did not reflect year-to-year economic changes except when the contracts were renewed, or when crises forced adjustment of the terms. These limitations are offset, however, by the fact that municipal taxes reflect long-run economic change and, when contracts were short, reflect shorter cyclical fluctuations in the economy. We must, however, take note of possible complications, including fraud, bankruptcy of tax farmers, evasion, arrangements with wholesalers and transporters, arbitrary exactions by collectors, and the tendency for authorities to settle for negotiated revenue levels. We cannot do much to the figures to compensate for these potential distortions, but it is important to note that the figures themselves are less secure than they may appear.

Another problem, especially with taxes calculated as a percentage of the value of the merchandise, is the degree to which the nominal yield of the tax reflects changes in price rather than changes in the volume of the commodity taxed. To avoid this problem where possible, the tax figures used in Chapter 6 are for duties that were collected at a fixed monetary rate per unit of the commodity. The nominal value of such taxes was thus tied to the actual volume of goods taxed. Elsewhere in the text, including Chapters 2, 10, 11, and 12, it has been necessary to use taxes collected entirely or partly *ad valorem*. In those instances it was necessary to make tentative adjustments based on available price indices in order to find a better approximation of the real trend of commercial activity. The following sections of this appendix detail the sources and some of the numbers on which the summary calculations presented in the body of Chapter 6 were based.

B. Sources on wine consumption

1. Long-term wine consumption estimates

In Chapter 6, section I, B estimates are based on a combination of tax revenues and actual consumption totals. The archives provided official figures for the volume of wine consumption for a number of years. These could be used to test the estimates developed from tax yields. The sources for actual volume are:

1621: AHN, *Consejos, Sala de Alcaldes, libros, año* 1621, fol. 270.

1630–32: AVM, *Secretaria*, sig. 3–231–1. For 1631, see also AHN, *Consejos, Sala de Alcaldes, libros, año* 1782.

1635–36: AVM, *Secretaria*, sig. 2–232–1.

1638: AHN, *Consejos, Sala de Alcaldes, libros, año* 1781.

1698–99: AHN, *Consejos*, leg. 7222.

1731–36: AVM, *Contaduria*, sig. 4–107–4.

1757: Matilla Tascón, "El primer catastro de la villa de Madrid," pp. 465–466.

1772–1847, various years: Madoz, *Diccionario geográfico*, vol. 10, pp. 993–1036. For 1772–74, there is a close fit with tax figures in AVM, *Contaduria*, sig. 3–326–1; and the total for 1829 coincides with AVM, *Contaduria*, sig. 3–191–4.

2. Wine tax revenues and volume estimates

The seventeenth-century wine consumption estimates given in Chapter 6 were derived from the revenues received by the city from a small wine tax imposed at the end of the sixteenth century. Between 1583 and 1680, the wine consumed in Madrid was subjected to 13 different taxes. The oldest, the one used here, was also the simplest and was collected at the rate of 2 *maravedises* for each of the 8 *azumbres* in an *arroba* or *cántara* of wine. As a result, it was always collected at the rate of 16 *maravedises* per *arroba*, unaffected by changes in price or alterations in the size of the *azumbre*, as was the case with some later *sisas*. This history of these taxes and their variants is presented in some detail in ar. eighteenth-century report found in AVM, *Secretaria*, sig. 2–218–13. Throughout the period in which this *sisa* was traced, there are clear references to the tax rate and to the tax as a separate item in the contracts and accounts. The rate was not affected by the radical inflations and deflations of the coinage, and the nominal value was tied to the volume of wine, whether collected in devalued or revalued *maravedises*. Thus, aside from fraud and the profits of the tax farmers, the principal variable in determining the value of the *sisa* was the volume of wine sold in Madrid. In compiling this series, the annual revenues from the *sisa* were recorded for as many years as possible for the period before the practice of letting four-year contracts began. Time, and the state of the archives, dictated that only scattered *sisa* values were collected for subsequent years.

Modest tax reforms were begun during the reign of Charles II, and in the first decades of the eighteenth century the system of *sisas* was considerably reformed. Madoz, in his *Diccionario geográfico,* vol. 10, pp. 1006–1007, details these changes in a brief history of the *sisas* of Madrid. When the series on wine is again fairly complete, it appears in the accounts as one large tax of about 9.8 *reales* per *arroba* with two smaller supplements, the first and second *quartillo* (quarter-*real) en arroba.* Since the series for the first *quartillo* is the most complete, that is the one used as the basis for our eighteenth-century volume estimates. Again the conversion is straightforward, since if the tax was one-fourth *real* per *arroba,* an estimate of volume could be obtained by multiplying the tax yield by four. While the accuracy of specific figures obtained this way can be challenged, the technique establishes the magnitude of consumption and its trends through almost 75 years.

With the exception of 1681–86 and 1698–99, all tax figures used below come from AVM, *Secretaría,* sigs. 3–229, 3–230, 3–231, 3–233, 3–234, 3–254, 3–255, 3–256, 3–257, 3–262; and *Contaduría,* sigs. 1–109–1, 1–110–1, 1–496–2, 1–422–1, 1–144–2, 2–119–1, 1–172–2, 3–326–1, and 4–107–4. For 1681–86 and 1698–99, they come from AHN, *Consejos,* leg. 7222.

The averages given in Table D.1 are derived from the yearly consumption totals that were developed, based upon manipulation of the sources along with such official figures for actual consumption as the documents provided.

While some of the differences between estimated and recorded volume are considerable, most of them can probably be explained by differences in the twelve-month period actually used. For some purposes, January to December was used, for others July to June. The estimates for 1766–67 are less firm, since they are based on a rough conversion of the larger wine tax to *arrobas,* using the ratio found for the 1770's. If anything, the figures are high, since that ratio appears greater in later situations.

The test for the reliability of the estimates is simple—dividing the recorded figures by the estimates to find the margin of error between the two. For the early period, the recorded volume of consumption was below the tax-derived estimate as follows:

1631	2.0%
1632	15.8

1635	8.5%
1636	1.1
1637	2.3
1639	2.4

The figure for 1632 is high, but the accounts make it pretty certain that there is a six-month overlap on the two figures, with the higher total reflecting a twelve-month period including the new harvest of that year, while the lower figure reflected a bad harvest in the preceding year. For most of the eighteenth-century cases in which similar comparisons can be made, the differences are small enough to suggest the same original source for tax and consumption figures.

No great claims are made for the literal accuracy of these figures; the trends are more important. In some cases the figures may include only wine actually taxed, while in others the recorded volume includes exempt wine as well. The years 1630–40 include all types, as do also the much lower figures for 1770–80. Madoz believed that large quantities escaped the tax and were unrecorded in the 1840's. He estimated that the 580,000 *arrobas* of the time really represented 700,000–850,000. For all of these problems we see no way to refine the data further, and we must proceed on the assumption that in any given quarter-century or so the problems are not great enough to obscure the basic tendencies.

C. Sources on olive oil consumption

1. *Sources for Table D.2*

The sources for Table D.2 are generally the same as for wine in the sixteenth and seventeenth centuries. The eighteenth- and nineteenth-century totals and estimates rely on AVM, *Contaduría*, sigs. 2–119–1 and 3–191–4; Madoz; and Manuel Espadas Burgos, "Abasto y hábitos alimenticios," pp. 274–275.

2. *Oil tax revenues and volume estimates*

All of the figures from 1584 to 1648 are based on the *sisa ordinaria del aceite* imposed at the same time as the first wine *sisa*, at the rate of one *maravedi* per *panilla*. There were 100 *panillas* in an *arroba,* and 34 *maravedises* in the *real*, so the conversion from tax figure to volume estimate requires that the tax figure be divided by 2.94. There are no recorded volume figures available for this period to test for the accuracy of this process.

The estimates of the later eighteenth century are based on the single oil *sisa* of the period. The actual yield of that tax was 5.808 times the estimated number of *arrobas*. This ratio was found by dividing the total amount of oil for the five years for which we have recorded totals (1780–84) into the total revenues for those years. Two sets of consumption figures for those years were

Table D.1. *Average Wine Consumption in Madrid, Sixteenth through Nineteenth Centuries*

Years	Volume Estimated(a)	Recorded	No. Years Documented
1584-85	776,050 ar.		2
1586-90	749,417		3
1593	853,188		1
1603-05	226,667		3
1606-10	983,447		5
1611-15	1,207,473		2
1616-20	1,423,888		3
1621-25	1,552,129		4
1626-30	1,627,240		5
1631-35	1,392,063	1,261,777 ar.	4,3
1636-40	1,100,640	1,119,844	4,4
1641-43	855,525		3
1646-50	707,817		5
1651-55	710,073		4
1656-60	734,910		5
1661-65	750,337		5
1666	750,337		1
1671-74	696,468		4
1681-85	554,930		4
1686	529,256		1
1698/9	506,400	458,578	1,1
1731-35	469,165	409,777	3,3
1736-40	482,090	467,090	4,1
1741-45	459,582		5
1746-50	487,571		5
1751-55	416,466		5
1756-60	462,414	500,000	5,1
1761-63	545,969		3
1766-70	449,181		3
1771-75	507,681	496,040	5,4
1776-80	525,360	491,861	5,3
1781-85	446,640		5
1786-90	523,213	508,930	5,1
1791-95	526,794		5
1796-1800	498,172		5
1801-05	497,695		5
1806-08	511,384		3
1818		599,642	1

Table D.1. *Average Wine Consumption in Madrid, Sixteenth through Nineteenth Centuries (cont.)*

Years	Volume Estimated (a)	Recorded	No. Years Documented
1824-25		581,056	2
1826-29		541,755	4
1836-40		439,596	5
1841-45		464,878	4
1846-47		543,209	2

a. To obtain the revenue figure in *reales* from which the estimates are derived, the estimates for 1584-1686 should be divided by 2.125 and the estimates for 1733-1808 should be divided by 4.0.

found, one in Madoz and the other in the municipal archives, with somewhat different yearly totals. The five-year total for the archival data, however, was 99.98% of that for the Madoz data, indicating a common source for both.

C. Sources for estimates of meat consumption

1. Conversion from number of cattle to pounds of meat

To establish total consumption in homogeneous figures, it was necessary to determine average weight of meat from the different types of cattle. The averages are shown in Tables D.3 and D.4. Accordingly, in the conversions from animals slaughtered to pounds of meat, we assume that a sheep yielded 21 pounds of mutton, a cow 350 pounds of beef, and a calf 73 pounds of veal.

2. Explanation of annual totals not given as such in sources

1601: AVM, *Contaduría,* sig. 3–588–5. Sources detail a full week's consumption for February 17–22 as 63 cows and 1,344 sheep. Using the above conversions, multiplying by 52 yielded the estimate given.

1607–08: The documents associated with the *sisa* records already cited indicate that between April 1, 1607, and February 14, 1608, 138,752 sheep were slaughtered, an average of 3,016 per week over 46 weeks. Over 52 weeks, this gives 158,519 head. Supposing the same proportion of sheep to cattle as in 1757, this gives 6,171 beef cattle as the base for calculation. This ratio of sheep to cattle is not very different from the single week for 1601 cited above.

1632: AVM, *Secretaría,* sig. 2–231–3 includes a list of the sheep slaughtered weekly for 27 weeks after August 1. This gives an average of 4,345 per week, an estimated 224,940 sheep over the year. With the same ratio of beef cattle as before, this implies 9,257 cattle.

1743: Palacio Atard, *Los españoles,* p. 298, cites a list of cattle slaughtered

Table D.2. *Average Olive Oil Consumption in Madrid, Sixteenth through Nineteenth Centuries*

Years	Volume		No. Years
	Estimated	Recorded	Documented
1584	30,260 ar.		1
1587-90	31,280		3
1593	24,820		1
1603-05	9,327		3
1606-10	31,926		5
1611-15	44,030		2
1616-20	51,000		3
1621-25	50,456		5
1626-30	47,064		5
1631-35	37,196		5
1635-40	46,703		5
1641-45	58,004		5
1646-47	43,690		2
1757		96,000 ar.	1
1770	138,376		1
1771-75	126,602		5
1776-80	132,579	125,429	5,1
1781-85	131,515	131,907	5,4
1786-90	149,854		5
1791-95	171,048		5
1796-1800	163,435		5
1801-05	128,114		5
1806-08	125,006		3
1818-20		147,360	2
1824-25		133,306	2
1826-29		127,785	4
1838-40		186,741	3
1841-45		230,656	4
1846-47		304,530	2

during 12 weeks in 1743. This averages 4,998 sheep and 140 cattle per week, or 259,896 and 7,280 head per year respectively.

1751: Madoz gives 315,581 sheep and 10,567 beef cattle for the year.

1763: Palacio Atard, *Los españoles,* p. 299, indicates 311,186 sheep and 9,503 beef cattle.

1766: Madoz indicates 325,000 sheep, 9,000 beef cattle, and 1,807 calves

Table D.3. *Salable Meat from Livestock Slaughtered in Sixteenth-Century Valladolid*

Type	Year	Average Yield
Cattle	1566	373 lbs.
Cattle	1586	270
Sheep	1566-67	26
Sheep	1586	29-30

Source: Bennassar, *Valladolid*, p. 72.

Table D.4. *Salable Meat from Livestock Slaughtered in Madrid, Early Nineteenth Century*

Type	Year	Number in Sample	Average Yield
Cattle:	1801	8,589	408 lbs.
	1807	14,628	298
	1844	21,446	403
	1845	24,305	404
	1846	25,427	404
Sheep:	1801	230,649	22.0 lbs.
	1807	278,553	21.3
	1834	22,794	25.9
	1835	29,361	21.6
	1843	3,700	28.1
	1844	173,842	25.0
	1845	153,835	24.3
	1846	181,720	26.0
Calves:	1844	9,873	71.7 lbs.
	1845	10,222	72.8
	1846	14,348	73.5

Sources: For 1801 and 1807: Vicente Palacio Atard, *Los españoles de la Ilustración*, pp. 299-300; for other years: Madoz, vol. 10, pp. 1023, 1031, 1033-1036.

for the year. These look suspiciously like estimates or stereotypical figures rather than actual ones.

1789: Palacio Atard, *Los españoles,* p. 299, gives 320,767 sheep, 9,793 lambs, 16,288 beef cattle, and 3,642 calves. Except for a slight discrepancy on calves, this matches the summary of consumption in AVM, *Secretaría,* sig. 4–5–67.

1796–1801: Palacio Atard, *Los españoles,* p. 300, gives 484,024 sheep and 13,204 beef cattle as the annual average for this period. This is higher than the estimate of 313,382 and 14,213 beef cattle built up from partial figures from 1797–98, but the latter was a bad year for food supply according to AHN, *Consejos,* leg. 6785.

1807: Palacio Atard, *Los españoles,* p. 300, gives 278,553 sheep and 14,678 beef cattle.

These estimates obviously have to be taken as order-of-magnitude figures, although they do not conflict with available figures on pounds of meat sold. Palacio Atard gives as his principal sources AHN, *Consejos,* legs. 6783, 6791–5, and 6796; and AGS, *Gracia y justicia,* leg. 1001.

3. The shift from mutton to beef

As Chapter 6 suggests, the proportion between mutton and beef in urban consumption changed radically at the beginning of the nineteenth century. Table D.5 summarizes the shift.

4. Revenue figures supporting meat consumption figures

Our figures on seventeenth-century meat consumption are supported by a series of revenue figures from the *sisa del rastro,* 1590–1728, which are published in my article, "Madrid y Castilla, 1560–1850," pp. 116–117.

For the eighteenth century, we have comparable figures for revenue from the *sisa del carne mayor,* 1741–1808. The records show a *sisa del carne mayor* and a *sisa del carne menor,* the latter appearing in 1770, probably because of the different nature of the source. Since we are interested in trends, and since the smaller tax regularly ran 8% to 12% the value of the larger, only the larger tax is listed in Table D.6.

Pork consumption was listed separately in the sources, and is given in Table

Table D.5. *Shift from Consumption of Mutton to Consumption of Beef in Madrid, 1766-1867*

Year	Total Beef and Mutton	Mutton
1766	12,056,911 lbs.	72%
1796-1801	14,990,048	69
1825	10,865,935	40
1829	10,874,660	34
1847	16,566,420	23
1865-67	21,611,443	21.5

Sources: For 1766-1847, previously cited sources. For 1865-67, Antonio Fernández García, *El abastecimiento de Madrid en reinado de Isabel II*, pp. 98-99.

Table D.6. *Average Value of the* Sisa del
Carne Mayor, *1741-1808*

Years	Revenue (in thousands)	No. Years Documented
1741-45	3,269 rs.	4.5
1745-49	3,675	4
1752-55	3,139	4
1756-60	3,463	5
1761	3,358	1
1770	3,417	1
1771-75	3,434	5
1776-80	3,479	5
1781-85	3,252	5
1786-90	3,840	5
1791-95	3,849	5
1796-1800	3,865	5
1801-05	3,491	5
1806-08	3,655	3

Sources: AVM, *Contaduría*, sigs. 2-419-1 and 2-234-1.

Table D.7. *Average Amount of Pork Taxed in Madrid, 1753-1806 and 1838-1848*

Years	Volume (in thousands)
1753-55	2,409 lbs.
1756-60	2,891
1761-65	2,828
1766-70	2,684
1771-75	3,139
1776-80	3,128
1781-85	3,282
1786-90	4,458
1791-95	6,637
1796-1800	5,685
1801-05	6,020
1806	5,797
1838-40	6,791
1841-45	6,662
1846-48	6,518

Sources: For 1753-1770: AVM, *Contaduría*, sig. 1-50-1; for 1770-1806: AVM, *Contaduría*, sig. 2-119-1; for 1838-48: Fernández García, *El abastecimiento*, p. 99. Also AHN, *Consejos*, legs. 6785 and 6788-38.

D.7, which indicates the number of pounds taxed between 1753 and 1806 and during the decade 1838–1848.

The sources present an interpretive problem in this case, because it is possible that they include a wider range of pork products after 1789. In that year a distinction appears between whole carcasses and pork taxed by weight, while the earlier sources are silent on this detail. A sharp upward trend of consumption is established well before 1789, in any case, so at the worst the rate of increase is somewhat overstated for the years around 1790.

III. Relative prices of basic commodities

The discussion of relative prices encountered from time to time in Chapter 6 is based on some simple calculations. For each year that prices are available, the price of a pound of bread was divided into the price of one *azumbre* of wine, one pound of beef, one pound of mutton, and one *panilla* of olive oil. Thus, for example, in 1556 an *azumbre* of wine was equivalent to 5.714 pounds of bread, a pound of beef to 2.517 pounds of bread, a pound of mutton to 4.724 pounds of bread, and a *panilla* of olive oil to 1.379 pounds of bread. The prices are derived from Earl Hamilton, *American Treasure* and *War and Prices,* with a few at the end taken from Gonzalo Anes Álvarez, *Economia e "Ilustración"* (1969), "Las fluctuaciones de los precios del trigo, de la cebada y del aceite en España, 1788–1808."

IV. Consumption of nonstaple commodities

Our sources yielded serial data on consumption or tax revenues linked with a number of commodities aside from wheat, wine, meat, olive oil, and charcoal. These include quite extensive series on wax, sugar, cacao, soap, and fish, two of which begin in the mid-eighteenth century and the remainder in 1770. Actual quantities are given in many cases. For others, the conversions from tax revenue were relatively direct: wax was taxed at the rate of one *quartillo* per pound, cacao at one *real* per pound, and sugar at about 9 *reales* per *arroba* (25 pounds). Additional sources provided more scattered evidence on fresh versus preserved and salted fish, chocolate, coffee, and distilled liquor. In tables D.8 and D.9 we attempt to summarize this data in support of some of the discussion of these commodities in Chapter 6, and at the same time provide a rough idea of the levels of consumption in the city at various times. Table D.8 indicates either the level of consumption in 1789 or the average annual consumption in 1786–89 as the base = 100 for the indices of consumption in Table D.9, which in turn are the basis for Figure 6.4. In this way, even without the detailed statistics, the reader can reconstruct a rough estimate of the level of consumption for any commodity through much of the century between 1750 and 1850.

Table D.8. *Base Consumption Levels for Indices of Consumption on Table 6.8*

Commodity	Base Years	Volume
Barley	1789	254,286 fn.
Cacao and chocolate	1786-90	1,070,709 lbs.
Coffee	1789	13,955 lbs.
Distilled liquors	1789	63,077 ar.
Fish (total)	1789	108,636 ar.
Fish (salt)	1786-90	66,969 ar.
Fish (fresh and preserved)	1789	42,498 ar.
Meat (beef and mutton)	1789	12,565,214 lbs.
Meat (beef, mutton, pork)	1789	19,739,939 lbs.
Olive oil	1786-90	149,855 ar.
Soap	1786-90	61,209 ar.
Sugar	1786-90	81,506 ar.
Wax	1789	347,525 ar.
Wheat	1789	742,874 fn.
Wine	1786-90	523,173 ar.

Sources: AVM, *Contaduría*, sigs. 2-119-1 (for all series, 1770-1808) and 2-299-1 (fish, 1737-39); AVM, *Secretaría*, sig. 4-5-67 (all commodities, 1789); AHN, *Consejos*, legs. 6788-39 (fish, 1760-64), 6792-1, fol. 37 (soap, 1749-68), 6792-13 (soap, 1801); Espadas Burgos, "Abasto y hábitos alimenticios;" Fernández García, *El abastecimiento*; Madoz, vol. 10, pp. 1037-1059, 1065-1072; Palacio Atard, *Los españoles*, pp. 248-306.

In addition to the consumption data for the limited range of items listed above, the documents contain detailed lists of urban imports for 1789, 1847, and 1848. These sources are based on fiscally inspired records and no doubt suffer from underreporting, but they do provide some insights into changing patterns of consumption between the eighteenth and nineteenth centuries. Some of the contrasts are discussed in the text, but often with a considerable degree of abstraction. To provide substance for the abstractions, Tables D.10 and D.11 indicate consumption figures for 1789, 1746, and 1848 for all commodities that could be compared directly without confusion due to nomenclature or contemporary classifications. Table D.10 deals with foodstuffs, Table D.11 with miscellaneous commodities and manufactures.

Table D.9. *Indices for Urban Consumption of Bulk Commodities in Madrid, 1756-1847*

Years	Wine	Wheat	Barley	Olive Oil	Salt Cod	Fresh and Preserved Fish
1756-60	88				58	
1760-64						
1767		74				
1776-80				88	84	
1786-90	100	100	100	100	100	100
1796-1800	95	126		109	130	
1815-20						
1818	115	63		98		65
1824-29	106	88		87		79
1830-31					62	
1836-40	84	100	98	126		71
1839-41						
1844-47	101	103	123	192	81	149

Years	Beef	Mutton	Pork	Beef, Mutton, and Pork	Beef and Mutton	Soap
1756-60						59
1760-64					82	
1767						
1776-80						67
1786-90	100	100	100	100	100	100
1796-1800	81	151	94	110	119	114
1815-20					85	
1818	102	70				
1824-29	113	60			84	93
1830-31						
1836-40	122	51	105	91	83	
1839-41						117
1844-47	174	60	106	110	112	155

Years	Wax	Sugar	Cacao and Chocolate	Coffee	Distilled Liquor
1756-60					
1760-64					
1767					
1776-80	88	74	77		
1786-90	100	100	100	100	100
1796-1800	90	88	91		
1815-20					
1818					
1824-29	57	77	62		
1830-31	60	102	82	544	95
1836-40			72		
1839-41	44	119	41		92
1844-47	48	159	87		96

Sources: Index figures are based on base-period consumption given in Table D.8 and other consumption data provided by sources for that table.

Table D.10. *Foodstuffs Imported into Madrid, 1789, 1847, and 1848*

Commodity	1789	1847	1848
Cereals, legumes, etc.			
Wheat and flour	773,639 fn.	541,885 fn.	955,912 fn.
Beans, peas, etc.	231,880	203,080	400,979
Potatoes	—	45,000	80,000
Barley, oats, rye	236,223	195,994	
Subtotal	1,241,742 fn.	985,959 fn.	1,436,891 fn.
Fish			
Salt fish	66,138 ar.	62,870 ar.	71,088 ar.
Fresh fish	32,553	24,253	29,279
Preserved fish	9,945	18,689	18,959
Freshwater fish	5,943	5,366	4,015
Subtotal	114,579 ar.	111,178 ar.	123,341 ar.
Meat			
Beef and veal	6,801,260 lb.	12,852,865 lb.	11,920,290 lb.
Mutton and lamb	8,146,484	3,782,102	4,163,326
Pork(a)	7,177,329	5,049,337	5,083,077
Subtotal	22,125,073 lb.	21,684,304 lb.	21,166,693 lb.
Fats and oil			
Olive oil	126,289 ar.	289,819 ar.	294,801 ar.
Lard	17,865	8,500	7,500
Tallow	14,007	5,729	5,601
Subtotal	158,161 ar.	304,048 ar.	307,902 ar.
Alcoholic beverages			
Wine	508,930 ar.	541,716 ar.	523,200 ar.
Vinegar	113,184	29,716	39,955
Distillates	63,078	46,565	52,200
Alcohol	3,358	252	—
Subtotal	688,550 ar.	618,249 ar.	615,355 ar.
Colonial commodities			
Sugar	73,999 ar.	85,000 ar.	172,080 ar.
Coffee	13,955 lb.	61,128 lb.	—
Cacao	1,198,837 lb.	761,816 lb.	724,875 lb.
Miscellaneous foodstuffs			
Eggs	1,045,680 dz.	1,707,678 dz.	1,865,986 dz.
Milk	10,515 ca.	36,745 ca.	54,302 ca.
Cheese	9,227 ar.	17,000 ar.	16,500 ar.
Honey	9,383 ar.	3,557 ar.	4,529 ar.
Candy, nougat	276,450 lb.	77,655 lb.	56,395 lb.

a. The meat total for 1789 is probably low in that it does not include any apparent reference to *chorizo* or other sausage products. In 1847-48 these items accounted for about 600,000 pounds of meat, or just under 3% of the total. It is likely that they had about the same importance earlier.

Table D.11. *Miscellaneous Commodities and Manufactures Imported into Madrid, 1789 and 1847*

Commodity	1789	1847
Rope sandals and shoes	23,437 pr.	69,000 pr.
Clay pottery	2,710 loads	3,500 loads
Beeswax	347,524 lb.	88,382 lb.
Brooms	8,519 dz.	8,960 dz.
Lavender	21,725 lb.	5,175 lb.
Aromatic and elastic gums	14,610 lb.	19,605 lb.
Gloves	45,176 pr.	7,800 pr.
Plaster	407,405 ar.	300,000 ar.
Soap	61,724 ar.	101,055 ar.
Esparto cording	30,136 ar.	144 ar.
Razors	5,568	10,188
Paper	104,877 reams	136,483 reams
Combs	128,844 pcs.	75,228 pcs.
Pens	46,652 pcs.	145,000 pcs.
Handkerchiefs		
Cotton	97,846 pcs.	292,800 pcs.
Silk	9,351 pcs.	8,700 pcs.
Subtotal	107,197 pcs.	301,500 pcs.
Stockings		
Cotton	107,817 pr.	72,978 pr.
Worsted	16,632 pr.	31,800 pr.
Silk	47,326 pr.	10,188 pr.
Subtotal	171,775 pr.	114,966 pr.

Sources: AVM, *Secretaría*, sig. 4-5-67; Madoz, vol. 10, pp. 1037-1059, 1065-1072.

Appendix E: Archival References for Market Trend Data

The index figures illustrated in the figures of Chapter 11 and the revenue and index figures in the tables of Chapters 10 and 12, as well as the market indicators for Chapter 2, are based on annual yields to municipal authorities from various taxes on commercial activities or on the projected return from rental contracts signed with tax farmers. No coherent series of this kind actually existed in the archives, so it was necessary to compile them year by year, tax by tax, from hundreds of rental contracts and municipal account books. The raw tax data and estimates for wheat, wine, and meat consumed in Madrid have been published elsewhere.[1] Some gaps in those early series have been filled, thanks to additional research, and those findings are incorporated into the indicators used in the text. These sources are listed in Appendix D.

Tax data present problems for long-term analysis because of the possibilities of distortion due to fraud, evasion, inflation, and increases in tax rates. For the centrally important series from Madrid, the possibility of tax increases is controlled by information on the nature of the taxes and two versions of a detailed history of their evolution.[2] Beyond that, the assumption of stable rates is based on extensive experience with data from 15 municipal archives in Spain.

Individual taxes were created to service particular royal or municipal loans or obligations, and were rarely changed in isolation. If tax rates were altered, it was in the context of a more sweeping municipal reform, and the structure of the municipal accounts themselves changed enough to be apparent when

---

1. Ringrose, "Madrid y Castilla, 1560–1850."

2. AHN, *Consejos*, leg. 511–5; *Alcaldes*, libro for 1623, fol. 545; AVM, *Secretaria*, sigs. 2–307–9, 2–487–28, 3–19–4, 3–11–1. Further indication of the nature of some of these municipal taxes in general is found in Antonia Heredía Herrera, "Los corredores de lonja en Sevilla y Cádiz" (1970), pp. 183–198.

constructing the serial data. As the list of taxes in Table E.1 indicates, enough such changes turned up to suggest that hidden modifications were few. The fee schedules of some taxes were partially or entirely expressed as *ad valorem* duties, creating the risk of an inflationary effect in the trends for the volume of commerce. The three food series from Madrid are immune to inflation effects, since the wheat figures are direct volume totals, and taxes on wine and meat were a fixed nominal sum per unit sold. Where the effects of inflation presented an interpretive risk, a version of the series adjusted by the most appropriate price series has been provided in the text.

In general, the serial data appear to be much superior to similar material from other countries. Rental contracts were generally annual or biennial until about 1650 and during much of the eighteenth century, reflecting cyclical trends much better than the *octroi* of Toulouse analyzed by Gebhardt and Mercadier.[3] For the most part, the absolute value of each annual figure is far less important than the assumption of reasonable consistency in the medium run and the analysis of relative changes.[4]

Table E.1 lists the taxes and commercially linked revenues for which serial data of some sort was developed. Not all of these were actually used in the text, since some were redundant. With the exception of the figures given in Appendix A, the raw figures will not be presented here, as they are quite extensive.[5]

3. Monique Gebhart and Claude Mercadier, *L'octroi de Toulouse à la veille de la Révolution.*
4. For a comment on developing and using such series, see Fernand Braudel, "Pour une histoire serielle: Seville et l'Atlantique, 1504–1650" (1963).
5. Some of the data for the period after 1650 has been published elsewhere; see Ringrose, "Perspectives on the Economy of Eighteenth-Century Spain" (1973).

Table E.1. *Tax Series Used In Preparing This Study*

Albacete

Almotacenía, 1543–1611
Correduría, 1543–1611
Almotacenía y Correduría, 1693–1701, 1762–98
Tierras de Labor, 1762–98

Sources: Municipal Archives of Albacete, uncatalogued municipal accounts.

Alcalá de Henares

Corredurías y Pesos, 1638–1720
Barca del Rio Henares, 1638–1720

Source: Municipal Archives of Alcalá de Henares, *Cuentas de Propios y Rentas.*

Benevente

Barca de Santa Cristina, 1690–1799
Barca de Villafer, 1690–1799
Renta de Lanas, 1690–1799
Pesos, Barras, Medidas y Contraste, 1690–1799

Source: Municipal Archives of Benevente. (Small, but totally uncatalogued as of 1965. Materials located by direct examination of the collection).

Burgos

Portazgo de Pancorbo, 1544, 1583–91, 1610–35, 1675–99
Portazgo de Barba del Mercadillo, 1675–99
Derecho de Barras y Puertas, 1675–99

Source: Municipal Archives of Burgos.

Cádiz

Aduanilla de Medio por Ciento, 1656–1801
Barca de Sancti Petri, 1656–1801
Pasaje de Puerto Santa María, 1656–1743
Pasaje de Puerto Real, 1656–1707

Source: Municipal Archives of Cádiz. Taken from a nearly complete series of books labeled *Cuentas de arbitrios y Propios de la Ciudad* for the years indicated.

Table E.1. *Tax Series Used in Preparing This Study* (*cont.*)

Cartagena

Renta Mayor de Medio por Ciento, 1602–1717
Mollages Dobles, 1602–1717
Correduría de Carros, 1611–84, 1705–20
Saca de Pescado, 1614–1720
Renta Mayor y Almotacenía, 1720–92
Correduría de Carros y Saca de Pescado, 1720–92
Renta de la Lonja, 1764–1802

Source: Municipal Archives of Cartagena, uncatalogued municipal accounts. (Catalogues existed and served to indicate what might be available, but the collection had been badly disrupted during the Civil War and as of 1965 had not been reordered.)

Córdoba

Derecho de Puertas, 1753–79

Source: Municipal Archives of Córdoba, sec.5, ser. 40, caja 26, docs. 21, 23, 29–31, 33, 36, 37.

Cuenca

Correduría Mayor y Sisa Vieja, 1577–1795

Source: Municipal Archives of Cuenca, legs. 147–154, 582, 1131, 1546, 1549.

Granada

Correduría de Azúcar, 1635–96, 1765–99, 1815–19
Correduría de Trigo, 1656–86, 1765–97, 1815–19
Alhóndiga, 1635–71, 1782–98, 1815–19

Source: Municipal Archives of Granada. (As of 1965, the catalogues did not correspond well with the actual shelving of materials, and materials had to be located by scanning labels.)

León

Peso de Mercancías, 1563–1635, 1648–56
Haber del Peso, 1721–81
Peso de Mercancías, Azucar y Cacao, 1753–97
Peso de San Francisco de Vino y Aceite, 1753–97

Source: Municipal Archives of León (scattered, uncatalogued accounts).

Table E.1. *Tax Series Used in Preparing This Study (cont.)*

Málaga

The accounting records showed three different formats and carry the possibility that the rates of taxation may also have changed. Hence it is necessary to assume that the data from each format constitute a separate series in which a given level of revenue from a given tax does not necessarily represent the same volume of traffic in each period.

First accounting format:
Lonja y Correduría de Pasas y Vino, 1618–83
Arbitrio de Gudiel sobre Pescado, Corambre, Especias, Hierro, Herraje, Miel, Cera, Madera, Tapicería, Lienzos, Paños, Sombreros y Medias, 1637–82
Arbitrio de Bacalao, 1638–1704
Second accounting format:
Lonja, Parte de Tierra, 1704–35
Correduría de Pasas y Vino, 1704–29
Arbitrio de Bacalao, 1710–24
Third accounting format:
Lonja, Parte de Tierra, 1743–63, 1785–1800
Lonja y Correduría de Pasas y Vino, 1752–63
Correduría de Pasas y Vino, 1770–1818
Arbitrio de Bacalao, 1768–1817

Sources: Municipal Archives of Málaga, legajos:				
7	36	67F	98F	125F
18	37	72F	99F	127F
21	42	75F	102F–105F	131F
23	44	78F	107F–109F	135F
24	45	92F	112F	206F
27	50	95F	115F–122F	212F
29–34	65F	96F	124F	

Palencia

Peso Real, 1662–1777
Corredurías del Pueblo, 1672–1778
Renta del Poyo, 1653–1776
Renta de la Greda, 1661–1779

Source: Municipal Archives of Palencia. (Account bundles were located by direct search with the aid of original inventories.)

Sevilla

Corredurías de Cargas de Mercancias que Salieron de la Ciudad, 1768–1806

Source: Municipal Archives of Sevilla, sec. 2 (*Contaduría*), carpetas 285–295, 326, 327. Toledo

Table E.1. *Tax Series Used in Preparing This Study* (*cont.*)

Almotacenia, 1540–1769
Peso del Mercado, 1540–1769
Renta de Paños, 1540–1769
Renta de Lienzos, 1540–1769
Renta de la Seda, 1625–83, 1715–69
Portazgo de Visagra, 1540–1769

Source: Municipal Archives of Toledo. (Bound account books labeled by date were stored in the back room of the archives. Michael Weisser tells me that the materials have been given a degree of organization since 1965.)

Zafra

Portazgo, 1536–1605 (scattered years), 1621–1726

Source: Medinaceli Archives, Casa de Piloto, Sevilla.

Appendix F: Toledo Population Figures

As with Madrid (see Chapter 2), the sources for the population of Toledo are varied and impressionistic, being based upon a handful of census-like documents created by the civil or religious hierarchies for their own purposes. Until Michael Weisser completes the work on Toledo which he has under way as this is being written, we will have to be satisfied with fragmentary data. Table F.1 summarizes figures encountered in various primary and secondary sources.

Table F.1. *Figures and Estimates for the Population of Toledo*

Year	Vecinos	Inhabitants	Source
1530	5,989	25-30,000	González, pp. 70-71
			Larraz López, pp. 94-95
			Madoz, vol. 10, p. 586
			Domínguez Ortiz, *XVII*, p. 137
1571	12,412	60,000	Domínguez Ortiz, *XVII*, p. 137
1591	10,933	55,000	González, pp. 70-71
			Madoz, vol. 10, p. 586
			Larraz López, pp. 94-95
			Domínguez Ortiz, *XVII*, p. 137
1597	-	80,000	Jiménez de Gregorio, p. 20
1630	-	20,000	Weisser
1646	5,000	22-25,000	González, pp. 70-71
			Madoz, vol. 10, p. 586
			Larraz López, pp. 94-95
			Jiménez de Gregorio, p. 20
			Domínguez Ortiz, *XVII*, p. 137
			(considers this high)
1669	-	10,000	Domínguez Ortiz, *XVII*, pp.129-134
			(considers this low)
1694	5,000	22-25,000	González, pp. 70-71
			Madoz, vol. 10, p. 586
			Larraz López, pp. 94-95
			Domínguez Ortiz, *XVII*, p. 137
1723	2,436	12,180	Jiménez de Gregorio, p. 20
1740	4,000	-	Estrada
1751	4,872	20-24,000	Estrada
1825	3,764	14,950	Miñano, vol. 8, p. 453
1842	-	14,778	Madoz, vol. 14, p. 839
1857	-	21,297	Martorell, pp. 98-99
1926	-	25,308	Martorell, pp. 98-99

Sources: Domínguez Ortiz, *La sociedad española en el siglo XVII*; Juan Antonio de Estrada, *Población general de España* (1768); Tomás González, *Censo español del siglo XVI* (1828); Fernando Jiménez de Gregorio, *Toledo a mediados del siglo XVIII* (1959); Larraz López, *La época del mercantilismo en Castilla, 1500-1700*; Pascual Madoz, *Diccionario estadístico-histórico de España* (1849); Martorell Téllez Girón, *Aportaciones al estudio de la población de Madrid en el siglo XVII* (1930); Sebastian de Miñano, *Diccionario geográfico-estadístico de España y Portugal* (1826-27); Weisser, "The Decline of Castile Revisited: The Case of Toledo."

Bibliography

I. Archives Consulted

Archivo del Banco de España (Madrid)
Archivo del Duque de Medinaceli
  (Sevilla)
Archivo General de Simancas (AGS)
  Direción General de Rentas (DGR),
    Única Contribución
  Diversos
  Expedientes de Hacienda
Archivo Histórico Nacional (Madrid)
  (AHN)
  Sección de Clero
  Sección de Consejos
  Sección de Consejos, Sala de Alcaldes
    y Corte
  Sección de Hacienda
  Sección de Osuna
Archivo de la Villa de Madrid (AVM)
  Sección de Contaduría
  Sección de Corregimiento
  Sección de Estadística
  Sección de Secretaría

Archivo de la Real Sociedad Económica
  Matritense
Biblioteca Nacional (Madrid) (BN)
  Sección de Manuscritos (MS)
Municipal Archives:
  Albacete
  Alcalá de Henares
  Benevente
  Burgos
  Cádiz
  Cartagena
  Córdoba
  Cuenca
  Granada
  León
  Málaga
  Palencia
  Sevilla
Real Academia de la Historia (Madrid)
  (RAH)

The most important archival collections for this project are in the AVM, the AGS, and the AHN. The more important clusters of sources, such as those involving food supply, economic structure of Madrid, and the tax series reflecting commercial activity are discussed in the appropriate places in the Appendices or in the footnotes. For examples of the potential of the *Catastro* for Spanish economic history, see Ringrose, *Transportation; El Antiguo Régimen: El Señorío de Buitrago*; and *El Antiguo Régimen: La Renta Nacional de Castilla.*

II. Published Primary Sources

Bourgoing, J. F. *The Modern State of Spain*. 4 vols. London, 1808 (translation of Paris ed. of 1807).

Caballero, Fermín. *Reseña geográfica-estadística de España*. 2nd ed. Madrid, 1868.

Canga Argüelles, José. *Diccionario de hacienda con aplicación a España*. 2 vols. Madrid, 1834; facsimile reprint: Madrid: Instituto de Estudios Fiscales, 1968.

Caxa de Leruela, Miguel. *Restauración de la abundancia de España*. Madrid, 1732.

Correo Mercantile. 1792–1794. Spanish commercial guide. In Bancroft Library.

Estrada, Juan Antonio de. *Población general de España*. 2 vols. Madrid, 1768.

Ford, Richard. *Handbook for Spain, 1845*. 3 vols. First published 1845. London: Centaur, 1965.

González, Tomás. *Censo español del siglo XVI*. Madrid, 1828.

Grandmaison, Geoffroy de, ed. *Correspondence du Comte de la Forest, ambassadeur de France en Espagne, 1808–1813*. 7 vols. Paris: Picard et Fils, 1905–1913.

Guia de Forasteros. Guide to government and business in Madrid, published yearly after 1740.

Iglesias, Josep, ed. *El cens de Comte de Floridablanca, 1787: Parte de Catalunya*. Barcelona: Fundació Salvador Casajuana, 1968.

Jovellanos, Gaspar Melchor de. *Informe de ley agraria*. Barcelona: Ediciones de Materiales, 1968.

Labrada, José Lucas. *Descripción económica del Reino de Galicia*. Vigo: Ed. Galaxia, 1971. (First published: El Ferrol, 1804.)

Larruga, Eugenio. *Memorias políticas y económicas sobre los frutos, comercio, fábricas y minas de España*. 45 vols. Madrid, 1787–1800.

León Pinelo, Antonio Rodríguez. *Anales de Madrid, 1598–1658*. Madrid: Instituto de Estudios Madrileños, 1971.

Mackenzie, Alexander. *Two Years in Spain, by a Young American*. Boston, 1828.

Madoz, Pascual. *Diccionario geográfico de España*. 16 vols. Madrid, 1847.

———. *Madrid: Audiencia, Provincia, Intendencia, Vicaría, Partido y Villa*. Madrid, 1848.

Manual de España. Madrid, 1810.

Matilla Tascón, Antonio. "El primer catastro de la villa de Madrid." *Revista del Archivo, Biblioteca y Museo* 69 (1961): 463–630.

———, ed. *Balanza de comercio exterior de España en el año 1795*. Madrid: Ministerio de Hacienda, 1965.

Mesonero Romanos, Ramón. "El extranjero en su patria." In Evaristo Correa Calderon, ed., *Escenas matritenses*. Salamanca: Anaya, 1970. (Written in 1833.)

———. *Manual de Madrid*. Madrid, 1833.

———. *Obras*, ed. Carlos Seco Serrano. 2 vols. In *Biblioteca de Autores Españoles* vols. 199–200. Madrid: Atlas, 1967. (First published ca. 1830–60.)

Miñano, Sebastian de. *Diccionario geográfico-estadístico de España y Portugal*. 8 vols. Madrid, 1826–27.

Moreau de Jonnes, Alexandre. *Statistique de l'Espagne*. Paris, 1834.

Pellicer de Ossau y Tovar, José. *Avisos históricos*. Madrid: Taurus, 1965.

Saavedra Fajardo, Diego. *Idea de un principe político-cristiano*. In his *Obras*, vol. 25

of *Biblioteca de autores españoles*. Madrid: Atlas, 1947. (First published in 1640.)

Sánchez, Pedro Antonio. *La economía gallega en los escritos de Pedro Antonio Sánchez,* ed. Xosé M. Beiras. Vigo: Ed. Galaxia, 1973. (Written ca. 1795–1806.)

Townsend, Joseph. *A Journey Through Spain in the Years 1786 and 1787,* 2nd ed. London, 1792.

Uztaríz, Gerónymo de. *Theórica y práctica de comercio y de marina.* (Facsimile reprint of 1742 edition.) Introduction by Gabriel Franco. Madrid: Aguilar, 1968.

Viñas y Mey, Carmelo, and Ramón Paz, eds. *Relaciones de los pueblos de España ordenadas por Felipe II, Provincia de Madrid,* and *Provincia de Toledo.* 4 vols. Madrid: CSIC, 1949, 1951, 1963.

III. Secondary Sources

Abrams, Philip. "Towns and Economic Growth: Some Theories and Problems." In Abrams and Wrigley, *Towns in Societies,* pp. 9–33.

———, and E. A. Wrigley, eds. *Towns in Societies, Essays in Economic History and Historical Sociology.* London: Cambridge University Press, 1978.

Alcalá-Zamora y Queipo de Llano, José. "Progresos tecnológicos y limitaciones productivas en la nueva siderurgia andaluza del siglo XVIII." *Hispania* 37 (1977): 379–414.

Alcazar Molina, Cayetano. *El Madrid del Dos de Mayo.* Madrid: Instituto de Estudios Madrileños, 1952.

Alfaya L., María Concepción. "Datos para la historia económica y social de España." *Revista de la Biblioteca, Archivo y Museo,* no. 3 (1926), pp. 203–204.

Andalucía moderna. 4 vols. Published as vols. 4–7 of *Actas del primer congreso de historia de Andalucia (1976).* 9 vols. Córdoba: Monte de Piedad y Caja de Ahorros de Córdoba, 1978.

Anes Álvarez, Gonzalo. "La agricultura española desde comienzos del siglo XIX hasta 1968." In *Ensayos sobre la economía española a mediados del siglo XIX.*

———. "Antecedentes próximos del motín contra Esquilache." *Moneda y Crédito,* no. 128 (1974): 219–224.

———. *El Antiguo Régimen: Los Borbones.* Vol. IV of *Historia de España Alfaguara.* Madrid: Alianza Editorial, 1975.

———. *Las crisis agrarias en la España moderna.* Madrid: Taurus, 1970.

———. *Economía e "Ilustración" en la España del siglo XVIII.* Barcelona: Ariel, 1969.

———. "Los pósitos en la España del siglo XVIII." *Moneda y Crédito,* no. 105 (1968): 39–69.

———. "Tendencias de la producción agrícola en tierras de la Corona de Castilla, siglos XVI a XIX." *Hacienda Pública Española,* no. 55 (1978): 97–112.

———, ed. *Memoriales y discursos de Francisco Martínez de la Mata.* Madrid: Ed. Moneda y Crédito, 1971.

————, and Jean Paul LeFlem. "Las crisis del siglo XVII: Producción agrícola, precios e ingresos en tierras de Segovia." *Moneda y Crédito,* no. 93 (1965).

Arangurén, José Luis. *Moral y sociedad: La moral social española en el siglo XIX.* Madrid: Cuadernos para el diálogo, 1970.

Artola, Miguel. *Antiguo Régimen y revolución liberal.* Barcelona: Ariel, 1978.

————. *La burguesía revolucionaria, 1808–1869.* Madrid: Alianza, 1973.

Baehrel, Rene. *Une croissance, la Basse-Provence rural, fin du XVIe siècle-1789.* Paris: SEVPEN, 1961.

Barbier, Jacques. "Peninsular Finances and Colonial Trade: The Dilemma of Charles IV's Spain." Paper presented to the American Historical Association, 1978.

Barea, Arturo. *The Forge.* Trans. Sir Peter Mitchell. London: Faber and Faber, 1944.

Barea Ferrer, José Luis. "Vicisitudes en torno a la construcción del nuevo puerto de Málaga en el siglo XVI." In *Andalucía moderna,* vol. 1, pp. 99–108.

Basas Ferñandez, Manuel. "Burgos, plaza de cambios en el siglo XVI." *Hispania* 38 (1968): 654–693.

————. *El Consulado de Burgos en el siglo XVI.* Seville: CSIC, 1963.

Bejarano, Francisco. *Historia del Consulado y de la Junta de Comercio de Málaga (1783–1859).* Madrid: CSIC, 1949.

————. *La industria de la seda en Málaga durante el siglo XVI.* Madrid: CSIC, 1951.

Beltrami, Daniele. *La penetrazione economica dei veneziani en Terraferma: Forze di Lavoro e proprietà fondiaria nelle campagne venete dei secoli XVII e XVIII.* Venice: Istituto per la Collaborazione Culturale, 1961.

————. *Saggio de storia dell'agricoltura nella Republica di Venezia durante l'et moderna.* Venice, 1955.

Beneyto Pérez, Juan. *Historia social de España y de Hispanoamérica.* Madrid: Aguilar, 1961.

Bennassar, Bartolomé. "L'alimentation d'une capitale espagnol au XVIe siècle: Valladolid." In Jean-Jacques Hémardinquer, ed., *Pour une histoire de l'alimentation.* Paris: Colin, 1970.

————. "Medina del Campo: Un example des structures urbaines de l'Espagne au XVIe siècle." *Revue d'Histoire Économique et Sociale* 39 (1961): 474–495.

————. *Recherches sur les grandes épidémies dans le nord de l'Espagne à la fin du XVIe siècle.* Paris: SEVPEN, 1969.

————. *Valladolid au siècle d'or; Une ville de Castille et sa campagne au XVIe siècle.* Paris: Mouton, 1967.

Bergier, Jean-François. *Genève et l'économie européenne de la renaissance.* Paris: SEVPEN, 1963.

————. *Problèmes de l'histoire économique de la Suisse. Population, vie rurale, échanges et trafics.* Berne, Switz.: Francke Editions, 1968.

Bernal, Antonio-Miguel. "Haciendas locales y tierras de propios, funcionalidad económica de los patrimonios municipales (siglos XVI-XIX)." *Hacienda Pública Española,* no. 55 (1978): 285–312.

————, and Antonio García-Baquero. *Tres siglos del comercio sevillano, 1598–1868:*

Cuestiones y problemas. Seville: Cámara Oficial de Comercio, Industria y Navegación de Sevilla, 1976.

Berry, Brian J. L. *Geografía de los centros de mercado y distribución al por menor.* Barcelona: Ed. Vicens Vives, 1971.

———, Edgar C. Conkling, and D. Michael Ray. *The Geography of Economic Systems.* Englewood Cliffs, N.J.: Prentice-Hall, 1976.

Bilbao, Luis María. "Crisis y reconstrucción de la economía vascongada en el siglo XVII." *Saioak: Revista de Estudios Vascos* 1 (1977): 157–180.

———. "Transformaciones económicas en el país vasco durante los siglos XVI y XVII." In *Historia del pueblo vasco,* pp. 111–143. San Sebastian: Ed. Rein, 1979.

Boserup, Ester. *Conditions of Agricultural Growth: The Economics of Agrarian Change Under Population Pressure.* Chicago: Aldine Press, 1965.

Brandes, Stanley. *Migration, Kinship and Community: Tradition and Transition in a Spanish Village.* New York: Academic Press, 1975.

Braudel, Fernand. *La Méditerranée et le monde méditerranéen a l'époque de Philippe II,* 2nd ed. 2 vols. Paris: Colin, 1966. In English: *The Mediterranean and the Mediterranean World in the Age of Philip II.* 2 vols. New York: Harper and Row, 1973.

———, and Frank Spooner. "Prices in Europe from 1450 to 1750." *Cambridge Economic History,* vol. 4. London: Cambridge University Press, 1967.

Brenner, Robert. "Agrarian Class Structure and Economic Development in Pre-Industrial Europe." *Past and Present,* no. 70 (1976).

———. "The Origins of Capitalist Development: A Critique of Neo-Smithian Marxism." *New Left Review* 104 (1977): 25–92.

Burguesia mercantil gaditana (1650–1868). Procedings of the *XXXI Congreso Luso-Español para el progreso de las ciencias.* Cádiz: Instituto de Estudios Gaditanos, 1976.

Bustelo García del Real, Francisco. "Algunos reflexiones sobre la población española de principios del siglo XVIII." *Anales de Economía,* no. 15 (1972): 89–106.

———. "La población española en la segunda mitad del siglo XVIII." *Moneda y Crédito,* no. 123 (1972): 53–104.

———. "Población y subdesarrollo en Galicia: sugerencias para un estudio histórico." *Hacienda Pública Española,* no. 55 (1978): 147–166.

———. "El Vecindario General de España de 1712 a 1717: Censo de Campoflorido." *Revista Internacional de Sociología* 32, nos. 7–8 (1973) and 11–12 (1974).

Caballero, Fermín. *Fomento de la poblaciion rural.* Madrid, 1863.

Cabero Diéguez, Valentín. *Evolución y estructura urbana de Astorga.* Salamanca: Universidad de Salamanca, 1973.

Cabrillana, Nicolás. "Villages désertés en Espagne." In *Villages désertés et histoire économique, XIe-XVIIIe siécles.* Paris: SEVPEN, 1965.

Callahan, William J. "Caridad, sociedad y economía en el siglo XVIII." *Moneda y Crédito,* no. 146 (1978): 65–76.

———. "Corporate Charity in Spain: The Hermandad del Refugio of Madrid, 1518–1814." *Histoire Sociale—Social History* 9 (1976): 159–186.

———. "Crown, Nobility, and Industry in Eighteenth-Century Spain." *International Review of Social History* 11 (1966): pp. 444–464.

———. *Honor, Commerce, and Industry in Eighteenth-Century Spain.* Harvard Graduate School of Business Administration, Boston, 1972.

———. "La política económica y las manufacturas del estado en el siglo XVIII." *Revista de Trabajo,* no. 38 (1972): 5–17.

———. *La Santa y Real Hermandad del Refugio y Piedad de Madrid, 1618–1832.* Madrid: Instituto de Estudios Madrileños, 1980.

Calonge Matellanes, María Pilar, Eugenio García Zarza, and María Elena Rodríquez Sánchez. *La España del antiguo régimen,* ed. Miguel Artola: III. *Castilla la Vieja.* Salamanca: Universidad de Salamanca, 1967.

Capella Martínez, Miguel. *La industria en Madrid.* Vol. 2. Madrid: Cámara Oficial de Comercio e Industria, 1963.

———, and Antonio Matilla Tascón. *Los Cinco Gremios Mayores de Madrid. Estudio crítico-histórico.* Madrid: Cámara Oficial de Comercio e Industria, 1957.

Carande, Ramón. *Carlos V y sus banqueros.* 3 vols. Madrid: Sociedad de Estudios y Publicaciones, 1965, 1967, 1969.

———. "Los moriscos de Henri Lapeyre, los de Julio Caro y algún morisco mas." *Moneda y Crédito,* no. 78 (1961): 9–26.

Carbajo Isla, María. "Primeros resultados cuantitativos de un estudio sobre la población de Madrid, 1742–1836." *Moneda y Crédito,* no. 107 (1968): 71–92.

Carlson, Charles L. "The Vulgar Sort: Common People in *Siglo de Oro* Madrid." Ph.D. dissertation, University of California, Berkeley, 1977.

Carmona García, Juan Ignacio. *Una aportación a la demografía de Sevilla en los siglos XVIII y XIX: Las series parroquiales de San Martín.* Seville: Diputación Provincial, 1976.

Caro Baroja, Julio. *Estudios sobre la vida tradicional española.* Barcelona: Ediciones 62, 1968.

———. *Los moriscos del Reino de Granada.* Madrid: Instituto de Estudios Políticos, 1957.

Carr, Raymond. *Spain: 1808–1939.* Oxford: Clarendon Press, 1966.

Casey, James. *The Kingdom of Valencia in the Seventeenth Century.* London: Cambridge University Press, 1979.

Castillo Pintado, Álvaro. "La coyuntura de la economía valenciana en los siglos XVI y XVII." *Anuario de Historia Económica y Social de la Facultad de Filosofía y Letras de la Universidad de Madrid* 2, no. 2 (1969); 239–288.

———. "Population et 'richesse' en Castille durant la seconde moitié du XVIe siècle." *Annales: Économies, Sociétés, Civilisations* (July-August 1965): 719–733.

Charlot, E., and J. Dûpaquier. "Mouvement annuel de la population de la ville de Paris de 1670 à 1821." *Annales de Démographie Historique* (1967): 511–519.

Chaunu, Huguette and Pierre Chaunu. *Seville et l'Atlantique.* 8 vols. Paris: SEVPEN, 1956.

Christaller, Walter. *Central Places in Southern Germany,* Trans. Carlisle W. Baskin. Englewood Cliffs, N.J.: Prentice-Hall, 1966. (First published in Germany in 1933.)

Cipolla, Carlo M. *Before the Industrial Revolution, European Society and Economy, 1000–1750.* New York: Norton, 1976.

———. "The Decline of Italy." *Economic History Review,* 2nd ser., 5 (1952–53). Also available in Brian Pullan, ed., *Crisis and Change in the Venetian Economy.* London: Metheun, 1968.

Clark, Peter, and Paul Slack. *English Towns in Transition, 1500–1700.* London: Oxford University Press, 1976.

Cobban, Alfred. *The Social Interpretation of the French Revolution.* Cambridge: The University Press, 1965.

Colmeiro, Manuel. *Historia de la economía política en España.* 2 vols. Madrid: Taurus, 1965.

Comellas García-Llera, José Luis. *Los Moderados en el poder, 1844–1854.* Madrid: CSIC, 1970.

"Comunion." *Encyclopedia Universal Ilustrada,* vol. 14, p. 884. Madrid: Espasa-Calpe, n.d.

Coronas Tejada, Luis. "Estudio demográfico de la ciudad de Jaén en el siglo XVII." In *Andalucía moderna,* vol. 1, pp. 215–218.

Cristobal y Mañas, Manuel. *La hacienda municipal de la villa de Madrid: estudio histórico-crítico.* Madrid: Imprenta Municipal, 1901.

Daumard, Adeline, ed. *Les fortunes françaises au XIXe siècle.* Paris: Mouton, 1973.

———, and François Furet. *Structures et relations sociales à Paris au milieu de XVIIIe siècle.* Paris: Colin, 1961.

Deane, Phyllis. *The First Industrial Revolution.* London: Cambridge University Press, 1965.

Deleito y Piñuelo, José. *Solo Madrid es Corte: La capital de dos mundos bajo Felipe IV.* Madrid: Espasa-Calpe, 1953.

Delgado Ribas, José María. "Cádiz y Málaga en el comercio colonial catalan posterior a 1778." In *Andalucía moderna,* vol. 3, pp. 127–140.

Devèze, Michel. *L'Espagne de Philippe IV, 1621–1665: "Siècle d'or et de misère.* 2 vols. Paris: Société d'Editions d'Ensignement Superior, 1971.

Deyon, Pierre. *Amiens, capitale provinciale: Étude sur la société urbaine au XVIIe siècle.* Paris: Mouton, 1967.

———. "Variations de la production textile aux XVIe et XVIIe siècles: Sources et premiers resultats." *Annales: Économies, Sociétés, Civilisations* 18 (1963), 939–955.

Diaz del Moral, Carmen. *La sociedad madrileña de fin de siglo.* Madrid: Ed. Turner, 1974.

Diaz-Trechuelo Spinola, María Lourdes. *La Real Compañia de Filipinas.* Seville: Escuela de Estudios Hispano-Americanos, 1965.

Domínguez Ortiz, Antonio. *El Barroco y la Ilustración,* vol. 4 of *Historia de Sevilla.* Seville: Universidad de Sevilla, 1976.

———. *Crisis y decadencia de la España de los Austrias.* Barcelona: Ariel, 1969.

———. *The Golden Age of Spain.* New York: Basic Books, 1971.

———. *La sociedad española del siglo XVII,* vol. 1. Madrid: CSIC, 1963.

———. *La sociedad española del siglo XVIII.* Madrid: CSIC, 1955.

382　*Bibliography*

――――. "Ventas y exenciones de lugares durante el reinado de Felipe IV." *Anuario de Historia del Derecho Español* 34 (1964), pp. 163–207.

Dunn, Edgar S., Jr. *The Location of Agricultural Production*. Gainesville: University of Florida Press, 1954.

La economía del Antiguo Régimen: La Renta Nacional de la Corona de Castilla, by "Group 75." Madrid: Universidad Autónoma de Madrid, 1977.

La economía del antiguo régimen: El Señorío de Buitrago, by "Grupo '73." Madrid: Universidad Autónoma de Madrid, 1974.

Elliott, J. H. *Imperial Spain*. London: Edward Arnold, 1965.

Elorza, Antonio. *La ideología liberal en la Ilustración española*. Madrid: Ed. Tecnos, 1970.

Enciso Recio, Luis Miguel. *Los establecimientos industriales españoles en el siglo XVIII: La mantelería de La Coruña*. Madrid: Ed. Rialp, 1963.

Ensayos sobre la economía española a mediados del siglo XIX. Madrid: Banco de España, 1970.

Entrambasaguas, Joaquín de. *El Madrid de Lope de Vega*. Madrid: Instituto de Estudios Madrileños, 1959.

Espadas Burgos, Manuel. "Abasto y hábitos alimenticios en el Madrid de Fernando VII." In *Cuadernos de Historia: IV, Estudios sobre la España liberal*. Madrid: CSIC, 1973.

――――. "El hambre de 1812 en Madrid." *Hispania* 110 (1968): 594–623.

――――, and María Ascensión Burgos. *Abastecimiento de Madrid en el siglo XVI*. Madrid: Instituto de Estudios Madrileños, 1961.

Estapé y Rodríguez, Fabian. *La reforma tributaria de 1845*. Madrid: Instituto de Estudios Fiscales, 1971.

Fayard, J., and Claude Larquié. "Hôtels madrilènes et démographie urbain au XVIIe siècle." *Mélanges de la Casa de Velazquez* 4 (1968): 229–258.

Fernández Albaladejo, Pablo. *El crisis del Antiguo Régimen en Guipúzcoa, 1700–1833*. Madrid: Akal Ed., 1976.

Fernández García, Antonio. *El abastecimiento de Madrid en el reinado de Isabel II*. Madrid: CSIC, 1971.

Fernández de Pinedo, Emiliano. *Crecimiento económico y transformaciones sociales del país vasco, 1100–1850*. Madrid: Siglo XXI Ed., 1974.

Fernández Vargas, Valentina. *La población de León en el siglo XVI*. Madrid: Universidad de Madrid, 1968.

Fisher, F. J. "The Development of London as a Centre of Conspicuous Consumption in the Sixteenth and Seventeenth Centuries." *Transactions of the Royal Historical Society*, 4th ser., 30 (1948). In E. M. Carus-Wilson, ed., *Essays in Economic History*, vol 2, pp. 197–207. London: Edward Arnold, 1962.

――――. "The Development of the London Food Market, 1540–1640." *Economic History Review* 5 (1935). In E. M. Carus-Wilson, ed., *Essays in Economic History*, vol. 1, pp. 135–151. London: Edward Arnold, 1954.

――――. "London as an 'Engine of Economic Growth.'" In Peter Clark, ed., *The Early Modern Town: A Reader*. New York: Longmans, 1976.

Flores, Antonio. *Ayer, Hoy y Mañana: Cuadros sociales de 1800, 1850 y 1899: I. Ayer o la sociedad de la fe en 1800*. Barcelona: Montaner y Simon, 1892.

————. *La sociedad de 1850*. Madrid: Alianza Editorial, 1968.

Fontana Lázaro, Josep. *Cambio económico y actitudes políticas en la España del siglo XIX*. Barcelona: Ariel, 1973.

————. "Colapso y transformación del comercio exterior español entre 1792 y 1827." *Moneda y Crédito*, no. 115 (1970): 3–23.

————. "La crisis agraria de comienzos del siglo XIX y sus repercusiones en España." *Hacienda Pública Española*, no. 55 (1978), 177–190.

————. *Hacienda y estado, 1823–1833*. Madrid: Instituto de Estudios Fiscales, 1973.

————. *La quiebra de la monarquía absoluta, 1814–1820*. Barcelona: Ariel, 1971.

Fornies Baigorri, Ascensión. *La vida comercial española, 1829–1885: Instituciones, doctrina y legislación mercantil*. Zaragoza: Instituto Fernándo el Católico, 1968.

Forster, Robert. *The Nobility of Toulouse in the Eighteenth Century*. New York: Octagon, 1971.

Fortea Pérez, José I. "La evolución demográfica de Córdoba en los siglos XVI y XVII." In *Andalucía moderna*, vol. 1, pp. 377–390.

Fourastié, Jacqueline. *Les formules des indices de prix*. Paris: Colin, 1966.

Fox, Edward W. *History in Geographic Perspective*. New York: Norton, 1971.

Freeman, Susan Tax. *Neighbors, The Social Contract in a Castilian Hamlet*. Chicago: University of Chicago Press, 1970.

García de Cortázar y Ruíz de Aguirre, José. *La época medieval*. Vol. 2 of *Historia de España Alfaguara*, ed. Miguel Artola. Madrid: Alianza, 1978.

————. *Vizcaya en el siglo XV: Aspectos económicos y sociales*. Bilbao: Caja de Ahorros Vizcaína, 1966.

García Fuentes, Lutgarda. "Sevilla y Cádiz en los exportaciones de productos agrarios a Indias en la segunda mitad del siglo XVII." In *Andalucía moderna*, vol. 1, pp. 402–406.

García Manrique, Eusebio, S.J. *Borja y Tarazona y el somontano del Moncayo*. Zaragoza: CSIC, 1960.

García Monerris, María Carmen, and José Luis Peset. "Los gremios menores y el abastecimiento de Madrid durante la Ilustración." *Moneda y Crédito*, no. 140 (1977).

García Pelayo, Manuel. "El estamento de la nobleza en el despotismo illustrado español." *Moneda y Crédito*, no. 17 (1946): 37–59.

García Sanz, Angel. "Agronomía y experiencias agronómicos en España durante la segunda mitad del siglo XVIII." *Moneda y Crédito*, no. 131 (1974): 29–54.

————. *Desarrollo y crisis del Antiguo Régimen en Castilla la Vieja: Economía y sociedad en tierras de Segovia de 1500 a 1814*. Madrid: Akal Ed., 1977.

————. "Renta y sociedad estamental en el marquesado de Cuéllar." *Estudios Segovianos* 25, nos. 74–75 (1973), 561–592.

García-Baquero González, Antonio. *Cádiz y el Atlántico, 1717–1778: El comercio colonial español bajo el monopolio gaditano*. 2 vols. Seville: Escuela de Estudios Hispano-Americanos, 1976.

————. "Comercio colonial, acumulación primitiva de capital y desindustrialización en la Baja Andalucía: El caso de Cádiz en el siglo XVIII." In *Andalucía moderna*, vol. 3.

———. *Comercio colonial y guerras revolucionarias*. Seville: Escuela de Estudios Hispano-Americanos, 1972.

García-Lombardero, Jaime. *La agricultura y el estancamiento económico de Galicia en la España del Antiguo Régimen*. Madrid: Siglo XXI Ed., 1973.

——— and Fausto Dopico. "La renta de la tierra en Galicia y la polémica por la redención de foros en los siglos XVIII y XIX." *Hacienda Pública Española*, no. 55 (1978): 191–200.

Garrido, F. *España contemporánea*. 2 vols. Barcelona, 1865.

Gebhart, Monique, and Claude Mercadier. *L'octroi de Toulouse a la veille de la Révolution*. Paris: Bibliothèque National, 1967.

Gentil da Silva, José. *En Espagne: Développement économique, subsistance, déclin*. Paris: Mouton, 1965.

Gilbert Sánchez de la Vega, Rafael. "La Recopilación de Hacienda en 1790." *Hacienda Pública Española*, no. 55 (1978): 201–208.

Giménez López, Enrique. "Aproximación al estudio de la estructura social de Alicante en el siglo XVIII." *Item*, no. 1 (Alicante, 1977): 9–28.

Girard, Albert. *Le commerce français à Séville et Cadix au temps des Habsbourg*. Reprinted New York: Burt Franklin, 1967. (First published, Paris, 1932.)

Gladstone, Lorna Jury. "Aristocratic Landholding and Finances in Seventeenth-Century Castile: The case of Gaspar Téllez Girón, Duke of Osuna (1656–1694)." Ph.D. dissertation, University of Virginia, Charlottesville, 1977.

González Bruguera, Francisco. "Les communeaux et le développement de la production agricole en Espagne, 1808–33." *Cahiers d'Histoire*, no. 2 (1969): 141–179.

González Enciso, Agustín. "Inversión pública e industria textil en el siglo XVIII. La Real Fábrica de Guadalajara." *Moneda y Crédito*, no. 133 (1975): 41–64.

González Muñoz, María C. *La población de Talavera de la Reina, siglos XVI-XX*. Toledo: Diputación Provincial, 1975.

Goodrich, Carter, ed. *Canals and American Economic Development*. New York: Columbia University Press, 1961.

Goubert, Pierre. *Cent mille provinciaux au XVIIe siècle. Beauvais et le beauvaisis de 1600 à 1730*. Paris: Flammarion, 1968.

Haggett, Peter. *Locational Analysis in Human Geography*. New York: St. Martin's, 1966.

Hamilton, Arthur. "A Study of Spanish Manners, 1750–1800, from the Plays of Ramón de la Cruz." *University of Illinois Studies in Language and Literature* 11 (1926): 363–428.

Hamilton, Earl J. *American Treasure and the Price Revolution in Spain, 1501–1650*. Cambridge, Mass.: Harvard University Press, 1934; reprinted New York: Octagon Books, 1965.

———. "El Banco Nacional de San Carlos, 1782–1829." In Pedro Schwartz Girón and Rafael Anes Álvarez, eds., *El Banco de España, Una historia económica*, pp. 197–231. Madrid: Banco de España, 1970.

————. "Foundation of the Bank of Spain," part 1: *Journal of Political Economy* 53 (1945): 97–114; part 2: 54 (1946): 17–37, 116–140.

————. *Money, Prices, and Wages in Valencia, Aragon, and Navarre, 1351–1500.* Cambridge, Mass.: Harvard University Press, 1936.

————. "Plans for a National Bank in Spain, 1701–1783." *Journal of Political Economy* 57 (1949): 315–336.

————. *War and Prices in Spain, 1651–1800.* Cambridge, Mass.: Harvard University Press, 1947.

Harris, Chauncy D., and Edward L. Ullman. "The Nature of Cities." *The Annals* 242 (1945): 1–10. Reprinted in Paul K. Hatt and Albert J. Reiss, eds., *Cities and Society*, pp. 237–247. New York: Free Press, 1957.

Hatt, Paul K., and Albert J. Reiss, eds. *Cities and Society.* New York: Free Press, 1957.

Hecksher, Eli. *Mercantilism.* 2 vols. London: Allen and Unwin, 1935.

Hennessy, A. M. *The Federal Republic in Spain: Pi y Margall and the Federal Republican Movement, 1868–74.* Oxford: Clarendon Press, 1962.

Henshall, Janet D. "Models of Agricultural Activity." In Richard J. Chorley and Peter Haggett, eds., *Socio-Economic Models in Geography.* London: Methuen, 1969.

Heredía Herrera, Antonia. "Los corredores de lonja en Sevilla y Cádiz." *Archivio Hispalense* (1970): 183–198.

Herr, Richard. *The Eighteenth-Century Revolution in Spain.* Princeton, N.J.: Princeton University Press, 1958.

————. "Hacía el derrumbe del Antiguo Régimen: Crisis fiscal y desamortización bajo Carlos IV." *Moneda y Crédito,* no. 118 (1970): 5–50.

————. *An Historical Essay on Modern Spain.* Englewood Cliffs, N.J.: Prentice-Hall, 1971.

————. "El significado de la desamortización en España." *Moneda y Crédito,* no. 131 (1974): 55–94.

————. "Spain." In David Spring, ed., *European Landed Elites in the Nineteenth Century*, pp. 98–126. Baltimore: Johns Hopkins University Press, 1977.

————. "La vente des propriétés de mainmorte en Espagne, 1798–1808." *Annales: Économies, Sociétés, Civilisations* 29 (1974): 215–228.

Herrero García, Miguel. *Las bebidas,* vol. 1 of *La vida española del siglo XVII.* Madrid: Gráfica Universal, 1933.

Hexter, Jack H. *Reappraisals in History.* Evanston, Ill.: Northwestern University Press, 1961.

Hibbert, A. B. "Medieval Town Patricians." *Past and Present* 3 (1953): 15–27.

Hicks, Sir John. *A Theory of Economic History.* London: Oxford University Press, 1969.

Hopfner, H. "La evolución de los bosques de Castilla la Vieja en tiempos históricos." *Estudios Geográficos* 15 (1954): 415–430.

Houston, J. M. *The Western Mediterranean World: An Introduction to its Regional Landscapes.* London: Longmans, 1964.

Huetz de Lemps, Alain. "Les terroirs en Vieile Castille et Leon: Un type de struc-

ture agraire." *Annales: Économies, Sociétés, Civilisations,* 17 (1962): 239–251.
————. "Le vignoble de la *Tierra de Medina* aux XVIIe et XVIIIe siècles." *Annales: Économies, Sociétés, Civilisations* 12 (1957): 403–417.
————. *Vignobles et vins du nord-ouest de l'Espagne.* vol, 1. Bordeaux: Feret et Fils, 1967.
Hull, Anthony. *Charles III and the Revival of Spain.* Washington, D.C.: University Press of America, 1980.
Hussey, Roland Dennis. *The Caracas Company, 1728–1784.* Cambridge, Mass.: Harvard University Press, 1934.
Iradiel Murugarren, Paulino. *Evolución de la industria textil castellana en los siglos XIII–XVI.* Salamanca: Universidad de Salamanca, 1974.
Jago, Charles J. "Aristocracy, War, and Finance in Castile, 1621–1665: The Titled Nobility and the House of Bejar During the Reign of Philip IV." Ph.D. dissertation, Cambridge University, 1969.
————. "Habsburg Absolutism and the Cortes of Castile." *American Historical Review* 86 (1981): 307–326.
————. "The Influence of Debt on the Relations between Crown and Aristocracy in Seventeenth-Century Castile." *Economic History Review,* 2nd ser. 26 (1973): 218–236.
Janke, Peter. *Mendizábal y la instauración de la monarquía constitucional en España, 1790–1853.* Madrid: Siglo XXI Ed., 1974.
Jiménez de Gregorio, Fernando. *Toledo a mediados del siglo XVIII, economia, sociedad y administración.* Toledo: Rafael Gomez-Menor, 1959.
John, A. H. "Aspects of English Economic Growth in the First Half of the Eighteenth Century." *Economica* (1961). In E. M. Carus-Wilson, ed., *Essays in Economic History,* vol. 2. London: Edward Arnold, 1962.
Jutglar, Antoni. *La era industrial en España.* Barcelona: Ed. Nova Terra, 1963.
————. *Ideologías y clases en la España contemporánea,* vol. 1. Madrid: Ed. Cuadernos para el Diálogo, 1968.
Kagan, Richard. *Students and Society in Early Modern Spain.* Baltimore: Johns Hopkins University Press, 1974.
Kamen, Henry. "The Decline of Castile: The Last Crisis." *Economic History Review,* 2nd ser., 17 (1964): 63–76.
————. *Spain in the Later Seventeenth Century.* London: Longmans, 1980.
Kany, Charles. *Life and Manners in Madrid, 1750–1800.* New York: AMS Press, 1970.
Katz, Michael. "Occupational Classification in History." *Journal of Interdisciplinary History* 3 (1973): 63–88.
Kennedy, Ruth Lee. "The New Plaza Mayor of 1620 and Its Reflection in the Literature of the Time." *Hispanic Review* 12 (1944): 49–57.
Kisza, John. "Mexico City and the Provinces in the Late Colonial Period: The Dynamics of Domination." Paper presented to the Pacific Coast Branch of the American Historical Association, 1978.
Klein, Julius. *The Mesta: A Study in Spanish Economic History, 1273–1836.* Cambridge, Mass.: Harvard University Press, 1920.

Konvitz, Josef W. *Cities and the Sea: Port City Planning in Early Modern Europe.* Baltimore: Johns Hopkins University Press, 1978.

Labrousse, Ernest. *Fluctuaciones económicas e historia social.* Madrid: Ed. Tecnos, 1962.

La Force, James C. *The Development of the Spanish Textile Industry, 1750–1800.* Berkeley and Los Angeles: University of California Press, 1965.

———. "Royal Textile Factories in Spain, 1700–1800." *Journal of Economic History* 24 (1964): 337–363.

———. "Technological Diffusion in the Eighteenth Century: The Spanish Textile Industry." *Technology and Culture* 5 (1964): 322–343.

Lapeyre, Henri. *Géographie de l'Espagne morisque.* Paris: SEVPEN, 1959.

Larquié, Claude. "Les esclaves de Madrid a l'epoque de la decadence, 1650–1700." *Revue Historique,* no. 495 (1966): 225–228.

———. "Etude de démographie madrilène: La paroisse de San Ginés de 1650–1700." *Mélanges de la Casa de Velazquez* 2 (1966): 225–278.

———. "Quartiers et paroisses urbaines: L'example de Madrid au XVIIe siècle." *Annales de Démographie Historique* (1974): 165–195.

Larraz López, José. *La época del mercantilismo en Castilla, 1500–1700.* Madrid: CSIC, 1943.

Laslett, Peter. *The World We Have Lost.* New York: Scribner's, 1965.

Lees, Andrew and Lynn Lees, eds. *The Urbanization of European Society in the Nineteenth Century.* Lexington, Mass.: D. C. Heath, 1976.

LeFlem, Jean Paul. "Las cuentas de la Mesta, 1510–1709." *Moneda y Crédito,* no. 121 (1972): 23–104.

Lequerica, José Félix de. *La actividad económica de Vizcaya en la vida nacional.* Madrid: Real Academía de Ciencias Morales y Políticas, 1956.

Le Roy Ladurie, Emmanuel. *Les paysans de Languedoc.* 2 vols. Paris: SEVPEN, 1966. Abridged English edition: *The Peasants of Languedoc.* Urbana: University of Illinois Press, 1976.

Lindert, Peter. "English Occupations, 1670–1811." *Journal of Economic History* 40 (1980): 685–712.

Lindert, Peter. "Working Paper no. 144." Department of Economics, University of California, Davis (1980).

Ling, Richard. "Long-Term Movements in the Trade of Valencia, Alicante, and the Western Mediterranean, 1450–1700." Ph.D. dissertation, University of California, Berkeley, 1974.

Linz, Juan. "Intellectual Roles in Sixteenth- and Seventeenth-Century Spain." *Daedalus* 101 (1972): 59–108.

Livi-Bacci, Massimo. "Fertility and Population Growth in Spain in the Eighteenth and Nineteenth Centuries." *Daedalus* 97 (1968): 523–535.

Llombart Rosa, Vicente. " 'Ley agraria' y 'Sociedades de agricultura': la idea inicial de Campomanes." *Información Comercial Española,* no. 512 (1976): 57–67.

López Gómez, Julia. "El puerto de Alicante." *Estudios Geográficos,* no. 60 (1951): 511–583.

López González, Juan Jaime. "El comercio y el movimiento portuario de Málaga durante el reinado de Carlos IV." In *Andalucía moderna,* vol. 3, pp. 303–313.

Lovett, Gabriel. *Napoleon and the Birth of Modern Spain.* 2 vols. New York: New York University Press, 1965.

Lynch, John. *Spain Under the Hapsburgs.* 2 vols. London: Oxford University Press, 1969.

Maclachlan, Jean O. *Trade and Peace with Old Spain.* New York: Octagon, 1974.

Maravall, José Antonio. *La oposición política bajo los Austrias.* Barcelona: Ariel, 1972.

Marcos González, María Dolores. *La España del Antiguo Régimen,* ed. Miguel Artola: VI. *Castilla la Nueva y Extremadura,* Salamanca: Universidad de Salamanca, 1971.

Martín Galindo, José Luis. "Evolución agrícola y ganadería en Maragatería." *Archivos Leoneses* 11 (1957): 110–137.

Martínez Cachero, Luis Alfonso. *Álvaro Flórez Estrada.* Oviedo: Instituto de Estudios Asturianos, 1961.

Martínez Quintero, M. E. "Descontento y actitudes políticas de la alta nobleza en los orígenes de la Edad Contemporánea." *Hispania* 37, (1977): 95–125.

Martorell Téllez Girón, Ricardo. *Aportaciones al estudio de la población de Madrid en el siglo XVII.* Madrid, 1930.

Masia Vilanova, Juan. "Dos épocas en las comunicaciones alicantinas." *Galatea,* no. 1 (1954): 14–17.

Mateos, María Dolores. *La España del Antiguo Régimen,* ed. Miguel Artola: 0. *Salamanca.* Salamanca: Universidad de Salamanca, 1966.

Antonio Matilla Tascón. "Las rentas vitalicias en el siglo XVIII." *Hacienda Pública Española,* no. 55 (1978): 275–284.

———. *La única contribución y el catastro de la Ensenada.* Madrid: Ministerio de Hacienda, 1947.

Mauleón Isla, Mercedes. *La población de Bilbao en el siglo XVIII.* Valladolid: Universidad de Valladolid, 1961.

McBride, Teresa. "Traditional Socialization and the Process of Modernization for Women: Domestic Service in Nineteenth-Century France." Paper presented at the Berkshire Conference on Women's History, 1974. Revised version: "The Modernization of "Womens' Work," *Journal of Modern History* (1977): 231–245.

Mejide Pardo, Antonio. *Economía marítima de la Galicia cantábrica en el siglo XVIII.* Valladolid: Universidad de Valladolid, 1971.

———. *La emigración gallega intrapeninsular del siglo XVIII.* Madrid: CSIC, 1960.

Melià Tena, Casimir. *L'economia del regne de València segons Cavanilles.* Valencia: L'Estel, 1978.

Melis, Federigo. *Mercaderes italianos en España, siglos XIV-XVI.* Seville: Universidad de Sevilla, 1976.

Merino, J. P. *Notas sobre la desamortización en Extremadura.* Madrid: Fundación Universitaria Española, 1976.

Mintz, Sidney W. "Peasant Markets." *Scientific American* 203 (1960): 112–122.

Molas Ribalta, Pedro. *Los gremios barceloneses del siglo XVIII: La estructura cor-*

porativa ante el comienzo de la Revolución Industrial. Madrid: Confederación Española de Cajas de Ahorros, 1970.

Mols, Roger. *Introduction à la démographie historique des villes d'Europe du XIV au XVIIIe siècle.* 3 vols. Louvain, Belgium: Publications Universitaires de Louvain, 1955.

Morazé, Charles. *The Triumph of the Middle Classes.* New York: Doubleday, 1968.

Morse, Richard M. "A Prolegomenon to Latin American Urban History." *Hispanic American Historical Review* 52 (1972): 359–394.

Nadal Oller, Jordi. *El fracaso de la revolución industrial en España.* Barcelona: Ariel, 1975.

———. "Industrialización y desindustrialización del suroeste español." *Moneda y Crédito,* no. 120 (1972): 3–80.

Nader, Helen. "Nobility as Borrowers and Lenders." Paper presented to the American Historical Association, 1976.

———. "Noble Income in Sixteenth-Century Castile: The Case of the Marquises of Mondéjar, 1480–1580." *Economic History Review,* 2nd ser., 30 (1977): 411–428.

Navarro Millares, Luis José. "Contactos comerciales entre el litoral catalán y puertos de Andalucía, 1799–1808." In *Andalucía moderna,* vol. 4, pp. 64–69.

Niehaus, Thomas K. "Population Problems and Land Use in the Writings of the Spanish Arbitristas: Social and Economic Thinkers, 1600–1650." Ph.D. dissertation, University of Texas, Austin, 1976.

North, Douglass C., and Robert Paul Thomas. "An Economic Theory of the Growth of the Western World." *Economic History Review,* 2nd ser., 23 (1970): 1–17.

Ortega y Gasset, José. *La redención de las provincias.* Madrid: Alianza Editorial, 1967.

Ortiz de la Tabla Ducasse, Javier. "Contrastes regionales en el comercio colonial: Exportación de Cádiz y Málaga a Nueva España, 1785–95." In *Andalucía moderna,* vol. 4, pp. 137–139.

Palacio Atard, Vicente. *El comercio de Castilla y el puerto de Santander en el siglo XVIII.* Madrid: CSIC, 1959.

———. *Los españoles de la Ilustración.* Madrid: Ed. Guadarrama, 1964.

———. "Problemas de abastecimiento en Madrid a finales del siglo XVIII." In *Villes de l'Europe méditerranéenne et de l'Europe occidentale, Annales de la Faculté des Lettres et Sciences Humaines,* nos. 9–10 (Nice, 1969): 279–288.

Parker, Geoffrey. *The Army of Flanders and the Spanish Road, 1567–1659.* London: Cambridge University Press, 1972.

Parry, J. H. *The Spanish Seaborne Empire.* New York: Knopf, 1966.

Patten, John. *English Towns, 1500–1700.* Kent, Eng.: Dawson-Archon Books, 1978.

Peña Sánchez, Martiniano. *Crisis rural y transformaciones recientes en Tierra de Campos.* Valladolid: Universidad de Valladolid, 1975.

Pérez, Ural A. "El precio de los granos en la península ibérica, 1585–1650." *Anuario del Instituto de Investigaciones Históricas* 8 (Rosario, 1965): 121–140.

Pérez de Castro, F. "El abasto de pan de la Corte madrileña en el año 1630." *Revista de la Biblioteca, Archivo y Museo* 15 (1946): 117–150.

Peset, Mariano, and José Luis Peset. *Muerte en España: Política y sociedad entre la peste y el cólera*. Madrid: Seminarios y Ediciones, 1972.

Phillips, Carla Rahn. *Ciudad Real, 1500–1750. Growth, Crisis, and Readjustment in the Spanish Economy*. Cambridge, Mass.: Harvard University Press, 1979.

———. "Ciudad Real in the Seventeenth Century." Paper presented to the Society for Spanish and Portuguese Historical Studies, 1972.

———. "Spanish Wool Exports in the Sixteenth and Seventeenth Centuries." Paper presented to the American Historical Association, 1978. Published as "The Spanish Wool Trade, 1500–1780." *Journal of Economic History* 42 (1982): 775–796.

Pike, Ruth. *Aristocrats and Traders: Sevillian Society of the Sixteenth Century*. Ithaca, N.Y.: Cornell University Press, 1972.

———. *Enterprise and Adventure: The Genoese in Seville and the Opening of the New World*. Ithaca, N.Y.: Cornell University Press, 1966.

Piuz, Anne-Marie. *Recherches sur le commerce de Genève au XVIIe siècle*. Geneva: Société d'Histoire et d'Archéologie, 1964.

Plaza Prieto, Juan. *Estructura económica de España en el siglo XVIII*. Madrid: Confederación Español de Cajas de Ahorro, 1975.

Polanyi, Karl. "The Economy as Instituted Process." In George Dalton, ed., *Primitive, Archaic, and Modern Economies*. New York: Doubleday & Co., 1968.

Ponsot, Pierre. "En Andalousie occidentale: Systèmes de transporte et développement économique, XVIe-XIXe siècle." *Annales: Économies, Sociétés, Civilisations* 31 (1976): 1195–1212.

———. "Revolution dans les campagnes espagnoles au XIXe siècle: Les désamortissements." *Etudes Rurales* 45 (1972): 104–123.

Poussou, J. P. "Les structures démographiques et sociales." In Charles Higounet and François-Georges Pariset, eds., *Histoire de Bordeaux*, V, *Bordeaux au XVIIIe siècle*. Bordeaux: Fédération Historique du Sud-Ouest, 1968.

Prados de la Escosura, Leandro. "El comercio exterior de España, 1790–1830: Una reconsideración." *Hacienda Pública Española*, no. 55 (1978): 339–350.

Pullan, Brian. *Rich and Poor in Renaissance Venice*. Cambridge, Mass.: Harvard University Press, 1971.

La Renta Nacional de la Corona de Castilla. See La economía del Antiguo Régimen.

Ringrose, David R. "España en el siglo XIX: Transportes, mercado interior e industrialización." *Hacienda Pública Española*, no. 27 (1974): 81–87.

———. "European Economic Growth: Comments on the North-Thomas Theory." *Economic History Review*, 2nd ser., 25 (1972): 285–292.

———. "The Government and the Carters in Spain, 1476–1700." *Economic History Review*, 2nd ser., 22 (1969): 45–57.

———. "The Impact of a New Capital City: Madrid, Toledo, and New Castile, 1560–1660." *Journal of Economic History* 33 (1973): 761–791.

———. "Madrid as an Agent of Economic Stagnation in Spain." *Journal of European Economic History* 10 (1981): 481–490.

———. "Madrid et l'Espagne du XVIIIe siècle: L'économie d'une capitale politique." *Mélanges de la Casa de Velazquez* 11 (1975): 593–605.

————. "Madrid y Castilla, 1560–1850: Una capital nacional en una economía regional." *Moneda y Crédito*, no. 111 (1969): 65–122.

————. "Perspectives on the Economy of Eighteenth-Century Spain." In *Historia Ibérica*, pp. 59–101. New York and Madrid: Las Américas and Anaya, 1973.

————. *Transportation and Economic Stagnation in Spain, 1750–1850*. Durham: Duke University Press, 1970. (In Spanish: *Los transportes y el estancamiento económico de España, 1750–1850*. Madrid: Ed. Tecnos, 1972.)

Rodríguez, Laura. *Reforma y Ilustración en la España del XVII: Pedro R. Campomanes*. Madrid: Fundación Universitaria Española, 1975.

————. "The Spanish Riots of 1766." *Past and Present*, no. 59 (1973): 117–146.

Romero de Solis, Pedro. *La población española en los siglos XVIII y XIX*. Madrid: Siglo XXI Ed., 1973.

Roupnel, Gaston. *La ville et la campagne au XVIIe siècle: Étude sur les populations du pays dijonnais*. Paris: SEVPEN, 1955.

Rozman, Gilbert. *Urban Networks in Ch'ing China and Tokugawa Japan*. Princeton, N.J.: Princeton University Press, 1973.

Rudé, George. *The Crowd in the French Revolution*. New York: Oxford University Press, 1959.

————. "The Growth of Cities and Popular Revolt, 1750–1850, with Particular Reference to Paris." In J. Bosher, ed., *French Government and Society, 1500–1800*, pp. 168–190. London: Athlone Press of the University of London, 1973.

Rueda Hernanz, Germán. "Aportación a la historia de la economía malagueña en el periodo de crisis de antiguo régimen, 1791–1833." In *Andalucía moderna*, vol. 4, pp. 206–209.

————. "La desamortización del siglo XIX en una zona de Castilla la Vieja." *Hacienda Pública Española*, no. 38 (1976): 201–229.

————. *La desamortización de Mendizábal en Valladolid*. Valladolid: Institución Cultural Simancas, 1980.

Rugg, Dean S. *Spatial Foundations of Urbanism*. Dubuque, Iowa: Wm. C. Brown, 1972.

Russell, Josiah Cox. *Medieval Cities and Their Regions*. Bloomington, Ind.: Indiana University Press, 1972.

Saez Bueza, Armando. *La población de Barcelona en 1863 y 1960*. Madrid: Ed. Moneda y Crédito, 1968.

Sainz de Robles, Federico Carlos. *Cielo y tierra de Madrid: Historia a scala reducida*. Madrid: Artes Gráficas Municipales, 1969.

Salomon, Noël. *La campagne de Nouvelle Castille à la fin du XVIe siècle, d'apres les "Relaciones Topográficas"*. Paris: SEVPEN, 1964.

Saltillo, Marqués del. "Ganaderos sorianos del siglo XVIII." *Celtiberia* 2 (1952): 387–389.

Salvador, Emilia. *La economía valenciana en el siglo XVI: Comercio de exportación*. Valencia: Universidad de Valencia, 1972.

Sánchez Ramos, Francisco. *La economía siderúrgica española*, vol. 1. Madrid: Instituto Sancho de Moncada, 1945.

Sánchez-Albornoz, Nicolás. *Las crises de subsistencias en España en el siglo XIX.* Rosario: Instituto de Investigaciones Históricas, 1963.

————. *España hace un siglo: Una economia dual.* Barcelona: Ediciones 62, 1968.

————. *Jalones en la modernización de España.* Barcelona: Ariel, 1975.

————. *Los precios agrícolas durante la segunda mitad del siglo XIX,* I. *Trigo y cebada.* Madrid: Banco de España, 1975.

Scheiber, Harry N. *The Ohio Canal Era: A Case Study of Government and the Economy, 1820–1861.* Athens: Ohio University Press, 1969.

Schmitt, Richard. *El clima de Castilla la Vieja y Aragón.* Zaragoza: CSIC, 1946.

Schnore, Leo F., ed.. *The New Urban History.* Princeton, N.J.: Princeton University Press, 1975.

Sella, Domenico. "Les mouvements longs de l'industrie lainere a Venise au XVIe et XVIIe siècles." *Annales: Économies, Sociétés, Civilisations* 12 (1959): 29–45.

Shafer, Robert Jones. *The Economic Societies in the Spanish World, 1763–1821.* Syracuse, N.Y.: Syracuse University Press, 1958.

Sjoberg, Gideon. *The Pre-Industrial City.* New York: Free Press, 1965.

Skinner, G. William, ed. *The City in Late Imperial China.* Stanford, Calif.: Stanford University Press, 1977.

Slicher van Bath, B. H. *The Agrarian History of Europe, 500–1850.* London: Edward Arnold, 1963.

Smailes, Arthur E. *The Geography of Towns.* London: Hutchinson University Library, 1964.

Smith, Robert S. *The Spanish Guild Merchant: A History of the Consulado, 1200–1700.* Durham, N.C.: Duke University Press, 1940.

Soltow, Lee. "Long-Run Changes in British Income Inequality." *Economic History Review,* 2nd ser., 21 (1968): 17–29.

Sombart, Werner. *Luxury and Capitalism.* Ann Arbor: University of Michigan Press, 1967.

Soubeyroux, Jacques. *Pauperisme et rapports sociaux à Madrid au XVIIIème siècle.* 2 vols. Paris: Librairie Honore Champion, 1978.

Stein, Barbara H. and Stanley Stein. *The Colonial Heritage of Latin America.* New York: Oxford University Press, 1970.

Stein, Stanley J. "Reality in Microcosm: The Debate Over Trade with America, 1785–1789." *Historia Ibérica,* pp. 111–119. New York and Madrid: Las Américas and Anaya, 1973.

Stone, Lawrence. *The Crisis of the Aristocracy, 1558–1641.* Oxford: Clarendon Press, 1965.

Tallada Pauli, José María. *Historia de las finanzas españolas en el siglo XIX.* Madrid: Espasa-Calpe, 1946.

————. "La política comercial y arancelaria española en el siglo XIX." *Anales de Economía* 3, no. 9 (1943): 47–71.

Terán, Miguel de. "Santander, puerto de embarque por las harinas de Castilla." *Estudios Geográficos* 8 (1947): 746–758.

Terrasse, Michel. "La région de Madrid d'apres les *Relaciones Topográficas.*" *Mélanges de la Casa de Velazquez* 4 (1968): 143–160.

Thomas, Diana Margaret. "The Royal Company of Printers and Booksellers of

Spain, 1763–1794." Ph.D. dissertation, University of California School of Library Science, Berkeley, 1974.

Tomás y Valiente, Francisco. *El marco político de la desamortización en España.* Barcelona: Ariel, 1971.

———. "Recientes investigaciones sobre la desamortización: intento de síntesis." *Moneda y Crédito,* no. 131 (1974): 95–160.

Tortella, Gabriel. *Los orígines del capitalismo en España: Banca, industria y ferrocarriles en el siglo XIX.* Madrid: Ed. Tecnos, 1973.

Ullman, Edward L. "A Theory of Location for Cities." *American Journal of Sociology* 46 (1941): 853–864. Reprinted in Paul K. Hatt and Albert J. Reiss, eds., *Cities and Society,* pp. 227–236. New York: Free Press, 1957.

Ulloa, Modesto. *La hacienda real de Castilla en el reinado de Felipe II.* Madrid: Fundación Universitaria Española, 1977.

———. "La producción y el consumo en la Castilla del siglo XVI." *Hispania* 31 (1971): 5–30.

Valle Buenestado, Bartolomé. "Notas sobre la evolución demográfica de la comarca de Pedroches, 1530–1857." In *Andalucía moderna,* vol. 4, pp. 289–308.

———. "Tres aspectos de la geografía agraria de Villanueva de Córdoba en el siglo XVIII." In *Andalucía moderna,* vol. 4, pp. 309–324.

Van Young, Eric. *Hacienda and Market in Eighteenth-Century Mexico.* Berkeley and Los Angeles: University of California Press, 1981.

———. "Urban Market and Hinterland: Guadalajara and Its Region in the Eighteenth Century." *Hispanic American Historical Review* 59 (1979): 593–635.

Venard, Marc. *Bourgeois et paysans au XVIIe siècle: Recherche sur le rôle des bourgeois parisiens dans la vie agricole au Sud de Paris au XVIIe siècle.* Paris: SEVPEN, 1957.

Verlinden, Charles. *The Beginnings of Modern Colonialization.* Ithaca, N.Y.: Cornell University Press, 1970.

———, J. Craeybeck, and E. Scholliers. "Price and Wage Movements in Belgium in the Sixteenth Century." In Peter Burke, ed., *Economy and Society in Early Modern Europe: Essays from Annales,* pp. 55–84. New York: Harper and Row, 1972.

———. "Italian Influence in Iberian Colonization." *Hispanic American Historical Review* 33 (1953): 199–211.

Vicens Vives, Jaime. *Approaches to the History of Spain,* Trans. Joan Connelly Ullman. Berkeley and Los Angeles: University of California Press, 1967.

———. *Manual de historia económica de España.* Barcelona: Ed. Vicens Vives, 1967.

Vilá Valenti, Juan. *La península ibérica.* Barcelona: Ariel, 1968.

Vilar, Jean. *Literatura y economía: La figura satírica del arbitrista en el siglo de oro.* Madrid: Revista de Occidente, 1973.

Vilar, Pierre. *Catalunya dins l'Espanya moderna.* 4 vols. Barcelona: Ediciones 62, 1968.

———. "Estructures de la societat espanyola cap al 1750." *Recerques: Historia, Economia, Cultura,* 1 (Barcelona: Ariel, 1970): 1–29.

———. *Spain, A Brief History.* Oxford: Pergamon Press, 1967.

Viñas y Mey, Carmelo. "Apuntes sobre historia social y económica de España." In Manuel Fernández Álvarez, ed., *Estudios sobre historia de España.* Madrid: Ed. Norte y Sur, 1965.

——. "Notas sobre la estructura social-demográfica del Madrid de los Austrias." *Revista de la Universidad de Madrid* 4 (1955): 461–496.

——. *El problema de la tierra en la España de los siglos XVI-XVII.* Madrid: CSIC, 1941.

Voltes Bou, Pedro. *Historia de la economía española en los siglos XIX y XX.* Madrid: Ed. Nacional, 1974.

Walker, Geoffrey J. *Spanish Politics and Imperial Trade, 1700–1789.* Bloomington: Indiana University Press, 1979.

Weber, Adna Ferrin. *The Growth of Cities in the Nineteenth Century.* Ithaca N.Y.: Cornell University Press, 1967. (First published: New York: Macmillan, 1899.)

Weber, Max. *The City.* New York: Free Press, 1958.

——. *Law in Economy and Society*, ed. Max Rheinstein. New York: Simon and Schuster, 1954.

Weisser, Michael R. "The Agrarian Ideal in Eighteenth-Century Spain." *Studies in Eighteenth-Century Culture* II (1982): 381–393.

——. "Crime and Subsistence: The Peasants of the *Tierra* of Toledo, 1550–1700." Ph.D. dissertation, Northwestern University, 1972.

——. "The Decline of Castile Revisited: The Case of Toledo." *Journal of European Economic History* 2 (1973): 615–640.

——. "The Demography of the Heartland of New Castile, 1550–1700." Unpublished typescript, 1974.

——. "Les marchands de Tolède dans l'économie castillane, 1565–1635." *Mélanges de la Casa de Velazquez* 7 (1971): 223–236.

——. *The Peasants of the Montes.* Chicago: University of Chicago Press, 1976.

——. "Toledo in the *Siglo de Oro.*" Paper presented to the Society for Spanish and Portuguese Historical Studies, 1972.

Woolfe, S. J. "Venice and the Terraferma: Problems of the Change from Commercial to Landed Activities." *Bollettino dell' Istituto di Storia della Societé dello Stato Veneziano* 4 (1962): 437–478.

Wrigley, E. A. "Demographic Models and Geography." In Richard J. Chorley and Peter Haggett, eds., *Socio-Economic Models in Geography.* London, 1971.

——. "Parasite or Stimulus: The Town in a Pre-Industrial Economy." In Abrams and Wrigley, *Towns in Societies,* pp. 295–310.

——. *Population and History.* New York: McGraw-Hill, 1969.

——. "A Simple Model of London's Importance in Changing English Society and Economy, 1650–1750." *Past and Present* 37 (1967): 44–70.

Yun Cabrera, Rafael. "La población de Pozoblanco a mediados del siglo XVIII." In *Andalucía moderna,* vol. 4, pp. 345–365.

Zelinsky, Wilbur. *A Prologue to Population Geography.* Englewood Cliffs, N.J.: Prentice-Hall, 1966.

Index